Unified Growth Theory

Unified Growth Theory

Oded Galor

PRINCETON UNIVERSITY PRESS | PRINCETON & OXFORD

© 2011 by Princeton University Press

Published by Princeton University Press, 41 William Street, Princeton,
New Jersey 08540

In the United Kingdom: Princeton University Press, 6 Oxford Street, Woodstock,
Oxfordshire OX20 1TW

press.princeton.edu

Jacket illustration: *Time Goes By,* 2007, GIMP-created image, © Manuel Lao

Library of Congress Cataloging-in-Publication Data

Galor, Oded, date.
  Unified growth theory / Oded Galor.
      p.   cm.
  Includes bibliographical references and index.
  ISBN 978-0-691-13002-6 (hardback : alk. paper)
    1. Economic development.   2. Technological innovations—Economic aspects.
I. Title.
HD75.G348   2011
338.9001—dc22   2010043076

British Library Cataloging-in-Publication Data is available

This book was composed in Times New Roman and Bell Gothic using ZzTEX
by Princeton Editorial Associates, Inc., Scottsdale, Arizona.
Printed on acid-free paper.   ∞

Printed in the United States of America
10 9 8 7 6 5 4 3 2 1

Dedicated to the members of two generations of my family who have profoundly affected my life—my sons Alon, Yuval, and Omri, and my parents Sarah and Joseph

Contents

CHAPTER 8
Concluding Remarks   285

Preface

Striving toward unification and simplification of the premises of the theory as a whole.
—Albert Einstein

This book is devoted to Unified Growth Theory—an intellectual endeavor conceived and developed by the author over the course of 20 years of research. The theory explores the fundamental forces that have generated the remarkable transition of the world economy from an epoch of stagnation to an era of sustained economic growth and triggered the emergence of the vast disparity in the standards of living across the globe.

The research agenda has been stimulated by the author's conviction that the understanding of comparative economic development would be hindered unless growth theory would reflect the principal growth engines over the entire process of development and would capture the central role played by historical and prehistorical factors in the prevailing disparity across countries and regions. Moreover, it was instigated by the recognition that the hurdles faced by less developed economies in reaching an era of sustained growth would remain obscure unless the forces that facilitated this transition among the currently developed economies would be thoroughly explored.

Chapter 1 introduces the empirical and theoretical motivations of the quest for a unified theory of economic growth. It examines the fundamental inconsistencies of non-unified growth theory with the process of development as a whole, underlines the importance of the establishment of a unified theory of economic growth, and describes the central hypotheses of Unified Growth Theory and their implications for comparative economic development.

Chapter 2 provides an overview of the three fundamental regimes that have characterized the process of development over the course of human history: the Malthusian Epoch, the Post-Malthusian Regime, and the Modern Growth Regime. It explores the forces that have generated the transition from stagnation to growth and have contributed to the emergence of the vast inequality across countries.

Chapter 3 develops the foundations of the influential Malthusian theory and examines its predictions regarding the evolution of population and income per capita in the pre-industrial era of human history. The analysis explores the hypothesis that although the growth of income per capita was minuscule during the Malthusian Epoch, the dynamism in population and technology over this period was instrumental for the emergence of economies from the Malthusian Epoch.

Chapter 4 examines the triggers for the onset of the demographic transition that has swept the world since the end of the nineteenth century and has been identified as one of the prime forces in the movement from stagnation to an era of sustained economic growth. The chapter explores various mechanisms that have been proposed as possible triggers for the demographic transition, assessing their empirical plausibility and significance in understanding the transition from stagnation to growth.

Chapter 5 develops the foundations of Unified Growth Theory. It underlines the significance as well as the intellectual challenge associated with the establishment of a unified theory of economic growth that captures each of the central phases in the process of development while orchestrating an endogenous transition across these distinct regimes. The chapter highlights the fundamental building blocks of Unified Growth Theory and their role in generating a dynamical system that accounts for (a) the epoch of Malthusian stagnation that has characterized most of human history; (b) the escape from the Malthusian trap and the associated spike in the growth rates of income per capita and population; (c) the emergence of human capital formation in the process of development; (d) the onset of the demographic transition; and (e) the emergence of the contemporary era of sustained economic growth.

Chapter 6 derives the implications of Unified Growth Theory for comparative economic development across the globe. It explores the role of cultural, institutional, and geographical factors in the differential pace of transition from stagnation to growth and the emergence of the contemporary disparity across countries. Furthermore, it establishes the persistent effect that deep-rooted factors (e.g., biogeographical endowments and migratory distance from the cradle of humanity in East Africa) have had on the course of comparative economic development from the dawn of human civilization to the modern era, and it examines the implications of Unified Growth Theory for understanding the origins of multiple growth regimes and convergence clubs.

Chapter 7 explores the dynamic interaction between human evolution and the process of economic development. It advances the hypothesis that during the Malthusian Epoch, when the subsistence consumption constraint affected the vast majority of the population, the forces of natural selection complemented the growth process and played a significant role in the transition of the world economy from stagnation to growth.

Finally, Chapter 8 offers some concluding remarks about the achievements of Unified Growth Theory thus far and the looming challenges in the exploration of the role of historical and prehistorical factors in contemporary economic development, as well as in the analysis of the interaction between human evolution and the process of development.

The philosophical foundations of this research agenda have been outlined by the author in his interview by Brian Snowdon (2008), "Towards a Unified Theory of Economic Growth." The theory was the subject of the author's Kuznets Lecture titled "Unified Growth Theory and Comparative Economic Development" (Yale University, 2009), Klein Lecture titled "Comparative Economic Development: Insights from Unified Growth Theory" (Osaka, 2008), opening lecture of the Israeli Economic Association Annual Meeting titled "From Stagnation to Growth" (Ma'ale Hahmisha, Israel, 2003), a keynote lecture at the DEGIT Annual Meeting (Vienna, 2001), and the keynote lecture of the Annual T2M Conferences (Paris, 2000). In addition, the theory was the focus of the author's lecture series for the Danish Doctoral Program (Copenhagen, 2008), the Minerva Summer Workshop in Economic Growth (Jerusalem, 2008), the International Monetary Fund Training Program (2006 and 2008), the Center for Economic Policy Research Summer Workshop in Economic History (Florence, 2007), and the Dutch Joint Doctoral Program (Groningen, 2000).

The research that led to this book has greatly benefited from the author's collaborations with Quamrul Ashraf, Stelios Michalopoulos, Omer Moav, Andrew Mountford, Dietrich Vollrath, and David Weil, and from extensive discussions with Carl-Johan Dalgaard, Peter Howitt, Ross Levine, and Yona Rubinstein. In addition, this research has profited from the interaction with doctoral students who attended the author's courses at Brown University, Providence, Rhode Island; the Hebrew University of Jerusalem; and the Massachusetts Institute of Technology, Cambridge, Massachusetts, and researchers who attended dozens of the author's lectures on segments of this book around the globe. In particular, the author is grateful to Charles Horioka and the members of the Institute of Social and Economic Research at Osaka University for fruitful discussions in the course of the Klein Lecture, and to Tim Guinnane, Mark Rosenzweig, Paul Schultz, and other members of the Growth Center at Yale University, New Haven, Connecticut, for stimulating discussions in the course of the Kuznets Lecture.

In addition, the final version of the manuscript benefited from numerous suggestions by William Fallon, Martin Fiszbein, Martin Guzman, Casper Hansen, Cory Harris, Mariko Klasing, Lars Lønstrup, Ryan Miller, Kuni Natsuki, Ehud Schwammenthal, Sarah Stein, and Harvey Stephenson and invaluable comments by anonymous reviewers, Boris Gershman, and Gareth Olds. Finally, support of the National Science Foundation through grants SBR-9709941, SES-0004304, and SES-0921573 and the Israel Science Foundation through grants 0341240, 848/00, and 795/03 for various segments of this research is gratefully acknowledged.

Providence, Rhode Island, January 2011

CHAPTER 1

Introduction

A complete, consistent, unified theory . . . would be the ultimate triumph of human reason.

—Stephen W. Hawking

The transition from an epoch of stagnation to an era of sustained economic growth has marked the onset of one of the most remarkable transformations in the course of human history. While living standards in the world economy stagnated during the millennia preceding the Industrial Revolution, income per capita has undergone an unprecedented tenfold increase over the past two centuries, profoundly altering the level and distribution of education, health, and wealth across the globe.

The rise in the standard of living has not been universally shared among societies. Variation in the timing of the take-off from stagnation to growth has led to a vast worldwide divergence in income per capita. Inequality, which had been modest until the nineteenth century, has widened considerably, and the ratio of income per capita between the richest and the poorest regions of the world has been magnified from a moderate 3:1 ratio in 1820 to a staggering 18:1 ratio in 2000 (Figure 1.1).

An equally striking development has emerged in the world distribution of population. The decline in population growth in Europe and North America toward the end of the nineteenth century and the long delay in the onset of a corresponding demographic transition in less developed regions, well into the second half of the twentieth century, have generated significant bifurcation in the global distribution of population. The share of world population that resides in the prosperous region of Europe has declined by nearly one-half over the past century, whereas the fraction of the human population that lives in the impoverished regions of Africa and Latin America has doubled.

Throughout most of human existence, the process of development was marked by Malthusian stagnation: resources generated by technological progress and land expansion were channeled primarily toward an increase in the size of the population, providing only a glacial contribution to the level of income per capita in the long run. While cross-country variations in technology and land productivity were reflected in differing population densities, their effect on variation in living standards was merely transitory.

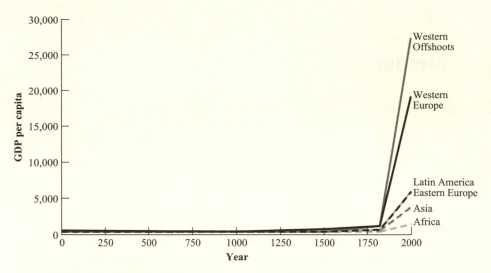

FIGURE 1.1. Evolution of regional income per capita over the past two thousand years.
Data source: Maddison (2001).
Note: The Western Offshoots are Australia, Canada, New Zealand, and the United
States.

In contrast, over the past two centuries, various regions of the world have
departed from the Malthusian trap and have witnessed a considerable increase
in growth rates of income per capita. The decline in population growth over
the course of the demographic transition has liberated productivity gains from
the counterbalancing effect of population growth and enabled technological
progress and human capital formation to pave the way for the emergence of
an era of sustained economic growth.

The transition from an epoch of Malthusian stagnation to an era of sustained
economic growth and the corresponding divergence in income per capita across
the globe have been the center of intensive research during the past decade. The
inconsistency of the predominant theories of economic growth with some of the
most fundamental characteristics of the growth process and their limited ability
to shed light on the origins of the vast global disparity in living standards have
led to the development of a unified theory of economic growth that captures the
growth process in its entirety.

Unified Growth Theory explores the fundamental factors that have contributed to the remarkable transition from stagnation to growth and examines
their significance for the understanding of the contemporary growth process of
developed and less developed economies. First, it unveils the factors that have
generated the Malthusian trap. What accounts for the epoch of stagnation that

has characterized most of human history? Why did episodes of technological progress in the pre-industrial era fail to generate sustained economic growth? Why has population growth counterbalanced the expansion of resources per capita that could have been generated by technological progress?

Moreover, the theory uncovers the forces that triggered the take-off from stagnation to growth. What is the origin of the sudden spurt in the growth rates of income per capita and population during the course of industrialization? What was the source of the striking reversal in the positive relationship between income per capita and population growth that existed throughout most of human history? Would the transition to the modern state of sustained economic growth have been feasible without the decline in population growth? What are the hurdles faced by less developed economies in their attempts to transition to a sustained-growth regime?

Further, Unified Growth Theory sheds new light on the origins of the perplexing divergence in income per capita across developed and less developed regions in the past two centuries. What accounts for the sudden take-off from stagnation to growth among some countries in the world and the persistent stagnation in others? Why has the positive link between income per capita and population growth reversed its course in some economies but not in others? Has the transition to a state of sustained economic growth in advanced economies adversely affected the process of development in less developed ones? Have variations in prehistoric biogeographical factors had a persistent effect on the composition of human capital and economic development across the world?

1.1 Toward a Unified Theory of Economic Growth

Non-unified theories of economic growth have been instrumental in advancing the understanding of the role that technological progress and the accumulation of factors of production have played in the modern era of economic growth. Nevertheless, they are inconsistent with the qualitative aspects of the growth process over most of human existence, and they fail to identify the forces that triggered the take-off from stagnation to sustained economic growth—insights that are instrumental for understanding the contemporary growth process and the origins of the great divergence in income per capita over the past two centuries.

The preoccupation of non-unified theories of economic growth with the growth process of developed economies in the past century and of less developed economies in the past few decades has become harder to justify in light of the disparity between the main features of the modern growth era and those that have characterized the growth process over most of human existence. It has become evident that as long as growth theory rests on distinct and disjoint theories to characterize the process of development during the Malthusian Epoch and the Modern Growth Regime, the understanding of the contemporary growth process will be limited and distorted.[1] "It is as though an artist were to gather the hands, feet, head and other members for his images from diverse models, each part perfectly drawn, but not related to a single body, and since they in no way match each other, the result would be monster rather than man" (Copernicus quoted in Kuhn [1957, p. 137]).

The advancement of Unified Growth Theory has been fueled by the conviction that the understanding of global variation in economic development would be fragile and incomplete unless the prevailing theory of economic growth reflects the principal driving forces behind the entire process of development and captures the central role that historical factors have played in bringing about the current disparities in living standards.[2] Moreover, it has been fostered by the realization that a comprehensive understanding of the hurdles faced by less developed economies would remain obscure unless the factors that facilitated the transition of the currently developed economies from stagnation to growth could be identified and modified to account for the differences in the growth structure of less developed economies in an increasingly interdependent world.

Unified Growth Theory provides a fundamental framework of analysis for the evolution of individuals, societies, and economies over the entire course of human history. The theory captures in a single analytical framework the main characteristics of the process of development: (i) the epoch of Malthusian stagnation that has characterized most of human history; (ii) the escape from the Malthusian trap and the associated spike in the growth rates of income per capita and population; (iii) the emergence of human capital formation in the process of development; (iv) the onset of the demographic transition; (v) the

---

[1] The evolution of theories in older scientific disciplines suggests that theories founded on the basis of a subset of the existing observations may be attractive in the short run but are nonrobust and nondurable in the long run. For instance, classical thermodynamics, which lacked microfoundations, was ultimately superseded by the micro-based statistical mechanics. Moreover, attempts to develop unified theories in physics have been based on the conviction that all physical phenomena should eventually be explainable by some underlying unity. In particular, Unified Field Theory proposes to unify by a set of general laws the four distinct forces that are known to control all observed interactions in matter: electromagnetism, gravitation, the weak force, and the strong force.

[2] Clearly, the understanding of the contemporary world would be limited and incomplete in the absence of a historical perspective. However, the intensity of recent explorations of the interaction between economic development and economic history could be attributed to increasing frustration with the failure of the ahistorical branch of growth theory to capture some of the most fundamental aspects of the growth process.

contemporary era of sustained economic growth; and (vi) the divergence in income per capita across countries.[3]

The theory unveils the principal economic forces that have generated the remarkable transition from stagnation to growth and underlines their significance for understanding the contemporary growth process of both developed and less developed economies. Moreover, it sheds light on the role of historical and prehistorical characteristics in the divergence of income per capita across regions of the world in the past two centuries.

Unified Growth Theory suggests that the transition from stagnation to growth has been an inevitable by-product of the process of development. It argues that the inherent Malthusian interaction between the rate of technological progress and the size and composition of the population accelerated the pace of technological progress and ultimately raised the importance of education in coping with the rapidly changing technological environment.[4] The rise in industrial demand for education brought about significant reductions in fertility rates. It enabled economies to divert a larger share of the fruits of factor accumulation and technological progress to the enhancement of human capital formation and income per capita, paving the way for the emergence of sustained economic growth.

The theory further explores the dynamic interaction between human evolution and the process of economic development and advances the hypothesis that the forces of natural selection played a significant role in the evolution of the world economy from stagnation to growth. The Malthusian pressures have acted as the key determinant of population size and conceivably, via natural selection, have shaped the composition of the population as well. Lineages of individuals whose traits were complementary to the economic environment generated higher levels of income, and thus a larger number of surviving offspring, and the gradual increase in the representation of their traits in the population contributed to the process of development and the take-off from stagnation to growth.

---

[3] The term "Unified Growth Theory" was coined by Galor (2005) to categorize theories of economic growth that capture the entire growth process in a single framework of analysis. The only unified theory of economic growth that captures the endogenous evolution of population, technology, human capital, and income per capita over the entire course of economic development, while generating both a spontaneous transition from Malthusian stagnation to sustained growth and a great divergence has been developed by Galor (2005, 2010), based on Galor and Weil (1999, 2000), Galor and Moav (2002), and Galor and Mountford (2008). This theory therefore is the central pillar of this book.

[4] The increased demand for human capital has not necessarily resulted in an increase in the rate of return on human capital due to institutional changes (e.g., the provision of public education) that lowered the cost of investment in human capital and facilitated a massive increase in the supply of education.

1.2 Origins of Global Disparity in Living Standards

Unified Growth Theory sheds light on the notable divergence in income per capita across the globe during the past two centuries. The theory advances the understanding of three fundamental aspects of comparative economic development. First, it identifies the factors that have governed the transition from stagnation to growth and have thus contributed to the observed worldwide differences in economic development. Second, it highlights the persistent effects that variations in historical and prehistorical conditions have had on the composition of human capital and economic development across countries. Finally, it uncovers the forces that have sparked the emergence of convergence clubs, and it explores the characteristics that have determined the association of different economies with each club.

1.2.1 Catalysts for the Engine of Transition from Stagnation to Growth

The first layer of Unified Growth Theory explores the underlying forces that have determined the timing and pace of the transition from an epoch of Malthusian stagnation to an era of sustained economic growth and have thus contributed to the disparity in economic development across countries. Country-specific characteristics that have affected the intensity of the pivotal interaction between the rate of technological progress and the size and composition of the population have generated variations in the transition from stagnation to growth and contributed to the gap in income per capita across countries.

Variation in rates of technological progress has reinforced the differential pace of the emergence of demand for human capital, the onset of the demographic transition, and the shift from stagnation to growth, and has thus contributed to the divergence in income per capita in the past two centuries. In particular, worldwide variation in the pace of technological progress has been triggered by cross-country differences in (i) the stock of knowledge and its rate of creation and diffusion among members of society; (ii) the level of protection of intellectual property rights, its positive effect on the incentive to innovate, and its adverse effect on the proliferation of existing knowledge; (iii) financial constraints and the level of competitiveness of the innovation sector; (iv) the composition of cultural and religious attributes and their effects on knowledge creation and diffusion; (v) the composition of interest groups in society and their incentives to block or promote technological innovations; (vi) the level of human diversity and the degree to which it complements the implementation and advancement of new technological paradigms; (vii) the propensity to trade and its effect on technological diffusion; and (viii) the abundance of natural resources essential for an imminent technological paradigm.

Once the technologically driven demand for human capital emerged in the second phase of industrialization, the prevalence of characteristics conducive to human capital formation has determined the swiftness of its accumulation, the timing of the demographic transition, the pace of the transition from stagnation to growth, and the observed distribution of income in the world economy. Thus, variations in country-specific characteristics that have contributed to human capital formation have differentially affected the timing and pace of the transition from agriculture to industry and comparative economic development as a whole.

In particular, global variation in human capital formation has been influenced by cross-country differences in (i) the prevalence of human capital–promoting institutions or policies (e.g., the availability, accessibility, and quality of public education); (ii) the ability of individuals to finance the cost of education as well as the foregone earnings associated with schooling; (iii) the impact of the level of inequality and of the degree of credit market imperfections on the extent of underinvestment in education; (iv) the stock of knowledge in society and its effect on the productivity of investment of human capital; (v) the composition of cultural and religious groups in a society and their effects on the incentives of individuals to invest in human capital; (vi) the impact of geographical attributes on health and thus human capital formation; (vii) the propensity to trade and the patterns of comparative advantage with respect to the production of skill-intensive goods; and (viii) preferences for educated offspring that may reflect cultural attributes, the composition of religious groups and social status associated with education.

1.2.2 Persistence of Prehistorical Biogeographical Conditions

In its second layer, Unified Growth Theory highlights the direct persistent effect that deep-rooted factors, determined as early as tens of thousands years ago, have had on the course of comparative economic development from the dawn of human civilization to the modern era.

The theory captures the thesis that part of the differences in the process of development across the globe can be traced to biogeographical factors that led to regional variation in the timing of the Neolithic Revolution (Diamond, 1997). According to this thesis, favorable biogeographical endowments that contributed to the emergence of agriculture gave some societies the early advantage of operating a superior production technology and generating resource surpluses. They permitted the establishment of a non-food-producing class, whose members were crucial for the development of written language and science and for the formation of cities, technology-based military powers, and nation states. The early dominance of these societies persisted throughout history, being further sustained by geopolitical and historical processes, such as colonization. The significance of the timing of agricultural transitions for precolonial economic development has been confirmed empirically, although evidence appears to suggest that over the past five hundred years the initial dominance brought about by an earlier transition to agriculture has dissipated.

Moreover, the theory is consistent with the thesis that the exodus of modern humans from Africa, nearly a hundred thousand years ago, appears central to understanding comparative economic development across the globe (Ashraf and Galor, 2009). In the course of the exodus of *Homo sapiens* out of Africa, variation in migratory distance from the cradle of humankind to settlements around the globe affected the level of genetic diversity and has had a long-lasting, hump-shaped effect on the pattern of comparative economic development that cannot be captured by contemporary geographical, institutional, and cultural factors. While the intermediate level of genetic diversity prevalent among Asian and European populations has been conducive to development, the high degree of diversity among African populations and the low degree among Native American populations have acted as detrimental forces in the development of these regions.

1.2.3 Convergence Clubs

In its third layer, Unified Growth Theory advances the understanding of the forces that have contributed to the existence of multiple growth regimes and the emergence of convergence clubs (i.e., groups of countries among which the disparity in income per capita tends to narrow over time). The theory attributes these phenomena to variation in the position of economies across the distinct phases of development. It suggests that the differential timing of take-offs from stagnation to growth has segmented economies into three fundamental growth regimes: slowly growing economies in the vicinity of a Malthusian steady state, fast growing countries in a sustained-growth regime, and a third group of economies in transition from one regime to the other. Moreover, it suggests that the presence of multiple convergence clubs may reflect a temporary state, as endogenous forces may ultimately permit members of the Malthusian club to shift their positions and join the members of the sustained-growth club.

CHAPTER 2

From Stagnation to Growth

Every phase of evolution commences by being in
a state of unstable force and proceeds through
organization to equilibrium.

—Kabbalah

This chapter provides an overview of the three fundamental regimes that have characterized the process of development over the course of human history: the Malthusian Epoch, the Post-Malthusian Regime, and the Modern Growth Regime.

Since the exodus of *Homo sapiens* from Africa approximately 100,000 years ago, human civilization has gradually evolved from nomadic tribes to complex industrial societies. During most of their existence, modern humans were associated with nomadic tribes that were engaged in hunting and gathering. The onset of the Neolithic Revolution about 10,000 years ago triggered the transition of societies to agricultural communities and the subsequent emergence of cities, states, and nations. Lastly, the Industrial Revolution 250 years ago marked the dawn of the recent industrial phase of modern societies (Figure 2.1).

The process of development during most of human existence was marked by Malthusian stagnation. Technological progress was insignificant by modern standards, and resources generated by technological progress and land expansion were channeled primarily into an increase in population. Variations in technology and land quality across countries were reflected in differences in population density, while the standard of living did not echo the degree of technological advancement.

In the past two centuries, in contrast, the pace of technological progress intensified in association with the process of industrialization. Various regions of the world departed from the Malthusian trap and experienced a considerable rise in the growth rate of income per capita and population. Unlike episodes of technological progress in the pre-Industrial Revolution era that failed to generate sustained economic growth, the increasing role of human capital in the production process during the second phase of industrialization, and the onset of a demographic transition, liberated gains in productivity from the counterbalancing effects of population growth. The decline in the growth rate of population and the associated enhancement of technological progress and

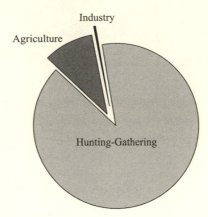

FIGURE 2.1. Modes of production since the exodus of *Homo sapiens* from Africa.

human capital formation paved the way for the emergence of the modern state of sustained economic growth.

The differential timing of the take-off from stagnation to growth across countries and the corresponding variation in the timing of the demographic transition have led to a significant divergence in income and to substantial changes in the distribution of population around the globe. Some regions have excelled in the growth of income per capita, while others have dominated population growth.

2.1 The Malthusian Epoch

During the Malthusian Epoch, humans were subjected to a persistent struggle for existence. Periods marked by an absence of changes in the level of technology or in the availability of land were characterized by a stable population size as well as a constant level of income per capita, whereas those characterized by improvements in the technological environment or in the availability of land generated temporary gains in income per capita, leading ultimately to larger but not richer populations. Technologically superior countries eventually developed denser populations, but their standards of living did not reflect the degree of their technological advancements.[1]

---

[1] Thus, as reflected in the viewpoint of a prominent observer of the period, "The most decisive mark of the prosperity of any country [was] the increase in the number of its inhabitants" (Smith, 1776, p. 128).

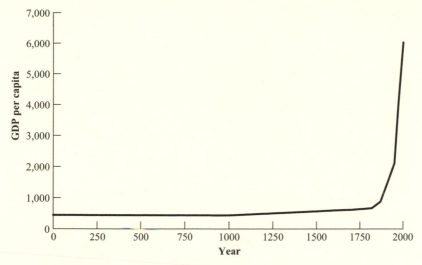

FIGURE 2.2. Evolution of world income per capita, 1–2001.
Data source: Maddison (2003).

2.1.1 Stagnation of Income per Capita in the Long Run

The average long-run growth rate of output per capita was negligible during the Malthusian Epoch, and standards of living did not differ greatly across countries. As depicted in Figure 2.2, the average level of income per capita during the first millennium fluctuated around $450 per year, and the average growth rate of output per capita in the world was nearly 0%. Similarly, in the years 1000–1820, the average level of income per capita in the world economy was below $670 per year, and the average growth rate of world income per capita was minuscule, creeping up at a rate of about 0.05% per year (Maddison, 2001).

This pattern of stagnation was observed across all regions of the world. As depicted in Figure 1.1, the average level of income per capita in Western and Eastern Europe, the Western Offshoots, Asia, Africa, and Latin America was in the range of $400–450 per year in the first millennium, and the average growth rate in each of these regions was nearly zero. This state of stagnation persisted until the end of the eighteenth century across most regions. In particular, the level of income per capita in 1820 ranged from about $420 per year in Africa, $580 in Asia, $690 in Latin America, and $680 in Eastern Europe, to $1,200 in the Western Offshoots and Western Europe. Furthermore, the average annual growth rate of output per capita over this period ranged from 0% in the impoverished region of Africa to 0.14% in the most prosperous region of Western Europe.

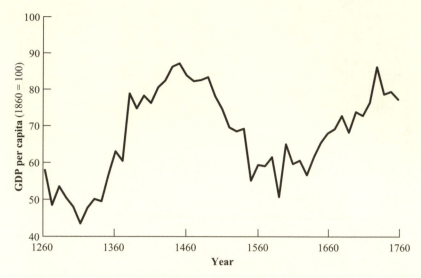

FIGURE 2.3. Fluctuations in gross domestic product (GDP) per capita: England, 1260–1760.
Data source: Clark (2005).

Nevertheless, wages and income per capita fluctuated significantly within regions, deviating from their sluggish long-run trend over decades and sometimes over several centuries. For example, as depicted in Figure 2.3, income per capita in England fluctuated considerably over most of the past millennium. In particular, it declined during the thirteenth century and increased sharply during the fourteenth and fifteenth centuries in response to the catastrophic population decline in the aftermath of the Black Death. This two-century rise in income per capita was followed by population growth, which brought about a decline in income per capita in the sixteenth century back to its fourteenth century level. Finally, income per capita increased once again in the seventeenth century and remained stable during most of the eighteenth century.

2.1.2 Population Dynamism

> *Population, when unchecked, increases in geometrical progression of such a nature as to double itself every twenty-five years.*
>
> —Thomas Malthus

Population growth during this time followed the Malthusian pattern as well. As depicted in Figure 2.4, the slow pace of resource expansion during the first

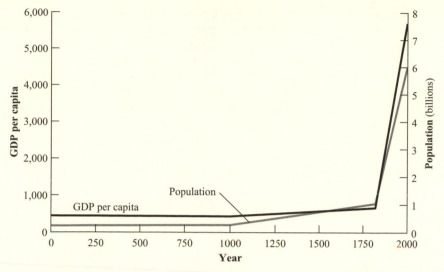

FIGURE 2.4. Evolution of world population and income per capita, 1–2000.
Data source: Maddison (2003).

millennium was reflected in a modest increase in the population of the world
from 231 million people in 1 CE to 268 million in 1000 CE, a minuscule average
growth rate of 0.02% per year.[2] The more rapid—but still sluggish—expansion
of resources during 1000–1500 permitted world population to increase from 268
million in 1000 CE to 438 million in 1500, a slow 0.1% average growth rate
per year. Resource expansion during 1500–1820 had a more significant impact
on world population, which increased from 438 million in 1500 to 1.04 billion
in 1820, an average pace of 0.27% per year. This positive association between
income per capita and the size of the population has been maintained in the past
two centuries as well, with world population surpassing the remarkable level of
six billion people (Maddison, 2001).[3]

Variation in population density across countries during the Malthusian
Epoch primarily reflected cross-country differences in technology and land

[2] Since output per capita grew at an average rate of 0% per year during 0–1000, the pace of
resource expansion was approximately equal to the pace of population growth, namely, 0.02% per
year.

[3] Lee (1997) reports positive income elasticity of fertility and negative income elasticity of
mortality from studies examining a wide range of pre-industrial countries. Similarly, Wrigley and
Schofield (1981) find a strong positive correlation between real wages and marriage rates in England
during 1551–1801, and Clark and Hamilton (2006) find that in England, at the beginning of the
seventeenth century, the number of surviving offspring is higher among households with higher
levels of income and literacy rates.

productivity. Due to the positive adjustment of population to an increase in income per capita, differences in technology or in land productivity across countries resulted in varying levels of population density rather than differences in living standards.[4] This pattern of increased population density persisted until the demographic transition, namely, as long as the positive relationship between income per capita and population growth was maintained. For instance, China's technological advances during 1500–1820 were associated with an increase in its share of world population from 23% to 37%, while its income per capita remained constant at about $600 per year.[5] Similarly, during 1600–1870, Britain's technological advancement relative to the rest of the world was accompanied by the doubling of its share of world population from 1.1% to 2.5%, and during 1820–1870, the land-abundant, technologically advanced United States experienced an increase in its share of world population from 1% to 3.2%.[6]

2.1.3 Fertility and Mortality

The relationship between fertility and mortality during the Malthusian Epoch appears ambiguous. Periods marked by resource expansion—and thus, plausibly, improved nourishment and health infrastructure—permitted a rise in the number of people who could be supported by the environment, inducing an increase in fertility rates along with a reduction in mortality rates. Moreover, eras characterized by rising mortality rates (e.g., the Black Death) induced an increase in fertility rates such that the number of surviving offspring was maintained at a level that could be supported by existing resources.

In particular, demographic patterns in England during the fourteenth and fifteenth centuries suggest that an increase in mortality rates, in conjunction with a rise in income per capita, was associated with a significant rise in fertility rates. However, the period 1540–1820 in England, which was marked by resource expansion, was characterized by a negative relationship between

---

[4] Consistent with the Malthusian paradigm, China's sophisticated agricultural technologies, for example, allowed high yields per acre but failed to raise the standard of living above subsistence. Similarly, introduction of the potato to Ireland in the middle of the seventeenth century was associated with a large increase in population over two centuries but without significant improvements in the standard of living. Furthermore, the destruction of potato crops by potato blight in the middle of the nineteenth century generated a massive decline in population due to the Great Famine and mass migration. Moreover, there is a positive association between the introduction of the potato, population, and urbanization across countries (Nunn and Qian, 2011).

[5] The Chinese population more than tripled during this period, increasing from 103 million in 1500 to 381 million in 1820.

[6] The population of the United Kingdom nearly quadrupled during 1700–1870, increasing from 8.6 million in 1700 to 31.4 million in 1870. Similarly, the population of the United States increased fortyfold, from 1 million in 1700 to 40.2 million in 1870, due to significant labor migration and high fertility rates.

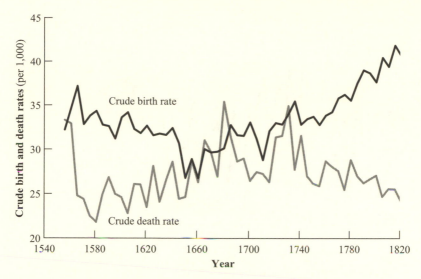

FIGURE 2.5. Fertility and mortality: England, 1540–1820.
Data source: Wrigley and Schofield (1981).

mortality and fertility rates. As depicted in Figure 2.5, an increase in mortality rates during 1560–1650 was associated with a decline in fertility rates, whereas the rise in income per capita during 1680–1820 was associated with a decline in mortality and an increase in fertility rates.

Life expectancy at birth fluctuated during the Malthusian Epoch, ranging from 24 years in Egypt during 33–258 CE to 42 years in England at the end of the sixteenth century. Throughout the initial process of European urbanization, the percentage of urbanized inhabitants in the population increased sixfold, from about 3% in 1520 to nearly 18% in 1750 (De Vries, 1984; and Bairoch, 1988). This rapid increase in population density, without significant changes in health infrastructure, generated a rise in mortality rates and a decline in life expectancy. In particular, as depicted in Figures 2.5 and 2.6, during 1580–1740, mortality rates increased in England by 50% and life expectancy at birth fell from around 40 to nearly 30 years (Wrigley and Schofield, 1981). However, a decline in mortality along with a rise in life expectancy began in the 1740s. Life expectancy at birth rose from around 30 to 40 in England and from 25 to 40 in France during 1740–1830 (Livi-Bacci, 2001).

2.1.4 Fluctuations in Income and Population

Fluctuations in population and wages during this epoch also exhibited the Malthusian pattern. Episodes of technological progress, land expansion,

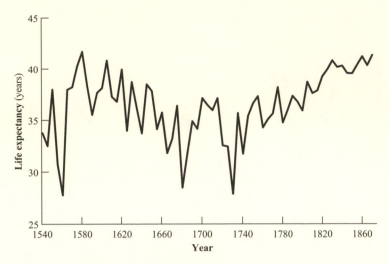

FIGURE 2.6. Life expectancy: England, 1540–1870.
Data source: Wrigley and Schofield (1981).

favorable climatic conditions, and major epidemics (which resulted in a decline of the adult population) brought about temporary increases in real wages and income per capita. In particular, as depicted in Figure 2.7, the catastrophic decline in the population of England during the Black Death (1348–1349) from about 6 million to about 3.5 million people demonstrates the causal effect of population decline in a Malthusian world. The land-labor ratio significantly increased and real wages tripled in the subsequent 150 years.[7] Ultimately, however, it appears that most of this increase in real resources per capita was channeled into an increase in the size of the population, bringing the real wage rate in the 1560s back to its pre-plague level.

2.1.5 Technological Progress

Technological progress during the Malthusian Epoch was positively affected by the size of the population. Population scale increased the supply of innovative ideas and their rate of diffusion. In addition, the size of the population affected the degree of specialization in the production process, the extent of learning by doing, and the scope for inter-regional trade and thus the degree of technological imitation and adoption. Moreover, increased population density contributed to population pressure and thus to the necessity of innovations (Boserup, 1965; Kremer, 1993).

---

[7] Voigtländer and Voth (2009) suggest that this major shock was instrumental for the rise in European income per capita above subsistence in the early modern period.

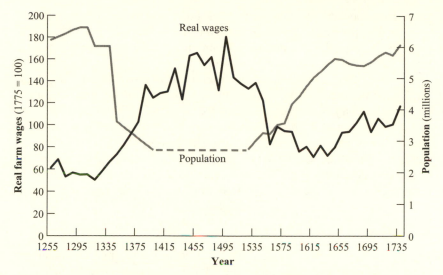

FIGURE 2.7. Population and real wages: England, 1250–1750.
Data source: Clark (2005).
Note: Reliable data on the evoluion of population during 1400–1525 is not available.

2.1.6 Main Characteristics of the Epoch

The evidence suggests that the process of development during most of human existence was marked by Malthusian stagnation. Resources generated by technological progress and land expansion were channeled primarily into increases in the size of the population, with only a minute contribution to the level of income per capita in the long run. While cross-country variations in levels of technology and land productivity were reflected by differences in population densities, their differential effect on living standards was merely transitory.

Nevertheless, the epoch of stagnation in income per capita masked a dynamism that may have ultimately brought about the take-off from this regime. In particular, Unified Growth Theory suggests that although growth of income per capita was minuscule during the Malthusian Epoch, the dynamism in population and technology that characterized this period was instrumental for the eventual emergence of economies from this stagnation.

2.2 The Post-Malthusian Regime

Ironically, shortly before the publication of Malthus's influential essay, some regions in the world began to emerge from the trap that he was describing. During the Post-Malthusian Regime, the Malthusian mechanism linking higher income to higher population growth continued to function. However, the effect that higher population had on diluting resources per capita, and thus on lowering income per capita, was counteracted by an acceleration in technological progress and capital accumulation, allowing income per capita to rise despite the offsetting effects of population growth.

The take-off of developed regions from the Malthusian Regime was associated with the Industrial Revolution and occurred during the first part of the nineteenth century. In contrast, the take-off of less developed regions took place toward the beginning of the twentieth century and was delayed in some countries until well into the twentieth century. The Post-Malthusian Regime ended with the onset of the decline in population growth that took place toward the end of the nineteenth century in Western Europe and the Western Offshoots and in the second half of the twentieth century in less developed regions.

2.2.1   Take-off in Income per Capita

During the Post-Malthusian Regime, the average growth rate of output per capita increased significantly, and living standards started to differ considerably across countries. The average growth rate of output per capita in the world soared from 0.05% per year during 1500–1820 to 0.5% per year in 1820–1870 and 1.3% per year in 1870–1913. The timing of the take-off and its magnitude differed across regions. As depicted in Figure 2.8, the take-off from the Malthusian Epoch and the transition to the Post-Malthusian Regime occurred at the beginning of the nineteenth century in Western Europe and the Western Offshoots; at the end of the nineteenth century in Latin America; and only in the second half of the twentieth century in Asia and Africa.

The differential timing of the take-off from the Malthusian Epoch increased the gap between the richest regions of the West and the impoverished region of Africa from about 3:1 in 1820 to approximately 5:1 in 1870. The level of income per capita across the globe in 1870, as depicted in Figure 1.1, ranged from about $440 in Africa, $540 in Asia, $700 in Latin America, and $870 in Eastern Europe, to $1,970 in Western Europe and $2,430 in the Western Offshoots.

2.2.2   Spike in Population Growth

The rapid increase in income per capita in the Post-Malthusian Regime was partly channeled into an increase in population. The Western European take-off, along with that of the Western Offshoots, brought about a sharp increase in population growth in these regions and consequently a modest rise in population growth in the world as a whole. The subsequent take-off of less developed regions and the associated increase in their population growth brought about an additional significant rise in world population growth. The rate of world population growth increased from an average of 0.27% per year during 1500–1820 to

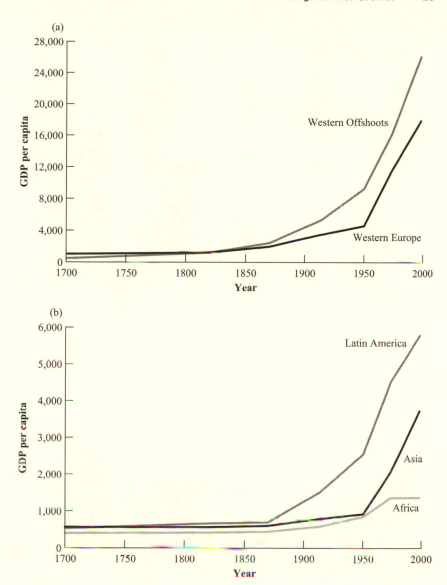

FIGURE 2.8. Differential timing of the take-off across regions: (a) early take-off; (b) late take-off.
Data source: Maddison (2001).

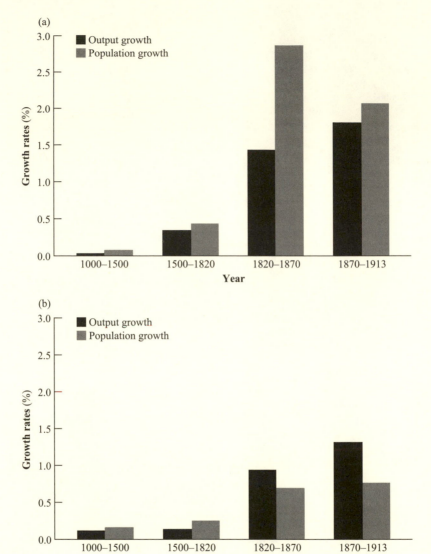

FIGURE 2.9. Regional growth of GDP per capita and population, 1500–2000: (a) Western Offshoots; (b) Western Europe; (c) Africa; (d) Latin America. *Data source:* Maddison (2001).

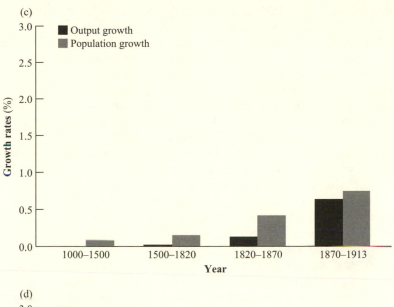

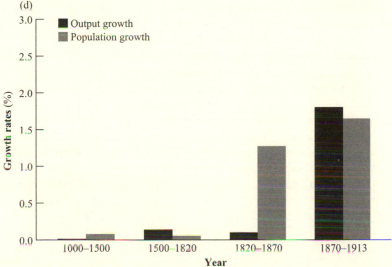

FIGURE 2.9 *(continued)*

0.4% per year in 1820–1870, and to 0.8% per year in 1870–1913. Furthermore, despite the decline in population growth in Western Europe and the Western Offshoots toward the end of the nineteenth century and the beginning of the twentieth century, the delayed take-off of less developed regions and the significant increases in their income per capita prior to their demographic transitions generated a further increase in the rate of world population growth. The rate increased to 0.9% per year during 1913–1950 and continued to increase, reaching 1.9% per year during 1950–1973. Ultimately, the onset of the demographic transition in most less developed economies during the second half of the twentieth century contributed to the decline of the world population growth rate to 1.7% per year in 1973–1998 (Maddison, 2001).

As depicted in Figure 2.9, the take-off in growth rates of income per capita in all regions of the world was associated with a corresponding take-off in population growth. In particular, the average growth rate of income per capita in Western Europe during 1820–1870 rose to an annual rate of 0.95% (from 0.15% during 1500–1820), while population growth significantly increased to about 0.7% (from 0.26% during 1500–1820). Similarly, the average growth of income per capita in the Western Offshoots during 1820–1870 rose to an annual rate of 1.4% (from 0.3% during 1500–1820), while population growth increased to about 2.9% (from 0.4% during 1500–1820). Other regions exhibit a similar pattern.

Ultimately, however, most regions experienced a demographic transition and subsequently a transition to an era of sustained economic growth, which enabled economies to convert a larger share of the fruits of factor accumulation and technological progress into growth of output per capita.

During the Post-Malthusian Regime, technological leaders and land-abundant regions improved their relative positions in the world in terms of both income per capita and population size. The increase in population densities of technological leaders persisted as long as the positive relationship between income per capita and population growth was maintained. Western Europe's technological advancement relative to the rest of the world increased its share of world population from 13% in 1820 to 15% in 1870, while the regional technological leader, the United Kingdom, increased its share of world population from 2% to 2.5% over this 50-year period. In addition, land abundance and technological advancement in the Western Offshoots and the associated effects on net reproduction rate and migration increased their share of world population over this period from 1.1% in 1820 to 3.6% in 1870.

Moreover, the rate of population growth relative to the growth rate of aggregate income declined gradually over this period. For instance, the growth rate of total output in Western Europe was 0.3% per year between 1500 and 1700, and 0.6% per year between 1700 and 1820. In both periods, two-thirds of the increase in total output was matched by increases in population growth, and the growth of income per capita was only 0.1% per year in the earlier period and 0.2% in the later one. In the United Kingdom, where growth was the fastest, the same rough division between total output growth and population growth can be observed: total output grew at an annual rate of 1.1% in the 120 years after 1700, while population grew at an annual rate of 0.7%. Population and income per capita continued to grow after 1820, but increasingly, the growth of total output was expressed as growth in income per capita. Population growth was 40% of total output growth during 1820–1870, dropping further after the demographic transition to about 20% of output growth during 1929–1990.

2.2.3 Fertility and Mortality

The rise in real income and relaxation in households' budget constraints during the Post-Malthusian Regime allowed for an increase in fertility rates along with increased investment in human capital. Despite the decline in mortality rates, fertility rates (as well as population growth) increased in most of Western Europe until the second half of the nineteenth century (Dyson and Murphy, 1985; Coale and Treadway, 1986). In particular, as depicted in Figure 2.10, despite a century-long decline in mortality rates, crude birth rates in England increased during the eighteenth century and the beginning of the nineteenth century. Thus, the net reproduction rate (i.e., the number of daughters per woman who reach reproduction age) increased from approximately the replacement level of one surviving daughter per woman in 1740 to about 1.5 on the eve of the demographic transition in 1870.

It appears that the significant rise in income per capita during the Post-Malthusian Regime increased the desired number of surviving offspring and thus, despite the decline in mortality rates, fertility in some regions increased, enabling households to reach this higher rate. In the absence of modern contraceptive methods, fertility was partly controlled during this period via adjustment in the age of marriage.[8] As depicted in Figure 2.11, the pattern of increased crude birth rates during 1700–1820 was associated with an earlier female age of marriage.[9]

---

[8] The importance of this mechanism of fertility control is implicitly reflected in the assertion by William Cobbett (1763–1835), a leader of the campaign against the changes brought by the Industrial Revolution: "men, who are able and willing to work, cannot support their families, and ought . . . to be compelled to lead a life of celibacy, for fear of having children to be starved." Quoted from "To Parson Malthus," *Political Register* (London, May 8, 1819).

[9] The same pattern is observed in the relationship between crude birth rates and crude marriage rates (per 1,000).

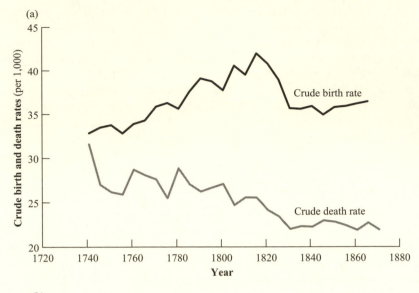

FIGURE 2.10. (a) Fertility and mortality, and (b) net reproduction rate: England, 1730–1871.
Data source: Wrigley and Schofield (1981).

FIGURE 2.11. Fertility rates and women's age of marriage: England 1610–1830. *Data source:* Wrigley and Schofield (1981).

2.2.4 Industrialization and Urbanization

The take-off from the Malthusian Epoch was associated with acceleration in the process of industrialization as well as a significant rise in urbanization. The take-off in developed regions was accompanied by a rapid process of industrialization. As depicted in Figure 2.12, the level of industrialization per capita (measured as the volume of industrial production per capita) increased significantly in the United Kingdom after 1750, rising by 50% during 1750–1800, quadrupling in 1800–1860, and nearly doubling in 1860–1913. Similarly the level of industrialization per capita accelerated in the United States, doubling during 1750–1800 as well as in 1800–1860 and increasing sixfold during 1860–1913. A similar pattern was experienced in Germany, France, Sweden, Switzerland, Belgium, and Canada, where industrialization nearly doubled during 1800–1860 and further accelerated during 1860–1913.

The take-off of less developed economies in the twentieth century was also associated with increased industrialization. However, as depicted in Figure 2.12, during the nineteenth century these economies experienced a decline in industrialization per capita. This decline presumably reflected the operation of two effects: the forces of globalization and colonialism that induced less developed economies to specialize in the production of raw materials and agricultural

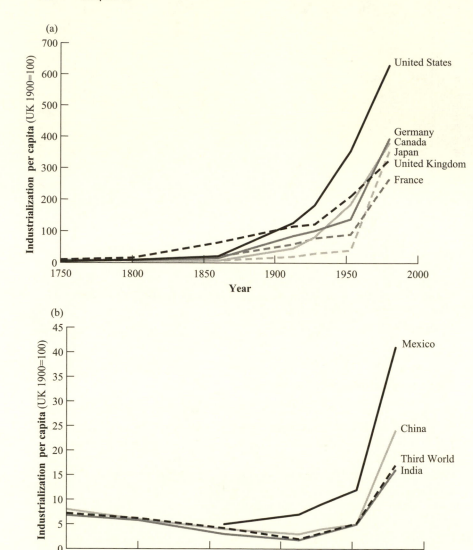

FIGURE 2.12. Levels of industrialization per capita (United Kingdom in 1900 = 100).
Data source: Bairoch (1982).
Notes: Countries are defined according to their 1913 boundaries. Germany from 1953 is defined as East and West Germany. India after 1928 includes Pakistan.

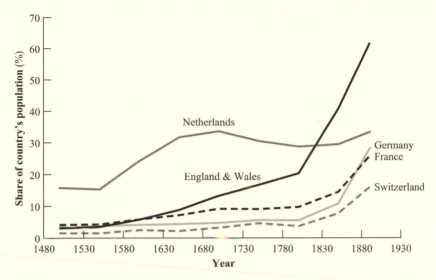

FIGURE 2.13. Percentage of country's population in cities with populations larger than 10,000.
Data sources: De Vries (1984); Bairoch (1988).

goods; and the adverse effect of significant increases in population on the level of industrial production per capita.[10]

The take-off from Malthusian stagnation and the acceleration in the process of industrialization considerably increased the level of urbanization. As reflected in Figure 2.13, the percentage of inhabitants in European cities with a population larger than 10,000 people nearly tripled over the years 1750–1870, from 17% to 54%. Similarly, the percentage of the English citizens who lived in cities with populations larger than 5,000 quadrupled during 1750–1910, from 18% to 75% (Bairoch, 1988).

This rapid process of industrialization and urbanization was accompanied by a decline in the share of agricultural production in total output, depicted in Figure 2.14. For instance, this share declined in England from 40% in 1790 to 7% in 1910.

2.2.5 Globalization and the Pace of Industrialization

The intensification of international trade during the nineteenth century asymmetrically affected the pace of industrialization in developed and less

---

[10] The sources of the decline in the industrialization of less developed economies are further explored in Chapter 6, following the thesis of Galor and Mountford (2008).

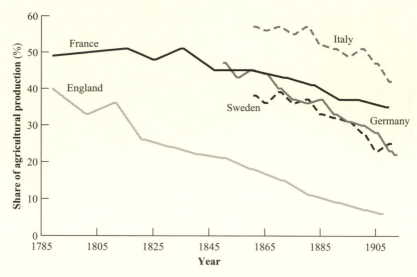

FIGURE 2.14. Decline in the percentage of agricultural production in total output: Europe, 1790–1910.
Data source: Mitchell (1975).

developed economies. During the nineteenth century, North-South trade, as well as North-North trade, expanded significantly due to the rapid industrialization of northwestern Europe as well as the reduction of trade barriers and transportation costs. The ratio of world trade to output rose from about 2% in 1800 to 10% in 1870, 17% in 1900, and 21% in 1913 (Estevadeordal et al., 2003). While much of the increased trade occurred among industrial economies, a significant proportion took place between industrial and nonindustrial economies. As shown in Table 2.1, a clear pattern of specialization emerged during this period. The United Kingdom and northwestern Europe were net importers of primary products and net exporters of manufactured goods, whereas the exports of Asia, Oceania, Latin America, and Africa were overwhelmingly composed of primary products (Findlay and O'Rourke, 2001).

Atlantic trade as well as that with Asia had major effects on European growth starting in the late sixteenth century (Acemoglu et al., 2005b). In addition, later expansion of international trade contributed further to the process of industrialization in the United Kingdom and continental Europe (Crafts and Thomas, 1986; O'Rourke and Williamson, 1999). For the United Kingdom, the proportion of foreign trade to national income grew from about 10% in the 1780s to about 26% during 1837–1845 and 51% during 1909–1913 (Kuznets, 1967). Other European economies experienced a similar pattern. The proportion of

TABLE 2.1
Regional shares of world trade in manufactures (%)

Region	1876–1880		1896–1900		1913	
	Exports	Imports	Exports	Imports	Exports	Imports
The United Kingdom and Ireland	37.8	9.1	31.5	10.4	25.3	8.2
Northwestern Europe	47.1	18.1	45.8	20.3	47.9	24.4
Other Europe	9.2	13.3	10.3	12.2	8.3	15.4
The United States and Canada	4.4	7.7	7.4	9.6	10.6	12.1
Rest of the world	1.5	51.8	5.0	47.5	7.9	39.9

Data source: Yates (1959).

foreign trade to national income on the eve of World War I was 54% in France, 38% in Germany, 34% in Italy, and 40% in Sweden (Kuznets, 1967). Furthermore, exports were critical for the viability of some industries, especially the cotton industry, where 70% of British output was exported in the 1870s (Mokyr, 1985).[11] Thus while technological advances could have spawned the Industrial Revolution without an expansion of international trade, the growth in exports increased the pace of industrialization and the growth rate of output per capita.[12]

In contrast, globalization appears to have had an adverse effect on the pace of industrialization in less developed economies. As depicted in Figure 2.12, during the nineteenth century these economies experienced a decline in per capita industrialization, due in part to the forces of globalization and colonialism, which induced them to specialize in the production of raw materials and agricultural goods.

2.2.6 Central Features of the Regime

The evidence suggests that during the Post-Malthusian Regime, the Malthusian mechanism linking higher income to higher population growth continued

---

[11] The quantitative study of Stokey (2001) suggests that trade was instrumental for the increased share of manufacturing in total output in the United Kingdom, as well as for the significant rise in real wages. Similarly, the empirical examination of O'Rourke and Williamson (2005) demonstrates that trade was a significant force behind the rise in British productivity.

[12] Pomeranz (2000) argues that technological and developmental differences between Europe and Asia were minor around 1750, but the discovery of the New World enabled Europe, via Atlantic trade, to overcome land constraints and take off technologically.

to function. Nevertheless, in the early process of industrialization, capital accumulation and acceleration of technological progress counteracted the effect that higher population growth had on diluting resources per capita, allowing income per capita to rise despite the offsetting effects of population growth.

In accordance with the main characteristics of Unified Growth Theory, the inherent Malthusian interaction between the rate of technological progress and the size and composition of the population accelerated the pace of technological progress and initially generated a considerable rise in the growth rates of income per capita and population. However, in light of the presence of Malthusian forces during this regime, a permanent break from the Malthusian trap could not have been orchestrated without the emergence of an additional force toward the end of the Post-Malthusian Regime—human capital formation.

2.3 Industrialization and Human Capital Formation

The second phase of industrialization was characterized by a gradual increase in the relative importance of human capital in the production process. As hypothesized by Unified Growth Theory, this important development was triggered by acceleration in the rate of technological progress and the role of human capital in adapting to a rapidly changing technological environment.

In the first phase of the Industrial Revolution, human capital played a limited role in the production process. Education was motivated by a variety of factors, including religion, social control, moral conformity, sociopolitical stability (i.e., the shadow of rebellion of the masses), social and national cohesion, and military efficiency. The extent to which public education was provided was not correlated with industrial development, and it differed across countries due to political, cultural, social, historical, and institutional factors. As argued by Landes (1969), although certain workers—supervisory and office personnel in particular—were required to read and do elementary arithmetical operations to perform their duties, a large fraction of the work of industry was performed by illiterates, especially in the early days of the Industrial Revolution.

In contrast, during the second phase of the Industrial Revolution, the demand for skilled labor in the growing industrial sector markedly increased. Human capital formation was designed primarily to satisfy increasing skill requirements in the process of industrialization, and industrialists became involved in shaping the educational system. Moreover, the reversal of the Malthusian relationship between income and population growth during the demographic transition was associated with a further increase in the level of resources invested in each child.

Evidence relating to the evolution of the return on human capital during this period is scarce and controversial.[13] One can mistakenly argue that the lack of clear evidence about the increase in return on human capital during this period indicates the absence of a significant increase in the demand for human capital. However, this partial equilibrium argument is flawed. The return on human capital is affected by the demand and supply of human capital. Technological progress in the second phase of the Industrial Revolution brought about an increase in demand for human capital, and indeed, in the absence of a supply response, one would have expected an increase in the return on human capital. However, the significant increase in schooling that took place during the nineteenth century (in particular, the introduction of public education), which lowered the cost of education, generated a significant increase in the supply of educated workers. Some of this supply response was a direct reaction to the increase in demand for human capital and thus may have only operated to partially offset the increase in the return on human capital. However, the introduction of public education generated an additional force that increased the supply of educated labor and operated to reduce the return on human capital.

2.3.1 Industrial Demand for Education

Education reforms in developed countries in the eighteenth and nineteenth centuries are indicative of the significance of industrial development in the formation of human capital during the second half of the nineteenth century. In particular, differences in the timing of the establishment of a national system of public education between England and continental Europe are instrumental in isolating the role that industrial forces played in human capital formation.

England
During the first phase of the Industrial Revolution (1760–1830), capital accumulation increased significantly without a corresponding increase in the supply of skilled labor. The investment-output ratio increased from 6% in 1760 to 12% in 1831 (Crafts, 1985, p. 73), whereas literacy rates remained largely unchanged, and the state devoted virtually no resources to raising the level of literacy among the masses (Mokyr, 2001). Literacy was largely a cultural skill or a hierarchical symbol and was of limited use in the production process. For instance, in 1841, only 5% of male workers and only 2% of female workers were employed in occupations in which literacy was strictly required (Mitch,

---

[13] Not surprisingly, existing evidence focusing on the return on old skills (e.g., construction) does not indicate that the return on such skills increased in England during the nineteenth century (Clark, 2005).

1992).[14] Workers developed skills primarily through on-the-job training, and child labor was highly valuable.

The development of a national public system of education in England lagged behind other Western European countries by nearly half a century (Sanderson, 1995).[15] England's early industrialization occurred without direct state intervention in the development of the minimal skills required for industrial production (Green, 1990). England initiated a sequence of reforms in its educational system after the 1830s, and literacy rates gradually increased. The process initially had nonindustrial motivations, such as religion, social control, moral conformity, enlightenment, and military efficiency, as was the case in other European countries (e.g., Germany, France, Holland, and Switzerland) that had supported public education much earlier. However, in light of the modest demand for skills and literacy by the capitalists, the level of governmental support was rather small.[16]

As the Industrial Revolution progressed to its second phase, the demand for skilled labor in the growing industrial sector markedly increased, and the proportion of children aged 5–14 in primary schools rose from 11% in 1855 to 25% in 1870 (Flora et al., 1983). Literacy became an increasingly desirable characteristic for employment, as indicated by job advertisements of the period (Mitch, 1993). In light of industrial competition from other countries, capitalists started to recognize the importance of technical education for the provision of skilled workers. As noted by Sanderson (1995, pp. 10–13), "Reading . . . enabled the efficient functioning of an urban industrial society laced with letter writing, drawing up wills, apprenticeship indentures, passing bills of exchange, and notice and advertisement reading." Moreover, manufacturers argued that "universal education is required in order to select, from the mass of the workers, those who respond well to schooling and would make a good foreman on the shop floor" (Simon, 1987, p. 104).

As it became apparent that skills were necessary for the creation of an industrial society, concerns that the acquisition of literacy would make the working

---

[14] Some have argued that the low skill requirements even declined over this period. For instance, Sanderson (1995) suggests that the emerging economy created a whole range of new occupations that required even less literacy and education than the old ones.

[15] For instance, in his parliamentary speech in defense of his 1837 education bill, Whig politician Henry Brougham reflected on this gap: "It cannot be doubted that some legislative effort must at length be made to remove from this country the opprobrium of having done less for education of the people than any of the more civilized nations on earth" (Green, 1990, pp. 10–11).

[16] Even in 1869, the English government funded only one-third of school expenditure (Green, 1990).

classes receptive to radical and subversive ideas dissipated, and capitalists lobbied for the provision of public education.[17] The pure laissez-faire policy failed to develop a proper educational system, and capitalists demanded government intervention in the provision of education. As Leeds iron-master and advocate of technical education James Kitson explained to the Select Committee on Scientific Instruction (1867–1868): "[T]he question is so extensive that individual manufacturers are not able to grapple with it, and if they went to immense trouble to establish schools they would be doing it in order that others may reap the benefit" (Green, 1990, p. 295).[18] An additional turning point in the attitude of English capitalists toward public education was the Paris Exhibition of 1867, where the limitations of English scientific and technical education became evident. Unlike the 1851 exhibition in which England won most of the prizes, the English performance in Paris was rather poor, and of the 90 classes of manufacturers, Britain dominated only in 10.[19]

In 1868, the government established the parliamentary Select Committee on Scientific Education. This was the origin of nearly 20 years of various parliamentary investigations into the relationship between the sciences, industry, and education designed to address the capitalists' outcry over the necessity of universal public education. A sequence of reports by the Committee in 1868, by the Royal Commission on Scientific Instruction and the Advancement of Science during 1872–1875, and by the Royal Commission on Technical Education in 1882 underlined the inadequate training for supervisors, managers, proprietors and workers. They argued that most managers and proprietors did not understand the manufacturing process and thus failed to promote efficiency, investigate innovative techniques, or value the skills of their workers (Green, 1990). In particular, W. E. Forster, the vice president of the committee of the Council of Education, told the House of Commons: "Upon the speedy provision of elementary education depends our industrial prosperity . . . if we leave our work-folk any longer unskilled . . . they will become overmatched in the

---

[17] There was a growing consensus among workers and capitalists about the virtues of reform. The labor union movement was increasingly calling for a national system of nonsectarian education. The National Education League (founded in 1869 by radical Liberals and Dissenters) demanded a free, compulsory, nonsectarian national system of education (Green, 1990).

[18] Indeed, the Factory Act of 1802 required owners of textile mills to provide elementary instruction for their apprentices, but the law was poorly enforced (Cameron, 1993).

[19] Lyon Playfair, who was one of the jurors, reported that "a singular accordance of opinion prevailed that our country has shown little inventiveness and made little progress in the peaceful arts of industry since 1862." The cause of this lack of progress "upon which there was most unanimity conviction is that France, Prussia, Austria, Belgium and Switzerland possess good systems of industrial education and that England possesses none" (Green, 1990, p. 296).

competition of the world" (Hurt, 1971, pp. 223–224). The reports made various recommendations that highlighted the need to redefine elementary schools, to revise the curriculum throughout the entire school system (particularly with respect to industry and manufacturing), and to improve teacher training.

In addition, in 1868 the Schools Inquiry Commission investigated secondary schools. It found that the level of instruction in the vast majority of schools was very unsatisfactory, reflecting the employment of untrained teachers and the use of antiquated teaching methods. Its main proposal was to organize a state inspection of secondary schools and provide efficient education geared to specific industrial needs. In particular, the Royal Commission on Technical Education of 1882 confirmed that England was being overtaken by the industrial superiority of Prussia, France, and the United States and recommended the introduction of technical and scientific education in secondary schools.

It appears that the English government gradually yielded to the capitalists and increased contributions to elementary as well as higher education. In the 1870 Education Act, the government assumed responsibility for ensuring universal elementary education. In 1880, just before the significant extension of the franchise in 1884—which made the working class the majority in most industrial counties—education was made compulsory throughout England. The 1889 Technical Instruction Act allowed new local councils to set up technical instruction committees, and the 1890 Local Taxation Act provided public funds that could be spent on technical education (Green, 1990). Finally, the 1902 Balfour Education Act marked the establishment of a national education system that provided free compulsory elementary education (Ringer, 1979; Green, 1990).

School enrollment of 10-year-olds increased from 40% in 1870 to 100% in 1900. The literacy rate among men, which was stable at around 65% during the first phase of the Industrial Revolution, increased significantly during the second phase, reaching nearly 100% at the end of the nineteenth century (Cipolla, 1969). Also, the proportion of children aged 5–14 in primary schools increased significantly in the second half of the nineteenth century, from 11% in 1855 to 74% in 1900 (Flora et al., 1983).

Continental Europe

Public education in the western countries of continental Europe (e.g., Prussia, France, Sweden, and the Netherlands) developed well before the Industrial Revolution, motivated by social, religious, political, and national factors. However, as was the case in England, massive educational reforms occurred in the second half of the nineteenth century due to the rising demand for skills in the process of industrialization. As noted by Green (1990, pp. 293–294), "In Continental Europe industrialization occurred under the tutelage of the state and began its accelerated development later when techniques were already becoming more scientific; technical and scientific education had been vigorously promoted from the center as an essential adjunct of economic growth and one that was recognized to be indispensable for countries which wished to close Britain's industrial lead."

In France, the initial development of the education system occurred well before the Industrial Revolution, but the process was intensified and transformed to satisfy industrial needs during the second phase of industrialization. The early development of elementary and secondary education in the seventeenth and eighteenth centuries was dominated by the church and religious orders. Some state interventions in technical and vocational training were designed to reinforce development in commerce, manufacturing, and military efficiency. After the French Revolution, the state established universal primary schools, but enrollment rates remained rather low. The state concentrated on the development of secondary and higher education, with the objective of producing an effective elite to operate the military and governmental apparatus. Secondary education remained highly selective, offering general and technical instruction largely to the middle class (Green, 1990). Legislative proposals during the National Convention quoted by Cubberley (1920, p. 516) are revealing about the underlying motives behind education in this period: "[C]hildren of all classes were to receive education, physical, moral and intellectual, best adapted to develop in them republican manners, patriotism, and the love of labor. . . . They are to be taken into the fields and workshops where they may see agricultural and mechanical operations going on."

The process of industrialization in France, the associated increase in the demand for skilled labor, and the breakdown of the traditional apprenticeship system significantly affected the state's attitude toward education. State grants for primary schools gradually increased in the 1830s, and some legislation was introduced to provide primary education in all regions, extend higher education, and provide teacher training and school inspections. The number of communities without schools fell by 50% from 1837 to 1850, and as the influence of industrialists on the structure of education intensified, education became more stratified according to occupational patterns (Anderson, 1975). This legislation reflected the increasing need for skilled labor in the economic environment of the period (Green, 1990). The eagerness of capitalists for rapid education reforms was reflected by the organization of industrial societies that financed schools specializing in chemistry, design, mechanical weaving, spinning, and commerce (Anderson, 1975).

As was the case in England, competition led industrialists to lobby for the provision of public education. The Great Exhibition of 1851 and the London Exhibition of 1862 created the impression that the technological gap between France and other European nations was narrowing and that French manufacturers should invest in the education of their labor force to maintain their technological superiority. Subsequently, reports on the state of industrial education by commissions established in 1862–1865 reflected the pleas of industrialists for the provision of industrial education on a large scale and for the implementation of scientific knowledge in the industry. "The goal of modern education . . . can no longer be to form men of letters, idle admirers of the past, but men of science, builders of the present, initiators of the future."[20] Education reforms in France were extensive in the second phase of the Industrial Revolution, and by 1881 a universal, free, compulsory, and secular primary school system had been established, emphasizing technical and scientific education. Illiteracy rates among conscripts tested at the age of 20 declined gradually from 38% in 1851–1855 to 17% in 1876–1880 (Anderson, 1975), and the proportion of children aged 5–14 in primary schools increased from 52% in 1850 to 86% in 1901 (Flora et al., 1983).

In Prussia, as in France, where the initial steps toward compulsory education took place at the beginning of the eighteenth century, well before the Industrial Revolution, education was viewed primarily as a way to unify the state. In the second part of the eighteenth century, education was made compulsory for all children aged 5–13. Nevertheless, these regulations were not strictly enforced partly due to the lack of funding (reflecting the difficulty of taxing landlords for this purpose) and partly due to their adverse effect on child labor income. At the beginning of the nineteenth century, motivated by the need for national cohesion, military efficiency, and trained bureaucrats, the education system was further reformed. Provincial and district school boards were established, education became compulsory (and secular) for a 3-year period, and the gymnasium was reconstituted as a state institution that provided 9 years of education for the elite (Cubberley, 1920; Green, 1990).

As in England and France, industrialization in Prussia triggered the implementation of universal elementary schooling. Taxes were imposed to finance the school system, and teachers' training and certifications were established. Secondary schools started to serve industrial needs as well; the *Realschulen*—which emphasized the teaching of mathematics and science—were gradually adopted, and vocational and trade schools were founded. Total enrollment in secondary school increased sixfold from 1870 to 1911 (Flora et al., 1983). Furthermore, the Industrial Revolution significantly affected the nature of education in German universities. German industrialists, who perceived advanced technology as a competitive advantage, lobbied for reforms in the operation of universities, and offered to pay to reshape their activities toward technological training and industrial applications of basic research (McClelland, 1980).

The evolution of education in the Netherlands also reflected the interest of capitalists in the skill formation of the masses. In particular, as early as the 1830s, industrial schools were established and funded by private organizations that represented industrialists and entrepreneurs. Ultimately, in the latter part of

---

[20] *L'enseignement Professionnel,* ii (1864, p. 332), quoted in Anderson (1975, p. 194).

the nineteenth century, the state—urged by industrialists and entrepreneurs—started to support these schools (Wolthuis, 1999).

United States

The process of industrialization in the United States also increased the importance of human capital in the production process. Evidence provided by Abramovitz and David (2000) and Goldin and Katz (2001) suggests that during 1890–1999, the contribution of human capital accumulation to the growth process of the United States nearly doubled.[21] As argued by Goldin (1998), the rise of the industrial, business, and commerce sectors in the late nineteenth century and early twentieth century increased the demand for managers, clerical workers, and educated sales personnel who were trained in accounting, typing, shorthand, algebra, and commerce. Furthermore, in the late 1910s, technologically advanced industries demanded blue-collar craft workers who were trained in geometry, algebra, chemistry, mechanical drawing, and related skills. The structure of education was transformed in response to industrial development and the increasing importance of human capital in the production process, and American high schools adapted to the needs of the modern workplace of the early twentieth century. Total enrollment in public secondary schools increased seventyfold from 1870 to 1950 (Kurian, 1994).[22]

2.3.2 Land Concentration and Human Capital Formation

The transition from an agricultural to an industrial economy altered the nature of the conflict among interest groups in society. The conflict of interest between the elite and the masses which had characterized the agricultural stage of development was transformed into a conflict between the entrenched landed

---

[21] Literacy rates in the United States were rather high prior to this increase in the demand for skilled labor. Literacy rates among the white population were already 89% in 1870, 92% in 1890, and 95% in 1910 (Engerman and Sokoloff, 2000). Education in earlier periods was motivated by social control, moral conformity, and social and national cohesion, as well as by skills required for trade and commerce. In particular, Bowles and Gintis (1975) and Field (1976) argue that educational reforms were designed to sustain the existing social order by displacing social problems into the school system.

[22] Due to differences in the structure of education finance between the United States and European countries, capitalists in the United States had only limited incentives to lobby for the provision of education and to support it financially. Unlike the central role that government funding played in the provision of public education in European countries, the evolution of the educational system in the United States was based on local initiatives and funding. The local nature of United States education initiatives induced community members, in urban as well as rural areas, to play a significant role in advancing their schooling systems. American capitalists, however, faced limited incentives to support the provision of education within a county in an environment where labor was mobile across counties and the benefits from educational expenditure in one county could be reaped by employers in other counties.

elites and emerging capitalist elites. The capitalists who were striving for an educated labor force supported policies that promoted public education, whereas landowners, whose interest lay in reducing the mobility of the rural labor force, favored policies that deprived the masses of education (Galor et al., 2009).[23]

Anecdotal evidence suggests that the degree of concentration of land ownership across countries and regions is inversely related to education expenditure and attainment. North and South America provide the most distinctive set of suggestive evidence regarding the relationship among the distribution of land ownership, education reforms, and the process of development. The original colonies in North and South America had vast amounts of land per person and levels of income per capita that were comparable to those of Western Europe. North and Latin America, however, differed in the distribution of land and resources. While the United States and Canada have been characterized by a relatively egalitarian distribution of land ownership, in the rest of the New World, land and resources have been persistently concentrated in the hands of the elite (Deininger and Squire, 1998).

Persistent differences in the distribution of land ownership between North and Latin America were associated with a significant divergence in education and income levels across these regions (Maddison, 2001). Although all economies in the Western hemisphere were developed enough in the early nineteenth century to justify investment in primary schools, only the United States and Canada were engaged in the education of the general population (Coatsworth, 1993; Engerman and Sokoloff, 2000).[24]

Variations in the degree of inequality in the distribution of land ownership among Latin American countries were reflected in differences in investment in human capital as well. In particular, Argentina, Chile, and Uruguay, in which inequality in the distribution of land ownership was less pronounced, invested significantly more in education (Engerman and Sokoloff, 2000). Similarly, Nugent and Robinson (2002) show that in Costa Rica and Colombia, where coffee is typically grown on small farms (reflecting lower inequality in the distribution of land), income and human capital are significantly higher than in Guatemala and El Salvador, where coffee plantations are rather large. Moreover, one of the principles championed by the progressives during the Mexican Revolution

---

[23] Interestingly, during the nineteenth century, the emergence of a broad-based demand for human capital–intensive services by the landowners in land-rich economies in Latin America (e.g., Argentina) triggered the establishment of an extensive public education system prior to the onset of significant manufacturing activities (Galiani et al., 2008).

[24] One may view the conflict that led to the Civil War in the United States as a struggle between the industrialists in the North, who were striving for a large supply of educated workers, and the landowners in the South, who wanted to sustain the existing system and to ensure a large supply of cheap uneducated labor.

of 1910 was compulsory free public education. However, the achievement of this goal varied greatly by state. In the north, where land distribution was more equitable, enrollment in public schools increased rapidly as industrialization advanced following the revolution. In contrast, in the south, where *haciendas* (employing essentially slave labor) dominated, there was virtually no increase in school enrollment following the revolution (Vaughan, 1982). Similarly, rural education in Brazil lagged behind some other Latin American countries due to the immense political power of local landlords. Hence, in 1950, 30 years after the Brazilian government had instituted an educational reform, nearly 75% of the nation was still illiterate (Bonilla, 1965).

2.3.3 Land Reforms and Education Reforms

Evidence from Japan, Korea, Russia, and Taiwan indicates that land reforms were followed by, or occurred simultaneously with, significant education reforms. There are two interpretations for these historical episodes. First, land reforms could have diminished the economic incentives of landowners to block education reforms. Second, an unfavorable shift in the balance of power from the viewpoint of the landed aristocracy could have brought about the implementation of both land and education reforms, consistent with the basic premise that landowners opposed spending on education, whereas others (e.g., the industrial elite) favored it.

Japan and the Meiji Restoration
Toward the end of the Tokugawa regime (1600–1867), although the level of education in Japan was impressive for its time, the provision of education was sporadic and had no central control or funding, reflecting partly the resistance of the landholding military class to education reforms (Gubbins, 1973). The opportunity to modernize the educational system arrived following the overthrow of the traditional feudal structure shortly after the Meiji Restoration of 1868. In 1871, an imperial decree initiated the abolishment of the feudal system. In a sequence of legislation during 1871–1883, decisions regarding land utilization and the choice of crops were transferred from landlords to farmers, prohibitions on the sale and mortgage of farmland were removed, a title of ownership was granted to the legal owners of the land, and ownership of communal pasture and forest land was transferred from wealthy landlords to the central government. This legislation resulted in the distribution of land among small family farms, a structure that persisted until the rise of a new landlord system during the 1930s (Hayami, 1975, chapter 3).

Education reform and land reform evolved simultaneously. In 1872 the Educational Code established compulsory and locally funded education for all children between the ages 6 and 14 (Gubbins, 1973). In addition, the central government funded a secondary school and university system. The Education Code of 1872 was refined in 1879 and 1886, setting the foundations for the structure of Japanese education until World War II. The progress in education attainment following the land reforms of the Meiji government was substantial: while in 1873 only 28% of school-age children attended schools, this ratio increased to 51% by 1883 and to 94% by 1903 (Passin, 1965).

Russia before the Revolution

Education in tsarist Russia lagged well behind comparable European countries at the close of the nineteenth century. Provincial councils dominated by wealthier landowners were responsible for their local school systems and were reluctant to favor the education of the peasants (Johnson, 1969). Literacy rates in rural areas were 21% in 1896, and the urban literacy rate was 56%. As the tsar's grip on power weakened during the early 1900s, the political power of wealthy landowners gradually declined, leading to a sequence of agrarian reforms that were initiated by Premier Pyotr Stolypin in 1906. Restrictions on the mobility of peasants were abolished, fragmented landholdings were consolidated, and the formation of individually owned farms was encouraged and supported through the provision of government credit. Stolypin's reforms accelerated the redistribution of land to individual farmers, and landholdings of the landed aristocracy declined from about 35–45% in 1860 to 17% in 1917 (Johnson, 1969).

In the wake of the agrarian reforms and the declining influence of the landed aristocracy, the provision of compulsory elementary education was proposed. The initial effort of 1906 languished, but the newly created representative body, the Duma, continued to pressure the government to provide free compulsory education. During 1908–1912, the Duma approved a sequence of significant increases in expenditures for education (Johnson, 1969). The share of the provincial council's budget that was allocated to education increased from 20% in 1905 to 31% in 1914 (Johnson, 1969), the share of the central government's budget devoted to the Ministry of Public Education increased threefold from 1.4% in 1906 to 4.9% in 1915, and the share of the entire population that was actively attending schools increased threefold from 1.7% in 1897 to 5.7% in 1915 (Dennis, 1961).

South Korea and Taiwan

The process of development in Korea was marked by major land reform followed by a massive increase in governmental expenditure on education. During the Japanese occupation in 1905–1945, land distribution in Korea became increasingly skewed, and by 1945 nearly 70% of Korean farming households were simply tenants (Eckert, 1990). During 1948–1950, the Republic of Korea instituted the Agricultural Land Reform Amendment Act which drastically affected landholdings.[25] The principle of land reform was enshrined in the constitution of 1948, and the actual implementation of the Agricultural Land Reform Amendment Act began in March 1950.[26] This act prohibited tenancy and land renting, put a maximum on the amount of land any individual could own, and dictated that individuals could only own land if they actually cultivated it. Owner cultivated farm households increased sixfold from 349,000 in 1949 to 1,812,000 in 1950, and tenant farm households declined from 1,133,000 in 1949 to essentially 0 in 1950 (Yoong-Deok and Kim, 2000).

Land reforms were accompanied by soaring expenditures on education. In 1949, a new Education Law was passed in South Korea that focused specifically on transforming the population into a technically competent workforce capable of industrial work. This legislation led to dramatic increases in the number of schools and students at all levels of education. Between 1945 and 1960, the number of elementary schools increased by 60%, and the number of elementary students went up by a staggering 165%. In secondary education, the growth was even more dramatic, with both the number of schools and the number of students growing by a factor of ten. The number of higher education institutions quadrupled, and the number of higher education students increased from only 7,000 in 1945 to more than 100,000 in 1960. In 1948, Korea allocated 8% of government expenditures to education. Following a slight decline due to the Korean War, educational expenditure increased to 9% in 1957 and to 15% in 1960, remaining at that level thereafter (Sah-Myung, 1983).

Taiwan experienced similar reforms during the same period, once Japanese colonization ended. The government of Taiwan implemented reforms during 1949–1953, enforcing rent reductions, selling public land to individual farmers who had previously been tenants, and permitting the purchase of rented land. In 1948, prior to these reforms, 57% of farm families were full or part owners and 43% were tenants or hired hands. By 1959, the share of full or part owners had increased to 81%, and the share of tenants had dropped to 19% (Chen, 1961).

A massive education reform accompanied these land reforms. The number of schools in Taiwan grew by 5% per year between 1950 and 1970, while the number of students grew by 6% per year. This pattern of growth mirrors that of South Korea, which had an especially impressive growth of 11% per year in the

---

[25] A major force behind this land reform was the aim of the post–World War II U.S. provisional government to remove the influence of large landowners (who were either Japanese or collaborators with the Japanese).

[26] Formally, education reform took place prior to the land reforms, but the provision for land reform was enshrined in the constitution prior to educational reform. The imminent land reform could have reduced the incentives for the landed aristocracy to oppose this education reform.

number of secondary students and 16% per year in higher education students. Funding for education grew from 1.8% of GNP in 1951 to 4.1% in 1970 (Lin, 1983).

In 1950, South Korea and Taiwan were primarily agricultural economies which had a GDP per capita (measured in 1990 international dollars) of about $770 and $940, respectively. South Korea and Taiwan's GDP per capita lagged well behind many countries in Latin America, such as Colombia ($2,150) and Mexico ($2,360), despite sharing with these countries a legacy of vast inequality in the distribution of agricultural land. In contrast to the Latin American countries, the implementation of land reforms in South Korea and Taiwan and their association with education reforms contributed to tremendous growth performance in the post-war period. With a level of income per capita in 1950 that placed them not only far behind the nations of Latin America but also behind Congo, Liberia, and Mozambique, these two countries have each grown at an average rate of nearly 6% per year between 1950 and 1998, leaving behind the countries of sub-Saharan Africa and overtaking the Latin American countries. In 1998, South Korea and Taiwan had GDP per capita levels that were 150% higher than that of Colombia and 100% higher than in Mexico (Maddison, 2001).

2.3.4 Political and Education Reforms

The nineteenth century was marked by significant political reforms along with the previously described education reforms and impressive human capital formation. One could therefore challenge the significance of the industrial motive for educational reform, and suggest that political reforms during the nineteenth century shifted the balance of power toward the working class and enabled workers to implement education reforms independently of the interests of the industrial elite. Have political institutions, rather than changes in economic incentives in the process of development, been the prime force behind the formation of human capital during this period?

In fact, political reforms that took place in the nineteenth century had no apparent effect on education reforms during this period, strengthening the hypothesis that industrial development, and the increasing demand for human capital, were indeed the trigger for human capital formation and the subsequent onset of the demographic transition. Education reforms took place in autocratic states that did not relinquish political power over the nineteenth century, and major reforms occurred in societies in the midst of democratization well before the stage at which the working class constituted the majority of voters.

In particular, as depicted in Figure 2.15, the most significant education reforms in England were completed before the voting majority shifted to the working class. The Reform Act of 1832 nearly doubled the total electorate, but even still only 13% of the voting-aged population was enfranchised. Artisans, the working classes, and some sections of the lower middle classes remained outside the political system. The franchise was extended further by the Reform Acts of 1867 and 1884, and the total electorate nearly doubled with each of these episodes. However, working-class voters did not become the majority in all urban counties until 1884 (Craig, 1989).

Figure 2.15 shows that a trend of significant increases in primary education was established well before the extension of the voting rights in the context of the 1867 and 1884 Reform Acts. In particular, the proportion of children aged 5–14 in primary schools increased fivefold (and surpassed 50%) over the three decades prior to the extension of the franchise in 1884 that granted the working class a majority in all urban counties. Furthermore, the political reforms do not appear to have had an effect on the pattern of education reform. In fact, the average growth rate of school attendance from decade to decade during 1855–1920 reached a peak around the Reform Act of 1884 and started declining thereafter. It is interesting to note, however, that the abolition of education fees in nearly all elementary schools occurred only in 1891, after the Reform Act of 1884, suggesting that the political power of the working class may have affected the distribution of education cost across the population, but the decision to educate the masses appears to be taken independently of the political power of the working class.

Thus, the onset of England's education reforms, and in particular the fundamental Education Act of 1870 and its major extension in 1880, occurred prior to the political reforms of 1884 that made the working class the majority in most counties. Moreover, while the shadow of the rebellion of the masses that may have prompted political reforms may have also contributed to education reforms (as established in Section 2.3.1), industrial demand for human capital in the second phase of industrialization dominated sociopolitical concerns in human capital formation.

In France, the trend of expanding education also preceded the major political reforms that gave the voting majority to the working class (Figure 2.15). Prior to 1848, restrictions limited the electorate to less than 2.5% of the voting-aged population. The 1848 revolution led to the introduction of universal voting rights for nearly all adult males and resulted in a majority for working-class voters. Nevertheless, the proportion of children aged 5–14 in primary schools had already doubled (and exceeded 50%) during the two decades prior to the extension of the franchise in 1848. Furthermore, the political reforms of 1848 did not appear to have an effect on the pattern of education expansion.

A similar pattern occurred in other European countries. Political reforms in the Netherlands did not affect the trend in education expansion, and the proportion of children aged 5–14 in primary schools exceeded 60% well before the major political reforms of 1887 and 1897. Similarly, the trends of political

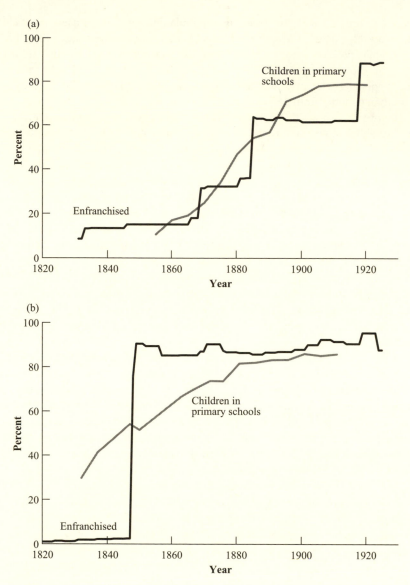

FIGURE 2.15. Evolution of voting rights and school enrollment: (a) England; (b) France.
Data source: Flora et al. (1983).

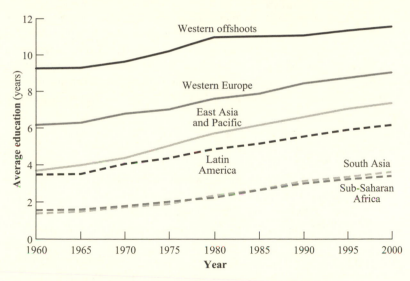

FIGURE 2.16. Evolution of average years of education, 1960–2000.
Data source: Barro and Lee (2001).

and education reforms in Sweden, Italy, Norway, Prussia, and Russia do not lend credence to the alternative hypothesis.

2.3.5 Human Capital Formation in Less Developed Economies

The process of industrialization was characterized by a gradual increase in the relative importance of human capital in less developed economies as well. As depicted in Figure 2.16, educational attainment increased significantly across all less developed regions during the Post-Malthusian Regime (Barro and Lee, 2001). Moreover, in line with the pattern that emerged among developed economies in the nineteenth century, the increase in educational attainment preceded or coincided with the decline in total fertility rates.

2.3.6 Main Insights

The evidence indicates that the inherent Malthusian interaction between the rate of technological progress and the size and composition of the population accelerated the pace of technological progress and ultimately triggered the process of industrialization. During the second phase of industrialization a major transformation in the production process had taken place. Industrial demand for human capital significantly increased, triggering the onset of human capital formation.

As will become apparent, human capital formation contributed greatly to the onset of the demographic transition that freed the growth process from the counterbalancing effect of population growth. Unified Growth Theory hypothesizes, therefore, that the rise in the industrial demand for human capital, and its impact on the formation of human capital, was an important force in the escape from the Malthusian trap and the transition to the Modern Growth Regime.

2.4 The Demographic Transition

The demographic transition swept the world in the course of the past two centuries. The unprecedented increase in population growth that occured during the Post-Malthusian Regime was ultimately reversed, bringing about significant reductions in fertility rates and population growth across various regions of the world, and enabling economies to convert a larger share of the fruits of factor accumulation and technological progress into growth of income per capita. The demographic transition enhanced the growth process via three channels: (1) reduced dilution of the stock of capital and land; (2) enhanced investment in the human capital of the population; and (3) altered age distribution of the population, temporarily increasing the size of the labor force relative to the population as a whole.

2.4.1 Decline in Population Growth

The timing of the demographic transition differed significantly across regions (Figure 2.17). The reduction in population growth occurred in Western Europe, the Western Offshoots, and Eastern Europe toward the end of the nineteenth century, whereas in Latin America and Asia this decline occurred only in the last decades of the twentieth century. Africa's population growth, in contrast, rose steadily during the twentieth century (Figure 2.18).

The Western Offshoots experienced the earliest decline in population growth, from an average annual rate of 2.9% during 1820–1870 to an annual average rate of 2.1% during 1870–1913 and 1.3% in 1913–1950.[27] In Western Europe, where land was less abundant and immigration was less significant, population growth declined from a (lower) average level of 0.8% per year during 1870–1913 to an average rate of 0.4% per year during 1913–1950. A similar reduction occurred in Eastern Europe as well.[28]

---

[27] Migration played a significant role in the rate of population growth of these land-abundant countries.

[28] A sharper reduction in population growth occurred in the United Kingdom, from 0.87% per year during 1870–1913 to 0.27% per year during 1913–1950.

FIGURE 2.17. Years elapsed since the onset of the demographic transition as of 2000.
Data source: Reher (2004).

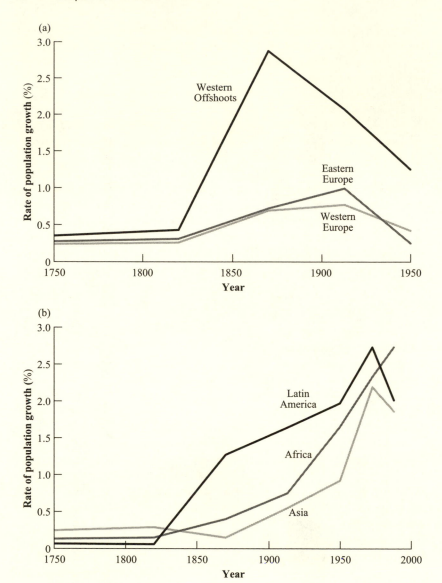

FIGURE 2.18. The demographic transition across regions: (a) early transitions; (b) late transitions.
Data source: Maddison (2001).

In contrast, in Latin America and Asia, the reduction in population growth started to take place in the 1970s.[29] Latin America experienced a decline in population growth from an average annual rate of 2.7% in 1950–1973 to an average annual rate of 2.0% during 1973–1998. Similarly, Asia (excluding Japan) experienced a decline in population growth from an average annual rate of 2.2% during 1950–1973 to an average annual rate of 1.9% during 1973–1998. The decline in fertility in these less developed regions, however, has been more significant in recent years, indicating a sharp forthcoming decline in population growth during the next decades.

In Africa, increased resources in the Post-Malthusian Regime have been channeled primarily into population growth. Africa's population growth rate has increased monotonically from a modest average annual rate of 0.4% during 1820–1870 to 0.7% during 1870–1913, 1.6% during 1913–1950, 2.3% during 1950–1973, and a rapid average annual rate of 2.7% during 1973–1998. Consequently, the share of the African population in the world has increased in the past century from about 7% in 1913 to 10% in 1973 and 13% in 1998.

2.4.2 Fertility Decline

During the demographic transition, the decline in population growth followed the decline in fertility rates. As depicted in Figure 2.19, during 1960–1999 the total fertility rate plummeted from 6 to 2.7 in Latin America and declined sharply from 6.1 to 3.1 in Asia. In contrast, in Africa, the total fertility rate declined only moderately over this period, from 6.5 to 5.0.[30] Furthermore, the total fertility rate in Western Europe and the Western Offshoots declined over this period below the replacement level (World Bank, 2001).

The demographic transition in Western Europe occurred near the turn of the nineteenth century. A sharp reduction in fertility took place simultaneously in several countries in the 1870s and resulted in a sharp decline of about one-third in fertility rates within a 50-year period. Moreover, a 10% decline in fertility rates occurred in 59% of all European countries during 1890–1920 (Coale and Treadway, 1986).

As depicted in Figure 2.20, during 1870–1920, crude birth rates (i.e., number of births per 1000 people) declined by 44% in England, 37% in Germany, and 32% in Finland and Sweden. Furthermore, despite the earlier onset of the demographic transition in France in the second half of the eighteenth century,

---

[29] As depicted in Figure 2.19, the decline in fertility in these countries started earlier. The delay in the decline in population growth can be attributed to an increase in life expectancy and in the relative size of the cohorts of women of reproductive age.

[30] The total fertility rate is the average number of children that would be born to a woman over her lifetime if she were to experience the current age-specific fertility rates throughout her lifetime and if she were to survive until the end of her reproductive life.

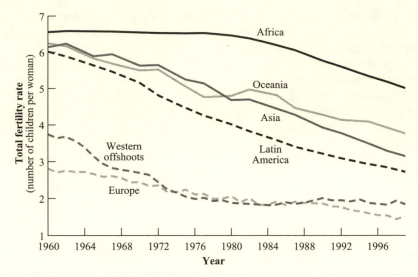

FIGURE 2.19. Evolution of the total fertility rate across regions, 1960–1999.
Data source: World Bank (2001).

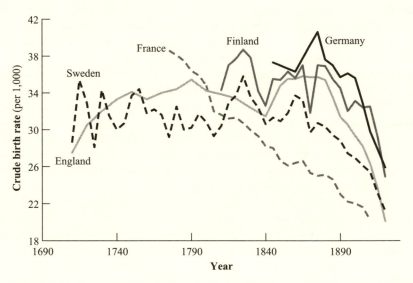

FIGURE 2.20. Demographic transitions in Western Europe: crude birth rates, 1710–1920.
Data sources: Andorka (1978).

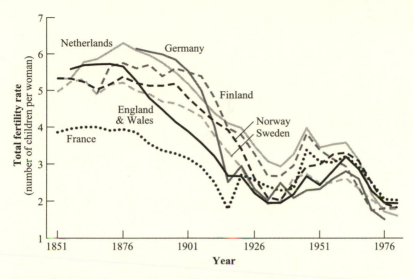

FIGURE 2.21. The demographic transition in Western Europe: total fertility rates, 1850–1980.
Data source: Chesnais (1992).

France experienced an additional significant reduction in fertility during 1870–1910, and its crude birth rates declined by 26%. Similar patterns are observed in the evolution of *total fertility rates* in Western Europe (Figure 2.21). Total fertility rates peaked in the 1870s and then declined sharply and simultaneously across Western European countries.

The decline in crude birth rates during the course of the demographic transition was accompanied by a significant decline in the net reproduction rates (i.e., the number of daughters per woman who reach reproductive age). Namely, the decline in fertility during the demographic transition outpaced the decline in mortality rates and brought about a decrease in the number of children who survived to the age of reproduction.

2.4.3 Mortality Decline

During the course of the demographic transition, the decline in mortality preceded the decline in fertility rates in most countries of the world, with the notable exceptions of France and the United States. The decline in mortality rates preceded that in fertility rates in Western European countries during 1730–1920 (Figures 2.20 and 2.22). In particular, the decline in mortality rates began in England 140 years prior to the decline in fertility, and in Sweden and Finland decades prior to the decline in fertility.

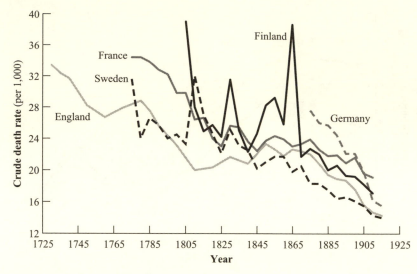

FIGURE 2.22. Mortality decline in Western Europe, 1730–1920.
Data source: Andorka (1978).

A similar pattern of mortality and fertility decline also emerged in less developed regions. As depicted in Figures 2.19 and 2.23, Africa experienced a sharp decline in infant mortality rates as of 1960, preceding the onset of decline in fertility rates in 1980. Moreover, evidence indicates a simultaneous reduction in mortality and fertility during 1960–2000 in all less developed regions.

2.4.4 Life Expectancy

The decline in mortality rates in developed countries since the eighteenth century (Figure 2.22) corresponded to a gradual increase in life expectancy, generating potentially a further incentive for investment in human capital. As depicted in Figure 2.24, life expectancy at birth in England increased at a stable rate from 32 years in the 1720s to about 41 years in the 1870s. This rate of rise in life expectancy increased toward the end of the nineteenth century, and life expectancy reached 50 years in 1906, 60 years in 1930, and 77 years in 1996.

While life expectancy increased significantly in developed regions in the nineteenth century (Figure 2.25), the rise in life expectancy in less developed regions occurred throughout the twentieth century, potentially contributing to human capital formation. In particular, life expectancy nearly tripled during the course of the twentieth century in Asia, rising from 24 years in 1900 to 66 years in 1999, reflecting the increase in income per capita as well as the diffusion

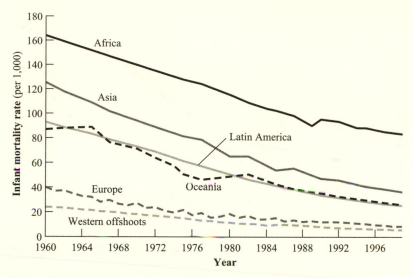

FIGURE 2.23. Decline in infant mortality rates across regions, 1960–1999.
Data source: World Bank (2001).

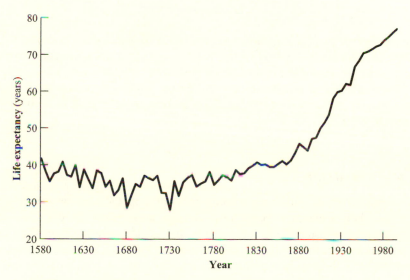

FIGURE 2.24. Evolution of life expectancy: England, 1580–1996.
Data sources: Wrigley and Schofield (1981) for 1580–1871; University of California, Berkeley, and Max Planck Institute (2003) for 1876–1996.

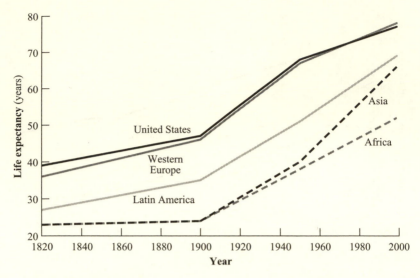

FIGURE 2.25. Evolution of life expectancy across regions, 1820–2000.
Data source: Maddison (2001).

of medical technology. Similarly, life expectancy in Africa more than doubled, from 24 years in 1900 to 52 years in 1999. In contrast, more rapid advancement in income per capita in Latin America generated an earlier rise in longevity. Life expectancy increased modestly during the nineteenth century and more significantly in the course of the twentieth century, from 35 years in 1900 to 69 years in 1999.

2.4.5 Central Characteristics

The demographic transition sweeping the world in the past two centuries brought about a significant reduction in fertility rates and population growth in various regions of the world. It enabled economies to convert a larger share of the gains from factor accumulation and technological progress into the material well-being of the population, rather than into its size.

In light of these observations, Unified Growth Theory underlines the role played by the rise in demand for human capital, and its impact on the formation of human capital and on the onset of the demographic transition, in the movement from stagnation to growth.

2.5   The Modern Growth Regime

The acceleration in technological progress and industrialization in the Post-Malthusian Regime and its interaction with the accumulation of human capital brought about a demographic transition, which paved the way for a transition to an era of sustained economic growth. Population growth no longer counterbalanced the rise in aggregate income triggered by rapid technological progress and factor accumulation, permitting sustained growth in income per capita.

The transition of the developed regions of Western Europe and the Western Offshoots to a state of sustained economic growth occurred toward the end of the nineteenth century, whereas the transition of some less developed countries in Asia and Latin America occurred toward the end of the twentieth century. Africa, in contrast, has not yet begun this transition.

2.5.1   Rapid Industrialization and Human Capital Formation

The transition to an era of sustained economic growth in developed and less developed regions was accompanied by rapid industrialization and human capital formation. As depicted in Figure 2.12, the level of industrialization per capita doubled during 1860–1913, and tripled in the course of the twentieth century. Similarly, the level of industrialization per capita in the United States increased sixfold during 1860–1913, and tripled during the twentieth century. A similar pattern was experienced in Germany, France, Sweden, Switzerland, Belgium, and Canada, where industrialization increased significantly during 1860–1913 as well as over the rest of the twentieth century. Moreover, less developed economies that made the transition to an era of sustained economic growth in recent decades have also experienced a significant increase in industrialization.

The transition to the Modern Growth Regime was also characterized by a gradual increase in the importance of the accumulation of human capital relative to physical capital, and by a sharp decline in fertility rates. In the first phase of the Industrial Revolution (1760–1830), capital accumulation as a fraction of GDP increased significantly, whereas literacy rates remained largely unchanged. However, in the second phase of the Industrial Revolution, the pace of capital accumulation subsided, and the education of the labor force markedly increased as skills became necessary for production. For instance, the investment ratio in England, which increased from 6% in 1760 to 11.6% in 1831, remained at around 11% on average during 1856–1913 (Matthews et al., 1982; Crafts, 1985). In contrast, the average years of schooling of males in the

FIGURE 2.26. The sharp rise in income per capita in the transition to sustained economic growth: England, 1435–1915.
Data sources: Feinstein (1972); Clark (2005).

labor force, which did not change significantly until the 1830s, had tripled by the beginning of the twentieth century (Matthews et al., 1982). School enrollment of 10-year-olds increased from 40% in 1870 to 100% in 1900. Overall, the significant rise in the level of income per capita in England as of 1865, as depicted in Figure 2.26, was associated with an increase in the standard of living (Voth, 2003, 2004).

The transition to sustained economic growth in the United States was also characterized by a gradual increase in the importance of the accumulation of human capital relative to physical capital. During 1890–1999, the contribution of human capital accumulation to the growth process in the United States nearly doubled, whereas the contribution of physical capital declined significantly. Goldin and Katz (2001) show that during 1890–1915, the growth rate of educational productivity was 0.29% per year, accounting for about 11% of the annual growth rate of output per capita over this period. During 1915–1999, the rate of growth of educational productivity was 0.53% per year, accounting for about 20% of the annual growth rate of output per capita. In contrast, Abramovitz and David (2000) report that the fraction of the growth rate in output per capita that was directly attributed to physical capital accumulation declined from an average of 56% in 1800–1890 to 31% during 1890–1927 and to 21% in 1929–1966.

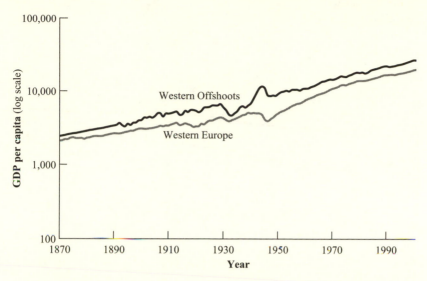

FIGURE 2.27. Sustained economic growth: Western Europe and the Western Offshoots, 1870–2001.
Data source: Maddison (2001).

2.5.2 Sustained Growth of Income per Capita

The acceleration of technological progress and the associated rise in demand for human capital brought about a demographic transition in Western Europe, the Western Offshoots, and in many of the less advanced economies, permitting a sustained increase in income per capita. Average income per capita in the past century has advanced at a stable rate of about 2% per year in Western Europe and the Western Offshoots (Figure 2.27). In contrast, some less developed regions experienced sustained growth rates of output per capita only in the past few decades. As depicted in Figure 2.28, the average growth rate of output per capita in Asia has been stable over the past 50 years, the growth rate in Latin America has been declining over this period, and the growth of Africa vanished in the past few decades.

2.5.3 Divergence in Income and Population across the Globe

The differential timing of the take-off from stagnation to growth across countries and the corresponding variations in the timing of the demographic transition led to a "Great Divergence" in income per capita as well as population growth across regions of the globe in the past two centuries. Some regions have

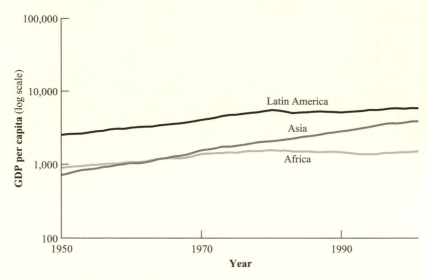

FIGURE 2.28. Income per capita in Africa, Asia, and Latin America, 1950–2001. *Data source:* Maddison (2003).

excelled in the growth of income per capita, while other regions have dominated in population growth.[31]

Income Distribution across Regions

Inequality in the world economy was insignificant until the nineteenth century. In contrast, the past two centuries have been characterized by a Great Divergence in income per capita among countries and regions. In particular, the ratio of GDP per capita between the richest and the poorest regions has widened considerably from a modest 3:1 ratio in 1820 to an incomprehensible 18:1 ratio in 2000 (Figures 2.29 and 2.30). Moreover, historical evidence indicates that, as late as the end of the first millennium CE, the civilizations of Asia were well ahead of Europe in both wealth and knowledge.[32] Nonetheless, by the time of the

---

[31] Contemporary variations in income per capita are attributed primarily to differences in productivity and human capital, as well as to misallocation of resources across sectors (Klenow and Rodriguez-Clare, 1997; Caselli, 2005; Caselli and Coleman, 2006; Hsieh and Klenow, 2009), rather than to differences in the marginal productivity of physical capital across countries (Caselli and Feyrer, 2007).

[32] It has been argued by historians that Chinese technology long anticipated advancements during the Industrial Revolution in Europe. For example, in textiles, China had been employing water-driven machinery in the twelfth century, 500 years prior to the appearance of similar technologies in Europe, while the early use of coal and coke for iron smelting in China resulted in iron

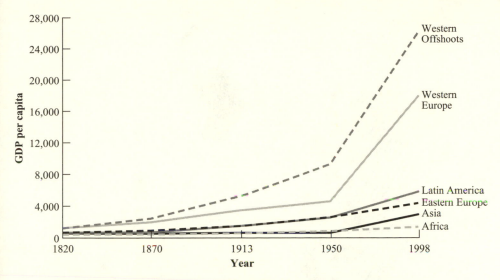

FIGURE 2.29. The Great Divergence. GDP per capita across regions, 1820–1998. *Data source:* Maddison (2001).

Industrial Revolution in the eighteenth century, Europe had already overtaken these societies (Landes, 1998).

Moreover, income inequality among the citizens of the world rose dramatically over the past two centuries. The Gini coefficient of the world income distribution increased from 43–45 in the early nineteenth century to about 65–70 today, and the Theil index increased from 58 in 1820 to 83–105 in 2002 (Bourguignon and Morrisson, 2002; Milanovic, 2009; Baten et al., 2010). This evolution was primarily due to the significant increase in inequality across countries as opposed to changes in inequality within countries. While inequality across nations accounted for only about 15 Gini points around 1820, it accounts for about 60 Gini points in 2002.[33]

---

production amounts in the eleventh century that were only matched in Europe 700 years later. Detailed historical accounts on the early dominance of Asian societies and the European overtaking have been given by Abu-Lughod (1989), Chaudhuri (1990), Goody (1996), Wong (1997), Frank (1998), Pomeranz (2000), and Hobson (2004).

[33] Some have argued that the divergence in income per capita in the past two centuries (Jones, 1997; Pritchett, 1997) is accompanied by the emergence of bimodality (convergence clubs) in the distribution of income across countries (Quah, 1997) and across people in the world economy (Baten et al., 2010). See, however, Dowrick and Nguyen (1989).

FIGURE 2.30. Income per capita across the globe, 2000.
Data source: World Bank (2001).

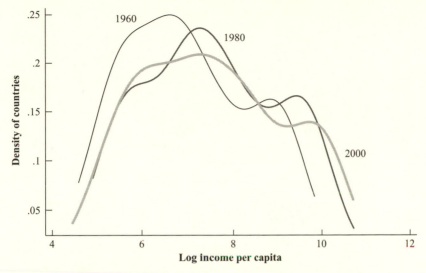

FIGURE 2.31. Distribution of income in the world economy, 1960–2000.
Data source: World Bank (2001).

Furthermore, inequality across countries has not narrowed in the world economy in the past four decades. As depicted in Figure 2.31, during 1960–2000, distribution of income per capita across countries has not contracted.[34] Moreover, convergence of poor economies toward rich ones has not been observed. As depicted in Figure 2.32, during 1960–2000, the relative income of countries in comparison to that of the United States has not reflected a tendency toward convergence. While convergence of poor economies toward the richer ones would have been represented by a clustering of poor economies above the 45° line, rich and poor economies alike are clustered around the 45°, indicating a persistence in the positions of economies relative to the United States.

Interestingly, cross-country evidence suggests that variations in contemporary income per capita and education across countries are significantly and positively associated with the time elapsed since the demographic transition (Figures 2.33 2.34).

---

[34] The pattern of global inequality across people rather than nations in the 1980s and 1990s appears to be sensitive to the price deflator used. While Sala-i-Martin (2006) argues that it declined, reflecting rapid growth in the populous countries of China and India, Milanovic (2009) shows that global inequality further increased during this period, using either the *World Development Indicator*'s GDP or household survey means and 2005 benchmark purchasing power parity (rather than that of 1990). For the evolution of inequality within countries during the course of the twentieth century, see Piketty and Saez (2006).

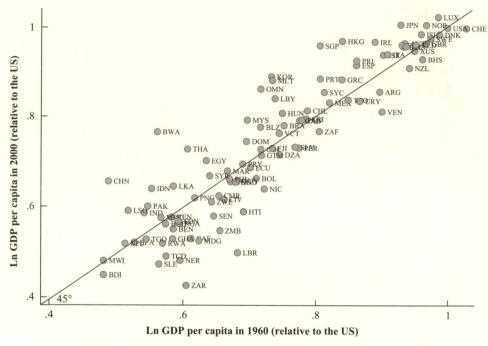

FIGURE 2.32. Income per capita (relative to the United States), 1960–2000. *Data source:* World Bank (2001).

Distribution of Population around the Globe

An equally momentous transformation occurred in the distribution of world population across regions, as depicted in Figure 2.35. The earlier take-off of Western European countries increased the amount of resources that could be devoted to family size, permitting an increase in their share of world population from 13% in 1820 to 15% in 1870. However, the early onset of the demographic transition in Western Europe and the long delay in the demographic transition of less developed regions led to a sharp decline in the share of Western European population in the world, from 15% in 1870 to 7% in 1998. In contrast, the prolongation of the Post-Malthusian Regime among less developed regions and the associated delay in their demographic transition channeled their increased resources toward a significant increase in their populations. Africa's share of world population increased from 7% in 1913 to 13% in 1998, Asia's share of world population increased from 52% in 1913 to 57% in 1998, and Latin American countries increased their share of world population from 2% in 1820

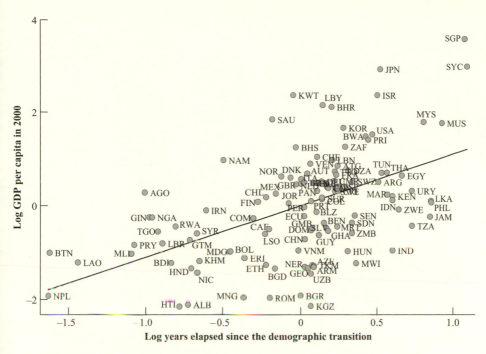

FIGURE 2.33. Income per capita in 2000 and its association with the time elapsed since the demographic transition.

Data sources: Reher (2004) for the demographic transition; World Bank (2001) for income.

Summary: The figure depicts the partial regression line for the effect of log years elapsed since the demographic transition on log income per capita in 2000 while controlling for absolute latitude and continental fixed effects. Thus, the x and y axes plot the residuals obtained from regressing the time elapsed since the demographic transition and log income per capita in 2000, respectively, on the aforementioned set of covariates.

to 9% in 1998. Thus, while the ratio of income per capita in Western Europe to that in Asia has tripled in the nineteenth and the twentieth centuries, the ratio of Asian to European population has doubled.[35]

---

[35] During 1820–1998, the ratio between income per capita in Western Europe and Asia (excluding Japan) grew 2.9 times, whereas the ratio between the Asian population (excluding Japan) and the Western European population grew 1.7 times (Maddison, 2001).

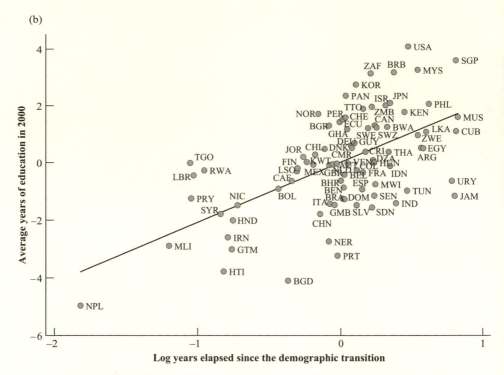

FIGURE 2.34. Education in 2000 and its assocation with the time elapsed since the demographic transition.

Data source: Reher (2004) for the time elapsed since the demographic transition.

Summary: The figure depicts the partial regression line for the effect of log years elapsed since the demographic transition on average years of education in 2000, while controlling for the absolute latitude and continental fixed effects. Thus, the *x* and *y* axes plot the residuals obtained from regressing the time elapsed since the demographic transition and average years of education in 2000, respectively, on the aforementioned set of covariates.

2.5.4 Insights for Comparative Development

The differential timing and pace of the take-off from stagnation to growth across countries and the corresponding variations in the timing of the demographic transition have led to a divergence in both income per capita and population growth across the globe in the past two centuries. Unified Growth Theory, therefore, explores the role played by country-specific characteristics (e.g., cultural, institutional, and geographical factors; inequality; and factor endowments) in

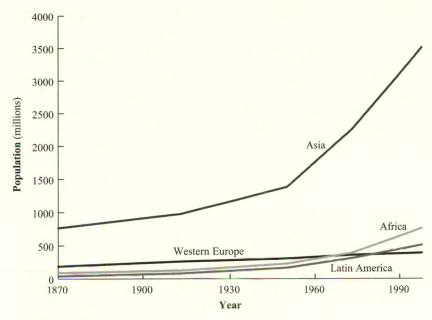

FIGURE 2.35. Divergence in regional populations.
Data source: Maddison (2001).

the differential timing and pace of the transition from stagnation to growth across countries.

2.6 Concluding Remarks

The evidence suggests that the process of development during most of human existence had been marked by Malthusian stagnation. Technological progress was insignificant by modern standards, and resources generated by technological progress and land expansion had been channeled primarily into an increase in the size of the population, with only a minute contribution to the level of income per capita in the long run. While cross-country variations in the levels of technology and land productivity were reflected in variations in population densities, their differential effect on living standards had been merely transitory. Nevertheless, the epoch of Malthusian stagnation in income per capita masked a dynamism that may have ultimately brought about the phase transition associated with the take-off from the Malthusian Epoch.

During the Post-Malthusian Regime, the Malthusian mechanism linking higher income to higher population growth continued to function. Nevertheless, early in the process of industrialization, capital accumulation and the acceleration in technological progress counteracted the effect that higher population had on diluting per capita resources, allowing income per capita to rise despite the offsetting effects of population growth. The inherent Malthusian interaction between the rate of technological progress and the size and composition of the population accelerated the pace of technological progress and initially generated a considerable rise in the growth rates of income per capita as well as population. However, in light of the presence of Malthusian forces during this regime, a permanent break from the Malthusian trap could not have taken place without the emergence of an additional force toward the end of the Post-Malthusian Regime—human capital formation.

In the second phase of industrialization, a major transformation in the production process took place. Industrial demand for human capital significantly increased, triggering human capital formation and ultimately a significant reduction in fertility rates and population growth. The demographic transition freed the growth process from the counterbalancing effect of population growth. It enabled economies to divert a larger share of the benefits of factor accumulation and technological progress to the enhancement of human capital formation and income per capita, thus paving the way for the emergence of sustained economic growth. Finally, the differential timing of the take-off from stagnation to growth across countries and the corresponding variations in the timing of the demographic transition have contributed to a divergence in income per capita and population growth across the globe in the past two centuries.

CHAPTER 3

The Malthusian Theory

The power of population is indefinitely greater than the
power in the earth to produce subsistence for man.
— Thomas Malthus

This chapter develops the foundations of the influential Malthusian theory and examines its predictions regarding the evolution of population and income per capita in the pre-industrial era of human history.

The Malthusian theory, inspired by Malthus (1798), suggests that worldwide stagnation in income per capita during the pre-industrial epoch reflected the counterbalancing effect of population growth on the expansion of resources. Resources generated by technological progress and land expansion were channeled into population growth and had a minuscule effect on income per capita in the long run. The positive effect of the standard of living on population growth along with diminishing labor productivity kept the long-run level of income per capita near a subsistence level. Periods marked by an absence of changes in the level of technology or the availability of land were characterized by a stable population size as well as a constant income per capita, whereas periods characterized by improvements in the technological environment or the availability of land generated only temporary gains in income per capita, eventually leading to a larger, but not richer, population. Thus, technologically superior economies ultimately had denser populations, but their standards of living did not reflect the degree of their technological advancement.[1]

The theory is strikingly simple, and yet it generates powerful predictions that are largely consistent with the significant role played by population growth over most of human history in mitigating the effect of technological progress on income per capita. The theory generates two major testable predictions. First, within an economy, the adoption or the advancement of superior production

---

[1] Specifically, according to Malthus (1798, p. 312), the expansion of resources led to an increase in population growth, reflecting the natural result of the "passion between the sexes." In contrast, when population size grew beyond the capacity sustainable by the available resources, it was reduced by the "preventive check" (i.e., intentional reduction of fertility) and by the "positive check" (i.e., the tools of nature: malnutrition, disease epidemics, war, and famine). As argued by Malthus, "The passion between the sexes has appeared in every age to be so nearly the same, that it may always be considered, in algebraic language, as a given quantity."

technologies led in the long run to a larger, but not richer, population. Second, differences in technologies or land productivity across countries were reflected in cross-country variations in population density rather than in income per capita.

Consistent with Malthusian predictions, Ashraf and Galor (2011) uncover statistically significant positive effects of land productivity and the technological level on population density in 1500 CE, 1000 CE, and 1 CE. In contrast, the effects of land productivity and technology on income per capita in these periods are not significantly different from zero. Moreover, the estimated effects on income per capita are about an order of magnitude smaller than the corresponding effects on population density.[2]

This empirical examination of the Malthusian theory exploits exogenous sources of cross-country variation in land productivity and technological levels to examine their hypothesized differential effects on population density versus income per capita.[3] Importantly, the qualitative results remain robust to controls for the confounding effects of a large number of geographical factors, including absolute latitude, access to waterways, distance to the technological frontier, and the share of land in tropical versus temperate climatic zones, which may have had an impact on aggregate productivity either directly (by affecting the productivity of land) or indirectly (by affecting the prevalence of trade and the diffusion of technologies).

3.1 The Basic Structure of the Model

This subsection outlines a Malthusian model developed by Ashraf and Galor (2011). Consider an overlapping-generations economy in which activity extends

---

[2] In contrast to Ashraf and Galor (2011), which tests the Malthusian prediction regarding the positive effect of the technological environment on population density but its neutrality for income per capita, Kremer (1993) examines the prediction of a Malthusian-Boserupian interaction. Accordingly, if population size has a positive effect on the rate of technological progress, as argued by Boserup (1965), this effect should manifest itself as a proportional effect on the rate of population growth, taking as given the positive Malthusian feedback from technology to population size. Based on this premise, Kremer's study defends the role of scale effects in endogenous growth models by empirically demonstrating that the rate of population growth in the world has indeed been proportional to the level of world population throughout human history. Thus, Kremer does not test the absence of a long-run effect of the technological environment on income per capita, nor does he examine the positive effect of technology on population size.

[3] Recent country-specific studies provide evidence in support of one of the elements of the Malthusian hypothesis—the positive effect of income on fertility and its negative effect on mortality. See Crafts and Mills (2009) for England in the sixteenth–eighteenth centuries, Kelly and O'Grada (2010) in the context of medieval and early modern England, and Lagerlöf (2009) for Sweden in the eighteenth–nineteenth centuries.

over infinite discrete time. In every period, the economy produces a single homogeneous good using land and labor as inputs. The supply of land is exogenous and fixed over time, whereas the evolution of labor supply is governed by households' decisions in the preceding period regarding the number of their children.

3.1.1 Production

Production occurs according to a constant-returns-to-scale technology. The output produced in period t, Y_t, is

$$Y_t = (AX)^\alpha L_t^{1-\alpha}, \quad \alpha \in (0, 1), \tag{3.1}$$

where L_t and X are, respectively, labor and land employed in production in period t, and A measures the technological level. The technological level may capture the percentage of arable land, soil quality, climate, cultivation and irrigation methods, as well as the knowledge required for engagement in agriculture (i.e., domestication of plants and animals). Thus, AX captures the effective resources used in production.

Output per worker produced in period t, $y_t \equiv Y_t/L_t$, is therefore

$$y_t = (AX/L_t)^\alpha. \tag{3.2}$$

3.1.2 Preferences and Budget Constraints

In each period t, a generation consisting of L_t identical individuals joins the workforce. Each individual has a single parent. Members of generation t (who join the workforce in period t) live for two periods. In the first period of life (childhood) they are supported by their parents. In the second period of life (parenthood) they inelastically supply their labor, generating an income that is equal to the output per worker, y_t, which they allocate between their own consumption and that of their children.

Individuals generate utility from consumption and the number of their (surviving) children:[4]

$$u^t = (c_t)^{1-\gamma}(n_t)^\gamma, \quad \gamma \in (0, 1), \tag{3.3}$$

where c_t is the consumption and n_t is the number of children of an individual of generation t.

---

[4] For simplicity, parents derive utility from the expected number of surviving offspring, and the parental cost of child rearing is associated only with surviving children. The incorporation of parental cost for nonsurviving children would not affect the qualitative predictions of the model.

Members of generation t allocate their income between their consumption, c_t, and expenditure on children, ρn_t, where ρ is the cost of raising a child.[5] Hence, the budget constraint for a member of generation t (in the second period of life) is

$$\rho n_t + c_t \leq y_t. \tag{3.4}$$

3.1.3 Optimization

Members of generation t allocate their income optimally between consumption and child rearing, so as to maximize their utility function (3.3) subject to the budget constraint (3.4). Hence, individuals devote a fraction $(1 - \gamma)$ of their income to consumption and a fraction γ to child rearing:

$$c_t = (1 - \gamma) y_t;$$
$$n_t = \gamma y_t / \rho. \tag{3.5}$$

Thus, in accordance with the Malthusian paradigm, income has a positive effect on the number of surviving children.

3.2 The Evolution of the Economy

3.2.1 Population Dynamics

The evolution of the working population is determined by the initial size of the working population and the number of (surviving) children per adult, n_t. Specifically, the size of the working population in period $t + 1$, L_{t+1}, is

$$L_{t+1} = n_t L_t, \tag{3.6}$$

where L_t is the size of the working population in period t; $L_0 > 0$.

Substituting (3.2) and (3.5) into (3.6), the time path of the working population is governed by the first-order difference equation

$$L_{t+1} = (\gamma/\rho)(AX)^\alpha L_t^{1-\alpha} \equiv \phi(L_t; A), \tag{3.7}$$

where, as depicted in Figure 3.1, $\partial\phi(L_t; A)/\partial L_t > 0$; $\partial^2\phi(L_t; A)/\partial L_t^2 < 0$; $\phi(0; A) = 0$; $\lim_{L_t \to 0} \partial\phi(L_t; A)/\partial L_t = \infty$; and $\lim_{L_t \to \infty} \partial\phi(L_t; A)/\partial L_t = 0$.

---

[5] If the cost of children is a time cost, then the qualitative results will be maintained as long as individuals are subjected to a subsistence consumption constraint (Chapter 5). If both time and goods are required to raise children, the results of the model will not be affected qualitatively. As the economy develops and wages increase, the time cost will rise proportionately with the increase in income, but the cost in terms of goods will decline. Hence, individuals will be able to afford more children.

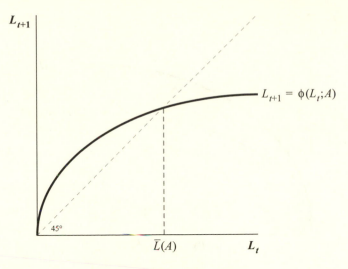

FIGURE 3.1. Evolution of population.

Hence, for a given level of technology, A, noting that $L_0 > 0$, there exists a unique stable steady-state level of the adult population, $\bar{L}$, (i.e., $\bar{L} = L_{t+1} = L_t$), such that[6]

$$\bar{L} = (\gamma/\rho)^{1/\alpha}(AX) \equiv \bar{L}(A), \tag{3.8}$$

and population density, $\bar{P}_d$:

$$\bar{P}_d \equiv \bar{L}/X = (\gamma/\rho)^{1/\alpha}A \equiv \bar{P}_d(A). \tag{3.9}$$

Importantly, as is evident from (3.8) and (3.9), an improvement in the technological environment, A, increases the steady-state levels of the adult population, $\bar{L}$, and population density, $\bar{P}_d$:

$$\frac{\partial \bar{L}}{\partial A} > 0 \quad \text{and} \quad \frac{\partial \bar{P}_d}{\partial A} > 0. \tag{3.10}$$

As depicted in Figure 3.2, if the economy is in a steady-state equilibrium, an increase in the technological level from A^l to A^h generates a transition process in which population gradually increases from its initial steady-state level, $\bar{L}(A^l)$, to a higher one, $\bar{L}(A^h)$. Similarly, consistent with the historical evidence in Section 2.1.4, a decline in the population (e.g., due to an epidemic,

[6] The trivial steady state, $\bar{L} = 0$, is unstable. Hence, given the initial positive size of the working population, this equilibrium will not characterize the population.

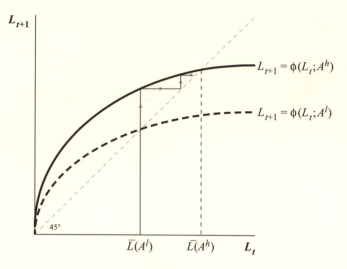

FIGURE 3.2. Effect of technological advancement on population.

such as the Black Death [1348–1350 CE]) would temporarily reduce population while temporarily increasing income per capita. The rise in income per capita, however, will generate a gradual increase in population back to the initial steady-state level, $\bar{L}$.

3.2.2 The Time Path of Income per Worker

The evolution of income per worker is determined by the initial level of income per worker and the number of (surviving) children per adult. Specifically, income per worker in period $t + 1$, y_{t+1}, noting (3.2) and (3.6), is

$$y_{t+1} = [(AX)/L_{t+1}]^\alpha = [(AX)/n_t L_t]^\alpha = y_t/n_t^\alpha. \tag{3.11}$$

Substituting (3.5) into (3.11), the time path of income per worker is governed by the first-order difference equation

$$y_{t+1} = (\rho/\gamma)^\alpha y_t^{1-\alpha} \equiv \psi(y_t), \tag{3.12}$$

where, as depicted in Figure 3.3, $\psi'(y_t) > 0$ and $\psi''(y_t) < 0$, so $\psi(y_t)$ is strictly concave, and $\psi(0) = 0$, $\lim_{y_t \to 0} \psi'(y_t) = \infty$ and $\lim_{y_t \to \infty} \psi'(y_t) = 0$.

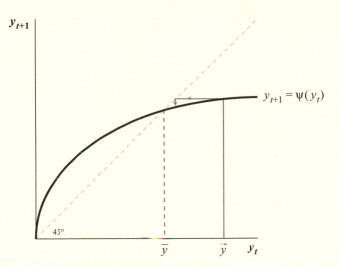

FIGURE 3.3. Evolution of income per capita.

Hence, noting that $y_0 > 0$, there exists a unique stable steady-state level of income per worker, $\bar{y}$:[7]

$$\bar{y} = (\rho/\gamma). \tag{3.13}$$

Importantly, as is evident from (3.2) and (3.13), while an advancement in the level of technology, A, increases the level of income per worker in the short run, y_t, it does not affect the steady-state level of income per worker, $\bar{y}$:

$$\frac{\partial y_t}{\partial A} > 0 \quad \text{and} \quad \frac{\partial \bar{y}}{\partial A} = 0. \tag{3.14}$$

As depicted in Figures 3.2 and 3.3, if the economy is in a steady-state equilibrium, an increase in the technological level from A^l to A^h generates a transition process in which income per worker initially increases to a higher level, $\tilde{y}$, reflecting higher labor productivity in the absence of population adjustment. However, as population increases, income per worker gradually declines to the initial steady-state equilibrium, $\bar{y}$. Similarly, consistent with the evidence in Section 2.1.4, a decline in population (e.g., due to an epidemic) would temporarily reduce population to $\tilde{L}$, while temporarily increasing income per capita

---

[7] The trivial steady-state equilibrium, $\bar{y} = 0$, is unstable. Thus, given $y_0 > 0$, this equilibrium will not characterize the population.

to $\bar{y}$. The rise in income per worker will generate a gradual increase in population back to the steady-state level, $\bar{L}$, and thus a gradual decline in income per worker back to $\bar{y}$.

3.3 Testable Predictions

The Malthusian theory generates the following testable predictions:

1. Within a country, an increase in productivity would lead in the long run to a larger population without altering the long-run level of income per capita.
2. Across countries, those characterized by superior land productivity or a superior level of technology would have, all else equal, higher population densities in the long run, but their standards of living would not reflect the degree of their technological advancement.

These predictions emerge from a Malthusian model as long as the model is based on two fundamental features: (i) a positive effect of the standard of living on population growth and (ii) decreasing returns to labor due to the presence of a fixed factor of production—land. Specifically, they would arise in the presence of a dynastic representative-agent Malthusian framework (Lucas, 2002), a reduced-form Malthusian-Boserupian interaction between population size and productivity growth (Kremer, 1993), exogenous technological progress (Hansen and Prescott, 2002), and endogenous technological progress that reflects the positive impact of population size and quality on aggregate productivity (Galor and Weil, 2000; Galor and Moav, 2002).

3.4 Empirical Framework

3.4.1 Empirical Strategy

The empirical examination of the central hypothesis of the Malthusian theory conducted by Ashraf and Galor (2011) exploits exogenous sources of cross-country variation in land productivity and technological levels to examine their hypothesized differential effects on population density and income per capita during 1–1500 CE.

In light of the potential endogeneity of population on technological progress, this research develops a novel identification strategy to examine the hypothesized effects of technological advancement on population density and income per capita. It establishes that the onset of the Neolithic Revolution, which marked the transition of societies from hunting and gathering to agriculture as early as 10,000 years ago, triggered a sequence of technological advancements that had a significant effect on the level of technology in the Middle Ages. In particular, as argued by Diamond (1997, 2002), an earlier onset of the Neolithic Revolution has been associated with a developmental head start that enabled the rise of a non-food-producing class whose members were essential for the advancement of written language, science, and technology, and for the formation of cities, technology-based military powers and nation states.[8] Thus, variation in the onset of the Neolithic Revolution across the globe, as depicted in Figure 3.4, is exploited as a proxy for the level of technological advancement during 1–1500 CE.

In addition, to address the possibility that the relationship between the timing of the Neolithic transition and population density in the Common Era may itself be spurious, being perhaps codetermined by an unobserved channel (e.g., human capital) the analysis appeals to the role of prehistoric biogeographical endowments in determining the timing of the Neolithic Revolution. Importantly, land productivity is largely independent of initial geographical and biogeographical endowments that were conducive to the onset of the Neolithic Revolution. While agriculture originated in regions of the world in which the most valuable domesticable wild plant and animal species were native, other regions proved to be more fertile and climatically favorable once the diffusion of agricultural practices brought the domesticated varieties to them (Diamond, 1997). Thus, the analysis adopts the numbers of prehistoric domesticable species of plants and animals that were native to a region prior to the onset of sedentary agricultural practices as instruments for the number of years elapsed since the Neolithic Revolution to demonstrate its causal effect on population density in the Common Era.[9]

Moreover, a direct measure of technological sophistication for 1000 CE and 1 CE is also employed as an alternative metric of the level of aggregate productivity to demonstrate the qualitative robustness of the baseline results.[10] Once again, the link running from prehistoric biogeographical endowments to the level of technological advancement in the Common Era, via the timing of the

---

[8] In the context of the Malthusian model presented earlier, the Neolithic Revolution should be viewed as a large positive shock to the level of technology, A, followed by a long discrete series of incremental aftershocks. Thus, at any given point in time, a society that experienced the Neolithic Revolution earlier would have a longer history of these aftershocks and would therefore reflect a larger steady-state population size (or, equivalently, a higher steady-state population density).

[9] The insufficient number of observations arising from the greater paucity of historical income data, compared to data on population density, does not permit a similar instrumental variable (IV) strategy to be pursued when examining the impact of the timing of the Neolithic Revolution on income per capita.

[10] The absence of sufficient variation in the underlying data obtained from Peregrine (2003) prevents the construction of a corresponding technology measure for 1500 CE.

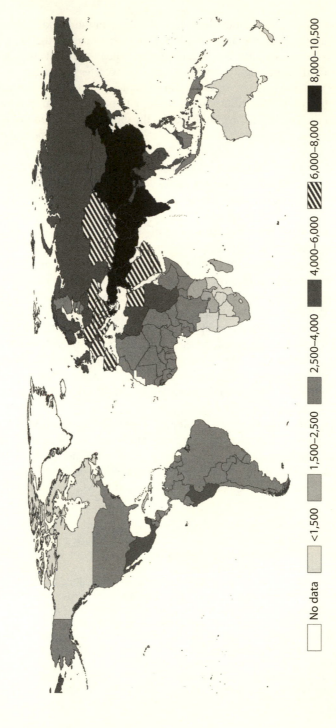

FIGURE 3.4. Years elapsed since the onset of the Neolithic Revolution. *Data source:* Putterman (2008).

Neolithic transition, enables the analysis to exploit the aforementioned bio-geographical variables as instruments for the indices of technological sophistication in 1000 CE and 1 CE to establish their causal effects on population density at these times.

Finally, to ensure that the results from the level regressions are not driven by unobserved time-invariant country fixed effects, a first-difference estimation strategy with a lagged explanatory variable is also employed. In particular, the robustness analysis exploits cross-country variation in the change in the level of technological sophistication between 1000 BCE and 1 CE to explain the cross-country variations in the change in population density and the change in income per capita over the 1–1000 CE time horizon.

3.4.2 The Data

The most comprehensive worldwide cross-country historical estimates of population and income per capita since 1 CE have been assembled by McEvedy and Jones (1978) and Maddison (2003), respectively.[11] Indeed, despite inherent problems of measurement associated with historical data, these sources remain unparalleled in providing comparable estimates across countries in the past 2,000 years and have, therefore, been regarded as standard sources for such data in the long-run growth literature.[12]

The measure of land productivity used in the analysis is the first principal component of the percentage of arable land and an index reflecting the overall suitability of land for agriculture, based on geospatial soil quality and temperature data, as reported by Ramankutty et al. (2002) and aggregated to the

---

[11] It is important to note that, while the urbanization rate in 1500 CE has sometimes been used as an indicator of pre-industrial economic development, it is not an alternative measure for income per capita. As suggested by the Malthusian hypothesis, technologically advanced economies have higher population densities and may thus be more urbanized, but the extent of urbanization has little or no bearing on the standard of living in the long run—it is largely a reflection of the level of technological sophistication. Indeed, the results are qualitatively unaffected, particularly with respect to the impact of technological levels (as proxied by the timing of the Neolithic Revolution), when the urbanization rate in 1500 CE is used in lieu of population density as the outcome variable.

[12] Nevertheless, the use of Maddison's (2003) income per capita data could have posed a significant hurdle if the data had in part been imputed with a Malthusian viewpoint of the pre-industrial world in mind. While Maddison (2008) suggests that this is not the case, the empirical investigation to follow performs a rigorous analysis to demonstrate that the baseline results remain robust under alternative specifications designed to address this particular concern surrounding Maddison's estimates of income per capita. Regarding the historical population data from McEvedy and Jones (1978), while some of their estimates remain controversial, particularly those for sub-Saharan Africa and pre-Columbian Mesoamerica, a recent assessment conducted by the U.S. Census Bureau finds that their aggregate estimates indeed compare favorably with those obtained from other studies. Moreover, the regional estimates of McEvedy and Jones are also very similar to those presented in the more recent study by Livi-Bacci (2001).

country level by Michalopoulos (2008).[13] The data on the timing of the Neolithic Revolution, constructed by Putterman (2008), measure the number of millennia elapsed, relative to 2000 CE, since the majority of the population residing within a country's modern national borders began practicing sedentary agriculture as the primary mode of subsistence.

The index of technological sophistication is constructed based on historical cross-cultural technology data, reported with global coverage in Peregrine's (2003) *Atlas of Cultural Evolution*. In particular, for a given time period and for a given culture in the archaeological record, the *Atlas of Cultural Evolution* draws on various anthropological and historical sources to report the level of technological advancement, on a 3-point scale, in each of four sectors of the economy, including communications, industry (i.e., ceramics and metallurgy), transportation, and agriculture. The index of technological sophistication is constructed following the aggregation methodology of Comin et al. (2010).[14]

3.4.3 The Neolithic Revolution and Technological Advancement

This section establishes that the Neolithic Revolution triggered a cumulative process of economic development, conferring a developmental head start to societies that experienced the agricultural transition earlier. In line with this assertion, Table 3.1 reveals preliminary results, indicating that an earlier onset of the Neolithic Revolution is indeed positively and significantly correlated with the level of technological sophistication in nonagricultural sectors of the economy in 1000 CE and 1 CE. For instance, the coefficient estimates for 1000 CE, all of which are statistically significant at the 1% level, indicate that a 1% increase in the number of years elapsed since the onset of the Neolithic Revolution is associated with an increase in the level of technological advancement in the communications, industrial, and transportation sectors of 0.37%, 0.07%, and 0.38%, respectively.

These findings lend credence to the use of the exogenous source of cross-country variation in the timing of the Neolithic Revolution as a proxy for the

---

[13] The use of contemporary measures of land productivity necessitates an identifying assumption that the spatial distribution of factors governing the productivity of land for agriculture has not changed significantly in the past 2,000 years. In this regard, it is important to note that the analysis at hand exploits worldwide variation in such factors, which changes dramatically only in geological time. Hence, while the assumption may not necessarily hold at a subregional level in some cases (e.g., in regions south of the Sahara, where the desert has been known to be expanding gradually in the past few centuries), it is unlikely that the moments of the global spatial distribution of land productivity are significantly different today than they were two millennia ago.

[14] Further details on definitions and sources of the primary and control variables employed by the analysis are collected in the appendix to this chapter.

TABLE 3.1
The Neolithic Revolution as a proxy for technological advancement

	(1) OLS	(2) OLS	(3) OLS	(4) OLS	(5) OLS	(6) OLS
	Dependent variable is level of					
	Log communications technology in		Log industrial technology in		Log transportation technology in	
	1000 CE	1 CE	1000 CE	1 CE	1000 CE	1 CE
Log years since Neolithic transition	0.368*** (0.028)	0.283*** (0.030)	0.074*** (0.014)	0.068*** (0.015)	0.380*** (0.029)	0.367*** (0.031)
Observations	143	143	143	143	143	143
R-squared	0.48	0.26	0.17	0.12	0.52	0.51

Summary: This table demonstrates that the timing of the Neolithic Revolution is positively and significantly correlated with the level of technology in multiple nonagricultural sectors of an economy in 1000 CE and 1 CE.

Notes: (i) The level of technology in communications is indexed according to the absence of both true writing and mnemonic or nonwritten records, the presence of only mnemonic or nonwritten records, or the presence of both; (ii) the level of technology in industry is indexed according to the absence of both metalworks and pottery, the presence of only pottery, or the presence of both; (iii) the level of technology in transportation is indexed according to the absence of both vehicles and pack or draft animals, the presence of only pack or draft animals, or the presence of both; (iv) robust standard error estimates are reported in parentheses; (v) *** denotes statistical significance at the 1% level, ** at the 5% level, and * at the 10% level, all for two-sided hypothesis tests; (vi) OLS denotes ordinary least squares.

variation in the level of technological advancement across countries during the agricultural stage of development.

3.4.4 Basic Regression Model

Formally, the baseline specifications adopted to test the Malthusian predictions regarding the effects of land productivity and the level of technological advancement on population density and income per capita are

$$\ln P_{i,t} = \alpha_{0,t} + \alpha_{1,t} \ln T_i + \alpha_{2,t} \ln X_i + \alpha'_{3,t}\Gamma_i + \alpha'_{4,t}D_i + \delta_{i,t}, \qquad (3.15)$$

$$\ln y_{i,t} = \beta_{0,t} + \beta_{1,t} \ln T_i + \beta_{2,t} \ln X_i + \beta'_{3,t}\Gamma_i + \beta'_{4,t}D_i + \varepsilon_{i,t}, \qquad (3.16)$$

where $P_{i,t}$ is the population density of country i in year t; $y_{i,t}$ is country i's income per capita in year t; T_i is the number of years elapsed since the onset of agriculture in country i; X_i is a measure of land productivity for country i, based on the percentage of arable land area and an index of agricultural suitability; Γ_i is a vector of geographical controls for country i, including absolute latitude and variables gauging access to waterways; D_i is a vector of continental dummies; and $\delta_{i,t}$ and $\varepsilon_{i,t}$ are country-specific disturbance terms for population density and income per capita, respectively, in year t.

3.5 Cross-Country Evidence

Consistent with the predictions of the Malthusian theory, the results demonstrate highly statistically significant positive effects of land productivity and the number of years elapsed since the Neolithic Revolution on population density in 1500 CE, 1000 CE, and 1 CE. The effects of these explanatory channels on income per capita in the corresponding periods, however, are not significantly different from zero, a result that fully complies with Malthusian priors. These results are shown to be robust to controls for other geographical factors, including absolute latitude, access to waterways, distance to the nearest technological frontier, percentage of land in tropical versus temperate climatic zones, and small-island and landlocked dummies, all of which may have had an impact on aggregate productivity either directly (by affecting the productivity of land) or indirectly (by affecting trade and the diffusion of technologies). Moreover, as foreshadowed by the initial findings in Table 3.1, the results are qualitatively unaffected when the index of technological sophistication, rather than the number of years elapsed since the Neolithic Revolution, is employed as a proxy for the level of aggregate productivity.

The detailed discussion of the empirical findings is organized as follows. Section 3.5.1 presents the results of testing the Malthusian prediction for population density in 1500 CE. Analogous findings for population density in 1000 CE and 1 CE are revealed in Section 3.5.2. The results of testing the Malthusian prediction for income per capita in the three historical periods are discussed in Section 3.5.3. This section also takes a closer look at the income per capita data and demonstrates the qualitative robustness of the baseline results with respect to alternative specifications designed to alleviate potential concerns regarding the possibility that historical estimates of cross-country living standards may in part reflect some prior conformity with a Malthusian view of the world. Section 3.5.4 reveals the qualitative robustness of the earlier findings when the index of technological sophistication is employed in lieu of the timing of the Neolithic transition as a proxy for the level of technological advancement. Additional results establishing robustness with respect to the technology diffusion hypothesis as well as other geographical factors are collected in Section 3.5.5. Finally, Section 3.5.6 concludes the discussion with findings from regressions based on the methodology of first differences, dispelling alternative theories and accounting for unobserved country fixed effects.

3.5.1 Population Density in 1500 CE

This section establishes the significant positive effects of land productivity and the level of technological advancement, as proxied by the timing of the Neolithic Revolution, on population density in 1500 CE. The results from regressions explaining log population density in 1500 CE are presented in Table 3.2. In particular, a number of specifications comprising different subsets of the explanatory variables in (3.15) are estimated to examine the independent and combined effects of the transition timing and land-productivity channels while controlling for other geographical factors and continental fixed effects.

Consistent with Malthusian predictions, Column 1 reveals the positive relationship between log years since transition and log population density in 1500 CE while controlling for continental fixed effects.[15] Specifically, the estimated OLS coefficient implies that a 1% increase in the number of years elapsed since the Neolithic transition increases population density in 1500 CE by 0.83%, an effect that is statistically significant at the 1% level.[16] Moreover, based on the R-squared of the regression, the transition-timing channel appears to explain 40% of the variation in log population density in 1500 CE, along with the dummies capturing unobserved continental characteristics.

The effect of the land-productivity channel, controlling for absolute latitude and continental fixed effects, is reported in Column 2. In line with theoretical predictions, a 1% increase in land productivity raises population density in 1500 CE by 0.59%, an effect that is also significant at the 1% level. Interestingly, in contrast to the relationship between absolute latitude and contemporary income per capita, the estimated elasticity of population density in 1500 CE with respect to absolute latitude suggests that economic development during this period was on average higher at latitudinal bands closer to the equator.[17] Thus,

[15] The results presented throughout are robust to the omission of continental dummies from the regression specifications. Without continental fixed effects, the coefficient of interest in Column 1 is 1.294 [0.169], with the standard error (in brackets) indicating statistical significance at the 1% level.

[16] Evaluating this effect at the sample means of 4,877 (for years since transition) and 6.06 (for population density in 1500 CE) implies that an earlier onset of the Neolithic Revolution by about 500 years is associated with an increase in population density in 1500 CE by 0.5 persons per square kilometer.

[17] An interesting potential explanation for this finding comes from an admittedly contested hypothesis in the field of evolutionary ecology. In particular, biodiversity tends to decline as one moves farther away from the equator—a phenomenon known as *Rapoport's Rule*—due to the stronger forces of natural selection arising from wider seasonal variation in climate at higher absolute latitudes. Lower resource diversity at higher absolute latitudes would imply lower carrying capacities of these environments due to the greater extinction susceptibility of the resource base under adverse natural shocks, such as disease and sudden climatic fluctuations. The lower carrying capacities of these environments would, in turn, imply lower levels of human population density.

TABLE 3.2
Determinants of population density in 1500 CE

	(1) OLS	(2) OLS	(3) OLS	(4) OLS	(5) OLS	(6) IV
	Dependent variable is log population density in 1500 CE					
Log years since Neolithic transition	0.833*** (0.298)		1.025*** (0.223)	1.087*** (0.184)	1.389*** (0.224)	2.077*** (0.391)
Log land productivity		0.587*** (0.071)	0.641*** (0.059)	0.576*** (0.052)	0.573*** (0.095)	0.571*** (0.082)
Log absolute latitude		−0.425*** (0.124)	−0.353*** (0.104)	−0.314*** (0.103)	−0.278** (0.131)	−0.248** (0.117)
Mean distance to nearest coast or river				−0.392*** (0.142)	0.220 (0.346)	0.250 (0.333)
Percentage of land within 100 km of coast or river				0.899*** (0.282)	1.185*** (0.377)	1.350*** (0.380)
Continent dummies	Yes	Yes	Yes	Yes	Yes	Yes
Observations	147	147	147	147	96	96
R-squared	0.40	0.60	0.66	0.73	0.73	0.70
First-stage F-statistic	—	—	—	—	—	14.65
Overidentifying p-value	—	—	—	—	—	0.440

Summary: This table establishes, consistently with Malthusian predictions, the significant positive effects of land productivity and the level of technological advancement, as proxied by the timing of the Neolithic Revolution, on population in 1500 CE while controlling for access to navigable waterways, absolute latitude, and unobserved continental fixed effects.
Notes: (i) Log land productivity is the first principal component of the log of the percentage of arable land and the log of an agricultural suitability index; (ii) the IV regression employs the numbers of prehistoric domesticable species of plants and animals as instruments for log transition timing; (iii) the statistic for the first-stage F-test of these instruments is significant at the 1% level; (iv) the p-value for the overidentifying restrictions test corresponds to Hansen's J statistic, distributed in this case as χ^2 with one degree of freedom; (v) a single continent dummy is used to represent the Americas, which is natural given the historical period examined; (vi) regressions (5) and (6) do not employ the Oceania dummy due to a single observation for this continent in the IV data-restricted sample; (vii) robust standard error estimates are reported in parentheses; (viii) *** denotes statistical significance at the 1% level, ** at the 5% level, and * at the 10% level, all for two-sided hypothesis tests.

while proximity to the equator was beneficial in the agricultural stage of development, it appears detrimental in the industrial stage. The R-squared of the regression indicates that, along with continental fixed effects and absolute latitude, the land-productivity channel explains 60% of the cross-country variation in log population density in 1500 CE.

Column 3 presents the results from examining the combined explanatory power of the previous two regressions. The estimated coefficients on the transition timing and land productivity variables remain highly statistically significant and continue to retain their expected signs while increasing slightly in magnitude in comparison to their estimates in earlier columns. Furthermore, transition timing and land productivity together explain 66% of the variation in log population density in 1500 CE, along with absolute latitude and continental fixed effects.

The explanatory power of the regression in Column 3 improves by an additional 7 percentage points once controls for access to waterways are accounted for in Column 4—the baseline regression specification for population density in 1500 CE. In comparison to the estimates reported in Column 3, the effects of the transition-timing and land-productivity variables remain reassuringly stable in both magnitude and statistical significance when subjected to the additional geographical controls. Moreover, the estimated coefficients on the additional geographical controls indicate significant effects, consistent with the assertion that better access to waterways has been historically beneficial for economic development by fostering urbanization, international trade, and technology diffusion. To interpret the baseline effects of the variables of interest, a 1% increase in the number of years elapsed since the Neolithic Revolution raises population density in 1500 CE by 1.09%, conditional on land productivity, absolute latitude, waterway access, and continental fixed effects. Similarly, a 1% increase in land productivity generates, *ceteris paribus*, a 0.58% increase in population density in 1500 CE.[18] These conditional effects of the transition timing and land productivity channels from the baseline specification are depicted as partial regression lines on the scatter plots in Figure 3.5(a) and (b), respectively.

The analysis now turns to addressing issues regarding causality, particularly with respect to the transition-timing variable. Specifically, while variations in land productivity and other geographical characteristics are inarguably exogenous to the cross-country variation in population density, the onset of the Neolithic Revolution and the outcome variable of interest may in fact be endogenously determined. Specifically, although reverse causality is not a source of concern, given that the vast majority of countries underwent the Neolithic

---

[18] In the absence of continental fixed effects, the coefficient associated with the transition-timing channel is 1.373 [0.118], while that associated with the land-productivity channel is 0.586 [0.058], with the standard errors (in brackets) indicating statistical significance at the 1% level.

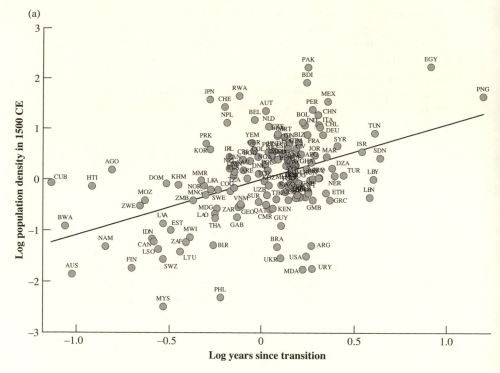

(a)

FIGURE 3.5. Transition timing, land productivity, and population density in 1500 CE:
(a) partial effect of transition timing on population density; (b) partial effect of land
productivity on population density.
Data source: Ashraf and Galor (2011).
Summary: The figure depicts the partial regression line for the effect of log transition
timing (log land productivity) on log population density in 1500 CE while controlling for
the influence of log land productivity (log transition timing), absolute latitude, access to
waterways, and continental fixed effects. Thus, the *x* and *y* axes in panel (a) [panel (b)]
plot the residuals obtained from regressing log transition timing [log land productivity]
and log population density, respectively, on the aforementioned set of covariates.

transition prior to the Common Era, the OLS estimates of the effect of the time
elapsed since the transition to agriculture may suffer from omitted variable bias,
reflecting spurious correlations with the outcome variable being examined.

To establish the causal effect of the timing of the Neolithic transition on
population density in the Common Era, the investigation appeals to Diamond's
(1997) hypothesis on the role of exogenous geographical and biogeographical
endowments in determining the timing of the Neolithic Revolution. According to the hypothesis, the emergence and subsequent diffusion of agricultural

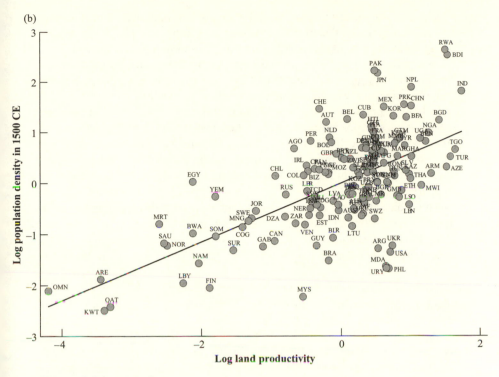

FIGURE 3.5 *(continued)*

practices were primarily driven by geographical conditions, such as climate, continental size, and orientation, as well as the availability of wild plant and animal species amenable to domestication. However, while geographical factors certainly continued to play a direct role in economic development after the onset of agriculture, it is postulated that the availability of prehistoric domesticable wild plant and animal species did not influence population density in the Common Era other than through the timing of the Neolithic Revolution. The analysis consequently adopts the numbers of prehistoric domesticable species of wild plants and animals, obtained from the dataset of Olsson and Hibbs (2005), as instruments to establish the causal effect of the timing of the Neolithic transition on population density.

The final two columns in Table 3.2 report the results associated with a subsample of countries for which data on the biogeographical instruments are available. To allow meaningful comparisons between IV and OLS coefficient estimates, Column 5 repeats the baseline OLS regression analysis on this particular subsample of countries, revealing that the coefficients on the explanatory variables of interest remain largely stable in terms of both magnitude and significance compared to those estimated using the baseline sample. This is a reassuring indicator that any additional sampling bias introduced by the restricted sample, particularly with respect to the transition-timing and land-productivity variables, is negligible. Consistent with this assertion, the explanatory powers of the baseline and restricted sample regressions are nearly identical.

Column 6 presents the IV regression results from estimating the baseline specification with log years since transition instrumented by the numbers of prehistoric domesticable species of plants and animals.[19] The estimated causal effect of the timing of the Neolithic transition on population density not only retains statistical significance at the 1% level but is substantially stronger in comparison to the estimate in Column 5. This pattern is consistent with attenuation bias afflicting the OLS coefficient as a result of measurement error in the transition-timing variable. To interpret the causal impact of the timing of the Neolithic Revolution, a 1% increase in years elapsed since the onset of agriculture causes, *ceteris paribus,* a 2.08% increase in population density in 1500 CE.

The coefficient on land productivity, which maintains stability in both magnitude and statistical significance across the OLS and IV regressions, indicates that a 1% increase in land productivity raises population density by 0.57%, conditional on the timing of the Neolithic transition, other geographical factors, and continental fixed effects. Finally, the rather strong F-statistic from the first-stage regression provides verification for the significance and explanatory power of the biogeographical instruments employed for the timing of the Neolithic Revolution, while the high p-value associated with the test for overidentifying restrictions is supportive of the claim that these instruments do not exert any independent influence on population density in 1500 CE other than through the transition-timing channel.

3.5.2   Population Density in Earlier Historical Periods

This section demonstrates the significant positive effects of land productivity and the level of technological advancement, as proxied by the timing of the Neolithic Revolution, on population density in 1000 CE and 1 CE. The results from regressions explaining log population density in 1000 CE and 1 CE are presented in Tables 3.3 and 3.4, respectively. As before, the independent and combined explanatory powers of the transition-timing and land-productivity channels are examined while controlling for other geographical factors and unobserved continental characteristics.

---

[19] Table 3.A in the appendix to this chapter summarizes the first-stage regression results from all IV regressions examined.

In line with the empirical predictions of the Malthusian theory, the findings reveal highly statistically significant positive effects of land productivity and an earlier transition to agriculture on population density in these earlier historical periods as well. Moreover, the positive impact on economic development of geographical factors capturing better access to waterways is also confirmed for these earlier periods.[20]

The stability patterns exhibited by the magnitude and significance of the coefficients on the explanatory variables of interest in Tables 3.3 and 3.4 are strikingly similar to those observed in the 1500 CE analysis (Section 3.5.1). Thus, for instance, while statistical significance remains unaffected across specifications, the independent effects of Neolithic transition timing and land productivity from the first two columns in each table increase slightly in magnitude when both channels are examined concurrently in Column 3. They remain stable thereafter when subjected to the additional geographical controls in the baseline regression specification of Column 4. This is a reassuring indicator that the variance-covariance characteristics of the regression samples employed for the different periods are not fundamentally different from one another, despite differences in sample size due to the greater paucity of population density data in the earlier historical periods. The qualitative similarity of the results across periods also suggests that the empirical findings are indeed more plausibly associated with the Malthusian theory, as opposed to being consistently generated by spurious correlations between population density and the explanatory variables of interest across the different historical periods.

To interpret the baseline effects of interest in Column 4 of the analysis for each historical period, a 1% increase in the number of years elapsed since the onset of the Neolithic Revolution raises population density in 1000 CE and 1 CE by 1.48% and 1.93%, respectively, conditional on the productivity of land, absolute latitude, access to waterways, and continental fixed effects.[21] Similarly,

---

[20] The inverse correlation between absolute latitude and population density is maintained in the 1000 CE analysis but appears ambiguous in the 1 CE analysis. This pattern may, in part, reflect increasing returns associated with societies residing closer to the equator during the Malthusian stage of development. In particular, as a result of agglomeration and latitudinally specific technology diffusion, the initial advantage enjoyed by equatorial societies during the Malthusian Epoch became more pronounced over time. Thus, the observed negative cross-sectional relationship between absolute latitude and population density, which is somewhat weak in 1 CE, becomes progressively stronger in 1000 CE and 1500 CE.

[21] In both the 1000 CE and 1 CE samples, evaluating this effect at the sample means for years since transition and population density implies that an earlier onset of the Neolithic by about 500 years is associated with an increase in population density by 0.5 persons per square kilometer. Despite differences in the estimated elasticities between the two periods, the similarity of the effects at the sample means arises due to counteracting differences in the sample means themselves. Specifically, while population density in 1000 CE has a sample mean of 3.59, the mean in 1 CE is only 2.54.

TABLE 3.3
Determinants of population density in 1000 CE

	(1) OLS	(2) OLS	(3) OLS	(4) OLS	(5) OLS	(6) IV
	Dependent variable is log population density in 1000 CE					
Log years since Neolithic transition	1.232*** (0.293)		1.435*** (0.243)	1.480*** (0.205)	1.803*** (0.251)	2.933*** (0.504)
Log land productivity		0.470*** (0.081)	0.555*** (0.065)	0.497*** (0.056)	0.535*** (0.098)	0.549*** (0.092)
Log absolute latitude		−0.377** (0.148)	−0.283** (0.116)	−0.229** (0.111)	−0.147 (0.127)	−0.095 (0.116)
Mean distance to nearest coast or river				−0.528*** (0.153)	0.147 (0.338)	0.225 (0.354)
Percentage of land within 100 km of coast or river				0.716** (0.323)	1.050** (0.421)	1.358*** (0.465)
Continent dummies	Yes	Yes	Yes	Yes	Yes	Yes
Observations	142	142	142	142	94	94
R-squared	0.38	0.46	0.59	0.67	0.69	0.62
First-stage F-statistic	—	—	—	—	—	15.10
Overidentifying p-value	—	—	—	—	—	0.281

Summary: This table establishes, consistently with Malthusian predictions, the significant positive effects of land productivity and the level of technological advancement, as proxied by the timing of the Neolithic Revolution, on population density in 1000 CE, while controlling for access to navigable waterways, absolute latitude, and unobserved continental fixed effects.

Notes: (i) Log land productivity is the first principal component of the log of the percentage of arable land and the log of an agricultural suitability index; (ii) the IV regression employs the numbers of prehistoric domesticable species of plants and animals as instruments for log transition timing; (iii) the statistic for the first-stage F-test of these instruments is significant at the 1% level; (iv) the p-value for the overidentifying restrictions test corresponds to Hansen's J statistic, distributed in this case as χ^2 with one degree of freedom; (v) a single continent dummy is used to represent the Americas, which is natural, given the historical period examined; (vi) regressions (5) and (6) do not employ the Oceania dummy due to a single observation for this continent in the IV data-restricted sample; (vii) robust standard error estimates are reported in parentheses; (viii) *** denotes statistical significance at the 1% level, ** at the 5% level, and * at the 10% level, all for two-sided hypothesis tests.

TABLE 3.4
Determinants of population density in 1 CE

	(1) OLS	(2) OLS	(3) OLS	(4) OLS	(5) OLS	(6) IV
	Dependent variable is log population density in 1 CE					
Log years since Neolithic transition	1.560*** (0.326)		1.903*** (0.312)	1.930*** (0.272)	2.561*** (0.369)	3.459*** (0.437)
Log land productivity		0.404*** (0.106)	0.556*** (0.081)	0.394*** (0.067)	0.421*** (0.094)	0.479*** (0.089)
Log absolute latitude		−0.080 (0.161)	−0.030 (0.120)	0.057 (0.101)	0.116 (0.121)	0.113 (0.113)
Mean distance to nearest coast or river				−0.685*** (0.155)	−0.418 (0.273)	−0.320 (0.306)
Percentage of land within 100 km of coast or river				0.857** (0.351)	1.108*** (0.412)	1.360*** (0.488)
Continent dummies	Yes	Yes	Yes	Yes	Yes	Yes
Observations	128	128	128	128	83	83
R-squared	0.47	0.41	0.59	0.69	0.75	0.72
First-stage F-statistic	—	—	—	—	—	10.85
Overidentifying p-value	—	—	—	—	—	0.590

Summary: This table establishes, consistently with Malthusian predictions, the significant positive effects of land productivity and the level of technological advancement, as proxied by the timing of the Neolithic Revolution, on population density in 1 CE, while controlling for access to navigable waterways, absolute latitude, and unobserved continental fixed effects.

Notes: (i) Log land productivity is the first principal component of the log of the arable percentage of land and the log of an agricultural suitability index; (ii) the IV regression employs the numbers of prehistoric domesticable species of plants and animals as instruments for log transition timing; (iii) the statistic for the first-stage F-test of these instruments is significant at the 1% level; (iv) the p-value for the overidentifying restrictions test corresponds to Hansen's J statistic, distributed in this case as χ^2 with one degree of freedom; (v) a single continent dummy is used to represent the Americas, which is natural, given the historical period examined; (vi) regressions (5) and (6) do not employ the Oceania dummy due to a single observation for this continent in the IV data-restricted sample; (vii) robust standard error estimates are reported in parentheses; (viii) *** denotes statistical significance at the 1% level, ** at the 5% level, and * at the 10% level, all for two-sided hypothesis tests.

a 1% increase in land productivity is associated with, *ceteris paribus,* a 0.50% increase in population density in 1000 CE and a 0.39% increase in population density in 1 CE.

For the 1000 CE analysis, the additional sampling bias introduced in the OLS estimates by moving to the IV-restricted subsample in Column 5 is similar to that observed earlier in Table 3.2, whereas the bias appears somewhat larger for the analysis in 1 CE. This difference is partly attributable to the smaller size of the subsample in the latter analysis. The IV regressions in Column 6, however, once again reflect the pattern that the causal effect of transition timing on population density in each period is stronger than its corresponding reduced-form effect, while the effect of land productivity remains rather stable across the OLS and IV specifications. In addition, the strength and credibility of the numbers of domesticable plant and animal species as instruments continue to be supported by their significance in the first-stage regressions and by the results of the overidentifying restrictions tests. The similarity of these findings with those obtained in the 1500 CE analysis reinforces the validity of these instruments and thereby lends further credence to the causal effect of the timing of the Neolithic transition on population density.

Finally, turning attention to the differences in coefficient estimates obtained for the three periods, it is interesting to note that, while the positive effect of land productivity on population density remains rather stable, the effect of the number of years elapsed since the onset of agriculture declines over time. For instance, comparing the IV coefficient estimates on the transition timing variable in Tables 3.3 and 3.4, the positive causal impact of the Neolithic Revolution on population density diminishes by 0.53 percentage points over the 1–1000 CE time horizon and by 0.85 percentage points over the subsequent 500-year period. This pattern is consistently reflected by all regression specifications examining the effect of the transition-timing variable.

Thus, it appears that the process of development initiated by the technological breakthrough of the Neolithic Revolution conferred social gains characterized by diminishing returns over time, and for a sufficiently large lag following the transition, societies should be expected to converge toward a similar Malthusian steady state, conditional on the productivity of land and other geographical factors.[22] In particular, as discussed in Section 6.4, the evidence appears to sug-

---

[22] Hence, the cross-sectional relationship between population density and the number of years elapsed since the Neolithic transition should be expected to exhibit some concavity. This prediction was tested by Ashraf and Galor (2011) using the following specification:

$$\ln P_{i,t} = \theta_{0,t} + \theta_{1,t} T_i + \theta_{2,t} T_i^2 + \theta_{3,t} \ln X_i + \theta_{4,t}' \Gamma_i + \theta_{5,t}' D_i + \delta_{i,t}.$$

Consistent with the aforementioned prediction, the OLS regression for 1500 CE yields $\theta_{1,1500} = 0.630$ [0.133] and $\theta_{2,1500} = -0.033$ [0.011], with the standard errors (in brackets) indicating that both estimates are statistically significant at the 1% level. Moreover, in line with the prediction that a concave relationship should not necessarily be observed in an earlier period, the regression for

TABLE 3.5
Differential effects of the Neolithic Revolution and land productivity on income per capita versus population density

	(1) OLS	(2) OLS	(3) OLS	(4) OLS	(5) OLS	(6) OLS
			Dependent variable is			
	Log income per capita in			Log population density in		
	1500 CE	1000 CE	1 CE	1500 CE	1000 CE	1 CE
Log years since Neolithic	0.159	0.073	0.109	1.337**	0.832**	1.006**
transition	(0.136)	(0.045)	(0.072)	(0.594)	(0.363)	(0.481)
Log land productivity	0.041	−0.021	−0.001	0.584***	0.364***	0.681**
	(0.025)	(0.025)	(0.027)	(0.159)	(0.110)	(0.255)
Log absolute latitude	−0.041	0.060	−0.175	0.050	−2.140**	−2.163**
	(0.073)	(0.147)	(0.175)	(0.463)	(0.801)	(0.979)
Mean distance to nearest	0.215	−0.111	0.043	−0.429	−0.237	0.118
coast or river	(0.198)	(0.138)	(0.159)	(1.237)	(0.751)	(0.883)
Percentage of land within	0.124	−0.150	0.042	1.855**	1.326**	0.228
100 km of coast or river	(0.145)	(0.121)	(0.127)	(0.820)	(0.615)	(0.919)
Continent dummies	Yes	Yes	Yes	Yes	Yes	Yes
Observations	31	26	29	31	26	29
R-squared	0.66	0.68	0.33	0.88	0.95	0.89

Summary: This table establishes, consistently with Malthusian predictions, the relatively small effects of land productivity and the level of technological advancement, as proxied by the timing of the Neolithic Revolution, on income per capita in 1500 CE, 1000 CE, and 1 CE, and their significantly larger effects on population density in the same periods, while controlling for access to navigable waterways, absolute latitude, and unobserved continental fixed effects.
Notes: (i) Log land productivity is the first principal component of the log of the arable percentage of land and the log of an agricultural suitability index; (ii) a single continent dummy is used to represent the Americas, which is natural, given the historical period examined; (iii) regressions (2) and (3), and (5) and (6) do not employ the Oceania dummy due to a single observation for this continent in the corresponding regression samples, restricted by the availability of data on income per capita; (iv) robust standard error estimates are reported in parentheses; (v) *** denotes statistical significance at the 1% level, ** at the 5% level, and * at the 10% level, all for two-sided hypothesis tests.

gest that over the past 500 years, this initial developmental dominance has been mitigated by additional factors. Consequently, while the data show a significant relationship between the timing of the transition to agriculture and development

1 CE yields $\theta_{1,1} = 0.755$ [0.172] and $\theta_{2,1} = -0.020$ [0.013], with the standard errors indicating that the first-order (linear) effect is statistically significant at the 1% level, whereas the second-order (quadratic) effect is insignificant.

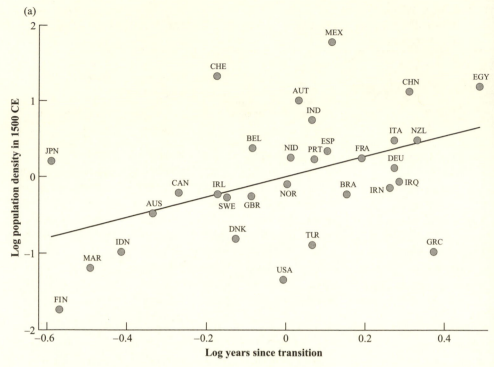

FIGURE 3.6. Transition timing, population density, and income per capita, 1500 CE: (a) partial effect of transition timing on population density; (b) partial effect of transition timing on income per capita.
Data source: Ashraf and Galor (2011).
Summary: The figure depicts the partial regression line for the effect of log transition timing on log population density and log income per capita in 1500 CE while controlling for the influence of log land productivity, absolute latitude, access to waterways, and continental fixed effects. Thus, the *x* and *y* axes in panel (a) [panel (b)] plot the residuals obtained from regressing log transition timing and log population density [log income per capita], respectively, on the aforementioned set of covariates.

outcomes in the precolonial era, Diamond's hypothesis about the persistent effect of the timing of the Neolithic Revolution on contemporary levels of income per capita across the globe is fragile (Ashraf and Galor, 2009).

3.5.3 Income per Capita versus Population Density

This section examines the Malthusian prediction regarding the neutrality of the standard of living with respect to land productivity and the level of technological advancement, as proxied by the timing of the Neolithic Revolution. Table 3.5

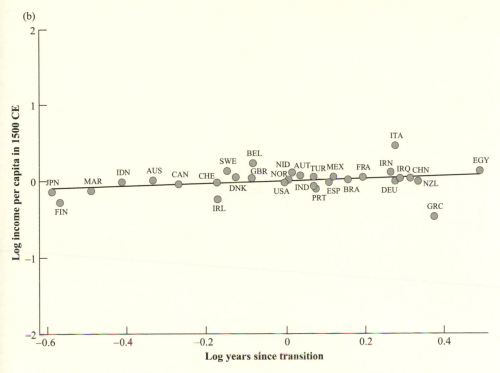

FIGURE 3.6 *(continued)*

presents the results from estimating the baseline empirical model, as specified in (3.16), for income per capita in 1500 CE, 1000 CE, and 1 CE. Since data for historical income per capita are available for a relatively smaller set of countries, the analysis at hand also conducts corresponding tests for population density using the income per capita data-restricted samples for the three historical periods. This permits an impartial assessment of whether higher land productivity and an earlier onset of the Neolithic Revolution are manifested mostly in terms of higher population density, as opposed to higher income per capita, as the Malthusian theory would predict.[23]

Columns 1–3 reveal that income per capita in each historical period is effectively neutral to variations in the timing of the Neolithic Revolution, the

[23] The insufficient number of observations arising from the greater scarcity of historical income data, compared to data on population density, prevents the analysis from pursuing an IV strategy that uses the numbers of prehistoric domesticable species of wild plants and animals as instruments for the timing of the Neolithic Revolution when examining its impact on income per capita.

(a)

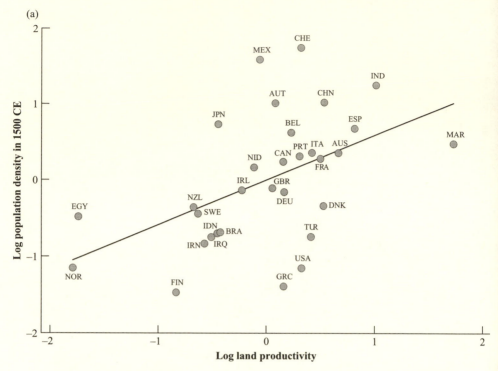

FIGURE 3.7. Land productivity, population density and income per capita in 1500 CE: (a) partial effect of land productivity on population density; (b) partial effect of land productivity on income per capita.

Data source: Ashraf and Galor (2011).

Summary: The figure depicts the partial regression line for the effect of log land productivity on log population density and log income per capita in 1500 CE while controlling for the influence of log transition timing, absolute latitude, access to waterways, and continental fixed effects. Thus, the *x* and *y* axes in panel (a) [panel (b)] plot the residuals obtained from regressing log land productivity and log population density [log income per capita], respectively, on the set of covariates.

agricultural productivity of land, and other productivity-enhancing geographical factors, conditional on continental fixed effects.[24] In particular, the effects of transition timing and land productivity on income per capita are not only substantially smaller than those on population density, they are also not statistically different from zero at conventional levels of significance. Moreover, the

---

[24] The rather high R-squared associated with each of these regressions is due to the inclusion of continental fixed effects in the specification.

(b)

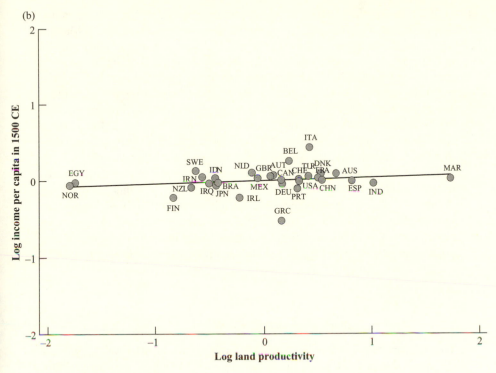

FIGURE 3.7 *(continued)*

other geographical factors, which arguably had facilitated trade and technology diffusion, do not appear to significantly affect income per capita.

In contrast, the regressions in Columns 4–6, which exploit the same variation in explanatory variables as in the preceding regressions on income per capita, reveal that the elasticities of population density in each period with respect to Neolithic transition timing and land productivity are not only highly statistically significant but are also larger by about an order of magnitude than the corresponding elasticities of income per capita. Thus, for 1500 CE, a 1% increase in the number of years elapsed since the Neolithic Revolution raises population density by 1.34% but income per capita by only 0.16%, conditional on land productivity, geographical factors, and continental fixed effects. Similarly, a 1% increase in land productivity is associated, *ceteris paribus,* with a 0.58% increase in population density in 1500 CE but only a 0.04% increase in income per capita in the same time period. The conditional effects of Neolithic transition timing and land productivity on income per capita versus population density in 1500 CE are depicted as partial regression lines on the scatter plots in Figures 3.6 and 3.7.

While the results revealing the cross-country neutrality of income per capita, despite differences in aggregate productivity, are fully consistent with Malthusian predictions, there may exist potential concerns regarding the quality of the income per capita data employed by the current analysis. In particular, contrary to Maddison's (2008) implicit assertion, if the historical income per capita estimates were in part imputed under the Malthusian prior regarding similarities in the standard of living across countries, then applying these data to test the Malthusian theory itself would clearly be invalid. However, a closer look at some properties of Maddison's (2003) data, as examined in the online appendix of Ashraf and Galor (2011), suggests that this need not be a concern.

Hence, the empirical analysis indicates that more productive societies sustained higher population densities, as opposed to higher standards of living, during 1–1500 CE. These findings are entirely consistent with the Malthusian prediction that in pre-industrial economies, resources temporarily generated by more productive technological environments were ultimately channeled into population growth, with negligible long-run effects on income per capita.

3.5.4 Effect of Technological Sophistication

This section demonstrates the qualitative robustness of the results regarding the significant positive effect of technology—as proxied by the timing of the Neolithic Revolution—on population density and its neutrality for income per capita under more direct measures of technological advancement. In particular, Table 3.6 presents the findings from estimating the baseline specification for population density and income per capita in the years 1000 CE and 1 CE, employing the index of technological sophistication corresponding to these periods, in lieu of the number of years elapsed since the Neolithic Revolution, as an indicator of the level of aggregate productivity.

As mentioned previously, the index of technological sophistication in each period is based on cross-cultural, sector-specific technology data from Peregrine (2003), aggregated to the country level by averaging across sectors and cultures within a country. Specifically, the index not only captures the level of technological advancement in communications, transportation, and industry, but also incorporates information on the prevalence of sedentary agricultural practices relative to hunting and gathering. Since the timing of the Neolithic transition is *a priori* expected to be highly correlated with the prevalence of agriculture across countries in both 1000 CE and 1 CE, its inclusion as an explanatory variable in the analysis would constitute the exploitation of redundant information and would potentially obfuscate the results of the analysis. The regressions in Table 3.6 therefore omit the timing of the Neolithic transition as an explanatory

TABLE 3.6
Robustness to direct measures of technological sophistication

	(1) OLS Full sample	(2) OLS Full sample	(3) OLS Income sample	(4) OLS Income sample	(5) OLS Income sample	(6) OLS Income sample
			Dependent variable is			
	Log population density in		Log income per capita in		Log population density in	
	1000 CE	1 CE	1000 CE	1 CE	1000 CE	1 CE
Log technology index in	4.315***	4.216***	0.064	0.678	12.762***	7.461**
relevant period	(0.850)	(0.745)	(0.230)	(0.432)	(0.918)	(3.181)
Log land productivity	0.449***	0.379***	−0.016	0.004	0.429**	0.725**
	(0.056)	(0.082)	(0.030)	(0.033)	(0.182)	(0.303)
Log absolute latitude	−0.283**	−0.051	0.036	−0.198	−1.919***	−2.350***
	(0.120)	(0.127)	(0.161)	(0.176)	(0.576)	(0.784)
Mean distance to nearest	−0.638***	−0.782***	−0.092	0.114	0.609	0.886
coast or river	(0.188)	(0.198)	(0.144)	(0.164)	(0.469)	(0.904)
Percentage of land within	0.385	0.237	−0.156	0.092	1.265**	0.788
100 km of coast or river	(0.313)	(0.329)	(0.139)	(0.136)	(0.555)	(0.934)
Continent dummies	Yes	Yes	Yes	Yes	Yes	Yes
Observations	140	129	26	29	26	29
R-squared	0.61	0.62	0.64	0.30	0.97	0.88

Summary: This table demonstrates that the relatively small effect of the level of technological advancement on income per capita in 1000 CE and 1 CE, and its significantly larger effect on population density in the same periods, remains qualitatively robust when more direct measures of technological sophistication for the corresponding years are used in lieu of the timing of the Neolithic Revolution.

Notes: (i) The technology index for a given time reflects the average degree of technological sophistication across communications, transportation, industrial, and agricultural sectors in that period; (ii) the almost perfect collinearity between the degree of technological sophistication in the agricultural sector and the timing of the Neolithic transition does not permit the use of the latter as a covariate in these regressions; (iii) log land productivity is the first principal component of the log of the arable percentage of land and the log of an agricultural suitability index; (iv) a single continent dummy is used to represent the Americas, which is natural, given the historical period examined; (v) regressions (3)–(6) do not employ the Oceania dummy due to a single observation for this continent in the corresponding regression samples, restricted by the availability of data on income per capita; (vi) the income sample restricts the dataset only to those observations for which per capita income is available; (vii) robust standard error estimates are reported in parentheses; (viii) *** denotes statistical significance at the 1% level, ** at the 5% level, and * at the 10% level, all for two-sided hypothesis tests.

variable for both population density and income per capita in the two periods examined.[25]

Echoing the qualitative robustness of the findings from previous sections, the log of the indices of technology in 1000 CE and 1 CE are indeed highly correlated with the log of the transition-timing variable. For instance, in the full cross-country samples, the log of the Neolithic transition-timing variable possesses correlation coefficients of 0.73 and 0.62 with the log of the indices of technology in 1000 CE and 1 CE, respectively. Similarly, in the income per capita data-restricted samples employed in Section 3.5.3, the corresponding correlation coefficients are 0.82 and 0.74.

Columns 1 and 2 in Table 3.6 reveal the full-sample regression results for population density in 1000 CE and 1 CE. Consistent with Malthusian predictions, the regressions indicate highly statistically significant positive relationships between technological sophistication and population density in the two periods. To interpret the coefficients of interest, a 1% increase in the level of technological sophistication in 1000 CE and 1 CE corresponds to a rise in population density in the respective periods of 4.32% and 4.22%, conditional on the productivity of land, geographical factors, and continental fixed effects. In addition, Columns 1 and 2 also indicate that the effects of the land-productivity channel on population density remain largely stable in comparison to previous estimates.

The results from replicating the 1000 CE and 1 CE analyses of Section 3.5.3, using the period-specific indices of technology as opposed to the timing of the Neolithic Revolution, are presented in Columns 3-6. For each period examined, the regressions for income per capita and population density reveal, exploiting identical variations in explanatory variables, that the estimated elasticity of population density with respect to the degree of technological sophistication is not only highly statistically significant but is also at least an order of magnitude larger than the corresponding elasticity of income per capita. Indeed, the conditional correlation between technology and income per capita is not statistically different from zero at conventional levels of significance. A similar pattern also emerges for the estimated elasticities of population density and income per capita in each period with respect to the land-productivity channel. These findings therefore confirm the Malthusian prior that, in pre-industrial times, variations in the level of technological advancement were ultimately manifested as variations in population density as opposed to differences in the standard of living across regions.

---

[25] Consistent with the symptoms of multicollinearity, inclusion of the transition-timing variable in these regressions results in the coefficients of interest possessing larger standard errors with relatively minor effects on the coefficient magnitudes themselves.

The remainder of the analysis in this section is concerned with establishing the causal effect of technology on population density in 1000 CE and 1 CE. Since the measures of technology employed by the preceding analysis are contemporaneous with population density in the two periods examined, the issue of endogeneity is perhaps more germane in this case than it was when examining the effect of the timing of the Neolithic Revolution on population density under the OLS estimator. In particular, the estimated coefficients associated with the period-specific technology indices in Columns 1 and 2 of Table 3.6 may, in part, be capturing reverse causality, due to the potential scale effect of population on technological progress, as well as the latent influence of unobserved country-specific characteristics that are correlated with both technology and population density. To address these issues, the analysis appeals to Diamond's (1997) argument, regarding the Neolithic transition to agriculture as a triggering event for subsequent technological progress. Thus the analysis exploits the exogenous component of cross-country variation in technology during the first millennium CE, as determined by the variation in prehistoric biogeographical endowments that led to the differential timing of the Neolithic Revolution itself.[26]

The analysis proceeds by first establishing the causal effect of the Neolithic Revolution on subsequent technological progress. Given the high correlation between the prevalence of sedentary agricultural practices in Peregrine's (2003) dataset and the timing of the Neolithic transition, the current analysis exploits, for each period examined, an alternative index of technological sophistication that is based only on the levels of technological advancement in communications, transportation, and industry but is otherwise identical in its underlying aggregation methodology to the index employed thus far. This approach permits a more transparent assessment of the argument that the Neolithic Revolution triggered a cumulative process of development, fueled by the emergence and propagation of a non-food-producing class in agricultural societies, which enabled sociocultural and technological advancements over and above subsistence activities.

Table 3.7 presents the results of regressions examining the impact of the timing of the Neolithic Revolution on the level of nonagricultural technological sophistication in 1000 CE and 1 CE while controlling for land productivity, absolute latitude, access to waterways, and continental fixed effects. In line with priors, the regressions in Columns 1 and 4 establish a highly statistically significant positive relationship between the timing of the Neolithic Revolution

---

[26] The potential issue of endogeneity arising from the latent influence of unobserved country fixed effects is also addressed by a first-difference estimation methodology employing data on population density and technological sophistication at two points in time. This strategy is pursued in Section 3.5.6.

TABLE 3.7

The Causal effect of the Neolithic Revolution on technological sophistication

	(1) OLS Full sample	(2) OLS Restricted sample	(3) OLS Restricted sample	(4) OLS Full sample	(5) OLS Restricted sample	(6) IV Restricted sample
	Dependent variable is log nonagricultural technology in					
	1000 CE			1 CE		
Log years since Neolithic transition	0.115*** (0.024)	0.146*** (0.030)	0.279*** (0.073)	0.152*** (0.027)	0.174*** (0.029)	0.339*** (0.074)
Log land productivity	−0.006 (0.008)	−0.012 (0.015)	−0.009 (0.014)	−0.024*** (0.008)	−0.027* (0.016)	−0.023 (0.019)
Log absolute latitude	0.012 (0.014)	0.000 (0.019)	0.005 (0.018)	0.039** (0.016)	0.026 (0.022)	0.032 (0.020)
Mean distance to nearest coast or river	0.008 (0.033)	0.117** (0.053)	0.129** (0.051)	0.007 (0.035)	0.050 (0.084)	0.066 (0.078)
Percentage of land within 100 km of coast or river	0.024 (0.038)	0.080 (0.052)	0.112* (0.058)	0.047 (0.048)	0.110 (0.070)	0.149** (0.076)
Continent dummies	Yes	Yes	Yes	Yes	Yes	Yes
Observations	143	93	93	143	93	93
R-squared	0.76	0.72	0.67	0.59	0.55	0.47
First-stage F-statistic	—	—	13.47	—	—	13.47
Overidentifying p-value	—	—	0.256	—	—	0.166

Summary: This table presents the causal effect of the timing of the Neolithic Revolution on the level of technology in nonagricultural sectors in 1000 CE and 1 CE while controlling for land productivity, access to navigable waterways, absolute latitude, and unobserved continental fixed effects.

Notes: (i) Unlike the regular technology index, the index of nonagricultural technology for a given period reflects the average degree of technological sophistication across only communications, transportation, and industrial sectors in that period; (ii) log land productivity is the first principal component of the log of the arable percentage of land and the log of an agricultural suitability index; (iii) the restricted sample refers to observations for which information on domesticable plants and animals is available; (iv) the IV regressions employ the numbers of prehistoric domesticable species of plants and animals as instruments for log transition timing; (v) the statistic for the first-stage F-test of these instruments is significant at the 1% level; (vi) the p-values for the overidentifying restrictions tests correspond to Hansen's J statistic, distributed in both instances as χ^2 with one degree of freedom; (vii) a single continent dummy is used to represent the Americas, which is natural, given the historical period examined; (viii) regressions (2) and (3), and (5) and (6) do not employ the Oceania dummy due to a single observation for this continent in the IV data-restricted sample; (ix) robust standard error estimates are reported in parentheses; (x) *** denotes statistical significance at the 1% level, ** at the 5% level, and * at the 10% level, all for two-sided hypothesis tests.

and the level of nonagricultural technological sophistication in each period, exploiting variation across the full sample of countries. To allow valid comparisons with the results from subsequent IV regressions, Columns 2 and 5 repeat the preceding OLS analyses on the subsample of countries for which data on the biogeographical instruments for the timing of the Neolithic Revolution are available. The results indicate that the OLS coefficients of interest from the preceding full-sample analyses remain robust to this change in the regression sample. Finally, Columns 3 and 6 establish the causal effect of the Neolithic Revolution on the level of nonagricultural technological sophistication in the two periods, employing the prehistoric availability of domesticable species of plants and animals as instruments for the timing of the Neolithic transition. Not surprisingly, as observed with earlier IV regressions, the causal impact of the Neolithic transition is, in each case, larger relative to its impact obtained under the OLS estimator. This pattern is consistent with measurement error in the transition-timing variable and the resultant attenuation bias afflicting OLS coefficient estimates.

In light of the causal link between the timing of the Neolithic transition and the level of technological advancement in the first millennium CE, the analysis may now establish the causal impact of technology on population density in the two periods examined. This is accomplished by exploiting exogenous variation in the level of technological advancement ultimately generated by differences in prehistoric biogeographical endowments that led to the differential timing of the transition to agriculture across countries. Table 3.8 reveals the results of this test where, as in Table 3.6, the measure of technology employed is the overall index that incorporates information on the prevalence of sedentary agriculture along with the level of advancement in nonagricultural technologies.

To facilitate comparisons of results obtained under the OLS and IV estimators, the full-sample OLS results from Table 3.6 for 1000 CE and 1 CE are again presented in Columns 1 and 4 of Table 3.8, while Columns 2 and 5 present the same regressions conducted on the IV-restricted subsample of countries. The causal effects of the level of technological advancement in 1000 CE and 1 CE, instrumented by the prehistoric availability of domesticable plant and animal species, on population density in the corresponding periods are revealed in Columns 3 and 6. The estimated IV coefficients indicate a much larger causal impact of technology on population density, with a 1% increase in the level of technological sophistication in 1000 CE and 1 CE raising population density in the respective time periods by 14.53% and 10.80%, conditional on the productivity of land, absolute latitude, access to waterways, and continental fixed effects. Thus, in line with the predictions of the Malthusian theory, the results indicate that, during the agricultural stage of development, temporary gains due to improvements in the technological environment were indeed channeled into population growth, thereby leading more technologically advanced societies to sustain higher population densities.

TABLE 3.8
The causal effect of technological sophistication on population density

	(1) OLS Full sample	(2) OLS Restricted sample	(3) OLS Restricted sample	(4) OLS Full sample	(5) OLS Restricted sample	(6) IV Restricted sample
	Dependent variable is log population density in					
	1000 CE			1 CE		
Log technology index in relevant period	4.315*** (0.850)	4.198*** (1.164)	14.530*** (4.437)	4.216*** (0.745)	3.947*** (0.983)	10.798*** (2.857)
Log land productivity	0.449*** (0.056)	0.498*** (0.139)	0.572*** (0.148)	0.379*** (0.082)	0.350** (0.172)	0.464** (0.182)
Log absolute latitude	−0.283** (0.120)	−0.185 (0.151)	−0.209 (0.209)	−0.051 (0.127)	0.083 (0.170)	−0.052 (0.214)
Mean distance to nearest coast or river	−0.638*** (0.188)	−0.363 (0.426)	−1.155* (0.640)	−0.782*** (0.198)	−0.625 (0.434)	−0.616 (0.834)
Percentage of land within 100 km of coast or river	0.385 (0.313)	0.442 (0.422)	0.153 (0.606)	0.237 (0.329)	0.146 (0.424)	−0.172 (0.642)
Continent dummies	Yes	Yes	Yes	Yes	Yes	Yes
Observations	140	92	92	129	83	83
R-squared	0.61	0.55	0.13	0.62	0.58	0.32
First-stage F-statistic	—	—	12.52	—	—	12.00
Overidentifying p-value	—	—	0.941	—	—	0.160

Summary: This table presents the causal effect of direct measures of technological sophistication in 1000 CE and 1 CE, as determined by exogenous factors governing the timing of the Neolithic Revolution, on population density while controlling for land productivity, access to navigable waterways, absolute latitude, and unobserved continental fixed effects.

Notes: (i) The technology index for a given period reflects the average degree of technological sophistication across communications, transportation, industrial, and agricultural sectors in that period; (ii) the almost perfect collinearity between the degree of technological sophistication in the agricultural sector and the timing of the Neolithic transition does not permit the use of the latter as a covariate in these regressions; (iii) log land productivity is the first principal component of the log of the arable percentage of land and the log of an agricultural suitability index; (iv) the restricted sample refers to observations for which information on domesticable plants and animals is available; (v) the IV regressions employ the numbers of prehistoric domesticable species of plants and animals as instruments for the log of the technology index in each of the two periods; (vi) in both cases, the statistic for the first-stage F-test of these instruments is significant at the 1% level; (vii) the p-values for the overidentifying restrictions tests correspond to Hansen's J statistic, distributed in both instances as χ^2 with one degree of freedom; (viii) a single continent dummy is used to represent the Americas, which is natural, given the historical period examined; (ix) regressions (2) and (3), and (5) and (6) do not employ the Oceania dummy due to a single observation for this continent in the IV data-restricted sample; (x) robust standard error estimates are reported in parentheses; (xi) *** denotes statistical significance at the 1% level, ** at the 5% level, and * at the 10% level, all for two-sided hypothesis tests.

3.5.5   Robustness to Technology Diffusion and Geographical Features

This section establishes the robustness of the results for population density and income per capita in 1500 CE with respect to the spatial influence of technological frontiers as well as other geographical factors (such as climate and small-island and landlocked dummies). All of these factors may have had an effect on aggregate productivity either directly, by affecting the productivity of land, or indirectly, by affecting the prevalence of trade and technology diffusion. Specifically, the technology diffusion hypothesis suggests that spatial proximity to societies at the world technology frontier confers a beneficial effect on development by facilitating the diffusion of new technologies from the frontier through trade as well as through sociocultural and geopolitical influences. In particular, the diffusion channel implies that, *ceteris paribus,* the greater the geographical distance from the technological leaders in a given period, the lower the level of economic development among the followers in that period.

To account for the technology-diffusion channel, the current analysis employs as a control variable the great-circle distance from the capital city of a country to the closest of eight worldwide regional technological frontiers. These centers of technology diffusion are derived by Ashraf and Galor (2009), who employ historical urbanization estimates provided by Chandler (1987) and Modelski (2003) to identify frontiers based on the size of urban populations. Specifically, for a given period, their procedure selects from each continent the two largest cities in that period that belong to distinct sociopolitical entities. Thus, the set of regional technological frontiers identified for 1500 CE comprises London and Paris in Europe, Fez and Cairo in Africa, Istanbul and Beijing in Asia, and Tenochtitlán and Cuzco in the Americas.

Column 1 of Table 3.9 reveals the qualitative robustness of the full-sample regression results for population density in 1500 CE under controls for distance to the closest regional frontier as well as small-island and landlocked dummies. To the extent that the gains from trade and technology diffusion are manifested primarily in terms of population size, as the Malthusian theory predicts, distance to the frontier has a highly statistically significant negative impact on population density. Nevertheless, the regression coefficients associated with the Neolithic transition-timing and land-productivity channels remain largely stable, albeit somewhat less so for the former, in comparison to their baseline estimates from Column 4 in Table 3.2. Indeed, the lower magnitude of the coefficient associated with the transition-timing channel is attributable to the fact that several frontiers in 1500 CE, including Egypt, China, and Mexico, were also centers of diffusion of agricultural practices during the Neolithic Revolution and, as such, distance to the frontier in 1500 CE is partly capturing the effect of the differential timing of the Neolithic transition itself.

The regression in Column 2 extends the robustness analysis of Column 1 by adding controls for the percentage of land in temperate and tropical zones. The

TABLE 3.9
Robustness to technology diffusion and geographical features

	(1) OLS Full sample	(2) OLS Full sample	(3) OLS Income sample	(4) OLS Income sample	(5) OLS Income sample	(6) OLS Income sample
			Dependent variable is			
	Log population density in 1500 CE		Log income per capita in 1500 CE		Log population density in 1500 CE	
Log years since Neolithic transition	0.828*** (0.208)	0.877*** (0.214)	0.117 (0.221)	0.103 (0.214)	1.498** (0.546)	1.478** (0.556)
Log land productivity	0.559*** (0.048)	0.545*** (0.063)	0.036 (0.032)	0.047 (0.037)	0.596*** (0.123)	0.691*** (0.122)
Log absolute latitude	−0.400*** (0.108)	−0.301** (0.129)	−0.020 (0.110)	0.028 (0.247)	−0.354 (0.392)	0.668 (0.783)
Mean distance to nearest coast or river	−0.403*** (0.152)	−0.388*** (0.144)	0.175 (0.286)	0.202 (0.309)	0.394 (0.994)	0.594 (0.844)
Percentage of land within 100 km of coast or river	0.870*** (0.272)	0.837*** (0.280)	0.160 (0.153)	0.245 (0.208)	1.766*** (0.511)	2.491*** (0.754)
Log distance to frontier	−0.186*** (0.035)	−0.191*** (0.036)	−0.005 (0.011)	−0.001 (0.013)	−0.130* (0.066)	−0.108* (0.055)
Small-island dummy	0.067 (0.582)	0.086 (0.626)	−0.118 (0.216)	−0.046 (0.198)	1.962** (0.709)	2.720*** (0.699)
Landlocked dummy	0.131 (0.209)	0.119 (0.203)	0.056 (0.084)	0.024 (0.101)	1.490*** (0.293)	1.269*** (0.282)
Percentage of land in temperate climate zones		−0.196 (0.513)		−0.192 (0.180)		−1.624* (0.917)
Percentage of land in tropical and subtropical climate zones		0.269 (0.307)		−0.025 (0.308)		1.153 (1.288)
Continent dummies	Yes	Yes	Yes	Yes	Yes	Yes
Observations	147	147	31	31	31	31
R-squared	0.76	0.76	0.67	0.67	0.94	0.96

Summary: This table demonstrates that the relatively small effects of land productivity and level of technological advancement, as proxied by the timing of the Neolithic Revolution, on income per capita in 1500 CE, but their significantly larger effects on population density in the same periods remain robust under additional controls for technology diffusion and climatic factors.
Notes: (i) Log land productivity is the first principal component of the log of the arable percentage of land and the log of an agricultural suitability index; (ii) a single continent dummy is used to represent the Americas, which is natural, given the historical period examined; (iii) the income sample restricts the dataset to those observations for which income per capita is available; (iv) robust standard error estimates are reported in parentheses; (v) *** denotes statistical significance at the 1% level, ** at the 5% level, and * at the 10% level, all for two-sided hypothesis tests.

findings demonstrate that the effects of the Neolithic transition-timing, land-productivity, and spatial technology-diffusion channels on population density are indeed not spuriously driven by these additional climatological factors.

Columns 3–6 reveal the robustness of the results for income per capita as well as population density in the income per capita data-restricted sample, under controls for the technology-diffusion channel and additional geographical factors. In comparison to the relevant baseline regressions presented in Columns 1 and 4 of Table 3.5, the coefficients associated with the transition-timing and land-productivity channels remain both qualitatively and quantitatively stable. In particular, the estimated elasticities of population density with respect to these channels are about an order of magnitude larger than the corresponding elasticities of income per capita regardless of the set of additional controls included in the specification.

With regard to the influence of technology diffusion, the qualitative pattern of the effects on population density versus income per capita is similar to that associated with the transition-timing and land-productivity channels. The finding that the negative elasticity of income per capita with respect to distance to the frontier is not only statistically insignificant but also at least an order of magnitude smaller than that of population density confirms Malthusian priors that the gains from trade and technology diffusion were primarily channeled into population growth, rather than into improvements in living standards, during pre-industrial times.[27] While this finding may also be consistent with a non-Malthusian migration-driven theory of population movements against a spatial productivity gradient, the results uncovered by the first-difference estimation strategy pursued in the next section provide evidence in favor of the proposed Malthusian interpretation.

3.5.6 Rejection of Alternative Theories

This section examines the robustness of the empirical findings to alternative theories and time-invariant country fixed effects. Specifically, the level regression results may be explained by the following non-Malthusian theory. In a world where labor is perfectly mobile, regions with higher aggregate productivity would experience labor inflows until regional wage rates were equalized, implying that, in levels, technology should be positively associated with population density but should not be correlated with income per capita across regions.

---

[27] Galor and Mountford (2008) reveal similar findings among non-OECD countries in 1985–1990, indicating that this phenomenon is more broadly associated with economies in the agricultural stage of development, even in the contemporary period.

Such a theory would also imply, however, that increases in the level of technology in any given region should generate increases in the standard of living in all regions. This runs contrary to the Malthusian prediction that increases in the level of technology in a given region should ultimately translate into increases in population density in that region, leaving income per capita constant at the subsistence level in all regions. Thus, examining the effect of a change in technology on changes in population density versus income per capita, as opposed to the impact of the level of technology on the levels of population density versus income per capita, constitutes a more discriminatory test of the Malthusian model.

Moreover, the results of the level regressions in Table 3.6, indicating the significant positive relationship between the level of technology and population density but the absence of a systematic relationship with income per capita, could potentially reflect spurious correlations between technology and one or more unobserved time-invariant country fixed effects. By investigating the effect of changes on changes, however, one may difference out time-invariant country fixed effects, thereby ensuring that the coefficients of interest in the regression will not be afflicted by any such omitted variable bias. In addition, while the relationship between contemporaneous changes in technology and population density or income per capita could reflect reverse causality, this endogeneity issue may be alleviated somewhat by examining the impact of the lagged change in technology on changes in population density versus income per capita.

The current investigation thus examines the effect of the change in the level of technology between 1000 BCE and 1 CE on the change in population density versus its effect on the change in income per capita over the 1–1000 CE time horizon. In particular, the analysis compares the results from estimating the following empirical models:

$$\Delta \ln P_{i,t} = \mu_0 + \mu_1 \Delta \ln A_{i,t-1} + \phi_{i,t}, \tag{3.17}$$

$$\Delta \ln y_{i,t} = \nu_0 + \nu_1 \Delta \ln A_{i,t-1} + \psi_{i,t}, \tag{3.18}$$

where $\Delta \ln P_{i,t} \equiv \ln P_{i,t+1} - \ln P_{i,t}$ (i.e., the difference in log population density in country i between 1 CE and 1000 CE); $\Delta \ln y_{i,t} \equiv \ln y_{i,t+1} - \ln y_{i,t}$ (i.e., the difference in log income per capita of country i between 1 CE and 1000 CE); $\Delta \ln A_{i,t-1} \equiv \ln A_{i,t} - \ln A_{i,t-1}$ (i.e., the difference in log technology of country i between 1000 BCE and 1 CE); and $\phi_{i,t}$ and $\psi_{i,t}$ are country-specific disturbance terms for the changes in log population density and log income per capita. In addition, the intercept terms, μ_0 and ν_0, capture the average trend growth rates of population density and income per capita respectively over the 1–1000 CE time horizon. These models are the first-difference counterparts of (3.15) and (3.16), given that (i) $\ln A_{i,t-1}$ is used in lieu of T_i, and (ii) the fixed effects of land productivity and the other geographical contols, including continental dummies, are time-invariant in those specifications.[28]

As discussed earlier, the alternative migration-driven theory predicts that an increase in technology in a given region will not differentially increase income per capita in that region due to the cross-regional equalization of wage rates, but it will increase income per capita in all regions. In light of the specifications defined above, this theory would therefore imply that $\nu_1 = 0$ and $\nu_0 > 0$ in (3.18). According to the Malthusian theory, however, not only will the long-run level of income per capita remain unaffected in the region undergoing technological advancement, it will remain unaffected in all other regions as well. The Malthusian theory thus implies that both $\nu_1 = 0$ and $\nu_0 = 0$.

Table 3.10 presents the results from estimating (3.17) and (3.18).[29] As predicted by the Malthusian theory, the slope coefficients in Columns 1 and 2 indicate that the change in the level of technology between 1000 BCE and 1 CE has a positive and statistically significant effect on the change in population density over the 1–1000 CE time horizon. In contrast, Column 3 reveals that the corresponding effect on the change in income per capita over 1–1000 CE is relatively marginal and not statistically significantly different from zero. Moreover, the intercept coefficient in Column 3 suggests that the standard of living in 1000 CE was not significantly different from that in 1 CE, a finding that

---

[28] In particular, (3.17) and (3.18) are obtained by applying the first-difference method to the following variants of (3.15) and (3.16):

$$\ln P_{i,t} = \gamma_0 + \mu_1 \ln A_{i,t-1} + \gamma_1 \ln X_i + \gamma_2' \Gamma_i + \gamma_3' D_i + \xi_{i,t}^P,$$

$$\ln y_{i,t} = \lambda_0 + \nu_1 \ln A_{i,t-1} + \lambda_1 \ln X_i + \lambda_2' \Gamma_i + \lambda_3' D_i + \xi_{i,t}^y,$$

with the respective error terms, $\xi_{i,t}^P$ and $\xi_{i,t}^y$, being modeled as:

$$\xi_{i,t}^P = \eta_i^P + \mu_0 t + \sigma_{i,t}^P,$$

$$\xi_{i,t}^y = \eta_i^y + \nu_0 t + \sigma_{i,t}^y,$$

where η_i^P and η_i^y are unobserved time-invariant country fixed effects on population density and income per capita in country i; μ_0 and ν_0 are global year fixed effects on population density and income per capita in year t; and $\sigma_{i,t}^P$ and $\sigma_{i,t}^y$ are country-year-specific disturbance terms for population density and income per capita. Thus, the error terms in (3.17) and (3.18) represent the changes over time in the aforementioned country-year-specific disturbance terms; that is, $\phi_{i,t} \equiv \sigma_{i,t+1}^P - \sigma_{i,t}^P$ and $\psi_{i,t} \equiv \sigma_{i,t+1}^y - \sigma_{i,t}^y$.

[29] These findings are qualitatively robust to the inclusion of continental dummies in the specifications.

TABLE 3.10
Effect of changes in technology on changes in income and population

	(1) OLS Full sample	(2) OLS Income sample	(3) OLS Income sample
	Dependent variable is differences in		
	Log population density between 1 CE and 1000 CE		Log income per capita between 1 CE and 1000 CE
Difference in log technology index between 1000 BCE and 1 CE	1.747*** (0.429)	3.133* (1.550)	0.073 (0.265)
Constant	0.451*** (0.053)	−0.026 (0.204)	−0.040 (0.064)
Observations	126	26	26
R-squared	0.17	0.34	0.00

Summary: This table establishes that the change in the level of technological sophistication that occurred between 1000 BCE and 1 CE was primarily associated with a change in population density as opposed to a change in income per capita over the 1–1000 CE time horizon. It also reveals that there was no trend growth in income per capita during this period, thereby demonstrating robustness to time-invariant country fixed effects and dispelling an alternative migration-driven theory that is consistent with the level regression results.

Notes: (i) The technology index for a given period reflects the average degree of technological sophistication across communications, transportation, industrial, and agricultural sectors in that period; (ii) the absence of controls from both regressions is justified by the removal of time-invariant country fixed effects through the application of the first-difference methodology; (iii) the income sample restricts the dataset to those observations for which income per capita was available; (iv) robust standard error estimates are reported in parentheses; (v) *** denotes statistical significance at the 1% level, ** at the 5% level, and * at the 10% level, all for two-sided hypothesis tests.

accords well with the Malthusian viewpoint. Overall, the results from the first-difference estimation strategy pursued in this section lend further credence to the Malthusian interpretation of the level regression results presented in earlier sections.

3.6 Concluding Remarks

This chapter examines the central hypothesis of the influential Malthusian theory, according to which improvements in the technological environment during the pre-industrial era had generated only temporary gains in income per capita, eventually leading to a larger, but not significantly richer, population. It exploits exogenous sources of cross-country variation in land productivity and technological levels to examine their hypothesized differential effects on population density versus income per capita.

Consistent with Malthusian predictions, the analysis uncovers statistically significant positive effects of land productivity and technological level on population density in 1500 CE, 1000 CE, and 1 CE. In contrast, the effects of land productivity and technology on income per capita in these periods are not significantly different from zero. Importantly, these qualitative results remain robust to controls for the confounding effects of a large number of geographical factors—including absolute latitude, access to waterways, distance to the technological frontier, and the share of land in tropical versus temperate climatic zones.

The analysis also dispels a non-Malthusian theory that may appear consistent with the level regression results. Specifically, in a world with perfect labor mobility, regions with higher aggregate productivity would have experienced labor inflows until regional wage rates were equalized, implying that technology should be positively associated with population density but should not be correlated with income per capita. However, labor inflows in response to technological improvements in a given region would result in higher income per capita in all regions, implying that changes in the level of technology should be positively associated with changes in the standard of living. On the contrary, using a first-difference estimation strategy with a lagged explanatory variable, the analysis demonstrates that, while changes in the level of technology between 1000 BCE and 1 CE were indeed associated with significant changes in population density over the 1–1000 CE time horizon, the level of income per capita across regions during this period was, in fact, largely unaffected, as suggested by the Malthusian theory.

Three additional findings should be noted. First, in contrast to the relationship between absolute latitude and contemporary income per capita, population density in pre-industrial times was on average higher at latitudinal bands closer to the equator. Second, the chapter also establishes the importance of technological diffusion in the pre-industrial world. Third, consistent with Diamond (1997), an earlier onset of the Neolithic Revolution contributed to the level of technological sophistication and thus population density in the pre-modern world.

The epoch of Malthusian stagnation in income per capita masked a dynamism that may have ultimately brought about the transition from stagnation to growth. Although the growth of income per capita was minuscule over this period, technological progress intensified and world population significantly increased—a dynamism that was instrumental for the emergence of economies from the Malthusian Epoch.

3.7 Appendix

3.7.1 First-Stage Regressions

First-stage regressions appear in Table 3.A.

3.7.2 Variable Definitions and Sources

Absolute latitude: The variable is calculated as the absolute value of the latitude of a country's centroid, as reported by the CIA's *World Factbook* online resource.

Distance to frontier in 1500 CE: The distance, in thousands of kilometers, from a country's modern capital city to the closest regional technological frontier in the year 1500 CE, is as reported by Ashraf and Galor (2009). Specifically, Ashraf and Galor employ historical urbanization estimates from Chandler (1987) and Modelski (2003) to identify frontiers based on the size of urban populations, selecting the two largest cities from each continent that belong to different sociopolitical entities. Thus, in 1500 CE, the set of regional frontiers comprises London (England), Paris (France), Cairo (Egypt), Fez (Morocco), Istanbul (Turkey), Beijing (China), Tenochtitlán (Mexico), and Cuzco (Peru). For additional details, the reader is referred to Ashraf and Galor (2009).

Income per capita in 1 CE, 1000 CE, and 1500 CE: The level of income per capita is as reported by Maddison (2003) for a given year. The interested reader is also referred to www.ggdc.net/maddison/other_books/HS-8_2003.pdf for a discussion of the data by the author.

Land productivity: This measure is composed of (1) the arable percentage of land, as reported by the *World Development Indicators* (World Bank, 2009), and (2) an index of the suitability of land for agriculture, based on geospatial soil pH and temperature data, as reported by Ramankutty et al. (2002) and aggregated to the country level by Michalopoulos (2008). In particular, log land productivity is the first principal component of the logs of these variables, capturing 83% of their combined variation.

Mean distance to nearest coast or river: The variable is defined as the distance, in thousands of kilometers, from a geospatial information system grid cell to the nearest ice-free coastline or sea-navigable river, averaged across the grid cells located within a country. This variable is obtained from the CID's research datasets in *General Measures of Geography*.

TABLE 3.A
First-stage regressions

	(1) OLS	(2) OLS	(3) OLS	(4) OLS	(5) OLS	(6) OLS
			Second-Stage Dependent Variable is			
	Log population density in 1500 CE	Log population density in 1000 CE	Log population density in 1 CE	Log technology index in 1500 CE	Log population density in 1000 CE	Log population density in 1 CE
			Endogenous Variable is			
					Log technology index in	
		Log years since Neolithic transition			1000 CE	1 CE
Excluded instruments						
Domesticable plants	0.012**	0.013**	0.012**	0.012**	0.001	0.007***
	(0.005)	(0.005)	(0.006)	(0.005)	(0.001)	(0.002)
Domesticable animals	0.067**	0.064**	0.048*	0.063**	0.020***	−0.002
	(0.029)	(0.028)	(0.029)	(0.028)	(0.006)	(0.008)
Second-stage controls						
Log land productivity	0.040	0.025	−0.011	0.023	0.002	−0.003
	(0.049)	(0.049)	(0.037)	(0.049)	(0.014)	(0.017)
Log absolute latitude	−0.127***	−0.130***	−0.083*	−0.120***	−0.015	−0.005
	(0.042)	(0.043)	(0.044)	(0.044)	(0.014)	(0.019)
Mean distance to nearest coast or river	0.127	0.103	0.094	0.079	0.112**	0.055
	(0.141)	(0.140)	(0.156)	(0.143)	(0.044)	(0.093)
Percentage of land within 100 km of coast or river	−0.165	−0.190	−0.227*	−0.171	0.044	0.061
	(0.137)	(0.136)	(0.136)	(0.137)	(0.036)	(0.063)
Continent dummies	Yes	Yes	Yes	Yes	Yes	Yes
Observations	96	94	83	93	92	83
R-squared	0.68	0.70	0.71	0.67	0.71	0.51
Partial R-squared	0.27	0.28	0.25	0.26	0.17	0.16
F-statistic	14.65	15.10	10.85	13.47	12.52	12.00

Summary: This table collects the first-stage regression results for all IV regressions examined in the text. Specifically, regressions (1), (2), and (3) represent, respectively, the first stage of regression (6) in Tables 3.2–3.4. Regression (4) corresponds to the first stage of *both* regressions (3) and (6) in Table 3.7. Finally, regressions (5) and (6) represent the first stage of regressions (3) and (6), respectively, in Table 3.8.

Notes: (i) Log land productivity is the first principal component of the log of the percentage of arable land and the log of an agricultural suitability index; (ii) the partial R-squared reported is for the excluded instruments only; (iii) the F-statistic is from the test of excluded instruments and is always significant at the 1 percent level; (iv) a single continent dummy is used to represent the Americas, which is natural, given the historical period examined; (v) the dummy for Oceania is not employed due to the presence of a single observation for this continent in the corresponding regression samples; (vi) robust standard error estimates are reported in parentheses; (vii) *** denotes statistical significance at the 1 percent level, ** at the 5 percent level, and * at the 10 percent level, all for two-sided hypothesis tests.

Nonagricultural technology index in 1 CE and 1000 CE: The index of nonagricultural technology for a given year is based on the same underlying data and aggregation methodology discussed above for the overall technology index. However, unlike the overall index, the nonagricultural counterpart incorporates data on the sector-specific technology indices for only the communications, industrial (i.e., ceramics and metallurgy), and transportation sectors.

Percentage of land in temperate climate zones: The percentage of a country's total land area in Köppen-Geiger temperate zones (including zones classified as Cf, Cs, Df, and Dw) is as reported by the CID's research datasets in *General Measures of Geography.*

Percentage of land in tropical and subtropical climate zones: The percentage of a country's total land area in Köppen-Geiger tropical and subtropical zones (including zones classified as Af, Am, Aw, and Cw), as reported by the CID's research datasets in *General Measures of Geography.*

Percentage of Land within 100 km of coast or river: The percentage of a country's total land area that is located within 100 kilometers of an ice-free coastline or sea-navigable river is defined as reported by the CID's research datasets in *General Measures of Geography.*

Plants and animals: This measure is the number of domesticable species of plants and animals, respectively, that were prehistorically native to the continent or landmass to which a country belongs. These variables are obtained from the dataset of Olsson and Hibbs (2005).

Population density in 1 CE, 1000 CE, and 1500 CE: Population density in a given year is calculated as population in that year, as reported by McEvedy and Jones (1978), divided by land area today, as reported by the World Bank's (2001) *World Development Indicators.* The cross-sectional unit of observation in the McEvedy and Jones dataset is a region delineated by its international borders in 1975. Historical population estimates are provided for regions corresponding to either individual countries or, in some cases, to sets comprised of two to three neighboring countries (e.g., India, Pakistan and Bangladesh). In the latter case, a set-specific population density figure is calculated based on total land area, and the figure is then assigned to each of the component countries in the set. The same methodology is also employed to obtain population densities for countries that exist today but were part of a larger political unit (e.g., the former Yugoslavia) in 1975. The population data reported by the authors is based on a wide variety of country- and region-specific historical sources, the enumeration of which would be impractical for this appendix. The interested reader is referred to McEvedy and Jones (1978) for more details on the original data sources cited therein.

Small-island and landlocked dummies: 0/1 indicators for whether a country is a small-island nation and whether it possesses a coastline. These variables are constructed by the authors based on information reported by the CIA's *World Factbook*.

Technology index in 1 CE and 1000 CE: The index of technology for a given year is constructed using worldwide historical cross-cultural data on sector-specific levels of technology, reported on a 3-point scale by the *Atlas of Cultural Evolution* (Peregrine, 2003). Following the aggregation methodology adopted by Comin et al. (2010), the index employs technology data on four sectors: communications, industry (i.e., ceramics and metallurgy), transportation, and agriculture.

The level of technology in each sector is indexed as follows. In the communications sector, the index is assigned a value of 0 in the absence of both true writing and mnemonic or nonwritten records, a value of 1 when only mnemonic or nonwritten records are present, and a value of 2 when both are present. In the industrial sector, the index is assigned a value of 0 in the absence of both metalworks and ceramics, a value of 1 if only ceramics is present, and a value of 2 if both are present. In the transportation sector, the index is assigned a value of 0 in the absence of both pack or draft animals, a value of 1 if only pack or draft animals are present, and a value of 2 if both are present. Finally, in the agricultural sector, the index is assigned a value of 0 in the absence of sedentary agriculture, a value of 1 when agriculture is practiced but only as a secondary mode of subsistence, and a value of 2 when agriculture is practiced as the primary mode of subsistence. In all cases, the sector-specific indices are normalized to assume values in the [0, 1] interval. The technology index for a given culture is thus the unweighted average across sectors of the sector-specific indices for that culture.

Given that the cross-sectional unit of observation in Peregrine's dataset is an archaeological tradition or culture, specific to a given region on the global map, and since spatial delineations in Peregrine's (2003) dataset do not necessarily correspond to contemporary international borders, the culture-specific technology index in a given year is aggregated to the country level by averaging across those cultures from Peregrine's map that appear within the modern borders of a given country.

Years since Neolithic transition: This measure is the number of thousand years elapsed, until 2000, since the majority of the population residing within a country's modern national borders began practicing sedentary agriculture as their primary mode of subsistence. These data, reported by Putterman (2008), are compiled using a wide variety of both regional and country-specific archaeological studies as well as more general encyclopedic works on the transition from hunting and gathering to agriculture during the Neolithic Revolution. The reader is referred to http://www.econ.brown.edu/fac/Louis_ Putterman/agricultural%20data%20page.htm for a detailed description of the primary and secondary data sources employed by the author in the construction of this variable.

CHAPTER 4

Theories of the Demographic Transition

> *Increased bearing is bound to be paid for by less efficient caring.*
>
> —Richard Dawkins

The demographic transition has swept the world since the end of the nineteenth century. The unprecedented increase in population growth during the Post-Malthusian Regime has been ultimately reversed, bringing about significant reductions in fertility rates and population growth in various regions of the world.

The demographic transition has enabled economies to convert a larger portion of the gains from factor accumulation and technological progress into growth of income per capita. It enhanced labor productivity and the growth process via three channels. First, the decline in population growth reduced the dilution of the growing stocks of capital and infrastructure, increasing the amount of resources per capita. Second, the reduction in fertility rates permitted the reallocation of resources from the quantity of children toward their quality, enhancing human capital formation and labor productivity. Third, the decline in fertility rates affected the age distribution of the population, temporarily increasing the fraction of the labor force in the population and thus mechanically increasing productivity per capita.

This chapter examines various mechanisms that have been proposed as possible triggers for the demographic transition and assesses their empirical significance in understanding the transition from stagnation to growth. Was the onset of the fertility decline an outcome of the rise in income during the course of industrialization? Was it triggered by the reduction in mortality rates? Was it fueled by the rise in the relative wages of women? Or was it an outcome of the rise in the demand for human capital in the second phase of industrialization?[1]

---

[1] The Princeton Project on the Decline of Fertility in Europe, carried out in the 1960s and 1970s, attempted to characterize the decline of fertility in Europe during the nineteenth and early twentieth centuries. The project suggests that social and economic forces played little role in the onset of fertility transition. The methodology used in this research has been discredited over the years (e.g., Guinnane et al., 1994; Brown and Guinnane, 2007), and economic forces are currently viewed as central to this transition.

4.1 The Rise in Income per Capita

The rise in income per capita prior to the decline in fertility has led some researchers to argue that the reduction in fertility was triggered by the rise in income in the process of industrialization. In particular, Becker (1960) advanced the argument that the decline in fertility was a by-product of the rise in income and the associated rise in the opportunity cost of raising children. His thesis suggests that the rise in income induced a fertility decline because the positive income effect on fertility was dominated by a negative substitution effect brought about by the rising opportunity cost of raising children. Similarly, Becker and Lewis (1973) postulated that the income elasticity with respect to investment in children's education was greater than that with respect to the number of children, and hence the rise in income led to a decline in fertility along with an increase in the investment in each child.

However, this preference-based theory is fragile from a theoretical viewpoint and unsatisfactory from an intellectual one. It hinges on the supposition that individuals' preferences reflect an innate bias against child quantity beyond a certain level of income.[2] Most critically, it generates testable predictions that appear inconsistent with the evidence.

4.1.1 The Theory and Its Testable Predictions

Consider a household that generates utility from consumption, c, and the number of (surviving) children, n. The household is endowed with one unit of time and it generates an income, y, if its entire unit of time is supplied to the labor market. Suppose that raising children is time intensive and the entire cost associated with raising each child is a fraction τ of the parental unit-time endowment.[3]

Hence, the household's consumption equals the household's labor income; that is, $c = (1 - \tau n)y$. Alternatively, the household's budget constraint can be written in the conventional form

$$\tau yn + c \leq y, \tag{4.1}$$

where the price of a child is the opportunity cost associated with raising it, τy.[4]

---

[2] One can attribute most changes in economic regimes to changes in the nature of preferences. However, since preferences, as opposed to choices, are largely unobservable, theories that rely on changes in preferences are not refutable.

[3] Alternatively, τy can be viewed as a monetary cost associated with paying for a fraction τ of a caretaker's time. The addition of nontime costs would not affect the qualitative insights.

[4] The price of consumption is normalized to 1.

A rise in the household's earning capacity (per unit of time), y, generates two conflicting effects. On the one hand, the increase in y generates a positive income effect, which operates to increase the number of children (as long as children are viewed as a normal good). On the other hand, the rise in y generates a negative substitution effect, which reflects the increase in the opportunity cost of raising a child, τy. If preferences are homothetic (i.e., preferences are not inherently biased toward either consumption or children as income increases), the income effect and substitution effect cancel one another. For instance, if the household's preferences are represented by a log-linear utility function,[5]

$$u = \gamma \ln n + (1 - \gamma) \ln c, \tag{4.2}$$

where $0 < \gamma < 1$ is a parameter, then the household's optimal number of children is independent of income:

$$n = \gamma / \tau. \tag{4.3}$$

Thus, *a priori,* in contrast to the prediction of the Beckerian theory, the rise in income may have no effect on the number of children. The Beckerian theory, therefore, is nonrobust, as it rests on an implicit set of assumptions that assure that the substitution effect dominates as income rises.

Nevertheless, independent of its theoretical fragility, one can examine the Beckerian theory based on its testable predictions. If indeed the substitution effect dominates at sufficiently high levels of income, then the theory suggests that the differential timing of the fertility decline across countries (in similar stages of development) would reflect differences in income per capita. Furthermore, the level of fertility among individuals in a given economy would reflect their income levels.

Thus, the theory generates two major testable implications:

a. Across countries that are similar in sociocultural characteristics (and thus in noneconomic factors that may affect fertility decisions), the timing of the fertility decline is inversely related to the level of income per capita.
b. Within an economy, the number of (surviving) children across households is inversely related to their levels of income.

---

[5] For simplicity, it is assumed that parents derive utility from the expected number of surviving offspring and that the parental cost of child rearing is associated only with surviving children. The introduction of costs associated with nonsurviving children, or risk aversion, would not affect the qualitative features of the theory.

4.1.2 The Evidence

Remarkably, the theory appears counterfactual on both counts. As depicted in Figures 4.1 and 4.2, the decline in fertility occurred in the same decade across Western European countries that differed significantly in their incomes per capita. In 1870, on the eve of the demographic transition, England and the Netherlands were the richest countries in Western Europe, enjoying GDP per capita of \$3,190 and \$2,760, respectively (Maddison, 2001).[6] In contrast, Germany and France, which experienced the onset of a decline in fertility in the same decade as England and the Netherlands, had in 1870 a significantly smaller GDP per capita of \$1,840 and \$1,880, respectively (i.e., only about 60% of the level in England). Moreover, Sweden and Norway's GDP per capita were only about 40% of that of England in 1870, and Finland's GDP per capita was merely a third of the level in England. Nevertheless, the onset of the fertility decline in these poorer economies occurred in the same decade as in England.[7]

The simultaneity of the demographic transition across Western European countries that differed significantly in their incomes per capita suggests that the high levels of income reached by these countries in the Post-Malthusian Regime played a very limited role, if any, in the onset of the demographic transition, refuting the first testable implication of the Beckerian theory. Moreover, the evidence presented by Murtin (2009) (based on a panel of countries during 1870–2000) shows that income per worker was positively associated with fertility rates, once controls were introduced for mortality rates and education.

Recent empirical examinations of the various factors that contributed to the demographic transition within an economy also refute the second implication of the Beckerian theory. In particular, cross-sectional evidence from France and England does not lend support to the theory. Murphy (2009) finds, based on panel data from France during 1876–1896, that income per capita had a positive effect on fertility rates during France's demographic transition, accounting for education, the gender literacy gap, and mortality rates. Moreover, a quantitative analysis of the demographic transition in England, conducted by Fernández-Villaverde (2001), suggests that, in contrast to the Beckerian theory, the force associated with a rise in income would have led to an increase in fertility rates rather than to the observed decline in fertility.

---

[6] GDP per capita was measured in 1990 international dollars.

[7] One could sensibly argue that the income thresholds at which the substitution effect dominates differ across this set of countries due to sociocultural and distributional factors. However, the likelihood that these differential thresholds would be reached in the same decade across a large number of countries appears remote.

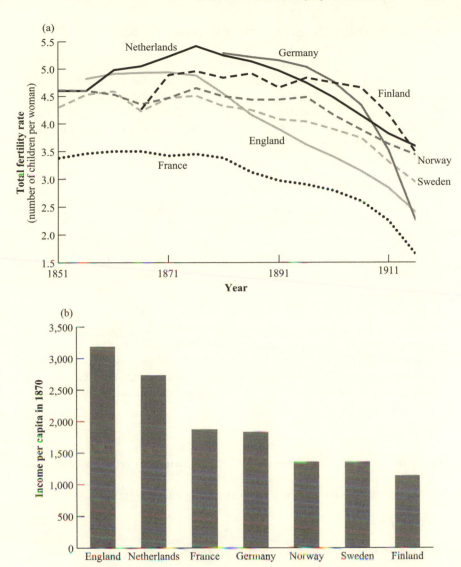

FIGURE 4.1. The demographic transition and income levels across Western Europe: (a) fertility rates, 1851–1915; (b) income per capita, 1870.
Data sources: Chesnais (1992); Maddison (2008).

4.2   The Decline in Infant and Child Mortality

The decline in infant and child mortality that preceded the reduction in fertility and population growth in most advanced economies, with the notable exceptions of France and the United States, has been viewed as a plausible explanation for the onset of the decline in population growth during the demographic transition. Nevertheless, this hypothesis appears to be nonrobust theoretically and inconsistent with historical evidence.

4.2.1   The Central Hypothesis

Consider a household that generates utility from consumption, c, and the number of surviving children, n. Suppose that each child faces a probability θ of surviving infancy. Given the (continuous) number of children that the household will bear, n^b, the number of surviving children is $n = \theta n^b$. The household's preferences are represented by a log-linear utility function,[8]

$$u = \gamma \ln n + (1 - \gamma) \ln c; \quad 0 < \gamma < 1. \tag{4.4}$$

Moreover, the household is endowed with one unit of time, and it generates an income, y, if its entire unit of time is supplied to the labor market.

Suppose that raising children is time intensive and the cost associated with raising each surviving child is a fraction τ of the parental unit-time endowment, whereas the cost of raising a nonsurviving child is 0. The household's budget constraint is therefore

$$\tau y n + c \leq y, \tag{4.5}$$

where the price of a surviving child is the opportunity cost associated with raising a child, τy.

The household's optimal number of surviving children is therefore

$$n = \gamma / \tau, \tag{4.6}$$

whereas the number of children born to the household, n^b, is

$$n^b = \gamma / (\tau \theta). \tag{4.7}$$

Hence, a decline in the child mortality rate, or equivalently an increase in the survival probability of a child, θ, mechanically reduces the level of household

---

[8] If the number of children is modeled as an integer rather than a continuous variable, then the maximization problem would have to be modified to account for uncertainty (e.g., Kalemli-Ozcan, 2002). Nevertheless, the qualitative prediction as outlined in this section would not be altered.

fertility, n^b, but (in the absence of uncertainty) has no effect on the number of surviving children, n.

The theory suggests that:

a. Mortality rates have a positive effect on total fertility rates.
b. Declines in mortality would not lead to a reduction in the number of surviving offspring unless the number of surviving children is uncertain and the following conditions are satisfied:
   (i) There exists a precautionary demand for children (i.e., individuals are risk averse with respect to the number of surviving offspring and thus hold a buffer stock of children in a high-mortality environment).
   (ii) Risk aversion with respect to consumption is not larger than risk aversion with respect to the number of surviving children.[9]
   (iii) Sequential fertility (i.e., replacement of nonsurviving children) is modest.
   (iv) Parental resources saved from the reduction in the number of children that do not survive to adulthood are not channeled toward childbearing.[10]

4.2.2   Evidence

While it is plausible that mortality rates were one of the factors that affected the level of fertility throughout human history, historical evidence does not lend credence to the argument that the decline in mortality accounts for the reversal of the positive historical trend between income and fertility and for the decline in population growth (i.e., fertility net of mortality).

The decline in mortality in Western Europe started nearly a century prior to the decline in fertility and was associated initially with increasing fertility rates in some countries. In particular, as depicted in Figure 4.2, the decline in mortality started in England in the 1730s and was accompanied by a steady increase in fertility rates until 1800. The sharp decline in fertility in the course of the demographic transition occurred during a period in which income per capita maintained its earlier positive trend, while mortality declines maintained the course that had existed in the 140 years preceding the decline in fertility.[11]

---

[9] In contrast, evolutionary forces would lead to the selection of preferences with higher risk aversion with respect to consumption (Galor and Michalopoulos, 2006).

[10] Furthermore, if the physiological constraint on the feasible number of births per woman is binding for some households under a high mortality regime, a reduction in mortality would operate to increase the number of surviving offspring.

[11] One could argue that the decline in mortality was not internalized into the decisions of households who had difficulties separating a temporary decline from a permanent one. However, this argument is highly implausible, given that mortality declined monotonically for nearly 140 years prior to the demographic transition. It is inconceivable that six generations of households did not update information about mortality rates in their immediate surroundings, keeping the collective memories about mortality rates prevalent more than a century earlier.

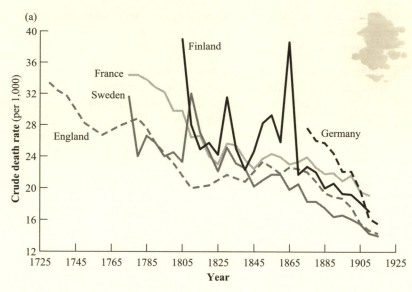

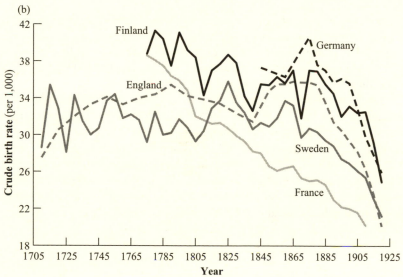

FIGURE 4.2. Mortality and fertility across Western Europe, 1705–1925.
Data sources: Chesnais (1992); Maddison (2008).

The sharp reversal in the fertility patterns in Western European countries in the 1870s, in the context of this stable pattern of mortality decline therefore suggests that the demographic transition was prompted by a different universal force.

Recent quantitative and empirical evidence supports the viewpoint that a decline in infant mortality rates was not the trigger for the decline in *net* fertility during the demographic transition. Doepke (2005), using mortality and fertility data from England during 1861–1951, finds that in the absence of changes in other factors, the decline in child mortality during this time should have resulted in a rise in net fertility rates, in contrast to the evidence. A similar conclusion about the insignificance of declining mortality for determining the decline in fertility during the demographic transition is reached in the quantitative analysis of Fernández-Villaverde (2001). Moreover, Murphy (2009) suggests, based on panel data from France during 1876–1896, that the mortality rate had no effect on fertility during France's demographic transition, accounting for education, income, and the gender literacy gap.[12]

Importantly, it is the reduction in net fertility and thus in population growth that is most relevant from the viewpoint of the theory of economic growth. However, in light of the implausible set of conditions that must be met for a decline in mortality rates to generate a decline in net fertility, the observed sharp decline in the number of surviving offspring (i.e., net reproduction rate) during the demographic transition raises further doubts about the significance of mortality declines in triggering the onset of the decline in population growth.[13]

4.3 The Rise in Demand for Human Capital

The gradual rise in demand for human capital during the second phase of industrialization and its close association with the timing of the demographic transition has led researchers to argue that the increasing role of human capital in the production process induced households to increase their investment in the human capital of their offspring, leading to the onset of the fertility decline.

---

[12] In contrast, Eckstein et al. (1999)'s structural quantitative analysis of the demographic transition in Sweden suggests that mortality decline played a role in the demographic transition. Their underlying theoretical structure requires conditions iii and iv (Section 4.2.1) as well as specific interactions among mortality, wages, and the return to human capital.

[13] The evolution of fertility and mortality in less developed economies has been partly affected by policies advanced by developed economies. A comprehensive overview of these patterns is provided by Schultz (1997).

Galor and Weil (1999, 2000) and Galor and Moav (2002) argue that the acceleration in the rate of technological progress during the second phase of the Industrial Revolution increased the demand for human capital and induced parents to invest more heavily in the human capital of their offspring.[14] This increase in the rate of technological progress and the associated increase in parental income and demand for human capital brought about two effects on population growth. On the one hand, the rise in income eased households' budget constraints and provided more resources for quality as well as quantity of children. On the other hand, it induced a reallocation of these increased resources toward child quality. In the course of transition from the Malthusian Epoch, the effect of technological progress on parental income dominated, and population growth as well as the average population quality increased. Ultimately, further increases in the rate of technological progress induced a reduction in fertility, generating a decline in population growth and an increase in the average level of education.

Suppose that individuals generate utility from the quantity and the quality of their children as well as from their own consumption. They choose the number of children and their quality in the face of a constraint on the total amount of time that can be devoted to child-raising and labor-market activities. A rise in parental income due to a rise in the demand for parental human capital would generate, in contrast to Becker and Lewis (1973), conflicting income and substitution effects that would not necessarily trigger a decline in fertility. However, the rise in the future demand for the children's human capital would lead to a pure substitution effect, which would induce parents to substitute quality for quantity of children.

---

[14] The effect of the rise in demand for human capital on parental choice of quality and quantity of offspring is discussed by Becker (1981). Becker et al. (1990) explore the role of luck in determination of the relative timing of the demographic transition and thus the wealth of nations. As they argue on page S13, "Many attempts to explain why some countries have had the best economic performance in the past several centuries give too little attention to accidents and good fortune." In their theory a major shock shifts the economy from the basin of attraction of a high-fertility to a low-fertility steady-state equilibrium, generating, counterfactually, a monotonic decline in fertility rates along with a monotonic rise in income per capita. However, existing evidence shows that the process of industrialization and the associated increase in income per capita were accompanied by a sharp increase in population growth, prior to its decline during the course of the demographic transition. Moreover, although they define the low output, high population growth steady state as a Malthusian steady-state equilibrium, it has none of the features of a Malthusian equilibrium; population growth rate is not at the replacement level and it is, counterfactually, higher than that in the beginning of the demographic transition. Furthermore, a small positive shock to income when the economy is in the "Malthusian" steady state initially decreases fertility, in contrast to the central aspect of the Malthusian equilibrium.

4.3.1 The Theory

Consider a household that generates utility from consumption, c, the number of (surviving) children, n, and the human capital of each child, h. Suppose that preferences are represented by a log-linear utility function[15]

$$u = (1 - \gamma) \ln c + \gamma [\ln n + \beta \ln h], \qquad (4.8)$$

where $0 < \gamma < 1$ and $0 < \beta < 1$ are constant parameters.

Let $\tau^q + \tau^e e$ be the time cost of raising a child with a level of education (quality) e. That is, τ^q is the fraction of the household's unit-time endowment that is required to raise a child, regardless of quality, and τ^e is the fraction of the household's unit-time endowment that is required for each unit of education per child.

The household is endowed with one unit of time. If it devotes its entire time to labor force participation it generates a wage income of y. The household's potential income, y, is divided between expenditure on child rearing (quantity and quality) and consumption, c. The household's budget constraint is therefore

$$yn(\tau^q + \tau^e e) + c \leq y, \qquad (4.9)$$

where the price of a child is the opportunity cost associated with raising it, $y(\tau^q + \tau^e e)$.

Suppose that individuals' level of human capital is determined by their quality (education) as well as by the technological environment. Technological progress reduces the adaptability of existing human capital to a new technological environment. Education, however, lessens the adverse effects of technological progress. In particular, the time required for adaptation to a new technological environment diminishes with the level of education and increases with the rate of technological change.

Suppose that the level of human capital of each child, h, is an increasing, strictly concave function of the parental time investment in the education of the child, e, and (due to the obsolescence of human capital in a changing technological environment) a decreasing, strictly convex function of the rate

---

[15] Once again, it is assumed that parents derive utility from the expected number of surviving offspring and the parental cost of child rearing is associated only with surviving children. The introduction of costs associated with non-surviving children, or risk aversion, would not affect the qualitative features of the theory.

of technological progress, g.

$$h = h(e, g), \tag{4.10}$$

where to assure an interior solution to the household optimization problem, it is further assumed that $\lim_{e \to 0} h_e(e, g) = \infty$, $\lim_{e \to \infty} h_e(e, g) = 0$, and $h(0, g) > 0$ (i.e., individuals have a basic level of human capital even in the absence of parental investment in quality).

Education lessens the obsolescence of human capital in a rapidly changing technological environment. That is, the marginal productivity of parental investment in a child's human capital increases in a more rapidly changing technological environment (i.e., $h_{eg}(e, g) \equiv \partial[\partial h(e, g)/\partial e]/\partial g > 0$).

The household's optimization implies, therefore, that the optimal level of children, n, and their quality, e, are given by

$$n = \gamma/(\tau^q + \tau^e e),$$
$$\tau^e h(e, g) = \beta h_e(e, g)(\tau^q + \tau^e e). \tag{4.11}$$

Hence, as follows from the properties of $h(e, g)$, and established in the appendix to this chapter, for a given $(g, \beta, \tau^e, \tau^q)$, the optimal level of children, n, and their quality, e, are uniquely determined:

$$e = e(g, \beta, \tau^e, \tau^q),$$
$$n = \gamma/[\tau^q + \tau^e e(g, \beta, \tau^e, \tau^q)]. \tag{4.12}$$

Hence, the optimal level of investment in child quality increases if:

a. The technological environment changes more rapidly (i.e., $\partial e(g, \beta, \tau^e, \tau^q)/\partial g > 0$);
b. Preferences for child quality are higher (i.e., $\partial e(g, \beta, \tau^e, \tau^q)/\partial \beta > 0$);
c. The cost of raising a child (regardless of quality) increases (i.e., $\partial e(g, \beta, \tau^e, \tau^q)/\partial \tau^q > 0$); or
d. The cost of educating a child decreases (i.e., $\partial e(g, \beta, \tau^e, \tau^q)/\partial \tau^e < 0$).

Similarly, the optimal number of children declines if:

a. The technological environment changes more rapidly (i.e., $\partial n/\partial g < 0$);
b. Preferences for child quality are higher (i.e., $\partial n/\partial \beta < 0$);
c. The cost of raising a child (regardless of quality) increases (i.e., $\partial n/\partial \tau^q < 0$); or

d. The cost of educating a child increases, and the elasticity of child quality with respect to the cost of child quality is smaller than one in absolute value (i.e., $\partial n / \partial \tau^e < 0$ if $[\partial e / \partial \tau^e][\tau^e/e] > -1$).[16]

Thus, the theory generates several testable implications regarding the effect of a rise in demand for education on the onset of the demographic transition:[17]

a. Across countries with similar sociocultural characteristics (and thus with similar noneconomic factors that may affect fertility decisions):
   (i) The timing of the fertility decline is inversely related to the rate of technological progress.
   (ii) The level of fertility is inversely related to investment in education.
b. Within an economy:
   (i) The level of fertility across households is inversely related to their level of investment in education.
   (ii) An increase in the preference for educated offspring decreases fertility.

4.3.2 Evidence: Education and the Demographic Transition

Consistent with the theory, the growth rates of income per capita among Western European countries were rather similar during their demographic transition, despite large differences in their levels of income per capita. The average growth rate among northwestern European countries during this period was 1.3% per year—ranging from 1.0% per year in England, 1.3% in Norway, 1.4% in Finland and France, 1.5% in Sweden, to 1.6% in Germany (Maddison, 2001). Moreover, the adverse effect of an increase in productivity in the advanced stages of development on net fertility has been established by Lehr (2009) using a pooled cross-sectional time series sample during 1960–1999, and by Herzer et al. (2010) based on a sample of countries during 1900–1999.

Furthermore, evidence from a panel of countries during 1870–2000 demonstrates that investment in education was indeed a dominating force in the decline in fertility. In particular, educational attainment has been negatively associated

---

[16] If the elasticity of child quality with respect to the cost of child quality is greater than one in absolute value, a decrease in the cost of education increases the overall investment in child quality.

[17] In contrast to Becker and Lewis (1973), a rise in parental income (possibly due to a rise in the return to their education) does not necessarily generate a substitution from child quantity to child quality. Instead, an increase in the household's earning capacity, y, due to the rise in the wage per efficiency unit of labor, generates two conflicting effects. On the one hand, the rise in y also generates a positive income effect that operates to increase the number of children. On the other hand, the rise in y generates a negative substitution effect that reflects an increase in the opportunity cost of raising a child, $y[\tau^q + \tau^e e]$. If preferences are homothetic, the income effect and the substitution effect cancel each other. Then the optimal number of children and their quality are independent of the parental level of income.

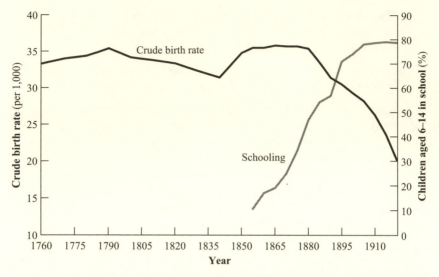

FIGURE 4.3. Investment in human capital and the demographic transition: England, 1760–1925.
Data sources: Wrigley and Schofield (1981); Flora et al. (1983).

with fertility, accounting for income per worker and mortality rates (Murtin, 2009). Importantly, cross-sectional evidence from France, Germany, and England supports the hypothesis that the rise in human capital formation has had an adverse effect on fertility. Becker et al. (2010) find that education stimulated a decline in fertility in Prussia during the nineteenth century.[18] Similarly, Murphy (2009) finds, based on panel data from France during 1876–1896, that the level of education attainment had an adverse effect on fertility rates during France's demographic transition, accounting for income per capita, the gender literacy gap, and mortality rates.

As depicted in Figure 4.3, the decline in fertility in England was associated with a significant increase in the investment in child quality as reflected by years of schooling. In particular, Klemp and Weisdorf (2010) establish a causal linkage between family sibship size and individual literacy using demographic data for 26 English parishes during 1580–1871. Exploiting exogenous variation in sibship size, stemming from parental fecundity, they find that each additional sibling reduces literacy among all family siblings. In addition, quan-

---

[18] They find that a lower cost of education, as proxied by lower land concentration, had an adverse effect on fertility and education in the middle of the nineteenth century and on the extensiveness of the fertility decline toward the end of that century.

titative evidence provided by Doepke (2004) suggests that educational policies aimed at promoting human capital formation played an important role in the demographic transition in England.

A direct test of the effect on fertility of the rise in the return to human capital has been conducted by Bleakley and Lange (2009) in the context of the eradication of hookworm disease in the American South (circa 1910). Noting that the eradication of this disease can be viewed as a positive shock to the return to child quality since (i) it raises the return to human capital investment, (ii) it had a very low fatality rate, and (iii) it had negligible prevalence among adults, they find that the rise in the return to child quality had a significant adverse effect on fertility rates.

Finally, the prediction of the theory regarding the adverse effect of increased preference for educated offspring on fertility rates is also supported by the empirical evidence (Becker et al., 2010).

4.3.3 Quantity-Quality Trade-off in the Modern Era

Empirical examinations of the presence of a quantity-quality trade-off in the contemporary period do not directly reflect on the importance of increased demand for education for the onset of the demographic transition. Nevertheless, they may provide an additional perspective about the mechanism as a whole.

Rosenzweig and Wolpin (1980), using the occurrence of multiple births as an exogenous source of variation in quantity, confirm the hypothesis that an exogenous increase in fertility decreases child quality. These findings were echoed by Hanushek (1992). Recently, however, Black et al. (2005) and Angrist et al. (2008) have used data on twins in Norway and Israel to assess the impact of an exogenous increase in the number of children on measures of the quality of nontwins. They have found little evidence of an adverse effect on the quality of nontwins.[19] In contrast, employing a similar methodology, Li et al. (2008) find a significant quantity-quality trade-off in rural China and weaker effects in urban areas. However, as asserted by Rosenzweig and Zhang (2009), since these studies ignore the impact on the quality of the twins themselves, it is essential to assess whether the closer spacing of twins and their inferior endowments affect investments in nontwins in the family and obscure the quantity-quality trade-off. Rosenzweig and Zhang (2009) find that parents do provide more human capital resources to children with higher endowments (i.e., nontwin children).

---

[19] Significant child allowances in these countries may mitigate the adverse effect on child quality and may therefore obscure the adverse effect of quantity on quality.

Furthermore, as elaborated in the derivation of the theory, an ideal test of the presence of a quantity-quality trade-off requires a change in the relative price of quantity or a change in the return to quality. In contrast, the effect of a change in an endogenous variable (i.e., quantity of children) requires a careful examination of the adjustment made by the household due to the exogenously imposed nonoptimal choice of quantity. The theory suggests that in sufficiently wealthy societies where intergenerational transfers take place (e.g., Israel and Norway) an unexpected birth is more likely to reduce future intergenerational transfers to the child as opposed to reducing child quality. The optimal level of investment in child quality, as other forms of investment, reflects the return on this investment. If a nonoptimal choice of quantity of children is imposed on the household (due to an unexpected birth of a child), it is not necessarily optimal for the household to reduce child quality. Instead, optimality would necessitate adjustments in other margins (intergenerational transfers or parental consumption). In particular, if parents intend to transfer income to their children in the future, the optimal investment in child quality equates the rate of return on investment in human capital to the rate of return on investment in physical capital (which is constant from the viewpoint of the individual). A shock to the quantity of children would generate an adjustment in the household's optimization. As such, a reduction in investment in child quality would be suboptimal, since it would result in a higher rate of return on investment in human capital than on physical capital.[20] The optimal adjustment would be a reduction in intergenerational transfers, leaving investment in child quality intact. Thus, although a quantity-quality trade-off may exist (i.e., an increase in the relative price of the quantity of children or the return to quality decreases the number of children and increases investment in each child), an exogenous change in child quantity does not affect child quality. The findings of Black et al. (2005) and Angrist et al. (2008) thus have limited bearing on the presence or absence of a quantity-quality trade-off.

4.4 The Rise in Demand for Human Capital: Reinforcing Mechanisms

The onset of the demographic transition is traced by Galor and Weil (2000) and Galor and Moav (2002) to the rise in the demand for human capital and the incentive that it provides parents to substitute quality for quantity of children. This link has been reinforced by various complementary mechanisms.

---

[20] See Galor and Moav (2004) for the optimal allocation of intergenerational transfers between investment in child human capital and the transfer of physical capital.

4.4.1 The Decline in Child Labor

The effect of the rise in the industrial demand for human capital on the reduction in the desired number of surviving offspring was enhanced by the reduction in the profitability of child labor. In the second stage of industrialization the wage differential between parental and child labor had increased, inducing parents to further reduce their number of children and to increase their investment in child quality (Hazan and Berdugo, 2002).[21] Moreover, the rise in the importance of human capital in the production process induced industrialists to support education reforms (Galor and Moav, 2006) and laws that abolished child labor (Doepke and Zilibotti, 2005), leading to a reduction in the prevalence of child labor, and thus, fertility.[22]

4.4.2 The Rise in Life Expectancy

Improvements in health infrastructure and the rise in life expectancy may have reinforced the impact of increased demand for human capital on the decline in the desired number of surviving offspring.[23] Despite gradual improvements in the health environment and in life expectancy prior to the demographic transition, investment in human capital was rather insignificant as long as technological demand for human capital was limited. However, in light of the technologically based rise in demand for human capital during the second phase of the Industrial Revolution, the effect of health on the productivity of workers and pupils has increased the potential rate of return on investments in children's human capital and thus has reinforced and complemented the incentive to invest in education and its associated effect on fertility rates.[24]

---

[21] Indeed, Horrell and Humphries (1995) suggest, based on data from England, that the earnings of children aged 10–14 (as a percentage of the father's earnings) declined by nearly 50% from 1817–1839 to 1840–1872 if the father was employed in a factory. Interestingly, the effect is significantly more pronounced if the father was employed in skilled occupations, reflecting the rise in the relative demand for skilled workers and its effect on the decline in the relative wages of children.

[22] Quantitative evidence suggests that child labor laws, and to a lesser extent educational policies, played an important role in the demographic transition in England (Doepke, 2004).

[23] Hazan (2009) has argued that increased life expectancy toward the end of the nineteenth century had no effect on the length of working life and thus could not be viewed as an incentive for investment in human capital. However, as established by Sheshinski (2009), when survival probabilities rise at all ages, behavioral response depends on changes in the hazard rate. An increase in life expectancy may lead to higher investment in education. Moreover, the increase in the health of children enhanced their productivity in human capital formation and thus increased the relative return to investment in child quality (Hazan and Zoabi, 2006).

[24] Young (2005) argues that a widespread community infection (i.e., the AIDS epidemic in Africa) lowers fertility, both directly, through a reduction in the willingness to engage in unprotected sexual activity, and indirectly, by increasing the scarcity of labor and the value of a woman's time.

4.4.3 Evolution of Preferences for Offspring Quality

The impact of the increased demand for human capital on the decline in the desired number of surviving offspring may have been magnified by the evolution of preferences toward child quality. These evolutionary processes conceivably have been driven by cultural and religious movements as well as by the forces of natural selection.

Galor and Moav (2002) propose that during the Malthusian Epoch individuals with a higher valuation for offspring quality gained an evolutionary advantage and their representation in the population gradually increased. They argue that the agricultural revolution facilitated division of labor, which fostered trade relationships among individuals and communities. It enhanced the complexity of human interaction and raised the return to human capital. The prevalence of preferences for child quality in the population lagged behind the evolutionarily optimal level, and individuals with traits of higher valuation for offspring quality generated higher income and, in the Malthusian Epoch (when income had a positive effect on fertility), a larger number of offspring.[25] Thus, the Malthusian pressure gradually increased the proportion of individuals whose preferences were biased toward child quality. This evolutionary process was reinforced by its interaction with economic forces. As the fraction of individuals with high valuation for quality increased, technological progress intensified, raising further the demand for human capital. The increase in the rate of return on human capital along with the increase in the bias toward quality in the population reinforced the substitution toward child quality, setting the stage for a more rapid decline in fertility and a significant increase in the investment in human capital.

Religious movements (e.g., Judaism [Botticini and Eckstein, 2005] and Protestantism [Becker and Woessmann, 2009]) and the Age of Enlightenment have also contributed to the demographic transition through their effects on preferences for education. In particular, as established empirically by Becker et al. (2010), a rise in preferences for education (proxied by concentric diffusion of Protestantism in Prussia around Luther's city of Wittenberg) had an adverse effect on fertility rates during the middle of the nineteenth century in Prussia.

4.5 The Decline in the Gender Gap

The rise in demand for human capital and its impact on the decline in the gender wage gap during the nineteenth and twentieth centuries have contributed to the onset of the demographic transition. In particular, the rise in women's relative

---

[25] As long as the bias toward child quality is moderate, the additional income generated dominates that bias toward quality and allows for a higher reproduction success rate.

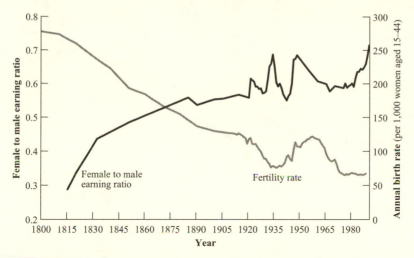

FIGURE 4.4. Female relative wages and fertility rates: United States, 1800–1990. *Data sources:* U.S. Bureau of the Census (1975); Hernandez (2000).

wages during the process of development, its positive impact on female labor force participation, and its adverse effect on fertility rates have been at the center of a complementary theory of the demographic transition that generates the observed hump-shaped relationship between income per capita and population growth.

A pattern of rising relative wages for women and declining fertility rates has been observed in a large number of developed and less developed economies. In particular, as depicted in Figure 4.4, this pattern was observed in the United States during 1800–1940.[26]

In addition, the process of development has been associated with a gradual decline in the gender gap in human capital formation. As depicted in Figure 4.5, the literacy rate among women in England, which was only 76% of that of men in 1840, grew rapidly during the nineteenth century and reached the male level in 1900.

4.5.1 The Theory and Its Testable Predictions

The role that the decline in the gender wage gap played in the onset of the demographic transition has been examined by Galor and Weil (1996). They

---

[26] For an extensive analysis of the pattern of fertility in the United States during 1826–1960, see Greenwood et al. (2005a) and Jones and Tertilt (2006).

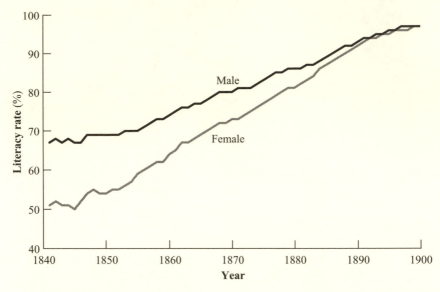

FIGURE 4.5. The decline in the gender gap in human capital: England, 1840–1900. *Data source:* Cipolla (1969).

argue that technological progress and capital accumulation in the process of industrialization increased the relative wages of women and triggered the onset of the demographic transition. They maintain that technological progress, along with physical capital accumulation, complemented mentally intensive tasks more than physically intensive tasks, raising the return to brain relative to brawn. Thus, in light of the comparative physiological advantage of men in physically intensive tasks and of women in mentally intensive tasks, the demand for women's labor gradually increased in the industrial sector, decreasing the gender wage gap.

In the early stages of industrialization, as long as the rise in women's wages was insufficient to induce a significant increase in women's labor force participation, fertility increased due to the income effect generated by the rise in men's wages in the increasingly more productive industrial sector. Ultimately, however, the rise in women's relative wages was sufficient to induce a significant increase in their labor force participation. This process increased the cost of child rearing proportionately more than the increase in household income, triggering a fertility decline. Moreover, the rise in demand for human capital in the process of development induced a gradual improvement in women's education. It raised the opportunity cost of raising children more than the increase in household income and reinforced the fertility decline and the rise in female labor force participation.[27]

Consider households that generate utility from consumption, c, and the number of (surviving) children, n. Each household consists of a man and a woman. The man's wage is w^M and the woman's wage is w^F (if they devote their entire time for labor force participation). Suppose that only women raise children and the cost associated with raising each child is a fraction τ of a woman's time endowment. Hence, the household's budget constraint is

$$\tau w^F n + c \leq w^F + w^M, \tag{4.13}$$

where the price of a child is the opportunity cost associated with raising a child, τw^F.

Hence, a rise in the wages of women, w^F, generates two conflicting effects. On the one hand, the rise in w^F generates a positive income effect that operates to increase the number of children (as long as children are viewed as a normal good). On the other hand, the rise in w^F generates a negative substitution effect that reflects the increase in the opportunity cost of raising children, τw^F. If preferences are homothetic, then the substitution effect necessarily dominates, since an increase in w^F increases the opportunity cost of raising children proportionately more than the household's income. Fertility therefore declines, and women's labor force participation increases.

Thus, unlike the single-parent model in which an increase in income generates conflicting income and substitution effects that cancel one another if preferences are homothetic, in the two-parent household model, if most of the burden of child rearing is placed on women, a rise in women's relative wages increases the opportunity cost of raising children more than household income, generating a pressure to reduce fertility.

4.5.2 The Evidence

The role of the decline in the gender wage gap in the demographic transition is supported empirically. Schultz (1985) finds that an increase in the relative wages of women played an important role in Sweden's fertility transition, and Murphy (2009) suggests, based on panel data from France during 1876–1896, that a reduction in the gender literacy gap had an adverse effect on fertility during France's demographic transition, accounting for income per capita, educational attainment, and mortality rates.[28]

---

[27] See also Goldin (1990) and Lagerlöf (2003b).

[28] In the contemporary era, Heckman and Walker (1990) find a negative effect of women's wages and a positive effect of men's income on birth rates.

4.6 The Old-Age Security Hypothesis

The old-age security hypothesis has been proposed as an additional mechanism for the onset of the demographic transition. It suggests that in the absence of capital markets, which permit intertemporal lending and borrowing, children serve as an asset that permit parents to transfer income to old age.[29] Hence, the establishment of capital markets in the process of development reduced this motivation for rearing children, contributing to the demographic transition.

Although old-age support is a plausible element that may affect the level of fertility, it appears as a minor force in the context of the demographic transition. First, since there are only rare examples in nature of offspring that support their parents in old age, it appears that old-age support cannot be the prime motivation for child rearing. Second, institutions supporting individuals in their old age were formed well before the demographic transition. For instance, evidence suggests that, as early as the sixteenth century, parents in England did not rely on support from children in their old age (Pelling and Smith, 1991; Hindle, 2004). In particular, the Poor Law Act of 1601 was interpreted by the English courts as giving the impoverished parent no claims for assistance from a child, but instead a claim for assistance from the community (Pelling and Smith, 1991).

The rise in fertility rates prior to the demographic transition, in a period of improvements in credit markets, raises further doubts about the significance of this mechanism. Moreover, cross-sectional evidence shows that in the pre-demographic transition era wealthier individuals, who presumably had better access to credit markets, had a larger number of surviving offspring, increasing the skepticism about the importance of this hypothesis.[30] Thus the decline in the importance of old-age support is unlikely to be a major force behind the significant reduction in fertility—at a rate of 30–50%—that occurred during the demographic transition.

4.7 Concluding Remarks

The demographic transition that has swept the world since the end of the nineteenth century has been identified as one of the prime forces in the movement from an epoch of stagnation to the modern state of sustained economic growth. The decline in population growth has enabled economies to divert a larger share

---

[29] See Neher (1971) and Caldwell (1976) for earlier studies and Boldrin and Jones (2002) for a recent quantitative analysis.

[30] It should be noted, however, that if the wealth of the rich is based on nonwage income, it would be associated with a pure income effect, which could result in higher fertility rates, despite a reduced need for old-age support.

of the gains from factor accumulation and technological progress to the enhancement of human capital formation and income per capita, thus paving the way for the emergence of sustained economic growth.

This chapter examined various mechanisms that have been proposed as possible triggers for the demographic transition, assessing their empirical significance in understanding the transition from stagnation to growth. The rise in income per capita prior to the decline in fertility has led some researchers to argue that the reduction in fertility was triggered by the rise in income during the process of industrialization. They have argued that increased income induced a fertility decline because the positive income effect on fertility was dominated by the negative substitution effect brought about by the rising opportunity cost of children. However, this preference-based theory is fragile from a theoretical viewpoint. It hinges on the supposition that individuals' preferences reflect an innate bias against children beyond a certain level of income. Most critically, however, it generates testable predictions that appear inconsistent with the evidence.

The decline in infant and child mortality has been viewed as a complementary explanation for the onset of the decline in fertility. Nevertheless, while it is plausible that mortality rates were among the factors that affected fertility levels throughout human history, historical evidence does not lend credence to the argument that the decline in mortality accounts for the reversal of the positive historical trend between income and fertility and for the decline in population growth (i.e., fertility net of mortality).

The old-age security hypothesis has been advanced as an additional mechanism for the onset of the demographic transition. It suggests that in the absence of capital markets, which permit intertemporal lending and borrowing, children serve as an asset that permits parents to transfer income to old age. Hence, the process of development and the establishment of capital markets reduced this motivation for rearing children, contributing to the demographic transition. However, empirical evidence suggests that this mechanism was only a minor force in the onset of the demographic transition.

Existing evidence lends credence to two triggers of the demographic transition that have been proposed thus far. The gradual rise in the demand for human capital in the second phase of industrialization and its close association with the timing of the demographic transition have led researchers to argue that the increasing role of human capital in the production process induced households to increase their investment in the human capital of their offspring, leading to the onset of the fertility decline. This central hypothesis is supported by a wide range of evidence from the time of the onset of the demographic transition. In addition, the decline in the gender wage gap in the process of development, and its potential impact on the rise in female labor force participation and the associated decline in fertility rates, have been at the center of a theory of the demographic transition that is consistent with the evidence.

4.8 Appendix

4.8.1 Optimal Investment in Child Quality

Lemma 4.1 *Given* $(g, \beta, \tau^e, \tau^q)$, *there exists a unique, interior, optimal level of investment in child quality*

$$e = e(g, \beta, \tau^e, \tau^q),$$

where $\frac{\partial e}{\partial g} > 0$, $\frac{\partial e}{\partial \beta} > 0$, $\frac{\partial e}{\partial \tau^q} > 0$, *and* $\frac{\partial e}{\partial \tau^e} < 0$.

Proof. As follows from (4.11), the necessary condition for the household's optimization with respect to e is given by the implicit function

$$G(e, g, \beta, \tau^q, \tau^e) \equiv \tau^e h(e, g) - \beta h_e(e, g)(\tau^q + \tau^e e) = 0. \tag{4.14}$$

Thus, noting the properties of $h(e, g)$,

$$\begin{aligned}
\lim_{e \to 0} G(e, g, \beta, \tau^q, \tau^e) &< 0, \\
\lim_{e \to \infty} G(e, g, \beta, \tau^q, \tau^e) &> 0,
\end{aligned} \tag{4.15}$$

whereas, noting that $0 < \beta < 1$,

$$\frac{\partial G(e, g, \tau^q, \tau^e)}{\partial e} = (1 - \beta)\tau^e h_e(e, g) - \beta h_{ee}(e, g)(\tau^q + \tau^e e) > 0. \tag{4.16}$$

Hence, it follows from the Intermediate Value Theorem that there exists a unique interior value of e such that $e = e(g, \beta, \tau^e, \tau^q)$.

Furthermore, noting that the strict concavity of $h(e, g)$ in e implies that $h(e, g) - h_e(e, g)e > 0$, it follows that

$$\begin{aligned}
\frac{\partial G(e, g, \tau^q, \tau^e)}{\partial g} &= \tau^e h_g(e, g) - \beta h_{eg}(e, g)(\tau^q + \tau^e e) < 0, \\
\frac{\partial G(e, g, \tau^q, \tau^e)}{\partial \beta} &= -h_e(e, g)(\tau^q + \tau^e e) < 0, \\
\frac{\partial G(e, g, \tau^q, \tau^e)}{\partial \tau^q} &= -\beta h_e(e, g)\tau^q < 0, \\
\frac{\partial G(e, g, \tau^q, \tau^e)}{\partial \tau^e} &= h(e, g) - \beta h_e(e, g)e > 0.
\end{aligned} \tag{4.17}$$

Thus, it follows from the Implicit Function Theorem that

$$\frac{\partial e}{\partial g} = -\frac{\partial G(e, g, \tau^q, \tau^e)}{\partial g} / \frac{\partial G(e, g, \tau^q, \tau^e)}{\partial e} > 0,$$

$$\frac{\partial e}{\partial \beta} = -\frac{\partial G(e, g, \tau^q, \tau^e)}{\partial \beta} / \frac{\partial G(e, g, \tau^q, \tau^e)}{\partial e} > 0,$$

$$\frac{\partial e}{\partial \tau^q} = -\frac{\partial G(e, g, \tau^q, \tau^e)}{\partial \tau^q} / \frac{\partial G(e, g, \tau^q, \tau^e)}{\partial e} > 0,$$

$$\frac{\partial e}{\partial \tau^e} = -\frac{\partial G(e, g, \tau^q, \tau^e)}{\partial \tau^e} / \frac{\partial G(e, g, \tau^q, \tau^e)}{\partial e} < 0.$$

(4.18)

4.8.2 Optimal Investment in Child Quantity

Lemma 4.2 *Given $(g, \beta, \tau^e, \tau^q)$, there exists a unique interior optimal number of children*

$$n = \frac{\gamma}{\tau^q + \tau^e e(g, \beta, \tau^e, \tau^q)},$$

where $\frac{\partial n}{\partial g} < 0$, $\frac{\partial n}{\partial \beta} < 0$, $\frac{\partial n}{\partial \tau^q} < 0$, and $\frac{\partial n}{\partial \tau^e} < 0$ if $[\partial e/\partial \tau^e][\tau^e/e] > -1$.

Proof. As follows from (4.11) and Lemma 4.1, the necessary condition for the household's optimization with respect to n is given by

$$n = \frac{\gamma}{\tau^q + \tau^e e} = \frac{\gamma}{\tau^q + \tau^e e(g, \beta, \tau^e, \tau^q)}.$$

(4.19)

Hence,

$$\frac{\partial n}{\partial g} = -\frac{\gamma \tau^e \frac{\partial e}{\partial g}}{[\tau^q + \tau^e e(g, \beta, \tau^e, \tau^q)]^2} < 0,$$

$$\frac{\partial n}{\partial \beta} = -\frac{\gamma \tau^e \frac{\partial e}{\partial \beta}}{[\tau^q + \tau^e e(g, \beta, \tau^e, \tau^q)]^2} < 0,$$

(4.20)

$$\frac{\partial n}{\partial \tau^q} = -\frac{\gamma [1 + \tau^e \frac{\partial e}{\partial \tau^q}]}{[\tau^q + \tau^e e(g, \beta, \tau^e, \tau^q)]^2} < 0,$$

whereas if $[\partial e/\partial \tau^e][\tau^e/e] > -1$ (i.e., if the elasticity of child quality with respect to the cost of child quality is smaller than one in absolute value), then

$$\frac{\partial n}{\partial \tau^e} = -\frac{\gamma [e + \tau^e \frac{\partial e}{\partial \tau^e}]}{[\tau^q + \tau^e e(g, \beta, \tau^e, \tau^q)]^2}$$

$$= -\frac{\gamma e [1 + \frac{\partial e}{\partial \tau^e} \frac{\tau^e}{e}]}{[\tau^q + \tau^e e(g, \beta, \tau^e, \tau^q)]^2} < 0.$$

(4.21)

CHAPTER 5

Unified Growth Theory

> *The theory that can absorb the greatest number of facts, and persist in doing so, generation after generation, through all changes of opinion and detail, is the one that must rule all observation.*
>
> —Adam Smith

This chapter develops the foundations of Unified Growth Theory. It underlines the significance as well as the intellectual challenge associated with the establishment of a theory of economic growth that captures each of the central phases in the process of development while orchestrating an endogenous transition across these distinct regimes. The chapter highlights the fundamental building blocks of Unified Growth Theory and their role in generating a dynamical system that accounts for (i) the epoch of Malthusian stagnation that characterized most of human history, (ii) the escape from the Malthusian trap and the spike in growth rates of income per capita and population, (iii) the emergence of human capital formation in the process of development, (iv) the onset of the demographic transition, and (v) the emergence of the contemporary era of sustained economic growth.

The advancement of Unified Growth Theory was fueled by the conviction that the understanding of global variation in economic development would be fragile and incomplete unless growth theory would reflect the principal driving forces over the entire process of development and would capture the central role played by historical and prehistorical factors in the prevailing disparity in economic development across countries and regions. Moreover, it was fostered by the realization that a comprehensive understanding of the hurdles faced by less developed economies in reaching an era of sustained economic growth would remain obscure unless the factors that brought about this transition among the currently developed economies could be identified and modified to account for the differences in the growth structure of less developed economies in an increasingly interdependent world.

Unified Growth Theory provides a fundamental framework of analysis for the evolution of individuals, societies, and economies over the entire course of human history. The theory—developed by Galor (2005, 2010) based on Galor and Weil (1999, 2000), Galor and Moav (2002), and Galor and Mountford (2008)—captures in a single analytical framework the main stages of development and the divergence in income per capita across countries.[1] The theory unveils the principal economic forces that have generated the remarkable transition from stagnation to growth and underlines their significance for understanding the contemporary growth process of both developed and less developed economies. Moreover, it sheds light on the role of historical and prehistorical characteristics in the divergence of income per capita between regions of the world in the past two centuries.

Unified Growth Theory reveals the factors that have generated the Malthusian trap. What accounts for the epoch of stagnation that characterized most of human history? Why did episodes of technological progress in the pre-industrial era fail to generate sustained economic growth? Why has population growth counterbalanced the expansion of resources per capita that could have been generated by technological progress? Moreover, the theory uncovers the forces that triggered the take-off from stagnation to growth. What is the origin of the sudden spurt in growth rates of income per capita and population during the course of industrialization? What was the source of the striking reversal in the positive relationship between income per capita and population that existed throughout most of human history? Would the transition to the modern state of sustained economic growth have been feasible without the decline in population growth? What are the hurdles faced by less developed economies in their attempts to transition to a sustained-growth regime?

Further, Unified Growth Theory sheds new light on the origins of the perplexing divergence in income per capita across developed and less developed regions in the past two centuries. What accounts for the sudden take-off from stagnation to growth among some countries in the world and the persistent stagnation in others? Why has the positive link between income per capita and population growth reversed its course in some economics but not in others? Has the transition to a state of sustained economic growth in advanced economies adversely affected the process of development in less developed ones? Have variations in prehistorical biogeographical factors had a persistent effect

---

[1] The term "Unified Growth Theory" was coined by Galor (2005) to categorize theories of economic growth that capture the entire growth process within a single unified framework of analysis. Some of the six salient characteristics of this process have been explored in the literature focusing on the transition from stagnation to growth (e.g., Jones 2001; Hansen and Prescott 2002; Lucas 2002; Lagerlöf 2003a; Doepke 2004; Voigtländer and Voth 2006, 2009; Ashraf and Galor 2007; Broadberry 2007; O'Rourke et al. 2008; Strulik and Weisdorf 2008; and Galor et al. 2009). However, the only unified theory of economic growth that captures the endogenous evolution of population, technology, human capital, and income per capita over the entire course of economic development and generates both a spontaneous transition from Malthusian stagnation to sustained growth and a great divergence is the one developed by Galor (2005, 2010). This theory therefore is the central pillar of the analysis.

on the composition of human capital and economic development around the world?

Importantly, Unified Growth Theory advances the understanding of three fundamental aspects of comparative economic development. First, it identifies the factors that have governed the pace of the transition from stagnation to growth and have thus contributed to the observed worldwide differences in economic development. Second, it underlines the persistent effects that variations in prehistorical biogeographical conditions have generated on the composition of human capital and economic development across the globe. Third, it uncovers the forces that have sparked the emergence of multiple growth regimes and convergence clubs and unveils the characteristics that determine the association of economies with each club.

5.1 The Fundamental Challenge

The establishment of a unified theory of economic growth has required major methodological and conceptual innovations in the construction of a unified microeconomic framework, and thus a single dynamical system, that captures the unique characteristics of each of the phases in the process of development while orchestrating an endogenous transition across these distinct regimes.

In light of historical evidence that the take-off from the Malthusian Epoch to an era of sustained economic growth, rapid as it may appear, was a gradual process (Crafts, 1985; Crafts and Harley, 1992), the Industrial Revolution cannot be plausibly viewed as an outcome of a major shock that shifted economies from the basin of attraction of the Malthusian equilibrium to that of the Modern Growth Regime. In particular, the simplest methodology for the generation of a phase transition, namely, a major shock in an environment characterized by multiple locally stable equilibria, appears inappropriate for generating the observed take-off from stagnation to growth.

Thus, the development of a unified theory of economic growth necessitated the construction of a dynamical system that permits economies to take off gradually but swiftly from a stable (absorbing) Malthusian equilibrium—an apparent contradiction to the notion of a stable equilibrium whose attractive forces do not permit a gradual escape. However, the epoch of Malthusian stagnation in income per capita masked a latent dynamism that ultimately brought about the phase transition associated with the take-off from the Malthusian equilibrium. In particular, although the growth of income per capita was minuscule over the Malthusian Epoch, in the course of the Malthusian interaction between technology and population, technological progress intensified and world population significantly increased—a dynamism that was instrumental for the escape of economies from this epoch.

Thus the phase transition associated with the take-off from the Malthusian Epoch was orchestrated by the impact of the evolution of these latent state variables on the dynamical system. In particular, the observed rapid, yet continuous, phase transition is captured by a single dynamical system, once the evolution of latent state variables in the Malthusian Epoch alters the qualitative structure of the dynamical system. The absorbing Malthusian equilibrium vanishes, and the economy gravitates toward a unique and stable sustained-growth steady-state equilibrium.

Galor and Weil (2000) and Galor and Moav (2002) develop unified growth theories in which the endogenous evolution of population, technology, and income per capita is consistent with the process of development in its entirety. These theories capture the fundamental regimes that have characterized the process of development as well as the fundamental driving forces that generated the transition from an epoch of Malthusian stagnation to an era of sustained economic growth. They introduce the methodological and conceptual innovation that the evolution of latent state variables was a critical force in the observed phase transition. During the Malthusian Epoch, the dynamical system is characterized by a stable Malthusian equilibrium. But eventually, due to a latent progression of the size of the population, the rate of technological progress and thus demand for human capital and the propensity of individuals to invest in human capital, the Malthusian steady-state equilibrium vanishes endogenously, leaving the arena open for the attractive forces of the emerging sustained-growth steady-state equilibrium.

5.2 Incompatibility of Non-Unified Growth Theories

Non-unified growth models have been instrumental in underscoring the role of factor accumulation and technological progress in the growth process during the modern era. Nevertheless, they are inconsistent with the qualitative aspects of the growth process over most of the course of human history. In particular, they fail to identify the forces that triggered the take-off from stagnation to sustained economic growth and the associated divergence in income per capita across countries—insights that are critical for understanding the contemporary growth process. Malthusian models, in contrast, capture the growth process during the Malthusian Epoch but are incompatible with the transition to the Modern Growth Regime.

5.2.1 The Malthusian Theory

The Malthusian theory captures the main attributes of the epoch of Malthusian stagnation that characterized most of human existence but is utterly inconsistent with the prime characteristics of the Modern Growth Regime. The theory suggests that stagnation in the evolution of income per capita over this epoch reflected the counterbalancing effect of population growth on the expansion of resources in an environment characterized by diminishing returns to labor. According to the theory, periods marked by the absence of changes in the level of technology or in the availability of land were characterized by stable population size as well as constant income per capita. In contrast, episodes of technological progress, land expansion, or favorable climatic conditions brought about temporary gains in income per capita, which triggered an increase in population that eventually led to the reversion of income per capita to its long-run level.

The Malthusian theory, as developed in Chapter 3, generates two testable predictions. First, within an economy, the adoption or advancement of superior production technologies leads to a larger, but not richer, population in the long run. Second, differences in technologies or in land productivity across countries are reflected in cross-country variations in population density rather than in income per capita. The predictions of the Malthusian theory are consistent with the pattern of development during the Malthusian Epoch, but they are irremediably inconsistent with the relationship between income per capita and population that has existed in the post-demographic transition era as well as in the Modern Growth Regime.

For instance, Kremer (1993), in an attempt to defend the role of the scale effect in endogenous growth models, examines a reduced-form dynamics of the coevolution of population and technology in a Malthusian environment, providing evidence for the presence of a scale effect in the pre-demographic transition era. This reduced-form Malthusian-Boserupian structure is well designed to capture either a Malthusian trap or a coevolution of population and technology in the Post-Malthusian Regime. However, it does not contain the ingredients that could generate a spontaneous take-off from a Malthusian trap or an endogenous onset of a demographic transition that could potentially lead to a sustained growth regime.[2]

Furthermore, models that are not based on Malthusian elements are unable to capture the epoch of Malthusian stagnation in which output per capita fluctuates around a subsistence level. In the absence of a positive effect of income on population growth and diminishing return to labor, the predictions of these models are at odds with the evolution of economies during the Malthusian Epoch, when technological progress had a negligible effect on the long-run level and growth rate of income per capita. For instance, Goodfriend and McDermott (1995) demonstrate that exogenous population growth increases population

---

[2] Artzrouni and Komlos (1990) simulate an escape from a Malthusian trap based on the Malthusian and Boserupian interaction between population and technology.

density and hence generates a greater scope for the division of labor, inducing the development of markets and economic growth. Their model, therefore, generates a take-off from a non-Malthusian stagnation to a Post-Malthusian Regime in which population and output are positively related. The model lacks Malthusian elements and therefore counterfactually implies strictly positive growth, with no extended period of stagnation, ever since the emergence of a market economy more than 5,000 years ago. Moreover, it does not identify the forces that would bring about the demographic transition and ultimately sustained economic growth. In particular, in the long run the economy remains in the Post-Malthusian Regime in which the growth of population and output are positively related.

5.2.2 Theories of Modern Economic Growth

The neoclassical growth model (Solow, 1956) has been instrumental in eluci-dating the role of factor accumulation and technological progress in the growth process during the modern era. Further, endogenous growth models (Lucas, 1988; Romer, 1990; Grossman and Helpman, 1991; Aghion and Howitt, 1992) have advanced the understanding of the determinants of technological progress and their role in sustaining economic growth in the long run.[3]

Nevertheless, non-unified growth models do not unveil the underlying forces behind the intricate patterns of the growth process over human history. They do not shed light on the underlying driving forces that triggered the transition from stagnation to growth, the hurdles faced by less developed economies in reaching a state of sustained economic growth, and the associated phenomenon of the Great Divergence in income per capita across countries.[4]

Furthermore, although the evolution of the demographic regime in the course of human history appears essential for understanding the evolution of income per capita over the process of development, non-unified endogenous and ex-ogenous growth models abstract from the determination of population growth

---

[3] Other notable contributions include Mankiw et al. (1992), Jones (1995), Dinopoulos and Thompson (1998), Peretto (1998), Segerstrom (1998), Young (1998), and Howitt (1999).

[4] As long as the neoclassical production structure of nondecreasing returns is maintained, non-unified growth models cannot be modified to account for the Malthusian Epoch by incorporation of endogenous population growth. For instance, suppose that the neoclassical growth model is augmented to account for endogenous population. Suppose further that the parameters of the model are chosen so as to assure that the level of income per capita reflects the level that existed during the Malthusian Epoch and population growth is near replacement level, as was the case during this era. This equilibrium would not possess the prime characteristic of a Malthusian equilibrium. Namely, technological progress would raise income per capita permanently, because adjustments in population growth would not offset this rise of income (as long as the return to labor is characterized by nondiminishing returns to scale).

over the growth process, and their predictions are inconsistent with the evolving demographic structure over the course of human history. In particular, the predictions of these models are at odds with the evolution of economies during the Malthusian Epoch, when capital accumulation and technological progress were counterbalanced almost entirely by an increase in the size of the population and had thus a negligible effect on the long-run level and growth rate of income per capita.

Furthermore, in contrast to the main predictions of these models, technological leaders largely experience a monotonic increase in the growth rates of their income per capita during the process of development. Their growth was slow in the early stages of development, it increased rapidly during the take-off from the Malthusian Epoch and continued to rise, often stabilizing at higher levels, in the sustained-growth regime.

Moreover, non-unified growth models with endogenous populations have been largely oriented toward the modern regime. They capture some aspects of the recent negative relationship between population growth and income per capita but fail to capture the significance of the positive effect of income per capita on population growth that had characterized most of human existence, as well as the economic factors that triggered the demographic transition and the take-off to an era of sustained economic growth.[5]

Thus, non-unified growth models do not possess the research methodology that can shed light on some of the most fundamental questions in today's world: (i) the origins of sustained differences in income per capita across the globe, (ii) the forces that led to the divergence in income per capita across countries and regions in the past 200 years, (iii) the barriers faced by less developed economies in reaching a state of sustained economic growth, and (iv) the central role played by historical and prehistorical factors in the prevailing disparity in economic development across countries and regions.

5.3 Central Building Blocks

The theory is based on the interactions among several building blocks: the Malthusian elements, the engines of technological progress, the origins of human capital formation, and the triggers of the demographic transition.

---

[5] Studies that capture aspects of the cross-sectional relationship between income per capita and fertility include Razin and Ben-Zion (1975), Barro and Becker (1989), and Becker et al. (1990), and more recently Dahan and Tsiddon (1998), Kremer and Chen (2002), McDermott (2002), and Manuelli and Seshadri (2009).

5.3.1 The Malthusian Elements

The process of development during most of human existence was marked by Malthusian stagnation. Resources generated by technological progress and land expansion were channeled primarily into an increase in population, with a minor long-run effect on income per capita. The positive effect of the standard of living on population growth along with diminishing labor productivity left income per capita near subsistence level (Malthus, 1798).

The Malthusian Epoch is captured in Unified Growth Theory by three central elements: (i) the production process is characterized by decreasing returns to labor due to the limited availability of land; (ii) parents generate utility from having children but child rearing is time intensive; and (iii) individuals are subject to a subsistence consumption constraint.[6] As long as the subsistence constraint binds, an increase in parental income results in an increase in the number of children. Hence, technological progress, which brings about temporary gains in income per capita, triggers an increase in population that offsets the gain in income per capita, due to decreasing returns to labor.

5.3.2 Engines of Technological Progress

The acceleration of technological progress in the course of industrialization is a fundamental force in the transition from stagnation to growth. While the size of the population stimulates technological progress in the early stages of development, human capital formation is the prime engine of technological progress in more advanced stages.

Unified Growth Theory supposes that in the Malthusian Epoch, when the technological frontier reflected the working environment of most individuals, the scale of the population affected the rate of technological progress via its effect on (i) the supply of innovative ideas, (ii) the demand for innovations, (iii) the rate of technological diffusion, (iv) the degree of specialization in the production process and thus the extent of "learning by doing," and (v) the scope for trade and thus the extent of technological imitation and adoption.[7] However, as advancements of the technological frontier become increasingly more complex in later stages of development, human capital becomes more

---

[6] The physiological foundations of the subsistence consumption constraint and the Malthusian equilibrium are explored by Dalgaard and Strulik (2010).

[7] The positive effect of the scale of the population on technological progress in the Malthusian Epoch is supported empirically (Boserup, 1965; Kremer, 1993). The role of the scale of the population in the modern era is, however, controversial. As technological progress becomes human capital intensive, if the scale of the population comes on the account of population quality, it may have an ambiguous effect on technological progress.

significant in the process of technological progress, and educated individuals are more likely to advance this frontier (see Nelson and Phelps 1966; Schultz 1975; Benhabib and Spiegel 2005).

5.3.3 The Origin of Human Capital Formation

The rise in industrial demand for human capital and its impact on human capital formation and the demographic transition are central components of the growth process and the transition to the Modern Growth Regime.

Unified Growth Theory postulates that changes in the economic environment that are triggered by technological progress raise human capital formation, since educated individuals have a comparative advantage in adapting to the new technological environment.[8] Thus, although the nature of the technology may be reflected in a long-run bias toward either unskilled or skilled labor, the introduction of these technologies increases the demand for human capital in the short run.[9]

5.3.4 The Trigger of the Demographic Transition

The demographic transition that marked the onset of the state of sustained economic growth is a focal point in the transition from stagnation to growth. The demographic transition brought about a reversal in the unprecedented increase in population growth that occurred during the Post-Malthusian Regime. As elaborated earlier, the reduction in fertility rates and population growth have enhanced the growth process via several channels. First, the decline in population growth reduced the dilution of capital, land, and infrastructure. Second, the reduction in fertility enhanced human capital formation via a reallocation of resources from the quantity of children to their quality. Third, the decline in fertility rates enhanced per capita labor productivity via its effect on the age distribution of the population, temporarily increasing the size of the labor force relative to the population as a whole. Thus, the demographic transition enabled economies to foster human capital formation and convert a larger share of the

---

[8] Consistent with this hypothesis, Hendricks (2010) finds that current variation in education across countries is primarily due to variation in skill intensities within industry rather than to variation in sectoral composition.

[9] The effect of technological transition on the return on human capital is at the center of the theoretical approach of Nelson and Phelps (1966), Galor and Tsiddon (1997), Galor and Moav (2000), and Hassler and Mora (2000). It is supported empirically by Schultz (1975) and Foster and Rosenzweig (1996). If the demand for education rises with the level (as opposed to the rate of change) of technology, the qualitative results would not be affected. Adopting this mechanism, however, is equivalent to assuming that changes in technology have been skill-biased throughout human history, in contrast to periods in which the characteristics of new technologies could be defined as unskilled-biased, most notably during the first phase of the Industrial Revolution.

gains from factor accumulation and technological progress into the material well-being of the population.

Unified Growth Theory postulates that the rise in demand for human capital triggered the decline in fertility in the course of the demographic transition. Individuals generate utility from the quantity and the quality of their children as well as from their own consumption. They choose the number of children and their quality in the face of a constraint on the total amount of time that can be devoted to child-raising and labor market activities. While a rise in parental income (due to the rise in demand for human capital) would generate conflicting income and substitution effects and would not necessarily trigger a decline in fertility, the effect of the rise in demand for human capital on potential future earnings of a child generates a pure substitution effect. It induces parents to substitute quality for quantity of children and thus operates to decrease fertility.

5.4 The Basic Structure of the Model

Consider an overlapping-generations economy in which activity extends over infinite discrete time. In every period, the economy produces a single homogeneous good using land and efficiency units of labor as inputs. The supply of land is exogenous and fixed over time, whereas the number of efficiency units of labor is determined by households' decisions in the preceding period regarding the number and level of human capital of their children.

5.4.1 Production of Final Output

Production occurs according to a constant-returns-to-scale technology that is subject to endogenous technological progress. The output produced in period t, Y_t, is

$$Y_t = H_t^{\alpha}(A_t X)^{1-\alpha}, \qquad \alpha \in (0, 1), \tag{5.1}$$

where H_t is the aggregate quantity of efficiency units of labor employed in period t, X is land employed in production in every period t, A_t is the endogenously determined level of technology in period t, and $A_t X$ therefore represents the effective resources employed in production in period t.

If individuals are fully employed, output per worker produced in period t, $y_t \equiv Y_t/L_t$, is

$$y_t = h_t^{\alpha} x_t^{1-\alpha}, \tag{5.2}$$

where $h_t \equiv H_t/L_t$ is the level of efficiency units of labor per full-time worker, and $x_t \equiv (A_t X)/L_t$ is the level of effective resources per worker in period t.

Suppose that there are no property rights over land.[10] If individuals are fully employed, their income, z_t, equals the output per full-time worker, y_t; that is,

$$z_t = y_t. \tag{5.3}$$

5.4.2 Preferences and Budget Constraints

In each period t, a generation that consists of L_t identical individuals joins the labor force. Each individual has a single parent. Members of generation t (those who join the labor force in period t) live for two periods. In the first period of life (childhood), $t - 1$, individuals consume a fraction of the parental unit-time endowment. The required time increases with child quality. In the second period of life (parenthood), t, individuals are endowed with one unit of time, which they allocate between child rearing and labor force participation. They choose the optimal mixture of quantity and quality of (surviving) children and supply their remaining time to the labor market, consuming their wages.

Preferences of members of generation t are represented by a utility function, u_t, defined over consumption above a subsistence level $\tilde{c} > 0$, as well as over the quantity and quality (measured by human capital) of their (surviving) children:[11]

$$u_t = (1 - \gamma) \ln c_t + \gamma \ln(n_t h_{t+1}), \quad 0 < \gamma < 1, \tag{5.4}$$

where c_t is the consumption of an individual of generation t, n_t is the number of (surviving) children of an individual of generation t, and h_{t+1} is the level of human capital (measured in efficiency units of labor) of each child in period $t + 1$, when they join the labor force.[12] The utility function is strictly monotonically increasing and strictly quasi-concave, satisfying the conventional boundary conditions that ensure, for a sufficiently high income, the existence of an interior solution for the utility maximization problem. However, for a sufficiently low level of income, the subsistence-consumption con-

---

[10] Allowing for capital accumulation and property rights over land would complicate the model to the point of intractability, but would not affect the qualitative results.

[11] For simplicity, parents derive utility from the expected number of surviving offspring, and the parental cost of child rearing is associated only with surviving children. The introduction of costs associated with nonsurviving children, or risk aversion, would not affect the qualitative features of the theory.

[12] Alternatively, the utility function could be defined over consumption above subsistence rather than over a consumption set that is truncated from below by the subsistence-consumption constraint. In particular, if $u_t = (c_t - \tilde{c})^{(1-\gamma)}(n_t h_{t+1})^\gamma$, the qualitative analysis would not be affected, but the complexity of the dynamical system would be greatly enhanced. The income expansion path would be smooth, transforming continuously from being nearly vertical for low levels of potential income to asymptotically horizontal for high levels.

straint is binding, and there is a corner solution with respect to the consumption level.

Individuals choose the number of children and their quality in the face of a constraint on the total amount of time that can be devoted to child-raising and labor market activities. Let $\tau + e_{t+1}$ be the time cost for a member of generation t of raising a child with a level of education (quality) e_{t+1}.[13] That is, τ is the fraction of the individual's unit-time endowment that is required to raise a child, regardless of quality, and e_{t+1} is the fraction of the individual's unit-time endowment that is devoted to the education of each child.[14]

Consider members of generation t who are endowed with h_t efficiency units of labor in period t. Define potential income, z_t, as the potential earning if the entire time endowment is devoted to labor force participation. The potential income, z_t, is divided between consumption, c_t, and expenditure on child rearing (quantity as well as quality), evaluated according to the value of the time cost, $z_t(\tau + e_{t+1})$, per child. Hence, in the second period of life (parenthood), the individual faces the budget constraint

$$z_t n_t (\tau + e_{t+1}) + c_t \leq z_t. \tag{5.5}$$

5.4.3 Production of Human Capital

Individuals' level of human capital is determined by their quality (education) as well as by the technological environment. Technological progress reduces the adaptability of existing human capital to the new technological environment. Education, however, lessens the adverse effects of technological progress on the effectiveness of the stock of human capital.

The level of human capital of a child of a member of generation t, h_{t+1}, is an increasing, strictly concave function of the parental time investment in the education of the child, e_{t+1}, and a decreasing strictly convex function of the

---

[13] The time required to produce a child can be purchased from other individuals. However, in the absence of heterogeneity across individuals or increasing returns in the production of human capital these transactions will not take place. As established in Chapter 7, the introduction of heterogeneity will not affect the qualitative analysis. Moreover, if there exists increasing returns in the production of education, or if both time and goods are required in order to produce child quality, the process would be intensified. As the economy develops and wages increase, and as the demand for human capital formation rises, the relative cost of child quality will diminish and individuals will substitute quality for quantity of children.

[14] τ is assumed to be sufficiently small so as to ensure that the population can have a positive growth rate. That is, $\tau < \gamma$.

rate of technological progress, $g_{t+1} \equiv (A_{t+1} - A_t)/A_t$:[15]

$$h_{t+1} = h(e_{t+1}, g_{t+1}). \tag{5.6}$$

Education lessens the adverse effect of technological progress. That is, technology complements skills in the production of human capital (i.e., $h_{eg}(e_{t+1}, g_{t+1}) > 0$). In the absence of investment in quality, each individual has a basic level of human capital that is normalized to 1 in a stationary technological environment; that is, $h(0, 0) = 1$.[16]

5.4.4 Optimization

Members of generation t choose the number and quality of their (surviving) children and their own consumption so as to maximize their intertemporal utility function subject to the subsistence-consumption constraint. Substituting (5.5) and (5.6) into (5.4), the optimization problem of a member of generation t is

$$\{n_t, e_{t+1}\} = \arg \max (1 - \gamma) \ln\{z_t[1 - n_t(\tau + e_{t+1})]\}$$
$$+ \gamma \ln\{n_t h(e_{t+1}, g_{t+1})\}, \tag{5.7}$$

subject to

$$z_t[1 - n_t(\tau + e_{t+1})] \geq \tilde{c};$$
$$(n_t, e_{t+1}) \geq 0.$$

Hence, as long as potential income in period t is sufficiently high to ensure that $c_t > \tilde{c}$ (i.e., as long as z_t is above the level of potential income at which the subsistence constraint is just binding, $z_t > \tilde{z} \equiv \tilde{c}/(1 - \gamma)$), the fraction of time spent by a member of generation t raising children is γ, while $1 - \gamma$ is devoted to labor force participation. However, if $z_t \leq \tilde{z}$, the subsistence constraint is binding; the fraction of time necessary to ensure subsistence consumption, $\tilde{c}$,

---

[15] It should be noted that the conditions placed on the function are sufficient but not necessary. As established by Lagerlöf (2006), a function that satisfies only a subset of these conditions will permit the derivation of all qualitative results.

[16] For simplicity, investment in quality is not beneficial in a stationary technological environment (i.e., $h_e(0, 0) = 0$). Moreover, in the absence of investment in education, there exists sufficiently rapid technological progress that, due to the erosion effect, renders the existing human capital obsolete (i.e., $\lim_{g \to \infty} h(0, g) = 0$). Furthermore, although the potential number of efficiency units of labor is diminished due to the transition from the existing technological state to a superior one (i.e., due to the erosion effect), each individual operates with a superior level of technology, and the productivity effect is assumed to dominate, that is, $\partial y_t/\partial g_t > 0$.

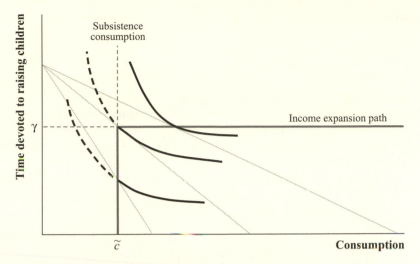

FIGURE 5.1. Preferences, constraints, and the income expansion path.
Summary: This figure depicts the household's indifference curves, budget constraints, and the subsistence-consumption constraint, $c \geq \tilde{c}$. The income expansion path is vertical as long as the subsistence-consumption constraint is binding (reflecting a corner solution for the individual optimization problem) and is horizontal at a level, γ, once this constraint is not binding (and the solution for the individual optimization problem is interior).

is larger than $1 - \gamma$, and the fraction of time devoted to child rearing is therefore below γ. That is,

$$n_t(\tau + e_{t+1}) = \begin{cases} \gamma, & \text{if } z_t \geq \tilde{z}; \\ 1 - (\tilde{c}/z_t), & \text{if } z_t \leq \tilde{z}. \end{cases} \tag{5.8}$$

Figure 5.1 shows the effect of an increase in potential income, z_t, on the individual's allocation of time between child rearing and consumption. The income expansion path is vertical as long as the subsistence-consumption constraint is binding. As the wage per efficiency unit of labor increases in this income range, the individual can generate subsistence consumption with a lower level of labor force participation, and the fraction of time devoted to child rearing increases. Once the level of income is sufficiently high such that the subsistence-consumption constraint is not binding, the income expansion path becomes horizontal at a level γ in terms of time devoted to child rearing.

Furthermore, as established in the appendix to this chapter, optimization with respect to e_{t+1} implies that the level of education chosen by members of generation t for their children, e_{t+1}, is an increasing function of g_{t+1}. In particular, there exists a critical level, $\hat{g}$, of the rate of technological progress such that

$$e_{t+1} = e(g_{t+1}) \begin{cases} = 0, & \text{if } g_{t+1} \leq \hat{g}; \\ > 0, & \text{if } g_{t+1} > \hat{g}, \end{cases} \qquad (5.9)$$

where $e'(g_{t+1}) > 0$, and $e''(g_{t+1}) < 0$, $\forall g_{t+1} > \hat{g} > 0$.[17]

Hence, the optimal level of investment in child quality and thus the optimal division of child-rearing time between quality and quantity is affected only by the rate of technological progress (via its effect on demand for education) and not by parental level of income.[18]

Furthermore, substituting (5.9) into (5.8), it follows that

$$n_t = \begin{cases} \dfrac{\gamma}{\tau + e(g_{t+1})} \equiv n^b(g_{t+1}), & \text{if } z_t \geq \tilde{z}; \\[3mm] \dfrac{1 - [\tilde{c}/z_t]}{\tau + e(g_{t+1})} \equiv n^a(g_{t+1}, z(e_t, g_t, x_t)), & \text{if } z_t \leq \tilde{z}, \end{cases} \qquad (5.10)$$

where $z_t = z(e_t, g_t, x_t)$, as follows from (5.3) and (5.6).

Hence, as follows from the properties of $e(g_{t+1})$, $n^b(g_{t+1})$, and $n^a(g_{t+1}, z_t)$:

1. An increase in the rate of technological progress reduces the number of children and increases their quality, that is,

$$\partial n_t / \partial g_{t+1} \leq 0 \text{ and } \partial e_{t+1} / \partial g_{t+1} \geq 0.$$

2. If the subsistence-consumption constraint is binding (i.e., if parental potential income is less than $\tilde{z}$), an increase in parental potential income raises the number of children but has no effect on their quality, that is,

$$\partial n_t / \partial z_t > 0 \quad \text{and} \quad \partial e_{t+1} / \partial z_t = 0, \quad \text{if } z_t < \tilde{z}.$$

3. If the subsistence-consumption constraint is not binding (i.e., if parental potential income is more than $\tilde{z}$), an increase in parental potential income does not affect the number of children or their quality, that is,

$$\partial n_t / \partial z_t = \partial e_{t+1} / \partial z_t = 0, \quad \text{if } z_t > \tilde{z}.$$

---

[17] $e''(g_{t+1})$ depends on the third derivatives of the production function of human capital. The function $e(g_{t+1})$ is assumed to be concave, which appears plausible.

[18] Hence, as is the case for other forms of investments, the optimal investment level depends on the rate of return on this investment and (in the absence of credit constraints) is independent of the investor's level of income. Moreover, if individuals are heterogenous in ability, accessibility and quality of education, cultural norms, and health status, the differential rate of return on this investment would result in heterogeneity in the level of investment in human capital.

5.5 Evolution of Technology, Population, and Effective Resources

5.5.1 Technological Progress

Suppose that technological progress, g_{t+1}, that takes place between periods t and $t + 1$ depends on the education per capita among the working generation in period t, e_t, and on the population size in period t, L_t:[19]

$$g_{t+1} \equiv \frac{A_{t+1} - A_t}{A_t} = g(e_t, L_t), \tag{5.11}$$

where for $e_t \geq 0$ and a sufficiently large population, L_t, $g(0, L_t) > 0$, $g_i(e_t, L_t) > 0$, and $g_{ii}(e_t, L_t) < 0$; $i = e_t, L_t$.[20] Namely, for a sufficiently large population, the rate of technological progress between periods t and $t + 1$ is a positive, increasing, strictly concave function of the size and level of education of the working generation in period t. Furthermore, the rate of technological progress is positive, even if labor quality is zero.

The state of technology in period $t + 1$, A_{t+1}, is therefore

$$A_{t+1} = (1 + g_{t+1})A_t, \tag{5.12}$$

where the state of technology in period 0 is given as A_0.

5.5.2 Population

The size of the working population in period $t + 1$, L_{t+1}, is

$$L_{t+1} = n_t L_t, \tag{5.13}$$

where L_t is the size of the working population in period t, and n_t is the number of children per person; L_0 is given. Hence, given (5.10), the evolution of the working population over time is

$$L_{t+1} = \begin{cases} n^b(g_{t+1})L_t, & \text{if } z_t \geq \tilde{z}; \\ n^a(g_{t+1}, z(e_t, g_t, x_t))L_t, & \text{if } z_t \leq \tilde{z}. \end{cases} \tag{5.14}$$

[19] While the role of the scale effect in the Malthusian Epoch is essential, none of the results depend on the presence or absence of the scale effect in the modern era. The functional form of technological progress given in (5.11) can capture both the presence or absence of this scale effect. In particular, the scale effect can be removed, once investment in education is positive, assuming, for instance, that $\lim_{L \to \infty} g_L(e_t, L) = 0$ for $e_t > 0$.

[20] For a sufficiently small population the rate of technological progress is strictly positive only every several periods. Furthermore, the number of periods that pass between two episodes of technological improvement declines with the size of population. These assumptions assure that in early stages of development the economy is in a Malthusian steady state with zero growth rate of output per capita, but ultimately the growth rate becomes positive and slow. If technological progress would occur in every period at a pace that increases with the size of population, the growth rate of output per capita would be positive in every period, despite the adjustment in the size of population.

5.5.3 Effective Resources

The evolution of effective resources per worker, $x_t \equiv (A_t X)/L_t$, is determined by the evolution of population and technology. The level of effective resources per worker in period $t + 1$ is

$$x_{t+1} \equiv \frac{(A_{t+1}X)}{L_{t+1}} = \frac{1 + g_{t+1}}{n_t} x_t, \tag{5.15}$$

where $x_0 \equiv A_0 X/L_0$ is given. Furthermore, as follows from (5.10) and (5.11),

$$x_{t+1} = \begin{cases} \dfrac{[1 + g(e_t, L_t)][\tau + e(g(e_t, L_t))]}{\gamma} x_t \equiv \phi^b(e_t, L_t)x_t, & \text{if } z_t \geq \tilde{z}; \\[3mm] \dfrac{[1 + g(e_t, L_t)][\tau + e(g(e_t, L_t))]}{1 - [\tilde{c}/z(e_t, g_t, x_t)]} x_t \equiv \phi^a(e_t, g_t, x_t, L_t)x_t, & \text{if } z_t \leq \tilde{z}. \end{cases} \tag{5.16}$$

5.6 The Dynamical System

The development of the economy is fully determined by a sequence $\{e_t, g_t, x_t, L_t\}_{t=0}^{\infty}$ that satisfies (5.9), (5.11), (5.14), and (5.16) in every period t and describes the joint evolution of education, technological progress, effective resources per capita, and population over time from historically given initial conditions e_0, g_0, x_0, and L_0.

The dynamical system is characterized by two regimes. In the first regime, the subsistence-consumption constraint is binding, and the evolution of the economy is governed by a four-dimensional nonlinear first-order autonomous system:

$$\begin{cases} x_{t+1} = \phi^a(e_t, g_t, x_t, L_t)x_t, \\ e_{t+1} = e(g(e_t, L_t)), \\ g_{t+1} = g(e_t, L_t), \\ L_{t+1} = n^a(g(e_t, L_t), \ z(e_t, g_t, x_t))L_t. \end{cases} \quad \text{for } z_t \leq \tilde{z} \tag{5.17}$$

In the second regime, the subsistence-consumption constraint is not binding, and the evolution of the economy is governed by a three-dimensional system:

$$\begin{cases} x_{t+1} = \phi^b(e_t, x_t, L_t)x_t, \\ e_{t+1} = e(g(e_t, L_t)), \qquad \text{for } z_t \geq \tilde{z}. \\ L_{t+1} = n^b(g(e_t, L_t))L_t, \end{cases} \tag{5.18}$$

In both regimes, however, the analysis of the dynamical system is greatly simplified because the evolution of e_t and g_t is independent of whether the subsistence-constraint is binding, and because, for a given population size L, the joint evolution of e_t and g_t is determined independently of x_t. The education level of workers in period $t + 1$ (as determined by parents in period t) depends only on the rate of technological progress expected between t and $t + 1$, while technological progress between t and $t + 1$, for a given population size L, depends only on the level of education in period t. Thus, for a given population size L, the dynamics of technology and education can be analyzed independently of the evolution of resources per capita.

5.6.1 The Dynamics of Technology and Education

The evolution of technology and education, for a given population size L, is characterized by the sequence $\{g_t, e_t; L\}_{t=0}^{\infty}$ that satisfies in every period t the equations[21]

$$g_{t+1} = g(e_t; L),$$
$$e_{t+1} = e(g_{t+1}).$$
(5.19)

In light of the properties of the functions $e(g_{t+1})$ and $g(e_t; L)$, this dynamical subsystem is characterized by three qualitatively different configurations, which are depicted in Figures 5.2(a), 5.3(a), and 5.4(a). The inherent Malthusian interaction between population size and the level of technology gradually increases the population and the rate of technological progress and generates an upward shift in the curve $g(e_t; L)$. Ultimately, the rate of technological progress exceeds the threshold level, $\hat{g}$, above which investment in human capital is beneficial, the Malthusian steady state vanishes, and the economy is attracted to the Modern Growth Regime.

In particular, for a range of small population sizes, depicted in Figure 5.2(a), the dynamical system is characterized by a globally stable steady-state equilibrium, $(\bar{e}(L), \bar{g}(L)) = (0, g^l(L))$, where $g^l(L)$ increases with population size, while the level of education remains unchanged. For a range of moderate population sizes, as depicted in Figure 5.3(a), the dynamical system is characterized by three steady-state equilibria: two locally stable steady-state equilibria, $(0, g^l(L))$ and $(e^h(L), g^h(L))$, and an interior unstable steady-state equilibrium, $(e^u(L), g^u(L))$, where $(e^h(L), g^h(L))$ and $g^l(L)$ increase monotonically with population size. Finally, for a range of large population sizes, as depicted in

---

[21] Although this dynamical subsystem consists of two independent one-dimensional nonlinear first-order difference equations, it is more revealing to analyze them jointly.

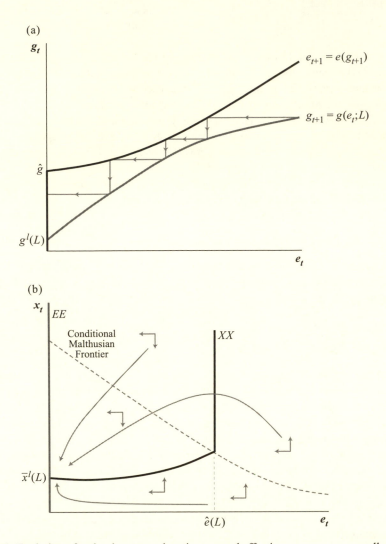

FIGURE 5.2. Evolution of technology, g_t; education, e_t; and effective resources, x_t: small population.
Summary: Panel (a) describes the evolution of education, e_t, and the rate of technological change, g_t, for a constant small population, L. The curve labeled $g_{t+1} = g(e_t; L)$ shows the effect of education on the growth rate of technology. The curve labeled $e_{t+1} = e(g_{t+1})$ shows the effect of expected technological change on optimal education choices. The point of intersection of the two curves is the globally stable steady-state equilibrium $(0, g^l(L))$. In early stages of development, the economy is in the vicinity of this steady-state equilibrium, where education is zero and the rate of technological progress is slow. Panel (b) describes the evolution of education, e_t, and effective resources per worker, x_t, for a constant small population, L. The EE locus is the set of all pairs $(e_t, x_t; L)$ for which education is constant over time. The XX locus is the set of all pairs $(e_t, x_t; L)$, given g_t, for which effective resources per worker are constant over time. The point of intersection of the two curves is a unique globally stable steady-state equilibrium. In early stages of development, the system is in the vicinity of this conditional Malthusian steady state. The Conditional Malthusian Frontier is the set of all pairs $(e_t, x_t; L)$, given g_t, below which the subsistence constraint is binding.

(a)

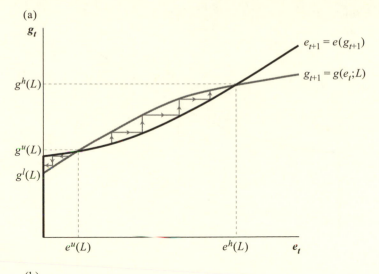

(b)

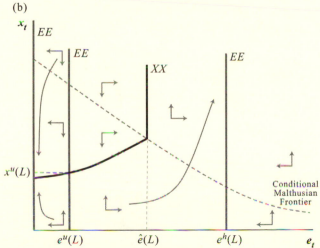

FIGURE 5.3. Evolution of technology, g_t; education, e_t; and effective resources, x_t: moderate population.

Summary: Panel (a) describes the evolution of education, e_t, and the rate of technological change, g_t, once the population has grown to moderate size, L. The system is characterized by multiple steady-state equilibria. The steady-state equilibria $(0, g^l(L))$ and $(e^h(L), g^h(L))$ are locally stable, whereas $(e^u(L), g^u(L))$ is unstable. Given the initial conditions, in the absence of large shocks, the economy remains in the vicinity of the low steady-state equilibrium $(0, g^l(L))$, where education is still zero but the rate of technological progress is moderate. Panel (b) describes the evolution of education, e_t, and effective resources per worker, x_t, for a constant moderate-sized population, L.

(a)

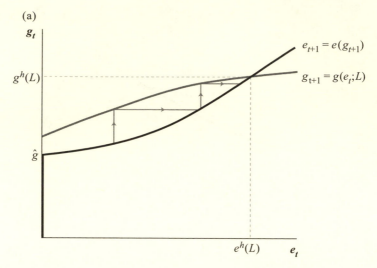

(b)

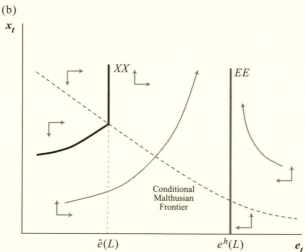

FIGURE 5.4. Evolution of technology, g_t; education, e_t; and effective resources, x_t: large population.

Summary: Panel (a) describes the evolution of education, e_t, and the rate of technological change, g_t, once the population grows to a high level, L. The system is characterized by a unique globally stable steady-state equilibrium, $(e^h(L), g^h(L))$. In mature stages of development, the economy converges monotonically to this steady state with high levels of education and technological progress. Panel (b) describes the evolution of education, e_t, and the rate of technological change, x_t, once the population has reached a high level, L. The dynamical system changes qualitatively, and the conditional Malthusian steady state vanishes. The economy evolves through a Post-Malthusian Regime until it crosses the conditional Malthusian Frontier, converging to the Modern Growth Regime.

Figure 5.4(a), the dynamical system is characterized by a globally stable steady-state equilibrium, $(e^h(L), g^h(L))$, where $e^h(L)$ and $g^h(L)$ increase monotonically with population size.

5.6.2 Global Dynamics

This analysis of the evolution of the economy is based on a sequence of phase diagrams that describe the evolution of the system, within each regime, for a given population size, and the transition between these regimes as the population increases in the process of development. Each of the phase diagrams is a projection of the three-dimensional system $\{e_t, g_t, x_t; L\}$ to the plane $(e_t, x_t; L)$.[22]

The phase diagrams, depicted in Figures 5.2(b), 5.3(b), and 5.4(b), contain three elements: the Malthusian Frontier, which separates the regions where the subsistence constraint is binding from those where it is not; the XX locus, which denotes the set of all triplets $(e_t, g_t, x_t; L)$ for which effective resources per worker are constant; and the EE locus, which denotes the set of all pairs $(e_t, g_t; L)$ for which the level of education per worker is constant.

The Malthusian Frontier
As established in (5.17) and (5.18), the economy exits from the subsistence-consumption regime when potential income, z_t, exceeds the critical level $\tilde{z}$. This switch of regime changes the dimensionality of the dynamical system from three to two, for a fixed level of L.

Let the Malthusian Frontier be the set of all triplets $(e_t, x_t, g_t; L)$ for which individuals' incomes equal $\tilde{z}$.[23] Using the definitions of z_t and $\tilde{z}$, it follows from (5.3) and (5.6) that the Malthusian Frontier is $MM \equiv \{(e_t, x_t, g_t; L) : x_t^{1-\alpha}h(e_t, g_t)^\alpha = \tilde{c}/(1-\gamma)\}$.

Let the Conditional Malthusian Frontier be the set of all pairs $(e_t, x_t; L)$ for which, conditional on a given technological level g_t, individuals' incomes equal $\tilde{z}$. Following the definitions of z_t and $\tilde{z}$, equations (5.3) and (5.6) imply that the Conditional Malthusian Frontier is $MM_{|g_t} \equiv \{(e_t, x_t; L) : x_t^{1-\alpha}h(e_t, g_t)^\alpha = \tilde{c}/(1-\gamma) \mid g_t\}$, where x_t is a decreasing, strictly convex function of e_t along the $MM_{|g_t}$ locus.

Hence, the Conditional Malthusian Frontier, as depicted in the bottom panels of Figures 5.2–5.4, is a strictly convex, downward sloping curve in the (e_t, x_t) space. Furthermore, it intersects the x_t axis and approaches asymptotically the

---

[22] See Galor (2007) for the analysis of discrete dynamical systems.

[23] Below the Malthusian Frontier, the effect of income on fertility will be positive, while above the frontier, there will be no effect of income on fertility. Thus, the Malthusian Frontier separates the Malthusian and Post-Malthusian Regimes, on the one hand, from the Modern Growth regime, on the other. Crossing this frontier is associated with the demographic transition.

e_t axis as x_t approaches infinity. The frontier shifts upward as g_t increases in the process of development.

The XX Locus

Let XX be the locus of all triplets $(e_t, g_t, x_t; L)$ such that the effective resources per worker, x_t, are in a steady state: $XX \equiv \{(e_t, x_t, g_t; L) : x_{t+1} = x_t\}$.

If the subsistence consumption constraint is not binding (i.e., if $z_t \geq \tilde{z}$), it follows from (5.16) that there exists a unique level, $e_t = \hat{e}(L)$, where $0 < \hat{e}(L) < e^h(L)$, such that $(\hat{e}(L), x_t) \in XX$, for all x_t for which $z_t \geq \tilde{z}$.[24] Moreover,

$$x_{t+1} - x_t \begin{cases} > 0, & \text{if } e_t > \hat{e}(L); \\ = 0, & \text{if } e_t = \hat{e}(L); \\ < 0, & \text{if } e_t < \hat{e}(L). \end{cases} \tag{5.20}$$

Hence, the XX Locus, as depicted in Figures 5.2(b)–5.4(b), is a vertical line above the Conditional Malthusian Frontier at level $\hat{e}(L)$.

If the subsistence constraint is binding, the evolution of x_t is based on the rate of technological change, g_t, and the effective resources per worker, x_t, as well as the quality of the labor force, e_t. Let $XX_{|g_t}$ be the locus of all pairs $(e_t, x_t; L)$ such that $x_{t+1} = x_t$, for a given level of g_t. That is, $XX_{|g_t} \equiv \{(e_t, x_t; L) : x_{t+1} = x_t \mid g_t\}$. It follows from (5.16) that for $z_t \leq \tilde{z}$, and for $0 \leq e_t \leq \hat{e}(L)$, there exists a single-valued function $x_t = x(e_t)$ such that $(x(e_t), e_t) \in XX_{|g_t}$. Moreover,

$$x_{t+1} - x_t \begin{cases} < 0, & \text{if } (e_t, x_t) > (e_t, x(e_t)) & \text{for } 0 \leq e_t \leq \hat{e}(L); \\ = 0, & \text{if } x_t = x(e_t) & \text{for } 0 \leq e_t \leq \hat{e}(L); \\ > 0, & \text{if } \{[(e_t, x_t) < (e_t, x(e_t)) & \text{for } 0 \leq e_t \leq \hat{e}(L)] \text{ or } [e_t > \hat{e}(L)]\}. \end{cases} \tag{5.21}$$

Hence, without loss of generality, the locus $XX_{|g_t}$ (i.e., the XX locus below the Conditional Malthusian Frontier) is depicted in Figure 5.2, as an upward sloping curve in the space (e_t, x_t), defined for $e_t \leq \hat{e}(L)$. $XX_{|g_t}$ is strictly below the Conditional Malthusian Frontier for values of $e_t < \hat{e}(L)$, and the two coincide at $\hat{e}(L)$. Moreover, the Conditional Malthusian Frontier, the XX locus above the Conditional Malthusian Frontier, and the $XX_{|g_t}$ locus coincide at $(\hat{e}(L), \hat{x}(L))$.

---

[24] To simplify the exposition without affecting the qualitative nature of the dynamical system, the parameters of the model are restricted to ensure that the XX locus is nonempty when $z_t \geq \tilde{z}$. That is, $\hat{g} < (\gamma/\tau) - 1 < g(e^h(L_0), L_0)$.

The EE Locus

Let EE be the locus of all triplets $(e_t, g_t, x_t; L)$ such that the quality of labor, e_t, is in a steady state: $EE \equiv \{(e_t, x_t, g_t; L) : e_{t+1} = e_t\}$.

As follows from (5.9) and (5.11), $e_{t+1} = e(g(e_t, L))$ and thus, for a given population size, the steady-state values of e_t are independent of the values of x_t and g_t. The locus EE evolves through three phases in the process of development, corresponding to the three phases that describe the evolution of education and technology, as depicted in Figures 5.2(b)–5.4(b).

In the early stages of development, when the population is sufficiently small, the joint evolution of education and technology is characterized by a globally stable temporary steady-state equilibrium, $(\bar{e}(L), \bar{g}(L)) = (0, g^l(L))$, as depicted in Figure 5.2(a). The corresponding EE locus, depicted in the space $(e_t, x_t; L)$ in Figure 5.2(b), is vertical at $e = 0$ for a range of small population. Furthermore, for this range, the global dynamics of e_t are given by

$$
e_{t+1} - e_t \begin{cases} = 0, & \text{if } e_t = 0; \\ < 0, & \text{if } e_t > 0. \end{cases} \tag{5.22}
$$

In later stages of development, as population increases sufficiently, the joint evolution of education and technology is characterized by multiple locally stable temporary steady-state equilibria, as depicted in Figure 5.3(a). The corresponding EE locus, depicted in the space $(e_t, x_t; L)$ in Figure 5.3(b), consists of three vertical lines corresponding to the three steady-state equilibria for the value of e_t, that is, $e = 0$, $e = e^u(L)$, and $e = e^h(L)$. The vertical lines $e = e^u(L)$ and $e = e^h(L)$ shift leftward and rightward, respectively, as population increases. Furthermore, the global dynamics of e_t in this configuration are given by

$$
e_{t+1} - e_t \begin{cases} < 0, & \text{if } 0 < e_t < e^u(L) \text{ or } e_t > e^h(L); \\ = 0, & \text{if } e_t \in \{0, \ e^u(L), \ e^h(L)\}; \\ > 0, & \text{if } e^u(L) < e_t < e^h(L). \end{cases} \tag{5.23}
$$

In mature stages of development, when the population is sufficiently large, the joint evolution of education and technology is characterized by a globally stable steady-state equilibrium, $(\bar{e}(L), \bar{g}(L)) = (e^h(L), g^h(L))$, as depicted in Figure 5.4(a). The corresponding EE locus, depicted in Figure 5.4(b) in the space $(e_t, x_t; L)$, is vertical at $e = e^h(L)$. This vertical line shifts rightward as population increases. Furthermore, the global dynamics of e_t in this configuration are given by

$$
e_{t+1} - e_t \begin{cases} > 0, & \text{if } 0 \le e_t < e^h(L); \\ = 0, & \text{if } e_t = e^h(L); \\ < 0, & \text{if } e_t > e^h(L). \end{cases} \tag{5.24}
$$

Conditional Steady-State Equilibria

In the early stages of development, when the population is sufficiently small, the dynamical system (Figure 5.2(b)) is characterized by a unique and globally stable conditional steady-state equilibrium given by the point of intersection of the EE and XX loci.[25] That is, conditional on a given technological level, g_t, the Malthusian steady-state equilibrium, $(0, \bar{x}^l(L))$, is globally stable.[26] In later stages of development, as population increases sufficiently, the dynamical system (Figure 5.3(b)) is characterized by two conditional steady-state equilibria. The Malthusian conditional steady-state equilibrium is locally stable, whereas the steady-state equilibrium $(e^u(L), x^u(L))$ is a saddle point.[27] For education levels above $e^u(L)$, the system converges to a stationary level of education $e^h(L)$ and possibly to a sustained positive growth rate of x_t. In mature stages of development, when the population is sufficiently large, the system converges globally to an education level $e^h(L)$ and possibly to a sustained positive growth rate of x_t (Figure 5.4(b)).

5.7   From Malthusian Stagnation to Sustained Growth

The economy evolves from an epoch of Malthusian stagnation through the Post-Malthusian Regime to the demographic transition and a Modern Growth Regime. This pattern and the prime driving forces in this transition emerge from the phase diagrams depicted in Figures 5.2–5.4.

Consider an economy in the early stages of development. The population is relatively small, and the implied slow rate of technological progress does not provide an incentive to invest in the education of children. As depicted in Figure 5.2(a), the interaction between education, e_t, and the rate of technological change, g_t, for a constant small population, L, is characterized by a globally stable steady-state equilibrium $(0, g^l(L))$, where education is zero and the rate of technological progress is slow. This steady-state equilibrium

---

[25] Since the dynamical system is discrete, the trajectories implied by the phase diagrams do not necessarily approximate the actual dynamic path, unless the state variables evolve monotonically over time. As shown, the evolution of e_t is monotonic, whereas the evolution and convergence of x_t may be oscillatory. Nonmonotonicity in the evolution of x_t may arise only if $e < \hat{e}$, and it does not affect the qualitative description of the system. Furthermore, if $\phi_x^a(l_t, g_t, x_t, L_t)x_t > -1$, the conditional dynamical system is locally nonoscillatory. The phase diagrams in Figures 5.2(b)–5.4(b) are drawn using assumptions that ensure no oscillations.

[26] The eigenvalues of the Jacobian matrix of the conditional dynamical system evaluated at the conditional steady-state equilibrium, $(0, \bar{x}(g_t))$, are both smaller than 1 in absolute value.

[27] Convergence to the saddle point takes place only if the level of education is e^u. That is, the saddle path is the entire vertical line that corresponds to $e_t = e^u$.

corresponds to a globally stable conditional Malthusian steady-state equilibrium, depicted in Figure 5.2(b). For a constant small population, L, and for a given rate of technological progress, effective resources per capita and level of education are constant, and output per capita is therefore constant as well. Moreover, shocks to population or resources are resolved in a classic Malthusian fashion.

As population grows slowly in reaction to technological progress, the $g(e_t; L)$ locus, depicted in Figure 5.2(a), gradually shifts upward, and the steady-state equilibrium shifts vertically upward, reflecting small increments in the rate of technological progress, while the level of education remains constant at zero. Similarly, the conditional Malthusian steady-state equilibrium (Figure 5.2(b)) shifts vertically upward as the XX locus shifts upward. However, output per capita remains initially constant at the subsistence level and ultimately creeps forward at a minuscule rate.

Over time, the slow growth in population that takes place in the Malthusian Regime raises the rate of technological progress and shifts the $g(e_t; L)$ locus in Figure 5.2 sufficiently upward, generating a qualitative change in the dynamical system, as depicted in Figure 5.3.

The dynamical system of education and technology for a moderate population is characterized by multiple history-dependent, stable, steady-state equilibria: $(0, g^l(L))$ and $(e^h(L), g^h(L))$ are locally stable, whereas $(e^u(L), g^u(L))$ is unstable. Given the initial conditions, in the absence of large shocks the economy remains in the vicinity of the low steady-state equilibrium $(0, g^l(L))$, where education is still zero but the rate of technological progress is moderate. These steady-state equilibria correspond to multiple locally stable, conditional Malthusian steady-state equilibria, depicted in Figure 5.3: a Malthusian steady state (characterized by constant resources per capita, slow technological progress, and no education) and a modern growth steady state (characterized by a high level of education, rapid technological progress, growing income per capita, and moderate population growth). However, since the economy starts in the vicinity of the Malthusian steady state, it remains there.[28]

As the rate of technological progress continues to rise in reaction to the increasing population, the $g(e_t; L)$ locus shifts upward further and ultimately, as depicted in Figure 5.4, the dynamical system experiences another qualitative change. The Malthusian steady-state equilibrium vanishes, and the conditional dynamical system is characterized by a unique, globally stable, modern steady-state equilibrium, $(e^h(L), g^h(L))$, with high levels of education and technological progress. The increase in the pace of technological progress has two

---

[28] Large shocks to education or technological progress would permit the economy to jump to the Modern Growth Regime steady state, but this possibility appears inconsistent with the evidence.

opposing effects on the evolution of population. On the one hand, it eases house-holds' budget constraints, allowing the allocation of more resources for raising children. On the other hand, it induces a reallocation of these additional re-sources toward child quality. In the Post-Malthusian Regime, due to the limited demand for human capital, the first effect dominates, and the rise in real income permits households to increase their family size as well as the quality of each child.[29] The interaction between investment in human capital and technologi-cal progress generates a virtuous circle: human capital formation prompts faster technological progress, further raising the demand for human capital, inducing further investment in child quality, and ultimately, as the economy crosses the Malthusian Frontier, triggering a demographic transition. The offsetting effect of population growth on the growth rate of income per capita is eliminated, and the interaction between human capital accumulation and technological progress permits a transition to a state of sustained economic growth.

In the Modern Growth Regime, resources per capita rise, as technological progress outpaces population growth. As the size of the population increases, its effect on the rate of technological progress declines asymptotically to zero. The $g(e_t; L)$ locus no longer shifts upward, and the level of education, technological progress, and the growth rates of resources per capita and thus output per capita converge to a constant, Modern Growth Regime, steady-state equilibrium.

5.8 Main Hypotheses

Unified Growth Theory generates several hypotheses about the evolution of population, human capital, and income per capita in the process of development. The theory generates testable predictions about (i) the fundamental factors that brought about the epoch of Malthusian stagnation that characterized most of human history, (ii) the causes of the remarkable escape from the Malthusian trap and the spike in growth rates of income per capita and population during the Post-Malthusian Regime, (iii) the economic forces that have led to the emergence of human capital formation in the process of development, (iv) the main trigger for the onset of the demographic transition, (v) the forces that have contributed to the emergence of the contemporary era of sustained economic

---

[29] Literally, income per capita does not change during the Post-Malthusian Regime; it remains fixed at the subsistence level. This is an artifact of the assumption that the only input into child quality and quantity is parental time, and that this time input does not produce measured output. If child rearing, especially the production of quality, requires goods, or if the time required to raise children can be purchased in the market (e.g., schooling), then the shift toward higher child quality that takes place during the Post-Malthusian Regime would be reflected in higher market expenditures (as opposed to parental time expenditures) and rising measured income.

growth, and (vi) the origins of the divergence in income per capita across countries.

H1 *In the early stages of development, economies were in the proximity of a stable Malthusian equilibrium. Resources generated by technological progress and land expansion were channeled into population growth and had a minuscule effect on income per capita in the long run. Periods marked by the absence of changes in the level of technology or in the availability of land were characterized by a stable population as well as constant income per capita. In contrast, episodes of technological progress, land expansion, and favorable climatic conditions brought about temporary gains in income per capita but ultimately triggered an increase in population, and thus a reduction in the land-labor ratio and income per capita toward its long-run level. Thus, technologically superior economies ultimately had denser populations, but their standard of living did not reflect the degree of their technological advancement.*

(i) During the initial phases of the Malthusian Epoch, the slow pace of technological progress (due to the limited size of the population) permitted nearly a full adjustment of the population to the expansion of resources and generated a proportional increase in output and population, keeping output per capita unchanged in the long run.

(ii) In the later phases of the Malthusian Epoch, the rise in the pace of technological progress (due to the increase in population size and density) generated an incomplete population adjustment, permitting a positive but very small growth rate of output per capita.

Hypothesis H1 is consistent with the time path of population and income per capita during 1–1500 CE. As reported in Section 2.1, the glacial pace of resource expansion in the first millennium was reflected in a minuscule growth of world population at an average rate of 0.02% per year, whereas the average growth rate of income per capita in the world economy was nearly zero. The more rapid, but still very slow, expansion of resources during 1000–1500 permitted world population to grow at a more rapid, but still very slow, rate of 0.1% per year, whereas the average growth rate of income per capita in the world economy grew at an average rate of about 0.05% per year. Moreover, cross-country evidence provided in Chapter 3 suggests that indeed, consistent with the prediction of Unified Growth Theory, the level of technology has a significant positive effect on population density in 1500 CE, 1000 CE, and 1 CE, whereas its effect on income per capita is an order of magnitude smaller and insignificantly different from zero.

H2 *The reinforcing interaction between population and technology during the Malthusian Epoch triggered a faster pace of technological progress and generated the transition to the Post-Malthusian Regime. Since the Malthusian mechanism was still in place, the expansion of resources that was brought about* *by the rapid pace of technological progress in the course of industrialization generated a spike in the growth rates of both income per capita and population. Although the expansion of resources was still partially counterbalanced by the enlargement of population, the delayed adjustment of population permitted the economy to experience rapid growth rates of income per capita.*

Hypothesis H2 is consistent with the evidence provided in Section 2.2 about the evolution of the world economy in the Post-Malthusian Regime. In particular, industrialization in Western European nations was associated with an increase in the growth rate of income per capita from an average annual rate of 0.15% during 1500–1820 to 0.95% during 1820–1870, and the average annual rate of population growth increased from 0.26% to 0.69%. A similar pattern was observed in all other regions during their periods of industrialization.

H3 *The acceleration in the rate of technological progress increased industrial demand for human capital toward the end of the Post-Malthusian Regime, inducing significant investment in human capital.*

Hypothesis H3 is consistent with the evidence, provided in Section 2.3, about the significant rise in industrial demand for human capital in the second phase of the Industrial Revolution and the subsequent marked increase in educational attainment.

H4 *The interaction between investment in human capital and technological progress generated a virtuous circle: human capital generated faster techno-logical progress, which in turn further raised the demand for human capital, inducing further investment in child quality, which ultimately triggered a de-cline in fertility rates and population growth.[30] The rise in demand for human capital in the second phase of industrialization induced the formation of human capital, which generated two opposing effects on population growth. On the one hand, the rise in income eased households' budget constraints, allowing the al-location of more resources for raising children. On the other hand, it induced a reallocation of resources toward child quality. In the Post-Malthusian Regime, due to the modest demand for human capital, the income effect dominated, and*

---

[30] It should be noted that the lack of clear evidence about the increase in the return on human capital in the second phase of the Industrial Revolution does not indicate the absence of a significant increase in demand for human capital during this period. The sizable increase in schooling that took place in the nineteenth century and, in particular, the introduction of public education, which lowered the cost of schooling (e.g., England's Education Act of 1870), generated a significant increase in the supply of educated workers that may have prevented a rise in return to education. Some of this supply response was a direct reaction of the potential increase in the return to human capital and thus may only operate to partially offset the increase in this return, but the reduction in the cost of education via public schooling generated an additional force that operated to reduce the return to human capital.

the rise in real income permitted households to increase the number as well as the quality of their children. But ultimately, the demand for human capital increased sufficiently so as to generate a decline in fertility.

This hypothesis is consistent with the evidence provided in Sections 2.2 and 2.3 that the rise in demand for human capital was associated initially with an increased investment in quality and quantity. Furthermore, Sections 2.4 and 4.3 show a wide array of evidence on the importance of human capital formation in the demographic transition, particularly in England, France, and Germany.

H5 *The onset of the demographic transition and the associated decline in population growth reduced the dilution of the stock of capital and land, enhanced investment in the human capital of the population, and altered the age distribution of the population, enhancing labor productivity per capita by temporarily increasing the size of the labor force relative to the population as a whole. Thus, this transition enabled economies to convert a larger share of the gains from factor accumulation and technological progress into growth of income per capita and paved the way for the emergence of sustained economic growth.*

Hypothesis H5 is consistent with the evidence provided in Section 2.4. In particular, as depicted in Figure 2.33, cross-country evidence suggests that contemporary income per capita and education are significantly and positively associated with the time elapsed since the demographic transition. In addition, the predicted timing of the acceleration in the growth rate of output per capita is consistent with the modern view of the British Industrial Revolution (e.g., Crafts, 1985; Crafts and Harley, 1992), which suggests that the first phase of the Industrial Revolution in England was characterized by a moderate increase in the growth rate of output per capita, whereas the take-off occurred only in the 1860s (Allen, 2006).

H6 *(i) Technological leaders experienced a monotonic increase in their growth rates of income per capita. Their growth was slow in the early stages of development, it increased rapidly during the take-off from the Malthusian Epoch, and it continued to rise, stabilizing at higher levels.*

(ii) Technological followers (who made the transition to sustained economic growth) experienced a nonmonotonic increase in their growth rates of income per capita. Their growth rates were slow in the early stages of development and increased rapidly in the early stages of the take-off from the Malthusian Epoch, boosted by the adoption of technologies from the existing technological frontier. However, once these economies reached the technological frontier, their growth rates dropped to the level of the technological leaders.

H7 *The differential timing of the take-off from stagnation to growth across economies triggered a divergence in income per capita across countries. It segmented economies into three clubs: a group of poor countries in the vicinity* *of the Malthusian equilibrium, a group of rich countries in the vicinity of the sustained growth equilibrium, and a third group in the transition from one club to the other.*

Hypotheses H6 and H7 are consistent with the evidence in Section 2.5 about the Great Divergence in the past centuries. Moreover, they are consistent with contemporary cross-country evidence that the growth process is characterized by multiple regimes (e.g., Durlauf and Johnson, 1995) and convergence clubs (Jones, 1997; Pritchett, 1997; Quah, 1997).

5.9 Complementary Mechanisms

The emergence of human capital formation and its impact on the demographic transition and the technological frontier are central forces in the transition from the Post-Malthusian Regime to the Modern Growth Regime in unified theories of economic growth in which population, technology, and income per capita are endogenously determined. Various complementary mechanisms that generate or reinforce the acceleration in technological progress, the rise in human capital formation, and the onset of the demographic transition have been proposed and examined quantitatively. These mechanisms have demonstrated that Unified Growth Theory can be augmented and fortified by additional characteristics of the transition from stagnation to growth without altering the fundamental hypothesis regarding the central role played by technological acceleration, the emergence of human capital formation, and the demographic transition in this process.

5.9.1 Sources of Human Capital Formation

The rise in demand for human capital, and thus the formation of human capi-tal, is attributed by Galor and Weil (2000), Galor and Moav (2002), and Galor (2005, 2010) to the acceleration of technological progress, underlying the role of educated individuals in coping with a rapidly changing technological envi-ronment. However, the link between industrial development and demand for hu-man capital could have been generated by various complementary mechanisms without altering the fundamental insights. In particular, the rise in demand for human capital could be reinforced by (i) capital accumulation in a technolog-ical environment characterized by capital-skill complementarity (Goldin and Katz, 1998; Fernández-Villaverde, 2001; Galor and Moav, 2004, 2006), (ii) the rise in the level of a skill-intensive industrial technology (Doepke, 2004), or (iii) increased specialization in the production of skill-intensive goods due to international trade (Galor and Mountford, 2008).

Moreover, while according to Unified Growth Theory, human capital formation is induced directly by the rise in demand for human capital, this mechanism is reinforced by several others:

a. The rising incentives of capitalists to support the provision of public education for the masses (Galor and Moav, 2006; Galor et al., 2009) and to establish child labor laws (Hazan and Berdugo, 2002; Doepke and Zilibotti, 2005).

b. The rise in demand for mental rather than physical labor in the course of development and its impact on women's labor force participation and thus the profitability of their investment in human capital (Galor and Weil, 1996).

c. The impact of technological progress in contraceptive methods and home appliances on women's labor force participation and the incentive to accumulate human capital (Goldin and Katz, 2002; Greenwood et al., 2005b) and its subsequent effect on preferences for educated wives who participate in the labor market (Fernández et al., 2004).

d. The effect of economic development on the extension of women's political rights (Doepke and Tertilt, 2009) and thus human capital formation.

e. An improvement in the health infrastructure and its effect on individuals' capacity to produce and benefit from human capital (Ehrlich and Lui, 1991; Galor and Weil, 1999; Boucekkine et al., 2003; Cervellati and Sunde, 2005; Soares, 2005; Hazan and Zoabi, 2006; Tamura, 2006; Chakraborty et al., 2008; Lorentzen et al., 2008).

f. The evolution of preferences for offspring quality (Galor and Moav, 2002).[31]

g. The reduction in the cost of education due to increased population density (Boucekkine et al., 2007).

5.9.2 Triggers of the Demographic Transition

The onset of the demographic transition is traced by Galor and Weil (2000) and Galor and Moav (2002) to the rise in demand for human capital and the inducement that it provides to substitute quality for quantity of children. However, the link among industrial development, technological progress, human capital formation, and the demographic transition could be generated by various complementary mechanisms without altering the fundamental insights.

In particular, the demographic transition could be generated by (i) female-biased technical change that increases the opportunity cost of child rearing more than household income (Galor and Weil, 1996); (ii) the decline in benefits from

---

[31] For the effect of institutions on the evolution of preferences see Bowles (1998).

child labor (Hazan and Berdugo, 2002; Doepke, 2004; Doepke and Zilibotti, 2005); (iii) the decline in mortality rates and improvement in health infrastructure (Galor and Weil, 1999; Kalemli-Ozcan, 2002; Lagerlöf, 2003a; Hazan and Zoabi, 2006; Tamura, 2006; Cervellati and Sunde, 2008; de la Croix and Licandro, 2009; and Bar and Leukhina, 2010); (iv) globalization and its effect on demand for human capital (McDermott, 2002; Galor and Mountford, 2006, 2008); (v) the evolution of preferences for offspring quality (Galor and Moav, 2002); or (vi) the transition from agriculture to industry (Strulik and Weisdorf, 2008).

5.9.3 Engines of Technological Progress

The rise in the pace of technological progress in the early stages of development is attributed to the inherent Malthusian interaction between population and technology, whereas its intensification in later stages of development is linked to the rise in human capital formation.[32] Alternatively, the acceleration can be generated by (i) a gradual movement from a slowly growing agricultural technology to rapidly evolving industrial technology (Hansen and Prescott, 2002); (ii) the evolution of markets (Desmet and Parente, 2009); (iii) institutions conducive to research and development (Mokyr, 2002; Acemoglu et al., 2005b; Milionis and Klasing, 2010); (iv) globalization (O'Rourke and Williamson, 2005; Galor and Mountford, 2006, 2008); (v) improved knowledge transmission (Mokyr, 2002; Lucas, 2009; Bar and Leukhina, 2010); or (vi) a selection of educated, entrepreneurial individuals in the process of development (Galor and Moav, 2002; Galor and Michalopoulos, 2006).

5.9.4 The Transition from an Agricultural to an Industrial Economy

The structure of the aggregate production function and its interaction with technological progress in Unified Growth Theory reflects implicitly a transition from an agricultural to an industrial economy that accompanied the transition from stagnation to growth. In Galor and Weil (2000), production occurs according to a constant-returns-to-scale technology that is subject to endogenous technological progress. The output produced in period t is $Y_t = H_t^\alpha (A_t X)^{1-\alpha}$, where H_t is the aggregate quantity of efficiency units of labor employed in period t, X is land employed in production in every period t, and A_t represents the endogenously determined technological level in period t. Hence $A_t X$ is the "effective resources" employed in production in period t. In the early stages of development, the economy is agricultural (i.e., the fixed amount of land is a binding constraint on the expansion of the economy). Population growth reduces labor productivity, since the rate of technological progress is not sufficiently high to compensate for the land constraint. However, as the rate of

---

[32] If the ability to innovate is limited at lower levels of income (e.g., due to malnutrition), the Malthusian trap will be prolonged (Guzman, 2010).

technological progress intensifies in the process of development, the economy becomes industrial. Technological progress counterbalances the land constraint, the role of land gradually diminishes, and effective resources expand at a rate that permits sustained economic growth.

An explicit modeling of the transition from agriculture to industry (e.g., Hansen and Prescott, 2002; Doepke, 2004; Ngai, 2004; Bertocchi, 2006; Galor and Mountford, 2008; Galor et al., 2009; Mourmouras and Rangazas, 2009) does not alter the fundamental insights of Unified Growth Theory. Namely, the acceleration in technological progress and its impact on demand for human capital and thus on the decline of population growth is a critical force in the transition from stagnation to growth. Nevertheless, it highlights the potential role of an increase in agricultural productivity in the process of industrialization (Gollin et al., 2002).

In particular, Hansen and Prescott (2002) develop a model that captures explicitly the shift from an agricultural sector to an industrial one. In the early stages of development, the industrial technology is not sufficiently productive, and production takes place solely in an agricultural sector, where population growth (which is assumed to increase with income) offsets increases in productivity. Exogenous technological progress in the latent constant-returns-to-scale industrial technology ultimately makes the industrial sector economically viable, and the economy gradually shifts resources from the agricultural to the industrial sector. Assuming that the positive effect of income on population is reversed, the rise in productivity in the industrial sector is not counterbalanced by population growth, permitting transition to a state of sustained economic growth.

Unlike unified theories in which the time paths of technological progress, population growth, and human capital formation are endogenously determined on the basis of explicit microfoundations, in Hansen and Prescott (2002): (i) technological progress is exogenous, (ii) population growth is assumed to follow the hump-shaped pattern that is observed over human history, and (iii) human capital formation (which appears central for the transition) is absent. Based upon this reduced-form approach, they demonstrate that there exists a rate of technological progress in the latent industrial sector, and a well-specified reduced-form relationship between population and output, under which the economy will shift from Malthusian stagnation to sustained economic growth. This reduced-form analysis, however, does not advance the objective of identifying the underlying microfoundations that led to the transition from stagnation to growth—the ultimate goal of Unified Growth Theory.

In accordance with the main hypothesis of Galor and Weil (2000), the transition from stagnation to growth in Hansen and Prescott (2002) is associated with an increase in productivity growth in the economy as a whole. Although productivity growth in each sector is constant, a shift toward the higher productivity growth sector that is associated with the transition increases the productivity in the economy, permitting the take-off to an era of sustained economic growth. Moreover, although formally the transition from stagnation to growth in Hansen and Prescott (2002) does not rely on the forces of human capital, if microfoundations for the critical factors behind the transition had been properly established, human capital would have played a central role in sustaining the rate of technological progress in the industrial sector and in generating the demographic transition. The lack of an explicit role for human capital in their structure is an artifact of the reduced-form analysis, which does not identify the economic factors behind the process of technological change in the latent industrial technology or those behind the assumed hump-shaped pattern of population dynamics.[33] Thus, Hansen and Prescott's explicit modeling of the transition from agriculture to industry does not alter the basic insights from the framework of Galor and Weil—a rise in productivity and a rise in demand for human capital are critical for take-off.[34]

Nevertheless, as discussed in the next chapter, a two-sector framework is instrumental in the exploration of the effect of international trade on the differential timing of the transition from stagnation to growth and the associated phenomenon of the Great Divergence (Galor and Mountford, 2008). Moreover, this framework is necessary to examine the incentives of landowners to block education reforms and the development of the industrial sector (Galor et al., 2009).

5.10 Calibrations of Unified Growth Theory

Lagerlöf (2006) provides a quantitative analysis of the benchmark model of Unified Growth Theory. The analysis demonstrates that the theory quantitatively replicates the observed time paths of population, income per capita, and human capital, generating: (i) a Malthusian Epoch; (ii) an endogenous take-off from Malthusian stagnation that is associated with an acceleration in technological progress and is accompanied initially by a rapid increase in population

---

[33] The demographic pattern assumed by Hansen and Prescott (2002) is critical for the transition from Malthusian stagnation to sustained economic growth. Moreover, human capital appears to be the implicit underlying force behind their transition. To generate the features of the Malthusian economy, they set the pace of population growth during this epoch at a level that would generate zero growth rate of output per capita. In the absence of change in this pattern of population growth, output per capita growth is not feasible. Thus, to generate output growth along with population growth during the take-off, they assume that at a certain stage, the rise in population growth did not fully offset the rise in output (suggesting that parental resources were channeled partly into child quality in light of a rising demand for human capital).

[34] A binding biological upper bound on the level of fertility on the eve of industrialization could have generated a take-off mechanically, due to the implied lack of population response to increased resources generated by technological change. However, the evidence shows that in Western Europe, fertility rates continued to increase for nearly a century after the initial take-off.

growth; and (iii) a rise in demand for human capital, followed by a demographic transition and sustained economic growth.

The calibration is based on specific functional forms for the production function of human capital and the rate of technological progress. First, as in the benchmark model, the level of human capital of a child of a member of generation t, h_{t+1}, is an increasing, strictly concave function of the parental time investment in the education of the child, e_{t+1}, and a decreasing, strictly convex function of the rate of technological progress, g_{t+1}. The specific functional form for the production function of human capital, (5.6), that is used in the calibration is

$$h_{t+1} = h(e_{t+1}, g_{t+1}) = \frac{e_{t+1} + \rho\tau}{e_{t+1} + \rho\tau + g_{t+1}}, \tag{5.25}$$

where $e_{t+1} + \rho\tau$ is the parental contribution to the education of each child, e_{t+1} is the parental direct investment in each child's education, and $\rho\tau$ is the contribution of the fixed time cost associated with child rearing, τ, to human capital formation, where $0 < \rho < 1$.

Second, as in the benchmark model, the rate of technological progress, g_{t+1}, that takes place between periods t and $t+1$, depends on the education per capita of the working generation in period t, e_t, and the size of the working population in period t, L_t. The specific functional form for the rate of technological progress, (5.11), that is used in the calibration is

$$g_{t+1} = g(e_t, L_t) = \begin{cases} (e_t + \rho\tau)\theta L_t, & \text{if } L_t < a^*/\theta; \\ (e_t + \rho\tau)a^* & \text{if } L_t \geq a^*/\theta, \end{cases} \tag{5.26}$$

where $\theta > 0$, and $a^* > 0$. Namely, the rate of technological progress between periods t and $t+1$ depends on the level of education per adult in period t, $e_t + \rho\tau$, as well as on the size of the adult population. Thus, $g_{t+1} > 0$ even if $e_t = 0$, but above a certain population size, further technological progress depends only on the level of education.

If the parameters of the model are chosen such that (i) labor share $\alpha = 0.6$, (ii) fixed time cost of children $\tau = 0.28$, (iii) contribution of the fixed time cost associated with child rearing to education $\rho = 0.851$, (iv) weight on children in the utility function $\gamma = 0.355$, (v) scale effect $\theta = 1$, (vi) upper limit on the contribution of population to technological progress $a^*/\theta = 7.54$, (vii) subsistence consumption $\tilde{c} = 1$, and (viii) land size $X = 1$, and if the initial conditions are such that (1) initial fertility $n_0 = 1$, (2) initial population $L_0 = 0.287$, (3) initial education $e_0 = 0$, (4) initial technological progress $g_0 = 0.048$, (5) initial technological level $A_0 = 0.951$, and (6) initial level of potential

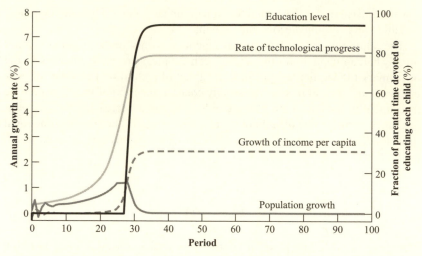

FIGURE 5.5. A quantitative analysis of Unified Growth Theory.
Summary: The figure describes the time path of the level of education, e_t, the average annual growth rates (in percentages) of population, L_t; technology, A_t; and potential income per worker, z_t. The growth rate of income increases from zero in the Malthusian Epoch to more than 2% in the era of sustained economic growth. The take-off from the Malthusian Epoch is associated initially with a rise in population growth, but human capital formation and the decline in population growth permit transition to an era of sustained economic growth.

income per worker $z_0 = 1.176$, then the patterns that emerge, as depicted in Figure 5.5, are consistent with those observed in human history.[35]

Calibrations of complementary models confirm the main insight of the benchmark model. They demonstrate the role of either the rise in the rate of technological progress or in demand for skilled workers at the onset of the demographic transition and the shift to an era of sustained economic growth. Hansen and Prescott (2002) calibrate their model so that (1) the initial Malthusian era is consistent with the growth facts describing the English economy prior to 1800, (2) the pure industrial regime matches the growth facts describing post–World War II industrialized economies, (3) the population growth rate reacts to changing living standards in a hump-shaped fashion, and (4) the implied annual rate of return on capital is consistent with available data. The analysis suggests that the transition from the point at which the industrial technology is

---

[35] Since the time spent raising children is constant in the steady state (i.e., since e and n are constant in the long run), the growth rate of z in the long run is equal to the growth rate in income per capita.

first used until more than 99% of the resources are allocated to the industrial sector takes about 105 years. Furthermore, as emphasized in the benchmark model of Unified Growth Theory, the rise in the growth rate of productivity associated with the transition from a low to a high productivity growth sector is associated initially with a rise followed by a decline in population growth and a monotonic increase in the growth rate of output per capita.[36] Augmenting Hansen and Prescott's framework by education and fertility choices, Doepke (2004) finds that, in line with the predictions of the Galor and Weil model, educational and child labor policies during this period are important for understanding the demographic transition.

Fernández-Villaverde (2001) constructs an overlapping-generations model with capital-skill complementarity and endogenous fertility, mortality, and education that is parametrized to match English data during the demographic transition of 1875–1920. The calibration shows that capital-specific technological change that matches the observed fall in the relative price of capital equipment accounts for more than 60% of the fall in fertility and more than 50% of the increase in income per capita over this period. Furthermore, the calibration shows that neutral technological change or the reduction in mortality cannot account for the fall in fertility.

5.11 Concluding Remarks

Unified Growth Theory unveils the principal economic forces that have generated the remarkable transition from stagnation to growth and underlines their significance for understanding the contemporary growth process of both developed and less developed economies. It identifies the role of historical and prehistorical characteristics in the divergence of income per capita across regions of the world in the past two centuries, and it sheds light on the interaction between economic development and human evolution and the potential role of evolutionary processes in the transition from stagnation to growth.

Consistent with the evidence, the theory suggests that the transition from stagnation to growth is an inevitable by-product of the process of development. It argues that the inherent Malthusian interaction between the rate of technological progress and the size and composition of the population accelerated the pace of technological progress and ultimately raised the importance of human capital in the rapidly changing technological environment. The rise in demand for human capital and its impact on human capital formation triggered a

---

[36] Bar and Leukhina's (2010) quantitative analysis of the evolution of the English economy does not support the conclusions of Hansen and Prescott (2002) that stagnation is generated because the industrial sector is idle and that the structural transformation and take-off in income growth transpire under constant, sector-specific productivity growth rates.

reduction in fertility rates and population growth and spurred further technological advances. The demographic transition has enabled economies to divert
a larger share of the gains from factor accumulation and technological progress
from fueling population growth to the enhancement of human capital formation and income per capita, thus paving the way for the emergence of sustained
economic growth.[37]

5.12 Appendix: Optimal Investment in Child Quality

The individual optimization (5.7) with respect to e_{t+1} implies that, independently of the subsistence-consumption constraint, the implicit functional relationship between e_{t+1} and g_{t+1} is given by

$$G(e_{t+1}, g_{t+1}) \equiv (\tau + e_{t+1})h_e(e_{t+1}, g_{t+1}) - h(e_{t+1}, g_{t+1}) \begin{cases} = 0, & \text{if } e_{t+1} > 0; \\ \leq 0, & \text{if } e_{t+1} = 0, \end{cases}$$

$$(5.27)$$

where $G_e(e_{t+1}, g_{t+1}) < 0$ and $G_g(e_{t+1}, g_{t+1}) > 0, \forall g_{t+1} \geq 0$ and $\forall e_{t+1} > 0$.

Furthermore, to ensure that for some positive level of g_{t+1} the chosen level
of education is 0 (i.e., investment in human capital is profitable only in a
sufficiently rapidly progressing technological environment), it is assumed that

$$G(0, 0) = \tau h_e(0, 0) - h(0, 0) < 0. \tag{5.A1}$$

Lemma 5.1 *If Assumption 5.A1 is satisfied, then the level of education chosen
by members of generation t for their children is an increasing function of* g_{t+1}:

$$e_{t+1} = e(g_{t+1}) \begin{cases} = 0, & \text{if } g_{t+1} \leq \hat{g}; \\ > 0, & \text{if } g_{t+1} > \hat{g} \end{cases}$$

where, $\hat{g} > 0$, *and*

$$e'(g_{t+1}) > 0 \,\forall g_{t+1} > \hat{g}.$$

Proof. As follows from the properties of $h(e_{t+1}, g_{t+1})$ and $G(e_{t+1}, g_{t+1})$,
given by (5.6) and (5.27), $G(0, g_{t+1})$ is monotonically increasing in g_{t+1}. Furthermore, $\lim_{g_{t+1} \to \infty} G(0, g_{t+1}) > 0$ and, as follows from Assumption 5.A1,
$G(0, 0) < 0$. Hence, there exists $\hat{g} > 0$ such that $G(0, \hat{g}) = 0$, and therefore, as
follows from (5.27), $e_{t+1} = 0$ for $g_{t+1} \leq \hat{g}$. Furthermore, e_{t+1} is a single-valued
function of g_{t+1}, where $e'_{t+1}(g_{t+1}) = -G_g(e_{t+1}, g_{t+1})/G_e(e_{t+1}, g_{t+1}) > 0$.

---

[37] Importantly, some have argued that economic growth is essential for greater opportunity,
tolerance of diversity, social mobility, commitment to fairness, and dedication to democracy
(Friedman, 2005).

CHAPTER 6

Unified Growth Theory and Comparative Development

> *If the misery of the poor be caused not by the laws of nature, but by our institutions, great is our sin.*
> —Charles Darwin

This chapter derives the implications of Unified Growth Theory for comparative economic development across the globe. It explores the role of cultural, institutional, and geographical factors in the differential pace of the transition from stagnation to growth across countries and the emergence of the contemporary global disparity in economic development. Further, it establishes the persistent effect of deep-rooted factors (e.g., migratory distance from the cradle of mankind in East Africa and the determinants of the onset of the Neolithic Revolution) on the global variations in the process of development. Finally, it explores the implications of Unified Growth Theory for the understanding of the origins of multiple growth regimes and convergence clubs.

Theories of comparative development highlight a variety of proximate and ultimate factors underlying some of the vast inequities in living standards across the globe. The importance of geographical, cultural, and institutional factors; human capital formation; ethnic, linguistic, and religious fractionalization; legal origins; colonialism; and globalization has been at the center of a debate regarding the origins of the differential timing of transitions from stagnation to growth and the remarkable transformation of the world income distribution in the past two centuries. While theoretical and empirical research has typically focused on the contemporaneous effects of such factors, attention has recently been drawn toward prehistorical factors that have been argued to affect the course of comparative economic development from the dawn of human civilization to the modern era.

The role of favorable geographical conditions in fostering the earlier European take-off from Malthusian stagnation and the divergence in income per capita around the globe has been given precedence by Jones (1981), Diamond (1997), Gallup et al. (1999), and Pomeranz (2000). They argue that the earlier rise of Europe can be attributed to its favorable biogeographical factors, natural resource base, abundant rainfall, temperate climate, lower disease burden, and geographical proximity to the New World, all of which facilitated the escape from the Malthusian trap.[1]

The persistent effect of institutions has been emphasized by North (1981), Knack and Keefer (1995), Hall and Jones (1999), Engerman and Sokoloff (2000), Acemoglu et al. (2001), Glaeser and Shleifer (2002), Mokyr (2002), Helpman (2004), and Greif (2006).[2] This research suggests that institutional factors that facilitated the protection of individual property rights, and enhanced technological innovations and the diffusion of knowledge, were the prime forces behind the earlier European transition to sustained economic growth and the divergence in economic performance around the globe.

Moreover, the endogenous nature of sociopolitical institutions, coupled with the inherent exogeneity of geography, has prompted some researchers to propose that initial geographical conditions gave rise to persistent differences in institutional quality across regions.[3] Engerman and Sokoloff (2000) argue that societies characterized by geographical factors conducive to income inequality implemented oppressive institutions designed to preserve the unequal distribution of wealth within their populations. Acemoglu et al. (2002) suggest that historical reversals in the economic performance of societies have a colonial legacy that reflects the imposition of extractive institutions by European colonizers in regions that were relatively affluent in the pre-colonial era.[4] Galor et al. (2009) underline the negative impact of inequality in the distribution of land ownership on the emergence of human capital–promoting policies.[5]

---

[1] The geographical hypothesis has also stressed an indirect role of geography in promoting the earlier European take-off. It has been argued, particularly by Jones (1981), that the natural barriers created by Europe's mountain chains and rivers prevented a single state from dominating the entire territory and eventually led to sociopolitical fragmentation and competition, encouraging innovative activities that contributed to an earlier take-off.

[2] See also Greif (1993), Sussman and Yafeh (2000), Shiue and Keller (2007), and Michalopoulos and Papaioannou (2010). The persistent effects of democratic institutions are examined by Persson and Tabellini (2006) and Acemoglu et al. (2008), and that of coercive labor institutions by Nunn (2008) and Dell (2010).

[3] Empirical investigations by Easterly and Levine (2003) and Rodrik et al. (2004) support the hypothesis that the geographical determinism of contemporary economic development operates primarily through the effects of initial geographical conditions on institutional quality.

[4] Additional aspects of the long-run effects of European colonialism on comparative economic development are examined at the country level for India by Banerjee and Iyer (2005) and at the cross-country level for Africa by Bertocchi and Canova (2002). In general, the findings in these studies are broadly consistent with the notion of a deleterious institutional legacy of European colonialism in the colonized regions.

[5] Brezis et al. (1993), in contrast, attribute technological leapfrogging to acquired comparative advantage of technological leaders in the use of existing technologies.

The significance of sociocultural factors in giving rise to the differential development trajectories of Europe and Asia has been the focus of an influential hypothesis raised originally by Max Weber in his works on the sociology of religion (Weber, 1905) and promoted more recently by Knack and Keefer (1997), Landes (1998), Barro and McCleary (2003), Fernández et al. (2004), Guiso et al. (2006), Ashraf and Galor (2007), and Tabellini (2010). The Weberian viewpoint attributes the rise of industrialization in the Western world to the proclivity of European culture for rationalism and an objective "disenchantment of the world." Moreover, the emphasis placed by Oriental culture on rigid aesthetic values of self-perfection and filial piety is held responsible for the delayed transition to a sustained growth regime in the East.[6]

The role of ethnic, linguistic, and religious fractionalization in the emergence of divergence has been linked to their effect on the quality of institutions. Easterly and Levine (1997) and Alesina et al. (2003) have demonstrated that geopolitical factors that brought about a high degree of fractionalization in some regions of the world led to the implementation of institutions detrimental for economic growth and, consequently, to a divergence in developmental paths across societies.

Finally, the importance of human capital formation and the onset of the demographic transition in giving rise to and sustaining the Great Divergence is stressed in Unified Growth Theory. The persistent effects of the level of human capital have been examined empirically by Glaeser et al. (2004) and those of the diversity of human capital by Ashraf and Galor (2009).

Unified Growth Theory sheds light on three aspects of comparative economic development. First, it generates a hypothesis about the factors that govern the pace of the transition from Malthusian stagnation to an era of sustained economic growth and thus the emergence of significant differences in economic development across countries and regions. Second, it suggests that initial biogeographical conditions determined tens of thousands of years ago have had a persistent effect on comparative economic development across the globe via their effect on the composition of the human population. Third, it advances the understanding of the origins of multiple growth regimes and convergence clubs that are often found in cross-country analyses of economic growth.

---

[6] In this context, the term "culture" refers to the set of society's norms, beliefs, customs, traditions, taboos, codes of conduct, and the like and is, therefore, distinct from the notion of institutions, which has traditionally been regarded in the literature as embodying the sociopolitical environment as determined by constitutions, rule of law, and property rights. North (1981), however, has advanced a broader notion of institutions in terms of a set of constraints imposed to structure socioeconomic interaction. These include both informal constraints, such as customs and traditions, as well as formal constraints, such as laws and property rights.

The theory suggests that the interaction between the rate of technological progress and the size and composition of the population has been pivotal in the transition from stagnation to growth. Nevertheless, this vital interaction between population and technological progress has been affected by a large number of country-specific characteristics (e.g., biogeographical, cultural, and institutional factors, as well as public policy and trade). They have affected the intensity of the positive feedback between population and technology in the Malthusian Epoch, the strength of the effect of human capital on technological progress in the Post-Malthusian Regime, and the significance of the rise in demand for human capital on the pace of human capital formation and fertility decline in the transition to the Modern Growth Regime. These country-specific characteristics have generated, therefore, variations in the pace of transition from stagnation to growth as well as differences in the steady-state levels of income per capita across countries.

Thus, country-specific characteristics that have affected the rate of technological progress—the level of protection of intellectual property rights; the stock of knowledge; the composition of ethnic, religious, and interest groups; the degree of diversity; the availability of complementary natural resources; and the propensity to trade—have contributed to the differential pace of the transition from stagnation to growth and comparative economic development across the globe. Further, once the technologically driven demand for human capital emerged in the process of development, setting the stage for a take-off from stagnation to growth, the prevalence of characteristics conducive to human capital formation influenced the swiftness of its accumulation, the timing of the demographic transition, the pace of the transition from stagnation to growth, and thereby the observed distribution of income in the world economy. In particular, country-specific characteristics that have affected human capital formation—the availability and accessibility of public education, credit-market imperfections, the stock of knowledge in society, religious composition, the degree of inequality in society, the distribution of ownership over factors of production, and the economy's comparative advantage—affected the differential pace of the transition from agriculture to industry and comparative economic development around the globe.

6.1 Country-Specific Characteristics and the Growth Process

In its first layer, Unified Growth Theory identifies the factors that have governed the pace of the transition from stagnation to growth and have thus contributed to the observed differences in economic development across countries. Unified Growth Theory contains two theoretical black boxes: the effect of population size and level of human capital on the rate of technological progress and the effect of the rate of technological progress on human capital formation. As these black boxes are opened and filled with additional characteristics that affect the incentives for and the constraints on technological innovations and human capital formation, variation in these characteristics across countries should account for variations in economic development around the globe.

6.1.1 Factors Contributing to Technological Progress

Suppose that, as postulated in the basic model, technological progress that takes place between periods t and $t + 1$ in country i, g_{t+1}^i, depends on the level of education per capita among the working generation in country i in period t, e_t^i, and the population size in country i in period t, L_t^i, as well as on country-specific factors, Ω_t^i, that affect technological progress. Then technological progress can be represented as

$$g_{t+1}^i = g(e_t^i, L_t^i, \Omega_t^i), \tag{6.1}$$

where for a sufficiently large population $g(0, L_t^i, \Omega_t^i) > 0$, $g_j(e_t^i, L_t^i, \Omega_t^i) > 0$, and $g_{jj}(e_t^i, L_t^i, \Omega_t^i) < 0$, $j = e_t^i, L_t^i, \Omega_t^i$. Hence, the rate of technological progress between periods t and $t + 1$ is a positive (even in the absence of investment in human capital), increasing, strictly concave function of the size and level of education of the working generation in period t, as well as of country-specific factors that are conducive to technological progress.

For given levels of population and human capital, (e_t^i, L_t^i), the rate of technological progress is governed by a number of country-specific characteristics:

a. The level of protection of intellectual property rights may have an ambiguous effect on technological progress, reflecting the trade-off between the positive effect of intellectual property rights on the incentive to innovate and its adverse effect on the proliferation of existing knowledge.[7]
b. The stock of knowledge in a society and its rate of creation and diffusion may create a platform on which faster technological innovations can emerge (Mokyr, 1990, 2002; Helpman and Trajtenberg, 1998).[8]

---

[7] The optimal level of protection of intellectual property rights may be altered in the process of development, and thus, countries in different stages of development may benefit from different policies on intellectual property rights (e.g., Diwan and Rodrik, 1991).

[8] Moreover, variation in the price of capital goods and thus in investment-specific technological change may foster technological progress (Greenwood et al., 1997)

c. Competition may discourage laggard firms from innovating but encourages neck-and-neck firms to innovate (Aghion et al., 2005).

d. The degree of credit-market imperfections and inequality in a society may affect human capital formation, entrepreneurial activities, and technological advancements (Galor and Zeira, 1993; Banerjee and Newman, 1993; Lloyd-Ellis and Bernhardt, 2000; Aghion et al., 2005; Levine, 2005).

e. The composition of cultural and religious groups in a society and their attitude toward knowledge creation and diffusion may affect the incentives to innovate and the proliferation rate of innovations (Weber, 1905).[9]

f. The composition of interest groups in society may affect the incentives to block or promote technological innovation (Acemoglu et al., 2005a).[10]

g. The degree of diversity in a society, as reflected by the composition of human capital, may provide a wider spectrum of traits that are complementary to the implementation of advanced technological paradigms, but it may reduce cooperation and thus the efficiency of the production process (Ashraf and Galor, 2009).

h. The intensity of concerns about relative standing may deter or enhance innovation, depending on economic, institutional, and cultural characteristics (Jones, 1981).[11]

i. The propensity of a country to trade, reflecting its geographical characteristics as well as its trade policy, may foster technological diffusion across nations (Grossman and Helpman, 1991; Hausmann et al., 2007).

j. The existence of complementary natural resources (Ashton, 1948) and alternative modes of production (Zeira, 1998) may affect the implementation of a looming technological paradigm.[12]

---

[9] The intensity of these forces may reflect geographical factors (Ashraf and Galor, 2007). For instance, Iyigun (2008) suggests that Ottoman advances in Europe benefited the Protestant Reformation. Thus, the intensity of some of these forces in Europe may have been affected by geographical proximity to the Ottoman Empire.

[10] Interest groups (e.g., colonialists, landed aristocracies, and monopolies) may block the introduction of new technologies to protect their political power and thus maintain their rent extractions (Olson, 1982; Krusell and Rios-Rull, 1996; Parente and Prescott, 2000; Persson and Tabellini, 2002; Acemoglu et al., 2005a; Brezis and Temin, 2008).

[11] Some observers have underlined the importance of competition across states in the early industrialization of Europe (Jones, 1981), while others have explored the impact of the importance that individuals attribute to their relative standing in society on the process of development (Gershman, 2010).

[12] Natural resource abundance may have an adverse effect on technological adoption (Berdugo et al., 2009), education, and economic development (Gylfason, 2001).

6.1.2 Reinforcing Elements in Human Capital Formation

Suppose that, as underlined in the basic model, the level of human capital of a child of a member of generation t in country i, h^i_{t+1}, is an increasing strictly concave function of the parental time investment in the education of the child, e^i_{t+1}, and a decreasing strictly convex function of the rate of technological progress, g^i_{t+1}. Suppose further that it is affected by country-specific characteristics, ϕ^i_t, that may affect the cost of education, its availability for different segments of society, and the efficiency of human capital formation. Namely,

$$h^i_{t+1} = h(e^i_{t+1}, g^i_{t+1}, \phi^i_t), \tag{6.2}$$

where ϕ^i_t is a vector of country-specific characteristics that affect the production of human capital.

Suppose that, as postulated in the basic model, individuals' preferences in country i are represented by a utility function, u^i_t, defined over consumption above a subsistence level, $\tilde{c} > 0$, as well as over the quantity and quality of their (surviving) children. Suppose further that the degree of preference for child quality, as captured by the preference parameter, $\mu^i_t \in (0, 1)$, varies across countries. Namely,

$$u^i_t = (1 - \gamma) \ln(c^i_t) + \gamma \ln[(n^i_t)^{1-\mu^i_t}(h^i_{t+1})^{\mu^i_t}], \qquad \gamma \in (0, 1), \tag{6.3}$$

where c^i_t is the consumption of a member of generation t, n^i_t is the number of (surviving) children of a member of generation t, and h^i_{t+1} is the level of human capital of each child in country i.

Investment in education, as follows from (5.7), (5.9), (6.2), and (6.3), depends on the rate of technological progress, g^i_{t+1}, as well as on a number of country-specific characteristics captured by the vector $\Psi^i_t \equiv [\phi^i_t, \mu^i_t]$, that is,

$$e^i_{t+1} = e(g^i_{t+1}; \Psi^i_t) \begin{cases} = 0, & \text{if } g^i_{t+1} \leq \hat{g}(\Psi^i_t); \\ > 0, & \text{if } g^i_{t+1} > \hat{g}(\Psi^i_t), \end{cases} \tag{6.4}$$

where $e_g(g^i_{t+1}; \Psi^i_t) > 0$ and $e_{gg}(g^i_{t+1}; \Psi^i_t) < 0$, $\forall g^i_{t+1} > \hat{g}(\Psi^i_t)$.

Hence, human capital formation would depend on a number of country-specific factors:[13]

---

[13] Hendricks (2010) finds that current variation in education across countries is primarily due to variation in skill intensities within industry rather than to variation in sectoral composition. The factors listed in the text may affect the skill-intensity within an industry as well as the prominence of the industrial sector.

a. The prevalence of human capital–promoting institutions or policies (e.g., the availability, accessibility, and quality of public education and child labor regulations) affects the extent of human capital formation (Hanushek and Woessmann, 2008). It may partly reflect the distribution of ownership over factors of production and the desirability of human capital formation for capitalists and landed aristocracy (see Acemoglu and Robinson, 2000; Bourguignon and Verdier, 2000; Gradstein and Justman, 2002; Galor and Moav, 2006; Gradstein, 2007; Galor et al., 2009).

b. The ability of individuals to finance the cost of education and the foregone earnings associated with schooling influence their capability to implement the desirable level of investment in education.

c. The degree of credit-market imperfections and inequality in a society affect the magnitude of underinvestment in education (see Galor and Zeira, 1993; Benabou, 1996; Durlauf, 1996; Fernández and Rogerson, 1996; Eckstein and Zilcha, 1994; Eicher and García-Peñalosa, 2001; Mookherjee and Ray, 2003; Galor and Moav, 2004; Banerjee and Duflo, 2005; Benabou, 2005).

d. The stock of knowledge in society contributes to the productivity of the acquisition of human capital.

e. The composition of cultural and religious groups in a society and their attitudes toward literacy and education may affect the incentive of individuals to invest in human capital formation.[14]

f. Geographical attributes and their effects on the health environment influence the extent of underinvestment in human capital.[15]

g. The propensity of a country to trade and its inherent comparative advantage affect skill intensity in production and may thus provide a further inducement for human capital formation.

h. The degree of investment in human capital is influenced by individuals' preferences for educated offspring, which may reflect cultural attributes, the composition of ethnic and religious groups in a society and their attitude toward education, and the social status associated with education (e.g., Galor and Moav, 2002; Alesina and Angeletos, 2005; Benabou and Tirole, 2006; Fernández and Fogli, 2009).

---

[14] Some religious movements have encouraged literacy, for example, Judaism (Botticini and Eckstein, 2005) and Protestantism (Becker and Woessmann, 2009).

[15] In particular, Gallup et al. (1999) establish the relationship between geographical variation in the prevalence of malaria and education, and Andersen et al. (2010) find that geographical variations in the prevalence of ultraviolet rays and their impact on the prevalence of cataracts had a significant impact on human capital formation and income per capita across countries.

6.1.3 The Dynamics of Technology and Education

The evolution of technology and education in country i for a given population size, L^i, and country-specific characteristics, Ω^i and Ψ^i, is characterized by the sequence $\{g_t^i, e_t^i; L^i, \Omega^i, \Psi^i\}_{t=0}^\infty$ such that in every period t,

$$g_{t+1}^i = g(e_t^i; L^i, \Omega^i);$$

$$\tag{6.5}$$

$$e_{t+1}^i = e(g_{t+1}^i; \Psi^i).$$

In light of the properties of the functions $e(g_{t+1}^i; \Psi^i)$ and $g(e_t^i; L^i, \Omega^i)$, this dynamical system is characterized by two qualitatively different configurations, as depicted in Figure 6.1. For a range of small population sizes, the dynamical system, depicted in Figure 6.1(a), is characterized by a globally stable (conditional) steady-state equilibrium, $(\bar{e}(L^i, \Omega^i, \Psi^i), \bar{g}(L^i, \Omega^i, \Psi^i)) = (0, g^l(L^i, \Omega^i))$, where $g^l(L^i, \Omega^i)$ increases with population size and with country-specific characteristics that are conducive to technological progress, while the absence of investment in education remains unchanged.

The inherent Malthusian interaction between population size and the rate of technological progress gradually increases both the population and the rate of technological progress, generating an upward shift in the curve $g(e_t^i; L^i, \Omega^i)$. Ultimately, the rise in the rate of technological progress (and thus in demand for human capital) increases sufficiently, and $g(e_t^i; L^i, \Omega^i)$ crosses the threshold level, $\hat{g}(\Psi_t^i)$, above which parental investment in the human capital of their offspring is beneficial. The Malthusian steady-state equilibrium vanishes, and the economy takes off to a state of sustained economic growth (Figure 6.1(b)). The economy converges to a globally stable (conditional) steady-state equilibrium, $(e^h(L^i, \Omega^i, \Psi^i), g^h(L^i, \Omega^i, \Psi^i))$, where $e^h(L^i, \Omega^i, \Psi^i)$ and $g^h(L^i, \Omega^i, \Psi^i)$ increase monotonically with population size and with country-specific characteristics that are conducive to technological progress and human capital formation.

Thus, variations in country-specific characteristics and their effects on the interaction between the rate of technological progress and human capital formation generate a differential pace of transition from stagnation to growth across countries. They determine the timing of the take-off (i.e., the time period in which the rate of technological progress in country i, $g^l(L^i, \Omega^i)$, exceeds the threshold rate of technological progress, $\hat{g}(\Psi^i)$, above which investment in human capital is profitable) and the (conditional) long-run steady-state equilibrium, $(e^h(L^i, \Omega^i, \Psi^i), g^h(L^i, \Omega^i, \Psi^i))$.

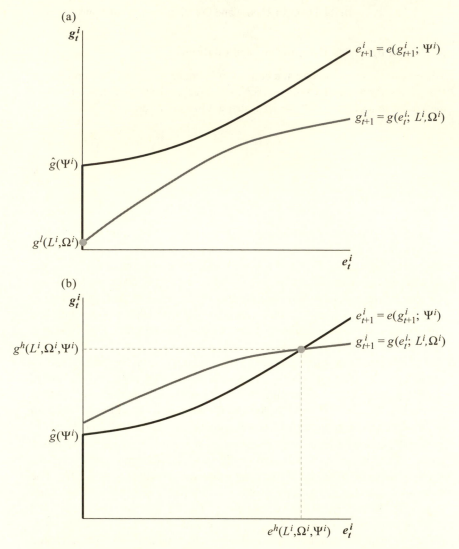

FIGURE 6.1. Evolution of technology, g_t^i, and education, e_t^i, in the development process of country i.

Summary: Panel (a) shows that in the early stages of development, population size is relatively small, and the economy is in a stable (conditional) Malthusian steady-state equilibrium characterized by low rate of technological progress, $g^l(L^i, \Omega^i)$, and no investment in education. Panel (b) shows that as population and the rate of technological progress increase in the course of the positive Malthusian feedback between population and technology, the curve $g_{t+1}^i = g(e_t^i; L^i, \Omega^i)$ shifts gradually upward, and ultimately its vertical intercept crosses the threshold rate of technological progress, $\hat{g}(\Psi^i)$, above which investment in human capital is profitable. The Malthusian steady-state equilibrium vanishes, and the economy takes off to a (conditional) sustained-growth steady-state $(e^h(L^i, \Omega^i, \Psi^i), g^h(L^i, \Omega^i, \Psi^i))$.

6.2 Variation in Technological Progress and Comparative Development

Unified Growth Theory establishes theoretically and quantitatively that the intensification of technological progress in the process of development and its effect on human capital formation and the onset of the demographic transition have been the prime forces in the transition of economies from stagnation to growth. Thus, country-specific characteristics that have affected the rate of technological progress have contributed to the differential pace of the transition from stagnation to growth and comparative economic development around the globe.

Consider two economies, A and B, that are identical in all respects, except for country-specific characteristics that contribute to technological progress. In particular, the countries are identical in the characteristics that are conducive to human capital formation (i.e., $\Psi^A = \Psi^B \equiv \Psi$). Thus, as follows from (6.4), for any given rate of technological progress, g_{t+1}, human capital formation is equal in the two economies. Namely, as depicted in Figure 6.2,

$$e_{t+1}^A = e_{t+1}^B = e(g_{t+1}; \Psi), \tag{6.6}$$

and the threshold level of the rate of technological progress above which parental investment in human capital is beneficial, $\hat{g}(\Psi)$, is also equal in the two countries.

Suppose further that country-specific characteristics that are conducive to technological progress, Ω^i, $i = A, B$, are more prevalent in country B. Hence, as depicted in Figure 6.2, for any given level of population, L, and human capital, e_t, the rate of technological progress is higher in country B, that is,

$$g_{t+1}^B = g(e_t; L, \Omega^B) > g_{t+1}^A = g(e_t; L, \Omega^A). \tag{6.7}$$

In the Malthusian regime, as depicted in Figure 6.2(a), while income per capita in the two economies may be equal, for a given level of population, the rate of technological progress is higher in country B. The steady-state equilibrium level of education and technology in country B is $(0, g^l(L, \Omega^B))$, whereas the level in country A is $(0, g^l(L, \Omega^A))$. The inherent Malthusian interaction between population size and the level of technology in each of the countries gradually increases the population size and the rate of technological progress. Thus, the potential demand for human capital also increases, generating an upward shift in the curves $g(e_t^A; L, \Omega^A)$ and $g(e_t^B; L, \Omega^B)$.

Ultimately, the rate of technological progress in country B increases sufficiently, and as depicted in Figure 6.2(b), crosses the threshold level $\hat{g}(\Psi)$, above which parental investment in human capital is beneficial. The (conditional) Malthusian steady-state equilibrium vanishes in country B, and the economy takes off to a (conditional) sustained-growth steady-state equilibrium

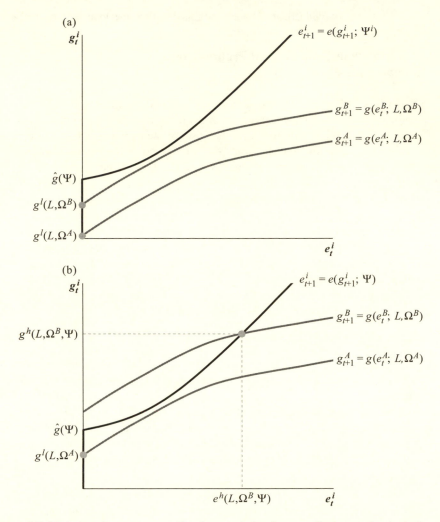

FIGURE 6.2. Variations in country-specific characteristics that contribute to technological progress and comparative development.

Summary: Panel (a) shows that in the early stages of development, prior to the emergence of demand for human capital, the two economies are in a (conditional) Malthusian steady-state equilibrium. Country B's characteristics, Ω^B, are more conducive to technological progress than those of country A, Ω^A, and, for a given population size, its rate of technological progress, $g^l(L, \Omega^B)$, is higher than that in country A, $g^l(L, \Omega^A)$. Panel (b) shows that as population and the rate of technological progress increase in the course of the positive Malthusian feedback between population and technology, the curves $g_{t+1}^B = g(e_t^B; L, \Omega^B)$ and $g_{t+1}^A = g(e_t^A; L, \Omega^A)$ shift gradually upward. Ultimately, the vertical intercept of $g_{t+1}^B = g(e_t^B; L, \Omega^B)$ crosses the threshold rate of technological progress, $\hat{g}(\Psi)$, above which investment in human capital is profitable, while the vertical intercept of $g_{t+1}^A = g(e_t^A; L, \Omega^A)$ remains below this threshold. The Malthusian steady-state equilibrium vanishes in country B, and the economy converges to a sustained-growth (conditional) steady-state equilibrium, $(e^h(L, \Omega^B, \Psi), g^h(L, \Omega^B, \Psi))$, whereas country A remains in the (conditional) Malthusian steady-state equilibrium, $(0, g^l(L, \Omega^A))$, for a longer time.

$(e^h(L, \Omega^B, \Psi), g^h(L, \Omega^B, \Psi))$. Country A, in contrast, experiences a later take-off. Moreover, if the country-specific characteristics of the two economies do not converge in the long-run, country B will have a superior steady-state equilibrium.

6.3 Variation in Human Capital and Comparative Development

> *Give a man a fish and you feed him for a day; teach a man to*
> *fish and you feed him for a lifetime.*
>
> —Maimonides

Unified Growth Theory establishes that once the technologically driven demand for human capital emerged, the prevalence of characteristics conducive to human capital formation influenced the swiftness of its accumulation, the timing of the demographic transition, the pace of the transition from stagnation to growth, and thereby the observed distribution of income in the world economy.[16] Thus, country-specific characteristics that have affected human capital formation have contributed to the differential pace of the transition from agriculture to industry and comparative economic development around the globe.

Consider two economies, A and B, identical in all respects except for specific characteristics that contribute to human capital formation. In particular, the two economies are identical in their country-specific characteristics that are conducive to technological progress (i.e., $\Omega^A = \Omega^B \equiv \Omega$). Thus, as follows from (6.1), for any given level of population, L, and human capital, e_t, the rates of technological progress in countries A and B, as depicted in Figure 6.3, are equal as well. Namely, for every $(e_t; L, \Omega)$,

$$g_{t+1}^A = g_{t+1}^B = g(e_t; L, \Omega). \tag{6.8}$$

Suppose further that country-specific characteristics that are conducive to human capital formation, Ψ^i, $i = A, B$, are more prevalent in country B. Thus, as follows from (6.4) and is depicted in Figure 6.3, for any given rate of technological progress, g_{t+1}, investment in human capital is at least as high in country B as it is in country A. Namely,

$$e_{t+1}^A = e(g_{t+1}; \Psi^A) \leq e_{t+1}^B = e(g_{t+1}; \Psi^B), \tag{6.9}$$

[16] Consistent with empirical evidence, increased demand for human capital has not necessarily resulted in an increase in the equilibrium rate of return to human capital due to a massive supply response generated by (i) the increase in the incentive for investment in education and (ii) institutional changes (e.g., the provision of public education) that lowered the cost of investment in human capital.

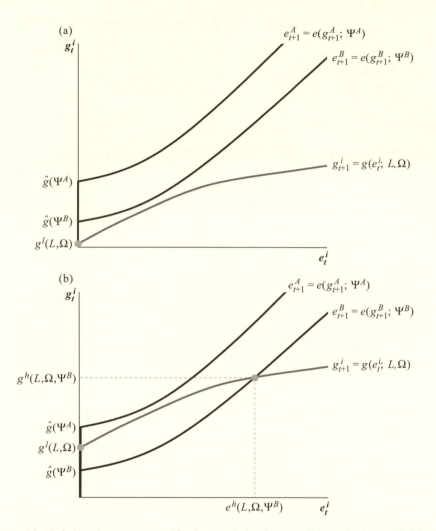

FIGURE 6.3. Variations in country-specific characteristics that contribute to human capital formation and comparative development.

Summary: Panel (a) shows that prior to the emergence of demand for human capital, the two economies are in the same (conditional) steady-state equilibrium, $(0, g^l(L, \Omega))$, but since country B's characteristics, Ψ^B, are more conducive to human capital formation than those in country A, Ψ^A, country B faces a lower threshold for take-off (i.e., $\hat{g}(\Psi^B) < \hat{g}(\Psi^A)$). Panel (b) shows that as population and the rate of technological progress increase in the course of the positive Malthusian feedback between population and technology, the curve $g^i_{t+1} = g(e^i_t; L, \Omega), i = A, B$, shifts gradually upward, and ultimately its vertical intercept crosses the threshold rate of technological progress, $\hat{g}(\Psi^B)$, above which investment in human capital in country B is profitable, while it remains below the corresponding threshold for country A, $\hat{g}(\Psi^A)$. The Malthusian steady-state equilibrium vanishes in country B, and the economy takes off to a (conditional) sustained-growth steady-state equilibrium, $(e^h(L, \Omega, \Psi^B), g^h(L, \Omega, \Psi^B))$, while country A temporarily remains in a (conditional) Malthusian steady-state equilibrium, $(0, g^l(L, \Omega))$.

and the threshold level of the rate of technological progress above which parental investment in human capital is beneficial is therefore lower in country B, that is,

$$\hat{g}(\Psi^B) < \hat{g}(\Psi^A). \tag{6.10}$$

In particular,

$$e_{t+1}^A = e(g_{t+1}; \Psi^A) \begin{cases} = e_{t+1}^B = 0, & \text{if } g_{t+1} \leq \hat{g}(\Psi^B); \\ < e_{t+1}^B = e(g_{t+1}; \Psi^B), & \text{if } g_{t+1} > \hat{g}(\Psi^B). \end{cases} \tag{6.11}$$

As depicted in Figure 6.3(a), prior to the emergence of demand for human capital, the two economies are in the same (conditional) steady-state equilibrium, $(0, g^l(L, \Omega))$, but country B faces a lower threshold for a take-off: $\hat{g}(\Psi^B) < \hat{g}(\Psi^A)$.

The positive Malthusian interaction between population size and the rate of technological progress in each of the countries gradually increases the value of these two variables and generates an upward shift in the curve $g_{t+1}^i = g(e_t^i; L, \Omega)$, reflecting a rise in demand for human capital. In particular, since $\hat{g}(\Psi^B) < \hat{g}(\Psi^A)$, individuals in country B are more responsive to the rise in demand for human capital, and that country experiences an earlier process of human capital formation and a faster transition to an era of sustained economic growth.

As depicted in Figure 6.3(b), once the rate of technological progress increases sufficiently and crosses its threshold level, $\hat{g}(\Psi^B)$, above which parental investment in human capital is profitable in country B, the Malthusian steady-state equilibrium vanishes in country B, and the economy takes off to a (conditional) sustained-growth steady-state equilibrium, $(e^h(L, \Omega, \Psi^B), g^h(L, \Omega, \Psi^B))$. In contrast, the rate of technological progress remains below the corresponding threshold for country A, $\hat{g}(\Psi^A)$. Thus the rise in demand for human capital is still insufficient to generate a take-off in country A, and the country remains temporarily in a (conditional) Malthusian steady-state equilibrium, $(0, g^l(L, \Omega))$. Moreover, if the country-specific characteristics of the two economies do not converge in the long-run, country B will have a superior long-run steady-state equilibrium.

6.3.1 The Emergence of Human Capital–Promoting Institutions

While the process of industrialization raised the importance of human capital in the production process, reflecting its complementarity with technology in a rapidly changing technological environment, human capital accumulation has not benefited all sectors of the economy. Inequality in the ownership of factors of production has generated an incentive for some sectors to block the implementation of institutional changes that promote human capital formation, resulting in a suboptimal level of investment in human capital from a growth perspective. In particular, variation in the distribution of ownership over natural resources across countries has contributed to the observed disparity in human capital formation and to the divergent development patterns around the globe.

Theory

As argued by Galor et al. (2009), the transition from an agricultural to an industrial economy introduced a new economic conflict in society. Unlike the agrarian economy, which was characterized by a conflict of interests between the landed aristocracy and the masses, the process of industrialization has brought about an additional conflict between the entrenched landed elite and the emerging capitalist elite. In light of a lower degree of complementarity between human capital and the agricultural sector, education has increased the productivity of labor in industrial production more than in agricultural and primary good production, inducing rural-to-urban migration and thus a decline in rental rates. Thus, while industrialists have had a direct economic incentive to support education policies that would foster human capital formation, landowners (as well as the owners of natural resources), whose interests lay in the reduction of the mobility of their labor forces, have favored policies that deprived the masses of education, as long as their stake in the productivity of the industrial sector were insufficient.[17]

The adverse effect of the implementation of public education on landowners' incomes from agricultural production has been magnified by the concentration of land ownership. Thus, as long as landowners affected the political process and thereby the implementation of growth-enhancing education policies, inequality in the distribution of land ownership has been a hurdle for human capital accumulation, slowing the process of industrialization and the transition to modern growth.[18]

Economies in which land and other natural resources have been more equally distributed have implemented earlier public education campaigns and have benefited from the emergence of a skill-intensive industrial sector and rapid development. In contrast, among economies marked by a more unequal distribution of ownership over natural resources, resource abundance that was a

---

[17] Landowners may benefit from the economic development of other segments of the economy due to capital ownership, the provision of public goods, and demand spillovers generated by economic development in the urban sector.

[18] Interestingly, during the nineteenth century, the emergence of a broad-based demand for human capital–intensive services by the landowners in land-rich economies in Latin America (e.g., Argentina) triggered the establishment of an extensive public education system prior to the onset of significant manufacturing activities (Galiani et al., 2008). Thus, lack of concentration of land ownership that was associated with a broad-based demand for human capital–intensive services by the landowners had a positive effect on human capital formation even before industrialization.

source of richness in the early stages of development has led in later stages to underinvestment in human capital, an unskilled labor-intensive industrial sector, and slower growth. Thus, variation in the distribution of ownership over land and other natural resources across countries, which could potentially be mapped into differences in geographical conditions, has contributed to disparity in human capital formation and the industrial composition of the economy and thus to divergent development patterns around the globe.

In contrast to the conflict-based political mechanism advanced by Engerman and Sokoloff (2002) and Acemoglu et al. (2005a), who underline the role of the conflict between the elite and the masses in the delayed implementation of growth-enhancing educational policies, Galor and Moav (2006) and Galor et al. (2009) emphasize a direct economic mechanism (i.e., the adverse effect of education reforms on land rental rates) that governs the relationship between inequality and the process of development. Thus, even if the political structure in the economy remains unchanged, economic development and gradual diversification of assets held by the landed aristocracy will ultimately trigger the implementation of growth-promoting education policies, once the stake of the landed aristocracy in the efficient operation of the industrial sector dominates their overall economic interest.

This theory can be integrated into the framework of Unified Growth Theory. Consider two economies, A and B, identical in all respects except for concentration in land ownership.[19] Suppose that land is more equally distributed in country B, and thus, the degree of equality in land ownership, Ψ^i, $i = A, B$, is more conducive to human capital formation in country B. As follows from (6.4) and depicted in Figure 6.4, for any given rate of technological progress, g_{t+1}, human capital formation is at least as high in country B as it is in country A (i.e., $e_{t+1}^A = e(g_{t+1}; \Psi^A) \le e_{t+1}^B = e(g_{t+1}; \Psi^B)$), reflecting the adverse effect of higher concentration of land ownership in country A. Moreover, the threshold level of the rate of technological progress (above which parental investment in human capital is beneficial) is lower in country B (i.e., $\hat{g}(\Psi^B) < \hat{g}(\Psi^A)$).

The process of development and the inherent Malthusian interaction between the size of the population and the rate of technological progress gradually increase the rate of technological progress and generate an upward shift in the curve $g(e_t^i; L, \Omega)$, reflecting a rise in the demand for human capital. In particular, since $\hat{g}(\Psi^B) < \hat{g}(\Psi^A)$, individuals in country B are more responsive to the rise in demand for human capital and, as depicted in Figure 6.4(a), the country experiences an earlier process of human capital formation and

---

[19] For an explicit theory that generates this reduced-form relationship between technology and human capital formation, see Galor et al. (2009).

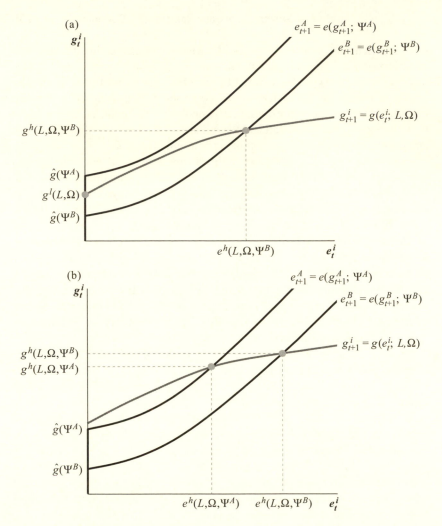

FIGURE 6.4. Adverse effects of inequality in land ownership on human capital formation and comparative development.

Summary: Panel (a) shows that as population and the rate of technological progress increase in the course of the positive Malthusian feedback between population and technology, the curve $g_{t+1}^i = g(e_t^i; L, \Omega)$, $i = A, B$, shifts gradually upward, and ultimately, its vertical intercept crosses the threshold rate of technological progress, $\hat{g}(\Psi^B)$, above which investment in human capital in country B is profitable, while it remains below the corresponding threshold for country A, $\hat{g}(\Psi^A)$. Country B takes off to a (conditional) sustained-growth equilibrium, $(e^h(L, \Omega, \Psi^B), g^h(L, \Omega, \Psi^B))$, while country A remains temporarily in a (conditional) Malthusian steady-state equilibrium, $(0, g^l(L, \Omega))$. Panel (b) shows that the continued positive Malthusian feedback between population and technology ultimately increases the rate of technological progress in country A beyond the threshold level, $\hat{g}(\Psi^A)$, above which investment in human capital in country A is profitable. The Malthusian steady-state equilibrium vanishes in country A, and the country takes off to a lower (conditional) sustained-growth equilibrium, $(e^h(L, \Omega, \Psi^A), g^h(L, \Omega, \Psi^A))$.

an earlier transition to a conditional sustained-growth steady-state equilibrium $(e^h(L, \Omega, \Psi^B), g^h(L, \Omega, \Psi^B))$.

Ultimately, however, the relentless interaction between population and technology increases the rate of technological progress in country A beyond the threshold level, $\hat{g}(\Psi^A)$, and as depicted in Figure 6.4(b), the country experiences human capital formation and a transition to a lower conditional steady-state equilibrium, $(e^h(L, \Omega, \Psi^A), g^h(L, \Omega, \Psi^A))$. Nevertheless, if the effect of the concentration of land ownership on human capital formation dissipates, as the share of the agricultural sector declines, the two economies will converge to the same long-run steady-state equilibrium.

Historical Evidence

Historical evidence suggests that the distribution of land ownership has indeed affected human capital formation and has been therefore a significant force in the emergence of sustained differences in human capital formation and growth patterns across countries. Anecdotal evidence, presented in Section 2.3.2, indicates that the degree of concentration of land ownership across countries and regions is inversely related to educational attainment. Moreover, evidence from Japan, Korea, Russia, and Taiwan, presented in Section 2.3.3, indicates that land reforms were followed by, or occurred simultaneously with, significant education reforms.

Two interpretations for those historical episodes are consistent with the proposed theory. First, land reforms diminished the economic incentives of landowners to block education reforms. Second, consistently with the basic premise that landowners opposed education spending whereas others (e.g., the industrial elite) supported it, an unfavorable shift in the balance of power from the viewpoint of the landed aristocracy brought about the implementation of both land and education reforms.

Empirical Examination

The central hypothesis, that land inequality adversely affected the timing of education reforms, is examined empirically by Galor et al. (2009), using variations in the concentration of land ownership and in public spending on education across states in the United States during the high school movement.[20]

During the first half of the twentieth century, the education system in the United States underwent a major transformation from insignificant to nearly

---

[20] The persistent adverse effect of landowners on economic development is established by Banerjee and Iyer (2005) in the context of colonial land revenue institutions set up by the British in India. They demonstrate that areas in which proprietary rights in land were historically given to landowners have significantly lower agricultural investment in the post-Independence period than areas in which these rights were given to cultivators. Moreover, these areas have significantly lower investments in health and education.

universal secondary education that was geared toward industrial needs. While in 1910, high school graduation rates were a mere 9–15% in the Northeast and the Pacific regions and 4% in the South, by 1950 graduation rates increased to nearly 60% in the Northeast and the Pacific regions and to about 40% in the South. Furthermore, there were significant regional variations in the timing and extensiveness of these changes (Goldin, 1998).

The high school movement and its qualitative effect on the structure of education in the United States reflected an educational shift toward nonagricultural learning that may have been viewed as a threat to the interest of landowners. The high school movement was undertaken with the intention of building a skilled workforce that could better serve the manufacturing sector. Over this period, firms increasingly demanded skilled workers that could be effective managers, sales personnel, and clerical workers, and courses in accounting, typing, short-hand, and algebra were highly valued in white-collar occupations. In addition, in the 1910s, some of the high-technology industries of the period started to demand blue-collar craft workers who were trained in mathematics, chemistry, and electricity (Goldin, 1998).

Consistent with the theory, the evidence suggests that inequality in the distribution of land ownership had a significant adverse effect on educational expenditures during this period.[21] Exploiting differences in education expenditures and land concentration across states during 1900–1940, Galor et al. (2009) identify a significant adverse effect of concentration of land ownership on education expenditures, controlling for the level of income per capita, race, and the urbanization rate within each state.[22]

6.3.2 Globalization and Divergence

The dramatic transformation of the distribution of income and population around the globe in the past two centuries is one of the most significant mysteries of the growth process. Some regions have excelled in growth of income per capita while others have dominated population growth.[23] This striking contrast between the development paths of large subsets of the world economy gives rise to fundamental questions about the determinants of economic growth in an interdependent world. Has the pace of transition to sustained economic growth

---

[21] For other studies of the relationship between land and economic performance in the United States during this time, see Gerber (1991) and Caselli and Coleman (2001).

[22] Consistent with the proposed theory and empirical findings, Wright (1970) suggests that Southern governments, influenced heavily by landholders, refused to expand enrollments and spending in education, because the North, which provided a significant outside option for educated workers, would reap the benefits from it.

[23] In the time period 1820–1998, the ratio between income per capita in Western Europe and Asia grew nearly threefold, whereas the ratio between the sizes of the Asian population and the Western European population grew nearly twofold (Maddison, 2001).

in advanced economies adversely affected the process of development in less developed economies? Have the forces of international trade contributed to the divergence in the timing of demographic transitions and the emergence of sustained economic growth across countries?

Theory

Galor and Mountford (2006, 2008) argue that international trade has played a significant role in the differential timing of demographic transitions across countries and has been a major determinant of the distribution of world population and of the divergence in income per capita across countries. The expansion of international trade enhanced specialization of industrial economies in the production of skill-intensive industrial goods. The associated rise in demand for skilled labor has induced a gradual investment in the quality of the population, expediting a demographic transition, stimulating technological progress, and further enhancing the comparative advantage of these industrial economies in the production of skill-intensive goods. In nonindustrial economies, in contrast, international trade has generated an incentive to specialize in the production of unskilled labor-intensive nonindustrial goods. The absence of significant demand for human capital has provided limited incentives to invest in the quality of the population, and a larger share of their gains from trade has been utilized for a further increase in population size, rather than in income per capita.[24] The demographic transition in these nonindustrial economies has been significantly delayed, increasing further their relative abundance of unskilled labor, enhancing their comparative disadvantage in the production of skill-intensive goods, and delaying their development.

International trade therefore had an asymmetric effect on the evolution of industrial and nonindustrial economies. While in the industrial nations the gains from trade have been directed primarily toward investment in education and growth in output per capita, a greater portion of the gains from trade in nonindustrial nations has been channeled into population growth. Thus, in contrast to the existing literature on the dynamics of comparative advantage, the theory suggests that, even if trade equalizes the growth of total output in the trading countries (due to the terms-of-trade effect), income per capita of developed and less developed economies will diverge, since in developed economies the growth of total output will be generated primarily by an increase

[24] Evidence suggests that the returns on human capital may have been higher in less developed economies. One can therefore mistakenly suppose that the incentive to invest in child quality is universally higher in these economies. However, these higher rates of return are not applicable to most individuals. They reflect a suboptimal investment in human capital in an environment characterized by credit-market imperfections and limited access to schooling. International trade, therefore, reduces further the modest demand for human capital and the incentive to substitute child quality for quantity.

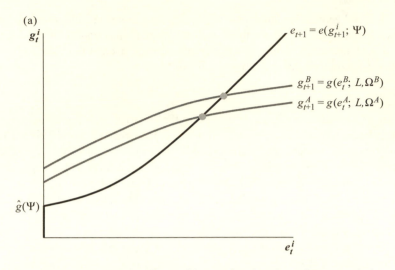

(a)

g_t^i

$e_{t+1} = e(g_{t+1}^i; \Psi)$

$g_{t+1}^B = g(e_t^B; L, \Omega^B)$

$g_{t+1}^A = g(e_t^A; L, \Omega^A)$

$\hat{g}(\Psi)$

e_t^i

FIGURE 6.5. Asymmetric effects of international trade on human capital formation and the growth process.

Summary: Panel (a) shows that prior to the emergence of international trade, the rate of technological progress in the two economies is above the threshold that justifies investment in human capital, but a decline in fertility has not yet occurred. Country B's characteristics, Ω^B, are more conducive to technological progress than those in country A, Ω^A, and thus, for any given population size, L, and human capital, e_t, the rate of technological progress in country B, $g_{t+1}^B = g(e_t; L, \Omega^B)$, is higher than that in country A, $g_{t+1}^A = g(e_t; L, \Omega^A)$. The countries are identical in characteristics that are conducive to human capital formation (i.e., $\Psi^A = \Psi^B \equiv \Psi$), and for any level of technological progress, g_{t+1}, human capital, $e_{t+1}^i = e(g_{t+1}; \Psi)$, $i = A, B$, is equal in the two countries. Panel (b) shows that trade generates asymmetric effects, Ψ^i, $i = A, B$, on demand for human capital in the two countries. The technologically advanced economy, B, specializes in skill-intensive industrial goods, increasing its demand for human capital, while country A specializes in unskilled labor-intensive goods, decreasing its demand for human capital. For any rate of technological progress, g_{t+1}, the curve $e_{t+1}^A = e(g_{t+1}; \Psi^A)$ shifts leftward, whereas $e_{t+1}^B = e(g_{t+1}; \Psi^B)$ shifts rightward relative to $e_{t+1}^i = e(g_{t+1}; \Psi)$. Trade intensifies human capital formation in country B, leading to its earlier demographic transition and a shift to modern growth, whereas it decelerates human capital formation in country A and delays its demographic transition and shift to modern growth. Country A experiences an inferior long-run equilibrium.

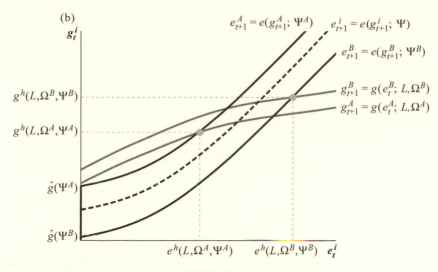

FIGURE 6.5 *(continued)*

in output per capita, whereas in less developed economies the contribution of population growth to the growth of total output will be more significant.[25]

The adverse effect of international trade on industrialization and thus on the timing of the demographic transition could have been mitigated by the positive effect of trade on technological diffusion across countries.[26] However, labor productivity greatly differed across countries, even among industries in which technologies were very similar. Moreover, since the rate of technological diffusion may depend on the appropriateness of the endowments of factors of production in the receiving country for this technology, an adverse effect of trade on the incentive to invest in human capital in less developed economies may have slowed down the rate of technological diffusion.

This theory can be incorporated into the basic framework of Unified Growth Theory.[27] Consider two economies, India (country A) and England (country B), in the midst of their processes of industrialization. Suppose that the countries are initially identical in those characteristics conducive to human capital formation

[25] For the dynamics of comparative advantage, see Findlay and Kierzkowski (1983), Grossman and Helpman (1991), Stokey (1991), Young (1991), and Matsuyama (1992), among others, and for the effect on divergence, see Krugman and Venables (1995), Baldwin et al. (2001), and O'Rourke and Williamson (2005).

[26] The determinants of international technological diffusion are explored by Keller (2004), Acemoglu et al. (2006), and Spolaore and Wacziarg (2009).

[27] For an explicit theory that generates this reduced-form relationship between technology and human capital formation, see Galor and Mountford (2008).

(i.e., $\Psi^A = \Psi^B \equiv \Psi$), and thus, for any given rate of technological progress, g_{t+1}, human capital formation is equal in the two countries. Hence, as depicted in Figure 6.5(a), for a given rate of technological progress, g_{t+1}, $e_{t+1}^A = e_{t+1}^B = e(g_{t+1}; \Psi)$, and the threshold level of the rate of technological progress (above which parental investment in human capital is beneficial), $\hat{g}(\Psi)$, is also equal in the two countries.

Suppose further that the two economies are identical in all other respects, except for country-specific factors, Ω^i, $i = A, B$, that contribute to a faster technological progress in country B. Hence, for any given level of human capital, e_t, and population size, L, the rate of technological progress in country B is larger than that in country A (i.e., $g_{t+1}^B = g(e_t; L, \Omega^B) > g_{t+1}^A = g(e_t; L, \Omega^A)$). Moreover, the rate of technological progress in the two economies is assumed to be above the threshold that justifies investment in human capital, but a decline in fertility has not yet occurred in the two economies.

Once international trade is established between India (A) and England (B), it induces the technologically advanced economy, England, to specialize in the production of industrial skill-intensive goods, increasing its demand for human capital, whereas it induces India to specialize in the production of unskilled-intensive, primary goods, decreasing its demand for human capital. International trade generates, therefore, an asymmetric effect on the demand for human capital in the two countries, as captured by the parameters Ψ^i, $i = A, B$. For any given rate of technological progress, g_{t+1}, investment in human capital increases (relative to autarky) in England (i.e., $e_{t+1}^B = e(g_{t+1}; \Psi^B) > e(g_{t+1}^i; \Psi)$) and decreases in India (i.e., $e_{t+1}^A = e(g_{t+1}; \Psi^A) < e(g_{t+1}^i; \Psi)$). As depicted in Figure 6.5(b), the curve $e_{t+1}^A = e(g_{t+1}; \Psi^A)$ therefore shifts leftward relative to the autarkic position, $e(g_{t+1}^i; \Psi)$, whereas the curve $e_{t+1}^B = e(g_{t+1}; \Psi^B)$) shifts rightward.

Thus, international trade intensifies human capital formation in England, leading to an earlier demographic transition and an earlier transition to an era of sustained economic growth. In contrast, international trade decelerates human capital formation in India, delaying its transitions. Furthermore, if the asymmetric effects of international trade on human capital formation in the two economies persist, India will experience an inferior long-run equilibrium relative to England.

Anecdotal Evidence

The contrasting process of development of England and India over the nineteenth and twentieth centuries is consistent with the proposed theory and provides an interesting case study. During the nineteenth century, England traded manufactured goods for primary products with India. As documented in Figure 2.12 in Chapter 2, industrialization per capita in India significantly regressed over this century, whereas industrialization per capita in England accelerated. The process of industrialization in England led to a significant increase in demand for skilled labor in the second phase of the industrial revolution, triggering a demographic transition in the 1870s and a transition to a state of sustained economic growth. In India, in contrast, the lack of demand for skilled labor delayed the demographic transition and the transition to a sustained-growth regime until the second half of the twentieth century. Thus, while the gains from trade were utilized in England primarily to increase output per capita, in India they were more biased toward increasing population size.

Another interesting case study providing supporting evidence for the proposed hypothesis is the economic integration of the Israeli and West Bank economies in the aftermath of the 1967 war. Trade and factor mobility between the skill-abundant economy of Israel and the unskilled labor–abundant economy of the West Bank shifted the latter's economy toward further specialization in the production of primary goods and triggered an astonishing increase in crude births rates from 22 per 1,000 people in 1968 to 42 per 1,000 in 1990, despite a decline in mortality rates. Thus, the gains from trade and development in the West Bank economy were partly converted into an increase in population size, nearly doubling the population in about two decades. Consistent with the proposed theory, the Palestinian uprising in the early 1990s and the gradual separation of the two economies resulted in the reduction in the crude birth rates among the Palestinian population.

Empirical Examination

Galor and Mountford (2008) use cross-country regression analysis to examine empirically the hypothesis that the effect of international trade on demand for human capital induces a rise in fertility and decline in human capital formation in nonindustrial economies, and a decline in fertility and rise in human capital formation in industrialized ones. The evidence, depicted in Figures 6.6 and 6.7, suggests that, indeed, international trade has reinforced the initial patterns of comparative advantage, generated a persistent effect on the distribution of population in the world economy, and contributed to the divergence in income per capita across countries and regions.

The empirical analysis focuses on a recent period in which most countries had already experienced their demographic transition. In particular, it examines the effect of the share of trade in GDP in 1985 on the total fertility rate and on the change in the average years of schooling in industrial and nonindustrial economies during 1985–1990. The actual level of trade in each country is instrumented by a country's intrinsic propensity to trade in 1985, so as to overcome the potential existence of omitted variables, measurement errors, and reverse causality from fertility and human capital formation to trade patterns.[28]

---

[28] The instrument, constructed by Frankel and Romer (1999), is generated by aggregating the results from thousands of bilateral trade relationships, which are estimated using a regression of bilateral trade share in GDP on seven variables and some of their interactions. These seven variables

(a)

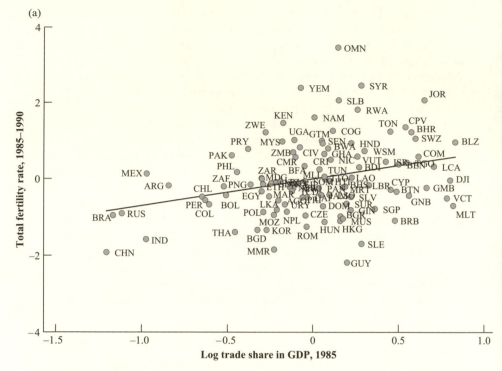

FIGURE 6.6. Effect of trade on fertility in (a) non-OECD and (b) OECD economies.
Data source: Galor and Mountford (2008).
Summary: The figure depicts the partial regression line for the effect of log trade share in GDP in 1985 on total fertility rate during 1985–1990 in non-OECD (panel a) and OECD economies (panel b) controlling for log GDP per capita and infant mortality rate in 1985. Thus, the *x* and *y* axes in panel (a) [panel (b)] plot the residuals obtained from regressing log trade share in GDP and total fertility rate in non-OECD [OECD] economies, respectively, on the aforementioned set of covariates.

Furthermore, in the absence of authoritative data on the factor content of trade that would have enabled the division of the world into economies exporting human capital–intensive goods and those exporting unskilled labor–intensive goods, the hypothesis is tested on a preexisting division of the world economy. This division considers OECD economies in 1985 as those which export human

---

are the bilateral distance between the two trading economies, a dummy for whether there is a common border between the two trading economies, a dummy for whether one or more economy is landlocked, and the country size variables (log area and log population for both countries).

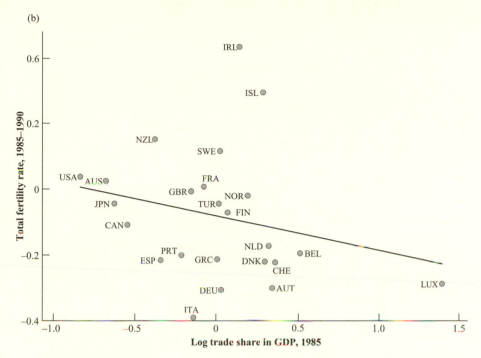

FIGURE 6.6 *(continued)*

capital–intensive goods and non-OECD economies in 1985 as those which export unskilled labor–intensive goods.[29]

The theory suggests that international trade, via its effect on patterns of specialization, would increase demand for human capital in OECD economies and decrease it in non-OECD economies. These asymmetric demand effects would generate a force tending to decrease fertility rates and increase human capital investment in OECD economies and tending to increase fertility rates and reduce human capital investment in non-OECD economies. In addition, however, the gains from international trade would be expected to generate a rise in income in both OECD and non-OECD countries. In the predemographic transition era, these gains in income would be channeled into increasing fertility rates. The rise in income would therefore enhance the increase in fertility rates in less developed economies and would offset some of the negative effect of the rise in demand for human capital on fertility in developed economies.

[29] The OPEC economies are omitted from the sample, since their trade patterns do not capture the characteristics underlined by the theory and the wealth effect associated with their oil revenues could potentially distort the relationships among trade, fertility, and education.

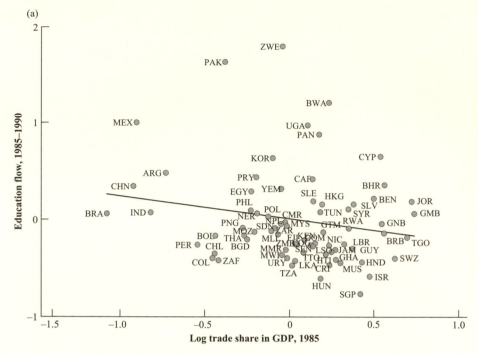

FIGURE 6.7. Effect of trade on education in (a) non-OECD and (b) OECD economies. *Data source:* Galor and Mountford (2008).
Summary: The figure depicts the partial regression line for the effect of trade share in GDP in 1985 on education flow during 1985–1990 in non-OECD economies (panel a) and OECD economies (panel b) while controlling for log GDP per capita. Thus, the *x* and *y* axes in panel (a) [panel (b)] plot the residuals obtained from regressing log trade share and education flow in GDP in non-OECD [OECD] economies, respectively, on the aforementioned set of covariates.

However, in the post-demographic transition era, which characterizes these data, the rise in income due to international trade generates, at the parental level, conflicting income and substitution effects with respect to the optimal number of children and their quality. Although, according to the theory, these effects offset one another, the rise in households' income increases the relative demand for human capital–intensive goods and generates a force tending to decrease fertility and raise human capital investment in non-OECD economies as well as in OECD economies that have not reached their balanced growth path.

Thus, in the post-demographic transition era, the overall effect of international trade on fertility is expected to be negative in OECD economies, whereas the net effect in non-OECD economies is determined by two conflicting forces.

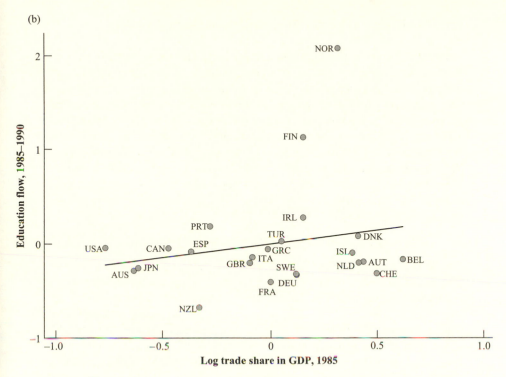

FIGURE 6.7 *(continued)*

Controlling for income, however, the effect of trade on fertility is predicted to be positive in non-OECD economies and negative in OECD economies. Similarly, controlling for income, the effect of trade on human capital formation is predicted to be negative in non-OECD economies and positive in OECD economics. Furthermore, some of the variation in fertility rates across countries would reflect variation in infant mortality rates. As long as parents generate utility from the number of surviving children, the theory predicts that infant mortality rates have a positive effect on fertility rates in both OECD and non-OECD economies.

The cross-country regression analysis supports the hypothesis that international trade generates opposing effects on fertility rates and education in developed and less developed economies. As depicted in Figures 6.6 and 6.7, international trade has a positive effect on fertility and a negative one on human capital formation in non-OECD economies, whereas in OECD economies, trade triggers a decline in fertility and an increase in human capital accumulation.

6.4 Persistence of Deeply Rooted Biogeographical Factors

In its second layer, Unified Growth Theory highlights the persistent direct effect that prehistorical biogeographical conditions (e.g., biodiversity, migratory distance from the geographical origin of *Homo sapiens* in East Africa, and genetic diversity) have had on the process of development over the entire course of human history. Recent studies suggest that variation in deeply rooted biogeographical factors is critical for understanding the course of comparative economic development from the dawn of human civilization to the modern era. They demonstrate that biogeographical factors in the distant past have generated a significant effect on the contemporary level of development across countries and regions of the world.[30]

6.4.1 The Neolithic Revolution and Comparative Development

The Socio-Technological Head-Start Channel
The influential thesis of Diamond (1997, 2002) suggests that contemporary differences in economic development can be traced to biogeographical factors that led to regional variation in the timing of the Neolithic Revolution. Diamond's hypothesis identifies the timing of the Neolithic transition to agriculture as a proximate determinant of institutional and economic development. It thereby designates initial geographical and biogeographical conditions (the size of the continent or landmass, orientation of the major continental axis, type of climate, and number of prehistorical plant and animal species amenable for domestication) governing the emergence and adoption of agricultural practices in prehistorical hunter-gatherer societies as the ultimate determinants in this channel.

In particular, Diamond argued that a larger continent or landmass implied greater biodiversity and hence, a greater likelihood that at least some species suitable for domestication would exist. In addition, a more pronounced East-West (relative to North-South) orientation of the major continental axis meant an easier diffusion of agricultural practices within the landmass, particularly among regions sharing similar latitudes and hence, similar environments suit-

---

[30] Deeply rooted biogeographical factors may have contributed to the emergence of cultural traits, ethnic and linguistic fractionalization, and social trust. Spolaore and Wacziarg (2009) argue that the genetic distance observed between populations captures their divergence in biological and cultural characteristics, acting as a barrier to the horizontal diffusion of technological innovations across populations. They show that F_{st} genetic distance, which reflects the time elapsed since two populations shared a common ancestor, bears a statistically significant positive relationship with both historical and contemporary pairwise income differences. Michalopoulos (2008) finds that variability in land quality can be viewed as the origin of ethnolinguistic fractionalization, and Durante (2009) demonstrates the role of climatic variability in the emergence of social trust.

able for agriculture. This orientation factor, compared across continents, is argued to have played a pivotal role in comparative economic development, favoring the early rise of complex agricultural civilizations on the Eurasian land-mass. Finally, certain climates are known to be more beneficial for agriculture than others. For instance, moderate zones encompassing the Mediterranean and marine west-coast subcategories in the Köppen-Geiger climate classification system are particularly amenable for growing annual heavy grasses, whereas humid subtropical, continental, and wet tropical climates are less favorable in this regard, with agriculture being almost entirely infeasible in dry and polar climates.[31]

Diamond's hypothesis suggests that the Neolithic Revolution conferred a developmental head start on societies that experienced an earlier transition from primitive hunting and gathering techniques to the more technologically advanced agricultural mode of production. Favorable biogeographical endow-ments that contributed to the emergence of agriculture gave some societies the early advantage of operating a superior production technology and generating resource surpluses. This head start permitted establishment of a non-food-producing class whose members were crucial for the development of written language and science and for the formation of cities, technology-based military powers, and nation states. The early dominance of these societies subsequently persisted throughout history, being further sustained by geopolitical and histor-ical processes, such as colonization.

This theory can be integrated into the framework of Unified Growth Theory. Consider two economies, A and B, identical in all respects except for the time in which the ancestors of their current population experienced the Neolithic Revolution. Suppose that the Neolithic Revolution occurred earlier in country B and thus the characteristics that are conducive to technological progress are more prevalent in country B (i.e., $\Omega^B > \Omega^A$). Hence, as follows from (6.1) and depicted in Figure 6.2, for any given population size, L, and human capital, e_t, the rate of technological progress in the post-Neolithic period is higher in country B (i.e., $g_{t+1}^B = g(e_t; L, \Omega^B) > g_{t+1}^A = g(e_t; L, \Omega^A)$).

Suppose further that the countries have identical characteristics that are conducive to human capital formation (i.e., $\Psi^A = \Psi^B \equiv \Psi$) and thus, as follows from (6.4), for any rate of technological progress, g_{t+1}, human capital formation is equal in the two economies. Namely, as depicted in Figure 6.2, $e_{t+1}^A = e_{t+1}^B = e(g_{t+1}; \Psi)$, and the threshold rate of technological progress (above which parental investment in human capital is beneficial) is also equal (i.e., $\hat{g}(\Psi^B) = \hat{g}(\Psi^A) = \hat{g}(\Psi)$).

---

[31] Olsson and Hibbs (2005) and Putterman (2008) provide support for the relationship between the presence of some of these factors and the timing of the onset of the Neolithic Revolution.

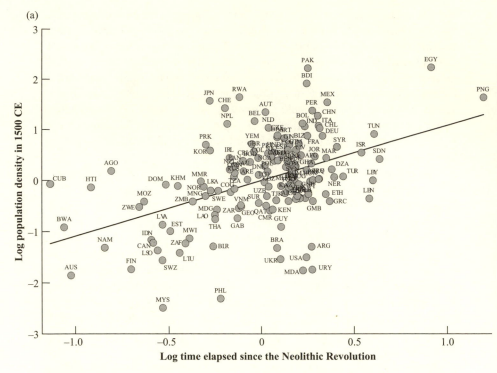

FIGURE 6.8. The Neolithic Revolution, technology, and population density. (a) Partial effect of transition timing on population density in 1500 CE. (b) Partial effect of transition timing on technological level in 1000 CE.

Data source: Ashraf and Galor (2011).

Summary: Panel (a) shows the partial regression line for the effect of log transition timing on log population density in 1500 CE, controlling for the influence of land productivity, absolute latitude, access to waterways, and continental fixed effects. Thus, the *x* and *y* axes plot the residuals obtained from regressing log time elapsed since the Neolithic Revolution and log population density, respectively, on the aforementioned set of covariates. Panel (b) shows the partial regression line for the effect of log transition timing on log technological level in 1000 CE, controlling for the influence of absolute latitude and continental fixed effects. Thus, the *x* and *y* axes plot the residuals obtained from regressing log time elapsed since the Neolithic Revolution and log technological level, respectively, on the aforementioned set of covariates.

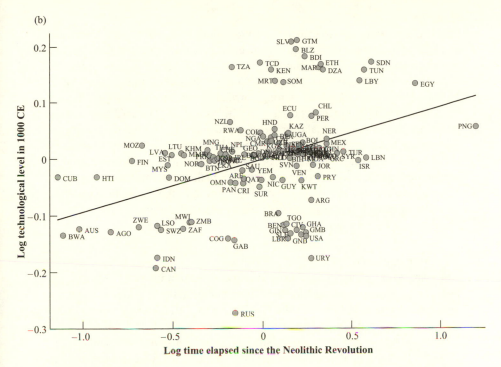

(b)

FIGURE 6.8 *(continued)*

In the Malthusian regime, while income per capita in the two economies may be equal, the rate of technological progress is higher in country B. As depicted in Figure 6.2, for a given level of population, the (conditional) steady-state equilibrium level of education and technology in country B is $(0, g^l(L, \Omega^B))$, whereas the level in country A is $(0, g^l(L, \Omega^A))$. The inherent Malthusian interaction between population size and the rate of technological progress in each of the countries gradually increases the level of both variables, generating an upward shift in the curves $g(e_t; L, \Omega^B)$ and $g(e_t; L, \Omega^A)$.

Inevitably, the rate of technological progress in country B increases sufficiently, and it crosses its threshold rate, $\hat{g}(\Psi)$, above which parental investment in human capital is beneficial. The Malthusian steady-state equilibrium vanishes in country B, and the economy takes off to a state of sustained economic growth. In contrast, in country A the pace of technological progress is slower, and it exceeds the threshold, $\hat{g}(\Psi)$, that would generate a take-off, after country B. However, as long as the effect of the socio-technological head start dissipates over time, the two economies will ultimately converge to the same long-run equilibrium.

Evidence

Empirical evidence provided by Ashraf and Galor (2009, 2011) and summarized in Chapter 3 establishes the significant impact of the timing of the Neolithic Revolution on the level of technology and economic development in the pre-industrial world (Figure 6.8). Moreover, Comin et al. (2010) find that the state of technology in 1000 BCE has a strong correlation with technology 2,500 years later, in 1500 CE. However, as established by Ashraf and Galor (2009), the evidence appears to suggest that over the past 500 years, this initial developmental dominance has been mitigated by additional factors. Consequently, while the data show a significant relationship between the timing of countries' transitions to agriculture and their development outcomes in the precolonial era, Diamond's hypothesis about the persistent effect of the timing of the Neolithic Revolution on contemporary levels of income per capita across the globe is fragile (Ashraf and Galor, 2009).[32]

The Life-Expectancy Channel

Galor and Moav (2008) hypothesize that social, economic, and environmental changes associated with the transition from hunter-gatherer tribes to sedentary agricultural communities (i.e., the Neolithic Revolution) triggered an evolutionary process that has generated a significant impact on contemporary human longevity. The rise in population density, domestication of animals, and increase in work effort during the Neolithic Revolution increased the exposure and vulnerability to infectious diseases and generated an evolutionary advantage to individuals characterized by more effective immune systems, contributing to contemporary human longevity.[33]

---

[32] Olsson and Hibbs (2005) and Putterman (2008) have suggested that there is empirical support for Diamond's hypothesis in that the timing of the Neolithic Revolution affected the contemporary variation in income per capita around the globe. However, as established by Ashraf and Galor (2009), these results are in fact nonrobust. Even the inclusion of continental fixed effects makes the (direct or indirect) effect of the Neolithic Revolution on contemporary outcome insignificantly different from zero.

[33] The effect of the Neolithic Revolution on the exposure and vulnerability of humans to infectious diseases is discussed by Diamond (1997), Olsson and Hibbs (2005), and Weisdorf (2005). Most comparisons between hunter-gatherers and farmers suggest that, in the same location, farmers suffered higher rates of infection due to (i) increased population density, (ii) poorer nutrition (caused by reduced meat intake), and (iii) greater interference with mineral absorption by a cereal-based diet. Consequently, Neolithic farmers were shorter and had a lower life expectancy relative to Mesolithic hunter-gatherers (e.g., Cohen, 1991). Available evidence, depicted in Figure 7.10, suggests that prehistorical hunter-gatherers often fared relatively well compared to later populations and that the Neolithic Revolution was indeed accompanied by a reduction in life expectancy. Moreover, skeletal remains from pre-Colombian America, analyzed by Steckel (2004), demonstrate a decline in the health environment from 6000 BCE to 1500 CE.

This evolutionary hypothesis is consistent with recent theories and evidence about the evolution of senescence, which demonstrate that some organisms that experience high mortality rates, attributed to external factors, could evolve to have a later onset of senescence (see Williams and Day, 2003; Reznick et al., 2004). Moreover, it is consistent with evidence suggesting that significant evolutionary processes in the human species occurred in a similar time span. Importantly, differences in the timing of the Neolithic Revolution across regions generated significant variation in the genetic composition of the contemporary human population, as reflected, for instance, by variations in the geographical distribution of lactose tolerance and genetic immunity to malaria associated with the sickle cell trait (Livingstone, 1958; Wiesenfeld, 1967; Durham, 1982).

This theory can be integrated into the framework of Unified Growth Theory. Consider two economies, A and B, identical in all respects except for the time at which the ancestors of their current population experienced the Neolithic Revolution. Suppose that the Neolithic Revolution occurred earlier in country B, and thus its characteristics are conducive to technological progress (i.e., $\Omega^B > \Omega^A$). Hence, as follows from (6.1) and depicted in Figure 6.9(a), for any given level of population, L, and human capital, e_t, the rate of technological progress is higher in country B (i.e., $g^B_{t+1} = g(e_t; L, \Omega^B) > g^A_{t+1} = g(e_t; L, \Omega^A)$).

Suppose further that an earlier onset of the Neolithic Revolution is associated with higher life expectancy and thus higher investment in human capital. As follows from (6.4) and depicted in Figure 6.9, for any given rate of technological progress, g_{t+1}, human capital formation is at least as high in country B as it is in country A (i.e., $e^A_{t+1} = e(g_{t+1}; \Psi^A) \le e^B_{t+1} = e(g_{t+1}; \Psi^B)$), and the threshold level of the rate of technological progress (above which parental investment in human capital is beneficial) is lower in country B (i.e., $\hat{g}(\Psi^B) < \hat{g}(\Psi^A)$).

In the Malthusian regime, while income per capita in the two economies may be equal, the rate of technological progress is higher in country B. As depicted in Figure 6.9(a), for a given level of population, the (conditional) steady-state equilibrium level of education and technology in country B is $(0, g^l(L, \Omega^B))$, whereas that in country A is $(0, g^l(L, \Omega^A))$. The inherent Malthusian interaction between population size and the rate of technological progress in each of the countries gradually increases both variables and generates an upward shift in the curves $g(e_t; L, \Omega^B)$ and $g(e_t; L, \Omega^A)$.

Inevitably, the rate of technological progress in country B increases sufficiently, and it crosses its threshold level, $\hat{g}(\Psi^B)$, above which parental investment in human capital is beneficial. The Malthusian steady-state equilibrium vanishes in country B, and the economy takes off to a state of sustained economic growth. In contrast, in country A, the pace of technological progress is slower and it exceeds the higher threshold, $\hat{g}(\Psi^A)$, that would generate a take-off, later than country B (Figure 6.9(b)). Moreover, even if the effect of the Neolithic Revolution on technological progress dissipates over time, as long

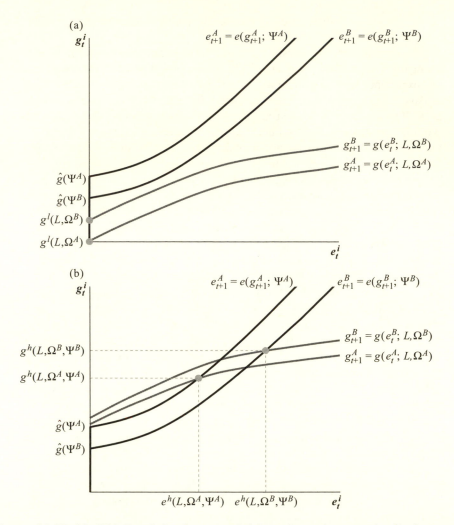

FIGURE 6.9. The Neolithic Revolution, human capital formation, and comparative development.
Summary: Panel (a) shows country A and country B in a Malthusian equilibrium. Country B
experiences the Neolithic Revolution earlier, and its characteristics, Ω^B, are more conducive
to technological progress than those of country A, Ω^A. For a given population size, its rate of
technological progress, $g^l(\text{L}, \Omega^B)$, is higher than that in country A, $g^l(\text{L}, \Omega^A)$. Moreover, since
country B experienced the Neolithic Revolution earlier, its life expectancy is higher; its characteristics,
Ψ^B, are more conducive to human capital formation than those in country A, Ψ^A; and it faces
a lower threshold for take-off (i.e., $\hat{g}(\Psi^B) < \hat{g}(\Psi^A)$). Panel (b) shows that as population and the
rate of technological progress increase in the course of positive Malthusian feedback between
population and technology, the curve $g^i_{t+1} = g(e^i_t; \text{L}, \Omega^i)$, $i = A, B$, shifts gradually upward, and
ultimately, its vertical intercept crosses the threshold rates of technological progress, $\hat{g}(\Psi^i)$, $i = A, B$,
above which investment in human capital is profitable. The Malthusian steady-state equilibria
vanish, and the economies take off to a (conditional) sustained-growth steady-state equilibrium,
$(e^h(\text{L}, \Omega^i, \Psi^i), g^h(\text{L}, \Omega^i, \Psi^i))$, where the earlier onset of the Neolithic in country B has a persistent
beneficial effect in the long run.

as its long-run effect on life expectancy and human capital formation persists, country B will have a superior long-run equilibrium.

Empirical Evidence

Galor and Moav (2008) exploit an exogenous source of variation in the time elapsed since the ancestors of the current population of each country experienced the Neolithic Revolution to identify the impact of the Neolithic Revolution on life expectancy. Moreover, they attempt to isolate the genetic channel through which this impact occurs by controlling for plausible alternative routes for the relationship between the timing of the Neolithic Revolution and contemporary life expectancy.

The Neolithic Revolution first occurred in the Middle East nearly 10,500 years ago, and then took place on average about 6,900 years ago in Asia, 6,300 in Europe, 3,800 in South America, 2,900 in Africa, and 2,300 years ago in North America. The hypothesis suggests that regions that experienced an earlier transition to agricultural communities were exposed to a longer period of evolutionary pressure that increased the representation of individuals who are genetically predisposed toward a more effective immune system, and thus toward higher life expectancy. In particular, it suggests that in a given socio-economic environment, descendants of people from regions that experienced the Neolithic Revolution earlier would have a higher life expectancy compared to descendants of people from regions that experienced the Neolithic Revolution later.

The average time elapsed since the ancestors of the present-day population of each country experienced the Neolithic Revolution is positively and significantly correlated with life expectancy in 2000.[34] Nevertheless, this correlation does not necessarily imply that an earlier onset of the Neolithic Revolution contributed to contemporary life expectancy. In particular, to establish a causal effect, one has to account for the possibility that omitted variables that may be conducive to longer life expectancy today may have also permitted an earlier onset of the Neolithic Revolution.

Moreover, even if a causal effect of an earlier onset of the Neolithic Revolution on contemporary life expectancy is established, it does not necessarily confirm the proposed genetic channel. An earlier onset of the Neolithic Revolution generated a socioeconomic process that may have had an impact on contemporary living standards and thereby on contemporary life expectancy,

---

[34] The average time elapsed since the population of each country experienced the Neolithic Revolution is computed based on the recently compiled dataset on the timing of the Neolithic Revolution across different regions of the world as well as the data on post-1500 migratory patterns across the globe (Putterman, 2008).

irrespective of its potential impact on the composition of genetic traits.[35] In particular, if the Neolithic Revolution affects life expectancy only through socioeconomic forces, then, as the beneficial effect of the Neolithic head start dissipates over the centuries, the Neolithic Revolution is unlikely to affect contemporary economic development.

Thus, the main empirical challenges are to (i) account for the contribution of geographical attributes and socioeconomic factors to the correlation between the timing of the Neolithic Revolution and contemporary life expectancy, (ii) overcome the potential effect of omitted variables that may govern the correlation between the Neolithic Revolution and contemporary life expectancy, and (iii) demonstrate that the timing of the Neolithic Revolution has a significant effect on life expectancy (beyond its effect thorough socioeconomic factors) that could be plausibly attributed to its impact on the genetic composition of the human population.

The findings indicate that a significant portion of the variation in life expectancy across countries can indeed be traced to the variation in the timing of the Neolithic Revolution. As depicted in Figure 6.10, every 1,000 years of earlier Neolithic transition of the ancestors of the current population of each country is estimated to contribute about 2 years to contemporary life expectancy, accounting for geographical characteristics, as well as for income, education, and health expenditure per capita. Thus, about 6 years of the existing 26-year gap in life expectancy between the European and the African population can be attributed to the fact that the ancestors of the current European population experienced the Neolithic Revolution about 3,000 years earlier than did those of the current African population.

To disentangle the genetic mechanism from the geographical and socioeconomic channels in the effect of the Neolithic Revolution on contemporary life expectancy, the analysis exploits the difference between the time elapsed since the Neolithic Revolution in each country, as defined by its current geographical territory, and the average time elapsed since the ancestors of the population of each country today experienced the Neolithic Revolution, capturing traits that are embodied in the current population and were transmitted intergenerationally. Indeed, the time elapsed since the Neolithic Revolution has a stronger and more significant effect on contemporary life expectancy via the portable (and thus plausibly the genetic) component. Moreover, the genetic interpretation of this effect is further strengthened by the finding that an earlier Neolithic transition reduces significantly the likelihood of mortality from infectious diseases compared to mortality from other sources.

---

[35] For instance, existing theories and evidence suggest that the advancement of health infrastructure, medical technology, and education contributed to the rise in life expectancy in recent centuries (Fogel, 1994; Galor and Weil, 1999; Boucekkine et al., 2003; Lagerlöf, 2003a; Cervellati and Sunde, 2005).

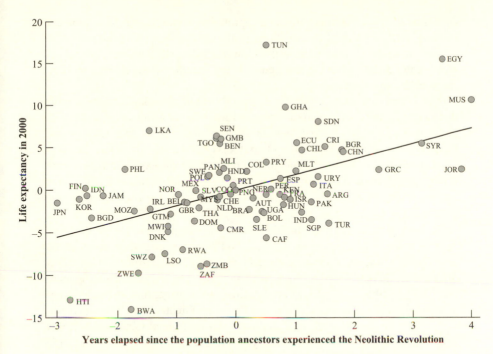

FIGURE 6.10. Years elapsed since the Neolithic Revolution and life expectancy in 2000.
Data source: Galor and Moav (2008).
Summary: The figure depicts the partial effect of the average time elapsed since the ancestors of the population of each country today experienced the Neolithic Revolution on life expectancy in 2000, controlling for geographical and socioeconomic factors. Thus, the *x* and *y* axes plot the residuals obtained from regressing time elapsed since the Neolithic Revolution and life expectancy, respectively, on the aforementioned set of covariates.

Hence, once the demand for human capital emerged in the process of industrialization, variation in the timing of the Neolithic Revolution across different regions could have contributed to existing variation in human capital formation and economic development around the globe.

6.4.2 The Out-of-Africa Hypothesis and Comparative Development

Ashraf and Galor (2009) argue that deep-rooted factors, determined tens of thousands of years ago, have had a significant effect on the course of economic development from the dawn of human civilization to the contemporary era. They advance the hypothesis that in the course of the exodus of *Homo sapiens* out of Africa, variation in migratory distance from the cradle of humankind to various settlements around the globe affected genetic diversity and had a direct, long-lasting, hump-shaped effect on the pattern of comparative economic development that cannot be captured by contemporary geographical, institutional, and cultural factors. Further, the optimal level of diversity has increased in the process of industrialization, as the beneficial forces associated with greater diversity have intensified in an environment characterized by more rapid technological progress.

The hypothesis rests on two fundamental building blocks. First, migratory distance from the cradle of humankind in East Africa had an adverse effect on the degree of genetic diversity within ancient indigenous settlements around the globe. Following the prevailing hypothesis, commonly known as the serial founder effect, it is postulated that, in the course of human expansion over planet Earth, as subgroups of the populations of parental colonies left to establish new settlements farther away, they carried with them only a subset of the overall genetic diversity.

Second, there exists an optimal level of diversity for each stage of development, reflecting the interplay between conflicting effects of diversity on the development process. The adverse effect pertains to the detrimental impact of diversity on the efficiency of the aggregate production process. Heterogeneity increases the likelihood of miscoordination and distrust, thus reducing cooperation and disrupting the socioeconomic order. Greater population diversity is therefore associated with the social cost of a lower total factor productivity, which inhibits the ability of society to operate efficiently with respect to its production possibility frontier.

The beneficial effect of diversity concerns the positive role of diversity in the expansion of the society's production possibility frontier. A wider spectrum of traits enhances the accumulation of universally applicable human capital and is more likely to be complementary to the development and successful implementation of advanced technological paradigms. Greater heterogeneity therefore fosters the ability of a society to incorporate more sophisticated and efficient modes of production, expanding the society's production possibility frontier and conferring the benefits of increased total factor productivity.[36]

Higher diversity in a society's population can therefore have conflicting effects on the level of its total factor productivity. Productivity is enhanced, on the one hand, by an increased capacity for technological advancement, while diminished, on the other, by reduced cooperation and efficiency.

However, if the beneficial effects of population diversity dominate at lower levels of diversity and the detrimental effects dominate at higher levels (i.e., if there are diminishing marginal returns to both diversity and homogeneity), the theory predicts an inverted-U relationship between genetic diversity and development outcomes over the course of the development process. Furthermore, the theory also predicts that the optimal level of diversity increases with

---

[36] Alesina and La Ferrara (2005) explore the conflicting effects of ethnic diversity on economic development.

the process of economic development, as the beneficial forces associated with greater population diversity intensified in an environment characterized by more rapid technological progress.[37]

The theory can be embedded in the framework of Unified Growth Theory. Consider two economies, A and B, identical in all respects except for the diversity of the human capital of their populations. In particular, suppose that the countries are identical in the characteristics that are conducive to human capital formation (i.e., $\Psi^A = \Psi^B \equiv \Psi$), and, as established in (6.4) and depicted in Figure 6.11, for any rate of technological progress, g_{t+1}, human capital formation is equal in the two countries (i.e., $e^A_{t+1} = e^B_{t+1} = e(g_{t+1}; \Psi)$). Moreover, the threshold level of the rate of technological progress (above which parental investment in human capital is beneficial), $\hat{g}(\Psi)$, is also equal in the two countries.

Suppose that, in light of the trade-off associated with diversity, there exists an optimal level of diversity, $\Omega^*_t = \Omega(g_t)$, in each period t. Furthermore, since the benefits associated with diversity increase in an environment characterized by more rapid technological progress, the optimal level of diversity is an increasing function of the rate of technological progress, i.e., $\Omega'(g_t) > 0$. Suppose further that, as long as the rate of technological progress in country B is below a critical level, $\tilde{g}$ (where $\tilde{g} < \hat{g}(\Psi)$), the level of diversity in country B, Ω^B, exceeds the optimal level (i.e., $\Omega^B > \Omega(g_t)$ for all $g_t < \tilde{g}$), and the lower level of diversity present in country A, Ω^A, is more conducive to technological progress. However, once the rate of technological progress in country B exceeds the critical level, $\tilde{g}$, the level of diversity in country B is more conducive to technological progress than that in country A.

Hence, as depicted in Figure 6.11(a), for any given level of population, L, and human capital, e_t,

$$g^B_{t+1} = g(e_t; L, \Omega^B) \begin{cases} < g^A_{t+1} = g(e_t; L, \Omega^A), & \text{if } g^l(L, \Omega^B) < \tilde{g}; \\ > g^A_{t+1} = g(e_t; L, \Omega^A), & \text{if } g^l(L, \Omega^B) > \tilde{g}. \end{cases} \tag{6.12}$$

In the Malthusian regime, while incomes per capita in the two economies may be equal, the rate of technological progress is higher in country A. In particular, for a given level of population, the steady-state equilibrium levels of education and technology in country B are $(0, g^l(L, \Omega^B))$, while the levels in country A are $(0, g^l(L, \Omega^A))$, where $g^l(L, \Omega^A) > g^l(L, \Omega^B)$.

The inherent Malthusian interaction between the size of the population and the rate of technological progress in each of the countries gradually increases both variables and generates an upward shift in the curves $g(e^B_t; L, \Omega^B)$ and

---

[37] As established by Ashraf and Galor (2007), cultural rather than genetic diversity may generate a similar pattern.

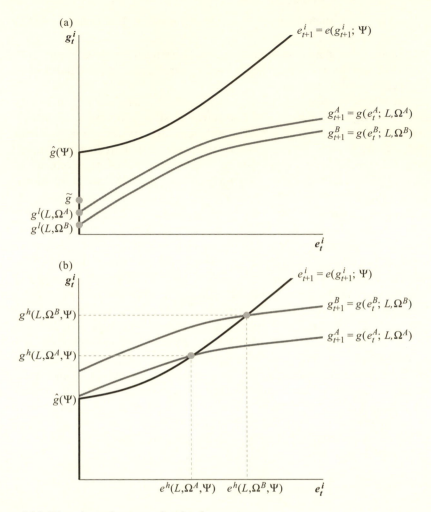

FIGURE 6.11. Diversity and comparative development.

Summary: Panel (a) shows that in the early stages of development, prior to the emergence of demand for human capital, the two economies, A and B, are in (conditional) Malthusian steady-state equilibrium. Country B's level of diversity, Ω^B, is less conducive to technological progress than that in country A, Ω^A, and for a given population size, L, its rate of technological progress, $g^l(L, \Omega^B)$, is lower than that in country A, $g^l(L, \Omega^A)$. Panel (b) shows that as population and the rate of technological progress increase during the positive Malthusian feedback between population and technology, the curves $g^B_{t+1} = g(e^B_t; L, \Omega^B)$ and $g^A_{t+1} = g(e^A_t; L, \Omega^A)$ shift upward. Ultimately, the vertical intercept of $g^B_{t+1} = g(e^B_t; L, \Omega^B)$ crosses the threshold rate of technological progress, $\tilde{g}$, above which diversity in country B is more conducive to technological progress than in country A. Technological progress accelerates in country B, shifting further upward the curve $g^B_{t+1} = g(e^B_t; L, \Omega^B)$. Eventually the vertical intercepts of $g^B_{t+1} = g(e^B_t; L, \Omega^B)$ and $g^A_{t+1} = g(e^A_t; L, \Omega^A)$ cross the threshold level, $\hat{g}(\Psi)$, above which investment in human capital is profitable. The Malthusian equilibrium vanishes in countries A and B, and the economies take off to a modern growth regime. During this development process, country B overtakes country A and converges to a superior (conditional) steady-state equilibrium.

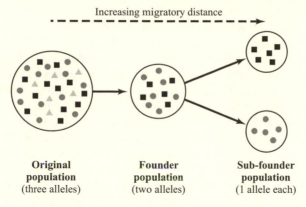

Original population (three alleles)   **Founder population** (two alleles)   **Sub-founder population** (1 allele each)

FIGURE 6.12. The serial founder effect.

$g(e_t^A; L, \Omega^A)$. Inevitably, the rate of technological progress in country B increases sufficiently and crosses the threshold level, $\tilde{g}$, above which the level of diversity in country B is more conducive to technological progress than is the level of diversity in country A.

Technological progress accelerates in country B, due to the scale and diversity effects, and for a given population size, the rate of technological progress in country B is higher than that of country A. Ultimately each of the two economies, at its own pace, crosses the critical rate of technological progress, $\hat{g}(\Psi)$, above which parental investment in human capital is beneficial. The Malthusian steady-state equilibrium vanishes in the two economies, and they take off to a state of sustained economic growth. During this development process, country B, because of its more beneficial level of diversity, overtakes country A and converges to a superior (conditional) steady-state equilibrium $(e^h(L, \Omega^B, \Psi), g^h(L, \Omega^B, \Psi)) > (e^h(L, \Omega^A, \Psi), g^h(L, \Omega^A, \Psi))$, as depicted in Figure 6.11(b).[38]

Migratory Distance from East Africa, the Serial Founder Effect, and Genetic Diversity

According to the prevailing hypothesis, commonly known as the serial founder effect, the populating of the world with humans occurred in a series of discrete steps. As illustrated in Figure 6.12, subgroups of the original population left their initial settlement to establish new settlements farther away, carrying only a subset of the overall genetic diversity of their parental colonies.

Empirical evidence suggests that, indeed, migratory distance from East Africa has an adverse linear effect on genetic diversity. This relationship has

---

[38] Population flows may affect the level of diversity in the process of development.

been established for 53 ethnic groups from the Human Genome Diversity Cell Line Panel for which Ramachandran et al. (2005) compute the expected heterozygosity (i.e., genetic diversity) from allelic frequencies associated with 783 chromosomal loci.[39] Migratory distance from East Africa for each of the 53 ethnic groups was computed using the great circle (or geodesic) distances from Addis Ababa, Ethiopia, to the contemporary geographic coordinates of these ethnic groups, subject to five obligatory intermediate waypoints (i.e., Cairo, Egypt; Istanbul, Turkey; Phnom Penh, Cambodia; Anadyr, Russia; and Prince Rupert, Canada) that capture paleontological and genetic evidence on prehistorical human migration patterns. For instance, given the spatial distribution of the 53 ethnic groups from the HGDP-CEPH sample, as depicted in Figure 6.13, the migration path from Addis Ababa to the Papuan ethnic group in modern-day New Guinea makes use of Cairo and Phnom Penh, whereas that to the Karitiana population in Brazil incorporates Cairo, Anadyr, and Prince Rupert as intermediate waypoints.[40]

The regression analysis, depicted in Figure 6.14, establishes that migratory distance from East Africa is a strong negative predictor of genetic diversity. Specifically, migratory distance alone explains 86% of the cross-group variation in within-group diversity.[41] In addition, the estimated OLS coefficient is highly statistically significant. It indicates that the predicted heterozygosity falls by

---

[39] For a more detailed description of the Human Genome Diversity Project (HGDP) Human Genome Diversity Cell Line Panel dataset, the interested reader is referred to Cann et al. (2002). A broad overview of the Human Genome Diversity Project is given by Cavalli-Sforza (2005).

[40] Based on mitochondrial DNA analysis, some recent studies (e.g., Oppenheimer, 2003; Macaulay et al., 2005) have proposed a southern exit route out of Africa whereby the initial exodus into Asia occurred not via the Levant but across the mouth of the Red Sea (between modern-day Djibouti and Yemen), thereafter taking a "beachcombing" path along the southern coast of the Arabian Peninsula to India and onward into Southeast Asia. Moreover, a subsequent northern offshoot from the Persian Gulf region ultimately lead to the settlement of the Near East and Europe. This scenario therefore suggests the use of Sana'a, Yemen, and Bandar Abbas, Iran, as intermediate waypoints instead of Cairo. Adopting this alternative route for computing migratory distances, however, does not significantly alter the qualitative results.

[41] These results are similar to those uncovered in an independent study by Prugnolle et al. (2005) that employs a subset of the HGDP-CEPH sample encompassing 51 ethnic groups whose expected heterozygosities are calculated from allelic frequencies for 377 loci. Despite their somewhat smaller sample at both the ethnic group and DNA analysis levels, Prugnolle et al. (2005) find that migratory distance from East Africa explains 85% of the variation in genetic diversity. In contrast, using an expanded dataset comprised of the 53 HGDP-CEPH ethnic groups and an additional 24 Native American populations, Wang et al. (2007) find that migratory distance explains a more modest 74% of the variation in genetic diversity, based on allelic frequencies for 678 loci. The authors attribute their somewhat weaker results to the fact that the additional Native American ethnic groups in their augmented sample were historically subjected to a high degree of gene flow from foreign populations (i.e., European colonizers), which obscured the genetic legacy of the serial founder effect in these groups.

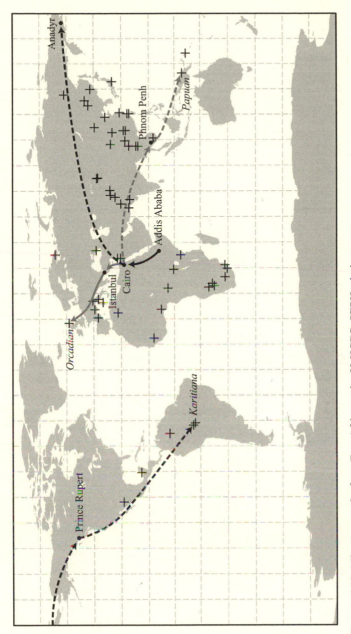

FIGURE 6.13. Migratory paths from East Africa to the 53 HGDP-CEPH ethnic groups.
Data sources: Cann et al. (2002); Ramachandran et al. (2005).

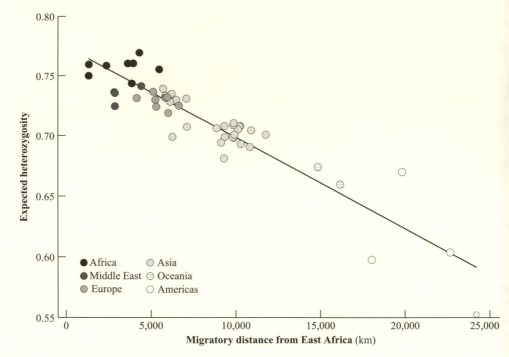

FIGURE 6.14. Expected heterozygosity and migratory distance in the HGDP-CEPH sample of 53 ethnic groups.
Data source: Ramachandran et al. (2005).

0.0755 percentage points for every 10,000 km increase in migratory distance from Addis Ababa.

Empirical Examination

Ashraf and Galor (2009) analyze the effect of genetic diversity on the process of development and contemporary income per capita around the globe. They exploit the explanatory power of migratory distance from East Africa for the cross-sectional variation in expected heterozygosity among ethnic groups in two dimensions. First, the strong capacity of migratory distance in predicting genetic diversity implies that the empirical analysis of the effect of genetic diversity need not be restricted to the 53 HGDP-CEPH ethnic groups that span only 21 countries; one can project genetic diversity for all countries. Second, given the potential endogeneity of *observed* genetic diversity and the level of economic development in the Malthusian era, the use of genetic diversity values *predicted* by migratory distance from East Africa alleviates concerns regarding endogeneity bias.

Consistent with the predictions of the theory, the empirical analysis finds that the level of genetic diversity within a society has a hump-shaped effect on development outcomes in the precolonial era, reflecting the trade-off between the beneficial and the detrimental effects of diversity on productivity. Moreover, the level of genetic diversity within a country today (i.e., genetic diversity and genetic distance among and between its ancestral populations) has a similar nonmonotonic effect on contemporary levels of income per capita. While the intermediate level of genetic diversity prevalent among Asian and European populations has been conducive to development, the high degree of diversity among African populations and the low degree among Native American populations have been detrimental to the development of these regions. Further, the empirical findings appear to suggest that the optimal level of diversity has increased in the course of industrialization. Importantly, as technological sophistication has increased in the transition to modern growth, the benefit of diversity has risen as well. As depicted in Figure 6.15, while the optimal level of diversity in 1500 corresponded to the levels that were present in Japan, China, and Korea, the optimal level of diversity in 2000 corresponds to that in the United States.[42]

Interestingly, the direct effect of genetic diversity on contemporary income per capita, once institutional, cultural, and geographical factors are accounted for, indicates that:

a. Increasing the diversity of the most homogeneous country in the sample (Bolivia) by 1 percentage point would raise its income per capita in 2000 by 39%.

b. Decreasing the diversity of the most diverse country in the sample (Ethiopia) by 1 percentage point would raise its income per capita by 21%.

c. Changing diversity by 1 percentage point (in either direction) from the optimal level of 0.7208 (which most closely approaches the U.S. diversity level of 0.7206) would lower income per capita by 1.9%.

d. Increasing the diversity of Bolivia to the optimum level of the United States would increase Bolivia's per capita income by a factor of 4.7, narrowing the income gap between the two countries from 12:1 to 2.5:1.

e. Decreasing the diversity of Ethiopia to the optimal level of the United States would increase Ethiopia's per capita income by a factor of 1.7, reducing the income gap between these two countries from 47:1 to 27:1.

[42] As established in Chapter 3, population density is the proper measure of economic development in the pre-Industrial Revolution era.

(a)

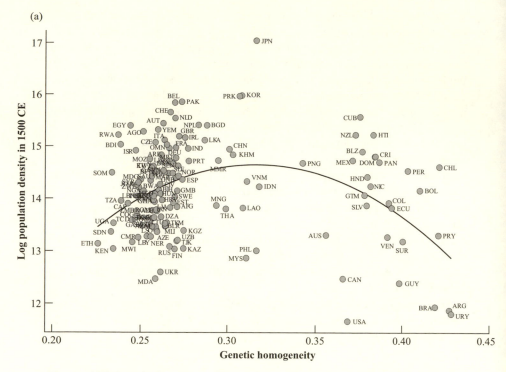

FIGURE 6.15. Genetic diversity and economic development in 1500 and 2000. (a) Genetic diversity and population density in 1500 CE. (b) Genetic diversity and income per capita in 2000.

Data source: Ashraf and Galor (2011).

Summary: The figure depicts the effect of genetic diversity on population density in 1500 CE (panel a) and income per capita in 2000 (panel b), controlling for the timing of the Neolithic Revolution, land productivity, and continental fixed effects.

Thus, as suggested by Unified Growth Theory, biogeographical factors, determined tens of thousands of years ago, have generated a significant effect on the course of economic development across countries and regions of the world.

6.5 Multiple Growth Regimes and Convergence Clubs

In its third layer, Unified Growth Theory advances the understanding of the forces that have contributed to the existence of multiple growth regimes and the emergence of convergence clubs (i.e., groups of countries among which the disparity in income per capita tends to narrow over a prolonged period of time).

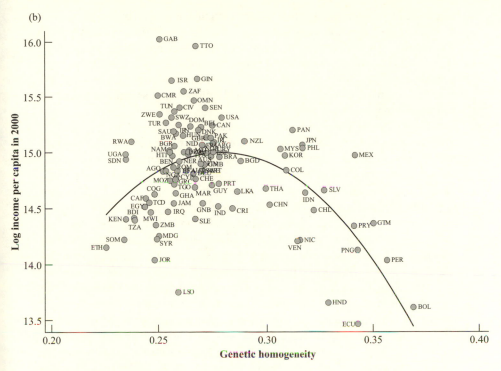

FIGURE 6.15 *(continued)*

The theory attributes these phenomena to variation in the position of economies along the distinct phases of development.

The quest for an empirical determination of the forces that have contributed to the existence of multiple growth regimes and the emergence of several convergence clubs, although central for understanding the process of development, has not been universally shared by researchers in the field of economic growth.[43] Contributors to the empirical literature on multiple growth regimes have faced mounting challenges to motivate their findings in the context of growth models that are widely perceived as plausible. The dominant tendency to rationalize and interpret these empirical explorations in the context of growth models characterized by multiple long-run equilibria based on initial conditions has been

[43] Growth nonlinearities and convergence clubs were explored theoretically by Galor and Ryder (1989), Azariadis and Drazen (1990), Galor (1992, 1996), and empirically by Durlauf and Johnson (1995), Quah (1997), Durlauf and Quah (1999), Kalaitzidakis et al. (2001), Bloom et al. (2003), Fiaschi and Lavezzi (2003), Durlauf et al. (2005), Feyrer (2008), and Owen et al. (2009), among others.

confronted by skepticism that has undermined this important endeavor and has deprived it from a central place in the growth literature.[44] If indeed there exists a threshold level of development that poor economies must surpass to join the club of the rich, and if this threshold is insurmountable (in the absence of large exogenous shocks), then how did the rich economies in today's world surpass it in the distant past, when their level of development was similar to that of countries in poverty traps today?

Unified Growth Theory provides a fundamental framework of analysis that uncovers the forces that contributed to the existence of multiple growth regimes and the emergence of several convergence clubs. Furthermore, it sheds light on the characteristics that determine the association of economies with each of the clubs. The theory suggests that, although the long-run equilibrium may not differ across economies, the differential timing of take-offs from stagnation to growth segmented economies into three fundamental growth regimes: slowly growing economies in the vicinity of a Malthusian regime, fast-growing countries in a sustained-growth regime, and economies transitioning from one regime to another. Thus economies fall into three fundamental groups: two convergence clubs of rich and poor economies and a third group of countries in the transition from one club to the other. Importantly, this segmentation does not reflect the long-run steady state of these economies, as would be implied by models characterized by multiple steady-state equilibria. Rather, it represents variation in the timing of the escape from a Malthusian trap and thus in the position of countries along the growth trajectory from the Malthusian Epoch to sustained economic growth. Convergence clubs, therefore, may be temporary, and endogenous forces would permit economies to shift from the Malthusian Epoch into the sustained-growth regime.

In contrast to existing research that links the thresholds permitting economies to switch from one club to another to critical *levels* of income and human capital, Unified Growth Theory suggests that they are associated primarily with critical *rates* of technological progress, population growth, and human capital formation. The theory suggests that two major transformations in the growth process determine the thresholds between the three fundamental regimes. The first threshold is associated with a rapid increase in the rates of technological progress and population growth, and the second with a significant rise in human capital formation along with a rapid decline in population growth. Variations in the levels of income, human capital, and population growth across

---

[44] A notable exception is Durlauf and Johnson (1995), who provide a broader interpretation that includes, in addition to multiple long-run equilibria, a world characterized by a unique long-run equilibrium but different stages of development.

countries would not be indicative of these thresholds and would only reflect country-specific characteristics rather than the actual stage of development.[45]

6.6 Concluding Remarks

Unified Growth Theory sheds light on the notable divergence in income per capita across the globe during the past two centuries. It advances the understanding of three fundamental aspects of comparative economic development. First, it identifies the factors that have governed the pace of the transition from stagnation to growth and have thus contributed to the observed worldwide differences in economic development. Second, it highlights the persistent effects that variations in prehistorical biogeographical conditions have had on the composition of human capital and economic development across countries. Third, it uncovers the forces that have sparked the emergence of convergence clubs and unveils the characteristics that determine the association of different economies with each club.

The theory implies that differences in the timing of the take-off from stagnation to growth contributed to the divergence in income per capita between countries. Thus, the first layer of the theory facilitates the identification of factors that have governed the pace of transition from an epoch of Malthusian stagnation to an era of sustained economic growth and have thus contributed to the observed differences in economic development across countries.

Global variation in country-specific characteristics that has influenced the rate of technological progress reinforced the differential pace of the emergence of demand for human capital, the onset of the demographic transition, and the pace of the shift from stagnation to growth, and has thus contributed to the divergence in income per capita in the past two centuries. In particular, worldwide variation in technological progress has been triggered by cross-country differences in the following characteristics.

a. The stock of knowledge and its rate of creation and diffusion across members of society.
b. The level of protection of intellectual property rights, its positive effect on the incentive to innovate, and its adverse effect on the proliferation of existing knowledge.

---

[45] For instance, although during the eighteenth century, education levels were significantly lower in England than in continental Europe, England was the first to industrialize and take off toward a state of sustained economic growth. Similarly, the demographic transition that marked a regime switch to a state of sustained economic growth occurred in the same decade across Western European countries that differed significantly in their incomes per capita.

c. Cultural and religious attributes and their effects on knowledge creation and diffusion.
d. The composition of interest groups in society and their incentives to block or promote technological innovation.
e. The level of human diversity and the degree to which it complements the implementation and advancement of new technological paradigms.
f. The economic, institutional, and cultural characteristics that determine the strength of concerns about relative standing and its role in deterring or enhancing innovation and effort.
g. The propensity to trade and its effect on technological diffusion.
h. The abundance of essential natural resources for an impending technological advancement.

Moreover, once the technologically driven demand for human capital emerged in the second phase of industrialization, the prevalence of characteristics conducive to human capital formation has determined the swiftness of its accumulation, the timing of the demographic transition, the pace of the transition from stagnation to growth, and the observed distribution of income in the world economy. Thus, variations in country-specific characteristics that have contributed to human capital formation have differentially affected the timing and pace of the transition from agriculture to industry and thus comparative economic development as a whole.

In particular, global variation in human capital formation has been triggered by cross-country differences in the following characteristics.

a. The prevalence of human capital–promoting institutions or policies (e.g., the availability, accessibility, and quality of public education and child labor regulations).
b. The ability of individuals to finance the cost of education as well as the foregone earnings associated with schooling.
c. The impact of the level of inequality and of the degree of credit-market imperfections on the extent of underinvestment in education.
d. The stock of knowledge in society and its effect on the productivity of investment of human capital.
e. The impact of geographical attributes on health and thus on human capital formation.
f. Preferences for educated offspring that may reflect cultural attributes and the composition of religious groups.

In its second layer, Unified Growth Theory highlights the persistent direct effect that differences in prehistorical biogeographical conditions (e.g., biodiversity, migratory distance from the geographical origin of *Homo sapiens* in East Africa, and genetic diversity) have had on global comparative development over the course of human history. Recent advances provide fascinating evidence that these initial endowments, determined as early as tens of thousands years ago, are critical for understanding comparative economic development from the dawn of human civilization to the modern era.

In its third layer, Unified Growth Theory advances the understanding of the forces that have contributed to the existence of multiple growth regimes and the emergence of several convergence clubs. The theory attributes these phenomena to variation in the position of economies among the distinct phases of development. The theory suggests that, although the long-run equilibrium may not differ among economies, the differential timing of take-offs from stagnation to growth has segmented economies into three fundamental growth regimes: slowly growing economies in the vicinity of a Malthusian steady state, fast-growing countries in a sustained-growth regime, and a third group of economies in transition from one regime to the other.

CHAPTER 7

Human Evolution and the Process of Development

> *It is not the strongest of the species that survive, nor the*
> *most intelligent, but the one most responsive to change.*
> —Charles Darwin

This chapter explores the dynamic interaction between human evolution and the process of economic development. It advances the hypothesis that during the Malthusian Epoch, when the subsistence consumption constraint affected the vast majority of the population, the forces of natural selection operated relentlessly and the survival of the fittest complemented the growth process and contributed to the transition of the world economy from stagnation to growth.

Humans were subjected to a persistent struggle for existence for most of their history. The Malthusian pressure affected the size of the population, and conceivably, via natural selection, its composition as well. Lineages of individuals whose traits were complementary to the economic environment generated higher income, and thus a larger number of surviving offspring, and the gradual increase in the representation of their traits in the population contributed significantly to the process of development and the take-off from stagnation to growth.

Evidence suggests that evolutionary processes in the composition of genetic traits may be rather rapid, and major evolutionary changes have occurred in the human population since the Neolithic Revolution. For instance, lactose tolerance has developed among Europeans and Near Easterners since the domestication of dairy animals in the course of the Neolithic Revolution, whereas in regions that were exposed to dairy animals in later stages, a larger proportion of the adult population suffers from lactose intolerance. Furthermore, genetic immunity to malaria provided by the sickle cell trait is prevalent among descendants of Africans whose engagement in agriculture improved breeding grounds for mosquitoes and thereby raised the incidence of malaria, whereas this trait is absent among descendants of nearby populations that did not make the transition to agriculture (Livingstone, 1958; Wiesenfeld, 1967; Durham, 1982). More generally, Voight et al. (2006) detected about 700 regions of the human genome where genes appear to have been reshaped by natural selection within the past

5,000–15,000 years. Moreover, a recent study by Mekel-Bobrov et al. (2005) reports that a variant of the gene ASPM (a specific regulator of brain size in the lineage leading to *Homo sapiens*) arose in humans merely about 5,800 years ago and has since swept to high frequency under strong positive selection.[1]

Nevertheless, despite the existence of compelling evidence about the interaction between human evolution and the process of economic development, only a few attempts have been made to explore this interaction—an exploration that may revolutionize our understanding of the process of long-run economic development as well as that of human evolution.[2]

7.1 Natural Selection and the Origins of Economic Growth

An evolutionary growth theory that captures the interplay between human evolution and the process of economic development in various phases of development was advanced by Galor and Moav (2002). The theory suggests that during the epoch of Malthusian stagnation, traits of higher valuation of offspring quality generated an evolutionary advantage and their representation in the population gradually increased. This selection process and its effect on investment in human capital stimulated technological progress and ultimately initiated a reinforcing interaction between investment in human capital and technological progress that brought about the demographic transition and the state of sustained economic growth.[3]

---

[1] There are numerous examples of rapid evolutionary changes among various species. The color change that peppered moths underwent during the nineteenth century is a classic example of evolution in nature (Kettlewell, 1973). Before the Industrial Revolution, light-colored English peppered moths blended with the lichen-covered bark of trees. By the end of the nineteenth century, a black variant of the moth, first recorded in 1848, became far more prevalent than the lighter varieties in areas in which industrial carbon removed the lichen and changed the background color. Moreover, evidence from Daphne Major in the Galapagos suggests that significant evolutionary changes in the distribution of traits among Darwin's finches occurred within a few generations due to a major drought (Grant and Grant, 1989). Other evidence, including changes in the color patterns of guppies within 15 generations due to changes in the population of predators, is surveyed by Endler (1986).

[2] The evolution of a wide range of attributes, such as time preference, risk aversion, and altruism, in a given economic environment, has been extensively explored in the economic literature (Weibull, 1997; Bowles, 1998; Robson, 2001; Alger and Weibull, 2010). In addition, Ofek (2001) and Saint-Paul (2007) examine the effect of the emergence of markets on the evolution of heterogeneity in the human population.

[3] The theory is applicable to either social or genetic intergenerational transmission of traits. A cultural transmission is likely to be more rapid and may govern some of the observed differences in fertility rates across regions. The interaction between cultural and genetic evolution is explored by Boyd and Richerson (1985) and Cavalli-Sforza and Feldman (1981); cultural transmission of preferences is examined by Bisin and Verdier (2000).

The Neolithic Revolution facilitated the division of labor and fostered trade relationships among individuals and communities, enhancing the complexity of human interaction and raising the return on human capital. Thus, individuals born to parents with traits of (moderately) higher valuation of offspring's quality generated higher income and, in the Malthusian Epoch, when child rearing was positively affected by aggregate resources, a larger number of offspring.

Malthusian pressure in the post-Neolithic Revolution era increased the representation of individuals whose preferences were biased toward child quality, positively affecting investment in human capital and subsequently the rate of technological progress. In the early stages of development, the proportion of individuals with higher valuation of quality was relatively low, investment in human capital was minimal, resources above subsistence were devoted primarily to child rearing, and the rate of technological progress was rather slow. Technological progress therefore generated proportional increases in output and population, and the economy was in the vicinity of a Malthusian equilibrium, where income per capita was constant, but the proportion of individuals with high valuation of quality was growing over time.[4]

As the fraction of individuals with high valuation of quality continued to increase, technological progress intensified, raising the rate of return on human capital and inducing households to reallocate these increased resources to child quality. In the early stages of the transition from the Malthusian Regime, the effect of technological progress on parental income dominated and the rate of population growth as well as the average quality increased, further accelerating technological progress. Ultimately, further increases in the rate of technological progress induced a universal investment in human capital along with a reduction in fertility rates, generating a demographic transition in which the rate of population growth declined along with an increase in the average level of education. The positive feedback between technological progress and the level of education reinforced the growth process, setting the stage for the transition to a state of sustained economic growth.[5]

During the transition from the Malthusian Epoch to the sustained-growth regime, once the economic environment improved sufficiently, the theory suggests that the significance of quality for survival declined, and traits of higher valuation of quantity gained the evolutionary advantage. Namely, as techno-

---

[4] Unlike the analysis in Chapter 5, in which the adverse effect of limited resources on population growth delays the process of development, in the evolutionary theory, the Malthusian constraint generates the necessary evolutionary pressure for the ultimate take-off.

[5] The theory suggests that waves of rapid technological progress in the pre-Industrial Revolution era did not generate sustained economic growth due to the shortage of preferences for quality in the population. Although in these previous episodes, technological progress temporarily increased the return on quality, the level of human capital that was generated by the response of the existing population to the incentive to invest in human capital was insufficient to sustain technological progress and economic growth.

logical progress brought about an increase in income, the Malthusian pressure relaxed and the domination of wealth in fertility decisions diminished. The inherent advantage of higher valuation of quantity in reproduction started to dominate, and individuals whose preferences were biased toward child quantity gained the evolutionary advantage. Nevertheless, the growth rate of output per worker has remained positive, since the high rate of technological progress sustained an attractive return on investment in human capital, even from the viewpoint of individuals whose valuation of quality is relatively low.

The theory suggests therefore that the transition from stagnation to growth is an inevitable by-product of the interaction between the composition of the population and the rate of technological progress in the Malthusian Epoch. However, for a given composition of population, the timing of the transition may differ significantly across countries and regions due to historical accidents, as well as to variation in geographical, cultural, social, and institutional factors; trade patterns; colonial status; and public policy.

7.2 Primary Ingredients

The theory is based on the interaction among several building blocks: the Darwinian elements, the Malthusian components, the nature of technological progress, the origins of human capital formation, and the factors that affect parental choice regarding the quantity and quality of offspring.

7.2.1 The Darwinian Elements

The theory incorporates the main ingredients of Darwinian evolution (i.e., variety, intergenerational transmission of traits, and natural selection) into an economic environment. Inspired by fundamental components of the Darwinian theory (Darwin, 1859), it is assumed that individuals do not operate consciously to ensure their evolutionary advantage. Nevertheless, those whose traits are most complementary to the environment would eventually dominate the population.

Individuals' preferences are defined over consumption above subsistence as well as over the quality and quantity of their children.[6] These preferences

---

[6] The subsistence consumption constraint is designed to capture the fact that the physiological survival of the parent is a precondition for survival of the lineage (dynasty). Resources allocated to parental consumption beyond the subsistence level may be viewed as a force that raises parental productivity and resistance to adverse shocks (e.g., famine and disease), generating a positive effect on the fitness of the parent and the survival of the lineage. This positive effect, however, is counterbalanced by the implied reduction in resources allocated to the offspring, generating a negative effect on the survival of the lineage.

capture the Darwinian survival strategy as well as the most fundamental trade-offs that exist in nature—the trade-off between resources allocated to the parent and the offspring and that between the number of offspring and resources allocated to each offspring.[7] The economy consists of a variety of individuals distinguished by the weight given to child quality in their preferences.[8] This trait is assumed to be transmitted intergenerationally, either culturally or genetically. The economic environment determines which type has evolutionary advantage, and the distribution of preferences in the population evolves over time due to differences in net fertility rates across types.[9]

The significance that individuals attribute to child quantity as well as to child quality reflects the well-known variety in the quality-quantity survival strategies (i.e., the K and r strategies) that exists in nature (e.g., MacArthur and Wilson, 2001). Human beings, like other species, confront the basic trade-off between offspring quality and quantity in their implicit Darwinian survival strategies. Although a quantity-biased preference has a positive effect on fertility rates and may therefore generate a direct evolutionary advantage, it adversely affects the quality of offspring, their income, and their fitness and may therefore generate an evolutionary disadvantage. "Increased bearing is bound to be paid for by less efficient caring" (Dawkins, 1989, p. 116). As has been established in the evolutionary biology literature since Lack (1954), the allocation of resources between offspring caring and bearing is subjected to evolutionary changes.[10]

[7] Resources allocated to quality of offspring in different stages of development take different forms. In early stages of development, it may be manifested in investment in the durability of the offspring through better nourishment and parental guidance, whereas in mature stages, investment in quality may capture formal education.

[8] The analysis abstracts from heterogeneity in the degree of the trade-off between resources allocated to parent and offspring. The introduction of this element would not alter the qualitative results.

[9] Recent research using historical and modern data from the United States and Europe suggests that fertility behavior has a significant hereditary component (Rodgers et al., 2001a). For instance, as established recently by Kohler et al. (1999) and Rodgers et al. (2001b), based on the comparison of fertility rates among identical and fraternal twins born in Denmark during 1870–1910 and 1953–1964, slightly more than one-quarter of the variance in completed fertility is attributable to genetic influence.

[10] Lack (1954) suggests that clutch sizes (i.e., number of eggs per nest) among owls and other predatory vole-eating birds, for instance, are positively related to food abundance. He argues that clutch size is selected such that under any feeding conditions, fertility rates ensure the maximal reproductive success. Furthermore, Cody (1966) documents the existence of significant differences between clutch sizes of the same bird species on islands and nearby mainland localities of the same latitude. In temperate regions, where food is more abundant on the mainland than on islands, the average clutch size is smaller on the islands. For instance, for *Cyanoramphus novaezelandeae*, the average mainland clutch is 6.5, whereas the island average is 4.

7.2.2 The Malthusian Components

The Malthusian Epoch is captured in Unified Growth Theory by three central elements: first, the production process is characterized by decreasing returns to labor due to the limited availability of land; second, parents generate utility from their children, and the production of children is time intensive; and third, individuals are subjected to a subsistence consumption constraint.[11] Thus, as long as the subsistence constraint is binding, an increase in income results in an increase in population growth. Technological progress, which brings about temporary gains in income per capita, therefore triggers an increase in population that offsets the gain in income but permits an increase in the average quality of the population. While population growth offsets the potential gain in income per capital during the Malthusian Epoch, ultimately, growth in income per capita is generated, despite decreasing returns to labor, since technological progress induces investment in human capital among a growing minority.

7.2.3 Determinants of Technological Progress
and Human Capital Formation

Technological progress is determined by the average level of human capital in society, reflecting the composition of the population and the average investment in human capital of each type.[12] Human capital formation is triggered by two forces. First, for a given average valuation of quality in the population, technological change raises demand for human capital and thus human capital formation. Technological progress reduces the adaptability of existing human capital to the new technological environment and educated individuals have a comparative advantage in adapting to this new environment.[13] Second, for a

---

[11] Bioeconomic foundations of the Malthusian equilibrium are explored by Dalgaard and Strulik (2010).

[12] This link between education and technological change was proposed by Nelson and Phelps (1966) and is supported empirically by Easterlin (1981), Foster and Rosenzweig (1996), as well as others. To focus on the role of the evolutionary process, the model abstracts from the potential positive effect of population size on the rate of technological progress. Adding this scale effect would simply accelerate the transition process. Consistently with Mokyr (2002), who argues that the effect of human capital accumulation on technological progress became significant only in the course of the Scientific Revolution that preceded the Industrial Revolution, the effect of human capital accumulation on the rate of technological progress need not be significant prior to the Scientific Revolution, as long as it becomes significant prior to the Industrial Revolution.

[13] See Nelson and Phelps (1966) and Schultz (1975). If the return on education rises with the level of technology rather than with the rate of technological progress, the qualitative analysis would not be affected. However, this alternative would imply that changes in technology were skill-biased throughout human history, in contrast to those periods in which technological change was skilled-saving, notably, in the first phase of the Industrial Revolution.

given rate of technological progress, and thus for a given demand for human capital, natural selection increases the representation of individuals with higher valuation of quality, stimulating human capital formation.

7.2.4 The Trigger of the Demographic Transition

Unified Growth Theory postulates that the rise in the demand for human capital triggered the decline in fertility in the course of the demographic transition. Individuals generate utility from the quantity and the quality of their children as well as from their own consumption. They choose the number of children and their quality in the face of a constraint on the total amount of time that can be devoted to child-raising and labor market activities. While a rise in parental income (due to the rise in demand for human capital) would generate conflicting income and substitution effects and would not necessarily trigger a decline in fertility, the effect of the rise in demand for human capital on the potential future earnings of a child generates a pure substitution effect. It induces parents to substitute quality for quantity of children and thus operates to decrease fertility.

Individuals choose the number of children and their quality based on their preferences for quality as well as their time constraints.[14] The onset of the demographic transition is triggered by human capital formation: for a given average valuation of child quality in the population, the rise in demand for human capital induces a larger fraction of parents to substitute quality for quantity of children, and for a given demand for human capital, natural selection increases the representation of individuals with higher valuation of quality, stimulating human capital formation and ultimately reducing fertility.[15]

7.3 The Basic Structure of the Model

Consider an overlapping-generations economy in which economic activity extends over infinite discrete time. In every period, the economy produces a single

---

[14] Anthropological evidence suggests that fertility control was indeed exercised even prior to the Neolithic Revolution. Reproductive control in hunter-gatherer societies is exemplified by pacing birth (e.g., birth every 4 years) conducted by tribes who live in small, semi-nomadic bands in Africa, Southeast Asia, and New Guinea to prevent the burden of carrying several children while wandering. They abstained from sexual intercourse for a 3-year period after each birth. Similarly, nomadic women of the Kung (a group of the San people of southern Africa) use no contraceptives but nurse their babies frequently, suppressing ovulation and menstruation for 2–3 years after birth, and reaching a mean interval between births of 44 months.

[15] The presence of a trade-off between quantity and quality of children in the pre-Industrial Revolution, pre-demographic transition period (i.e., when the income effect is still dominating), is established by Becker et al. (2010).

homogeneous good, using land and efficiency units of labor as inputs. The supply of land is exogenous, whereas the supply of efficiency units of labor is determined by households' decisions in the preceding period regarding the number of children and their level of human capital.

7.3.1 Production of Final Output

Production occurs according to a constant-returns-to-scale technology that is subject to endogenous technological progress. The output produced in period t, Y_t, is

$$Y_t = H_t^{1-\alpha}(A_t X)^\alpha, \tag{7.1}$$

where H_t is the aggregate quantity of efficiency units of labor in period t, X is land employed in production (which, for simplicity, is fixed over time), A_t represents the endogenously determined technological level in period t, and $\alpha \in (0, 1)$. The multiplicative form in which the level of technology, A_t, and land, X, appear in the production function implies that the relevant factor for the output produced is the product of the two, defined as effective resources.

Suppose that there are no property rights over land. The return on land is therefore zero, and the wage per efficiency unit of labor, w_t, is then equal to the output per efficiency unit of labor produced in period t. Hence,

$$w_t = x_t^\alpha, \tag{7.2}$$

where $x_t \equiv A_t X / H_t$ denotes effective resources per efficiency unit of labor in period t.[16]

The modeling of the production side is based on two simplifying assumptions. First, capital is not an input in the production function, and, second, the return on land is zero.[17]

---

[16] Unlike the formulation in Chapter 5, x_t denotes effective resources per efficiency unit of labor rather than per worker. Namely $x_t \equiv A_t X / H_t$ rather than $x_t \equiv A_t X / L_t$.

[17] Alternatively, one could have assumed that the economy is small and open to a world capital market in which the interest rate is constant. In this case, the quantity of capital is set to equalize its marginal product to the interest rate, while the price of land follows a path such that the total return on land (rent plus net price appreciation) is also equal to the interest rate. Capital has no role in the mechanism that is identified in this book, and the qualitative results are not affected if the supply of capital were endogenously determined. Allowing for capital accumulation in a closed economy framework, or property rights over land, would complicate the model to the point of intractability.

7.3.2 Preferences and Budget Constraints

In each period, a new generation of individuals is born. Each individual has a single parent.[18] Members of generation t (those who join the labor force in period t) live for two periods. In the first period of their life (childhood), $t - 1$, individuals consume a fraction of the parental unit-time endowment. The required time increases with children's quality. In the second period of life (parenthood), t, individuals are endowed with one unit of time, which they allocate between child rearing and labor force participation. They choose the optimal mixture of quantity and quality of children and supply their remaining time in the labor market, consuming their wages.

Every generation t consists of a variety of individuals (type i of generation t) distinguished by the trade-off between child quality and quantity in their preferences. Individuals within a dynasty are of the same type. That is, preferences are hereditary, and they are transmitted without alteration from generation to generation within a dynasty. The distribution of types evolves over time due to the effect of natural selection on the relative size of each dynasty. The type with the evolutionary advantage (i.e., the type characterized by higher fertility rates) is determined by the economic environment, and it may be replaced due to endogenous evolution of this environment.

Individuals' preferences are represented by a utility function defined over consumption above a subsistence level, $\tilde{c} > 0$, as well as over the quantity and quality (measured by human capital) of their (surviving) children:[19]

$$u_t^i = (1 - \gamma) \ln c_t^i + \gamma [\ln n_t^i + \beta^i \ln h_{t+1}^i], \tag{7.3}$$

where the parameter $\gamma \in (0, 1)$, c_t^i is the household consumption of a type i individual of generation t, n_t^i is the number of (surviving) children, $\beta^i \in (0, 1]$ is the relative weight given to quality in the preferences of dynasty i, and h_{t+1}^i is the level of human capital of each child.[20] The quality parameter, β^i,

---

[18] For simplicity, the model abstracts from marriages, assuming implicitly that marriages are largely assortative.

[19] Alternatively, the utility function could have been defined over consumption above subsistence rather than over a consumption set that is truncated from below by the subsistence consumption constraint. Under this formulation: $u_t^i = (1 - \gamma) \ln(c_t^i - \tilde{c}) + \gamma [\ln n_t^i + \beta^i \ln h_{t+1}^i]$. As will become apparent, the adoption of this formulation would not affect the qualitative analysis but would greatly add to the complexity of the dynamical system. Under each specification, the subsistence consumption constraint generates the Malthusian effect of income on population growth at low income levels. The effect of higher income on infant mortality and natural fertility would generate a similar effect.

[20] For simplicity, parents derive utility from the expected number of surviving offspring, and the parental cost of child rearing is associated only with surviving children. A more realistic cost structure would not affect the qualitative features of the theory.

is transmitted from generation to generation within a dynasty and remains stationary.[21] The utility function is strictly monotonically increasing and strictly quasi-concave, satisfying the conventional boundary conditions that assure, for sufficiently high income, the existence of an interior solution for the utility maximization problem. However, for a sufficiently low level of income, the subsistence consumption constraint is binding and there is a corner solution with respect to the consumption level.

Individuals choose the number of children and their quality in the face of a constraint on the total amount of time that can be devoted to child-raising and labor market activities. For simplicity, only time is required to produce child quantity and quality. Let $\tau + e_{t+1}^i$ be the time cost for member i of generation t of raising a child with a level of education (quality) e_{t+1}^i. That is, τ is the fraction of the individual's unit-time endowment that is required to raise a child, regardless of quality, and e_{t+1}^i is the fraction of the individual's unit-time endowment that is devoted for the education of each child; τ is assumed to be sufficiently small so as to ensure that the population has a positive growth rate. That is, $\tau < \gamma$.

Consider a member i of generation t who is endowed with h_t^i efficiency units of labor in period t. Define potential income, z_t^i, as the potential earning if the entire time endowment is devoted to labor force participation, earning the competitive market wage, w_t, per efficiency unit:

$$z_t^i \equiv w_t h_t^i = x_t^\alpha h_t^i \equiv z(x_t, h_t^i). \tag{7.4}$$

Potential income is divided between consumption, c_t^i, and child rearing (quantity as well as quality), evaluated according to the individual's opportunity cost $w_t h_t^i [\tau + e_{t+1}^i]$ per child. Hence, in the second period of life (parenthood), the individual faces the budget constraint:

$$w_t h_t^i n_t^i (\tau + e_{t+1}^i) + c_t^i \leq w_t h_t^i \equiv z_t^i. \tag{7.5}$$

7.3.3 Production of Human Capital

Individuals' levels of human capital are determined by their quality (education) as well as by the technological environment. Technological progress is

---

[21] The distribution of β^i changes due to the effect of natural selection on the distribution of types. Furthermore, although β^i is stationary within a dynasty, the optimization of individuals changes over time due to changes in the economic environment. For simplicity, it is assumed that the subsistence consumption constraint and the weight given to consumption in the utility function are homogenous among individuals, and hence they are not subjected to natural selection.

assumed to raise the value of education in the production of human capital. Technological progress reduces the adaptability of existing human capital to the new technological environment. Education, however, lessens the adverse effects of technological progress on the effectiveness of the stock of human capital. That is, skilled individuals have a comparative advantage in adapting to the new technological environment.

The level of human capital of a child of member i of generation t, h^i_{t+1}, is an increasing strictly concave function of the parental time investment in the education of the child, e^i_{t+1}, and a decreasing strictly convex function of the rate of technological progress, g_{t+1}:

$$h^i_{t+1} = h(e^i_{t+1}, g_{t+1}), \tag{7.6}$$

where $g_{t+1} \equiv (A_{t+1} - A_t)/A_t$.

Education lessens the adverse effect of technological progress. That is, technology complements skills in the production of human capital (i.e., $h_{eg}(e^i_{t+1}, g_{t+1}) > 0$). Furthermore, even in the absence of investment in quality, each individual has a positive level of human capital. In a stationary technological environment, this level of basic skills is normalized to 1 (i.e., $h(0, 0) = 1$). Finally, in the absence of investment in education, for sufficiently rapid technological progress, the erosion effect renders existing human capital obsolete (i.e., $\lim_{g \to \infty} h(0, g_{t+1}) = 0$).

Although the potential number of efficiency units of labor is diminished due to the transition from the existing technological state to a superior one (the erosion effect), each individual operates with a superior level of technology (the productivity effect). Hence, once the rate of technological progress reaches a positive steady-state level, the erosion effect is constant, and labor productivity grows at a constant rate.

7.3.4 Optimization

Members of generation t choose the number and quality of their children and their own consumption to maximize their utility function. Substituting (7.5) and (7.6) into (7.3), the optimization problem of a member i of generation t is

$$\{n^i_t, e^i_{t+1}\} = \operatorname*{argmax}\{(1 - \gamma) \ln w_t h^i_t [1 - n^i_t(\tau + e^i_{t+1})]$$

$$+ \gamma [\ln n^i_t + \beta^i \ln h(e^i_{t+1}, g_{t+1})]\} \tag{7.7}$$

subject to

$$w_t h^i_t [1 - n^i_t(\tau + e^i_{t+1})] \geq \tilde{c};$$

$$(n^i_t, e^i_{t+1}) \geq 0.$$

The optimization with respect to n_t^i implies that as long as the potential income of a member of type i of generation t is low, the subsistence constraint binds. The individual devotes a sufficient fraction of the time endowment for labor force participation so as to ensure consumption of the subsistence level, $\tilde{c}$, and uses the rest of the time endowment for child rearing. Once potential income is sufficiently high, the subsistence consumption constraint is no longer binding, and the individual devotes a fraction $1 - \gamma$ of the unit-time endowment for labor force participation, consuming $c_t^i > \tilde{c}$, and a fraction γ for child rearing.

Let $\tilde{z}$ be the level of potential income above which the subsistence constraint is no longer binding. That is, $\tilde{z} \equiv \tilde{c}/(1 - \gamma)$. It follows that for $z_t^i \geq \tilde{c}$,

$$n_t^i(\tau + e_{t+1}^i) = \begin{cases} \gamma, & \text{if } z_t^i \geq \tilde{z}, \\[2mm] 1 - \tilde{c}/z_t^i, & \text{if } z_t^i \leq \tilde{z}. \end{cases} \tag{7.8}$$

If $z_t^i \leq \tilde{c}$, then $n_t^i = 0$ and type i would become extinct.

It should be noted that for a given level of potential income, $z_t^i = x_t^\alpha h_t^i$, the parameter β^i does not affect the time allocation between child rearing and labor force participation. It affects, however, the division of time between the number of children and their quality. As will become apparent, individuals with a higher β^i spend more time on child quality at the expense of lower quantity.

As long as the potential income of member i of generation t, z_t^i, is below $\tilde{z}$, the fraction of time necessary to ensure subsistence consumption, $\tilde{c}$, is larger than $1 - \gamma$, and the fraction of time devoted to child rearing is therefore below γ. As the wage per efficiency unit of labor increases, the individual can generate subsistence consumption with lower labor force participation, and the fraction of time devoted to child rearing increases.

Figure 7.1 shows the effect of an increase in potential income, z_t^i, on the individual's choice of total time spent on children and consumption. The income expansion path is vertical until the level of income passes the critical level that permits consumption to exceed the subsistence level. Thereafter, the income expansion path becomes horizontal at a level γ in terms of time devoted to child rearing.[22]

Regardless of whether potential income is above or below $\tilde{z}$, increases in wages will not change the division of child-rearing time between quality and quantity. The division between time spent on quality and time spent on quantity

---

[22] If the utility function had been defined over consumption above subsistence rather than over the consumption set that is truncated from below by the subsistence consumption constraint— that is, if $u_t^i = (1 - \gamma) \ln(c_t^i - \tilde{c}) + \gamma[\ln n_t^i + \beta^i \ln h_{t+1}^i]$—then the income expansion path is a smooth convex approximation of the one depicted in Figure 7.1. For low levels of income, it is asymptotically vertical; for high levels, it is asymptotically horizontal.

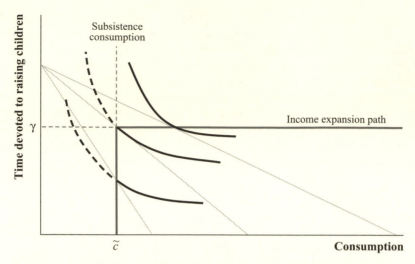

FIGURE 7.1. Preferences, constraints, and income expansion path.
Summary: The figure depicts the household's indifference curves, budget constraints, and the subsistence consumption constraint. The income expansion path is vertical as long as the subsistence consumption constraint is binding; it becomes horizontal once the subsistence consumption constraint ceases to bind.

is affected by the rate of technological progress, as well as the preference for quality, β^i. Specifically, using (7.8), the optimization with respect to e^i_{t+1} implies that, independently of the subsistence consumption constraint, the implicit functional relationship between investment in child quality, e^i_{t+1}, and the rate of technological progress, g_{t+1}, is given by

$$G(e^i_{t+1}, g_{t+1}; \beta^i) \equiv \beta^i h_e(e^i_{t+1}, g_{t+1})$$

$$- \frac{h(e^i_{t+1}, g_{t+1})}{(\tau + e^i_{t+1})} \begin{cases} = 0, & \text{if } e^i_{t+1} > 0, \\ \leq 0, & \text{if } e^i_{t+1} = 0, \end{cases} \tag{7.9}$$

where $G(e^i_{t+1}, g_{t+1}; \beta^i)$ is the difference in the benefits from a marginal increase in time investment in quality and one in quantity. For all $g_{t+1} \geq 0$, and $e_{t+1} \geq 0$, $G_e(e_{t+1}, g_{t+1}; \beta^i) < 0$, $G_g(e_{t+1}, g_{t+1}; \beta^i) > 0$, and $G_\beta(e_{t+1}, g_{t+1}; \beta^i) > 0$.

Individuals with a sufficiently low level of β^i do not invest in the human capital of their offspring when the future rate of technological progress is zero. To ensure that individuals with a sufficiently high level of β^i would invest in the human capital of their offspring even when the future rate of technological progress is zero, it is sufficient to assume that for individuals with the highest valuation of quality (i.e., $\beta^i = 1$) the benefit from an infinitesimal time investment in quality is larger than one in quantity, that is,

$$h_e(0, 0) > 1/\tau. \tag{7.A1}$$

As follows from Assumption (7.A1) and (7.9), $G(0, 0; 0) < 0$, and $G(0, 0; 1) = \tau h_e(0, 0) - h(0, 0) > 0$. Let $\underline{\beta}$ be the threshold level of the quality parameter, above which individuals of type i of generation t invest in the education of their offspring even when $g_{t+1} = 0$; that is, $G(0, 0; \underline{\beta}) = 0$. Hence, as follows from the properties of (7.9), there exists $\underline{g}(\beta^i) \geq 0$ such that $G(0, \underline{g}(\beta^i), \beta^i) = 0$ for all $\beta^i \leq \underline{\beta}$.

Under Assumption (7.A1), it follows from the properties of (7.6) and (7.9) that the quality of children, e^i_{t+1}, chosen by member i of generation t is an increasing function of the rate of technological progress, g_{t+1}, and the individual's valuation of quality, β^i:

$$e^i_{t+1} = \varepsilon(g_{t+1}; \beta^i) \equiv e^i(g_{t+1}) \begin{cases} = 0, & \text{if } g_{t+1} \leq \underline{g}(\beta^i) \text{ and } \beta^i \leq \underline{\beta}, \\ > 0, & \text{if } g_{t+1} > \underline{g}(\beta^i) \text{ or } \beta^i > \underline{\beta}, \end{cases} \tag{7.10}$$

where $\varepsilon_g(g_{t+1}; \beta^i) > 0$ and $\varepsilon_\beta(g_{t+1}; \beta^i) > 0$, $\forall g_{t+1} > \underline{g}(\beta^i)$ and $\forall \beta^i > \underline{\beta}$.

As is apparent from (7.9), $\varepsilon_{gg}(g_{t+1}; \beta^i)$ depends on the third derivatives of the production function of human capital. A concave reaction of the level of education to the rate of technological progress appears plausible; hence to simplify the exposition (without affecting the qualitative results), it is assumed that

$$\varepsilon_{gg}(g_{t+1}; \beta^i) < 0, \quad \forall g_{t+1} > \underline{g}(\beta^i) \text{ and } \forall \beta^i > \underline{\beta}. \tag{7.A2}$$

As follows from (7.10), the level of human capital of an individual of type i in period $t + 1$ is therefore

$$h^i_{t+1} = h(e^i_{t+1}, g_{t+1}) = h(\varepsilon(g_{t+1}; \beta^i), g_{t+1}) = h(e^i(g_{t+1}), g_{t+1}) \equiv h^i(g_{t+1}). \tag{7.11}$$

As is apparent from (7.9) and the properties of (7.6), $\partial h^i(g_t)/\partial g_t$ can be positive or negative. Since the response of education, e_{t+1}, to g_{t+1} may be viewed as a measure intended to offset the erosion effect of g_{t+1} on the level of human capital, it is natural to assume that

$$\partial h^i(g_{t+1})/\partial g_{t+1} < 0 \quad \forall g_{t+1} > 0. \tag{7.A3}$$

Furthermore, this assumption simplifies the geometrical analysis of the dynamical system without affecting the qualitative results. Substituting $e_{t+1}^i = \varepsilon(g_{t+1}; \beta^i)$ into (7.8), noting that $z_t^i = x_t^\alpha h(\varepsilon(g_t; \beta^i), g_t) = x_t^\alpha h^i(g_t)$, it follows that for $z_t^i \geq \tilde{c}$,

$$n_t^i \equiv n(g_{t+1}, z_t^i; \beta^i) = n(g_{t+1}, z(x_t, h^i(g_t)); \beta^i)$$

$$= \begin{cases} \gamma/[\tau + \varepsilon(g_{t+1}; \beta^i)], & \text{if } z_t^i \geq \tilde{z}, \\ (1 - [\tilde{c}/z_t^i])/[\tau + \varepsilon(g_{t+1}; \beta^i)], & \text{if } z_t^i \leq \tilde{z}, \end{cases} \quad (7.12)$$

where $n(g_{t+1}, z(x_t, h^i(g_t)); \beta^i)$ is increasing and strictly concave in x_t, as long as x_t is smaller than the level $[\tilde{z}/h^i(g_t)]^{1/\alpha}$ (above which the subsistence constraint is no longer binding for individuals of type i), and is independent of x_t otherwise.

Thus, as follows directly from (7.10) and (7.12):

1. Technological progress decreases the number of children of individual i and increases their quality (i.e., $\partial n_t^i/\partial g_{t+1} \leq 0$ and $\partial e_{t+1}^i/\partial g_{t+1} \geq 0$).
2. If parental potential income is below $\tilde{z}$ (i.e., if the subsistence consumption constraint is binding), an increase in parental potential income raises the number of children but has no effect on their quality (i.e., $\partial n_t^i/\partial z_t^i > 0$ and $\partial e_{t+1}^i/\partial z_t^i = 0$ if $z_t^i < \tilde{z}$).
3. If parental potential income is above $\tilde{z}$, an increase in parental potential income does not change the number of children or their quality (i.e., $\partial n_t^i/\partial z_t^i = \partial e_{t+1}^i/\partial z_t^i = 0$, if $z_t^i > \tilde{z}$).

Hence, if the subsistence consumption constraint is binding, an increase in the effective resources per worker raises the number of children but has no effect on their quality, whereas if the constraint is not binding, an increase in effective resources per worker does not change the number of children or their quality. Hence, for a given rate of technological progress, parental type, rather than parental income, is the sole determinant of offspring quality.

7.3.5 Distribution of Types and Human Capital Formation

In period 0, there is a small number L_0^a of identical adult individuals of type a—the quality type—with a high valuation of quality, $\beta^a > \bar{\beta}$, and L_0^b identical adult individuals of type b—the quantity type—with a low valuation of quality, $\beta^b < \underline{\beta}$.[23] Since the quality parameter is transmitted without alteration within a

---

[23] The existence of a large number of types would not affect the qualitative analysis. The presence of two types of individuals simplifies the exposition considerably and permits the analysis

dynasty, and since the properties of (7.10) and (7.12) imply that, given the rate of technological progress, parental type is the sole determinant of offspring education, it follows that in each period t, the population of generation t, L_t, consists of two homogeneous groups of types a and b of size is L_t^a and L_t^b, respectively. That is, $L_t = L_t^b + L_t^a$.[24]

It should be noted that the parameter γ, which reflects the trade-off between resources allocated to parent and offspring, is assumed for simplicity to be identical for all individuals. As follows from the optimization of each individual, independently of β^i, the parameter γ, has no effect on the distribution of resources between quality and quantity of offspring. Heterogeneity in γ would be reflected in the height of the vertical portion of the income expansion path in Figure 7.1. The incorporation of heterogeneity, therefore, would not alter the process of development, as long as the economy is in the Malthusian regime and the subsistence constraint binds for the entire population.

However, once Malthusian pressure is relaxed, a high value of γ would generate an evolutionary advantage. Resources allocated to parental consumption beyond subsistence may be viewed as a force that raises parental resistance to adverse shocks (e.g., famine and epidemics), generating a positive effect on parental fitness and the survival of the lineage. This positive effect, however, is counterbalanced by the implied reduction in resources allocated to offspring, generating a negative effect on the survival of the lineage. Provided that the resistance to shocks is an increasing and concave function of consumption, consumption increases with income, although the average propensity to consume declines.

The optimal investment in child quality by members of each dynasty of type i is affected by their attitude toward child quality and the rate of technological progress. Suppose that $\beta^b < \underline{\beta} < \beta^a$. Under Assumption (7.A1), as depicted in

---

of the effect of a single quality parameter on the evolution of this complex three-dimensional system. Since the process of evolution is inherently associated with an improvement in the fitness and hence the evolutionary advantage of certain mutants, the underlying assumption is that when mutation starts affecting the economy in period 0, it introduces a type that at least temporarily has an evolutionary advantage (i.e., a type with a parameter β that is closer to the evolutionary optimal level relative to the preexisting type, b).

[24] Until period $t = -2$, the population of the world is homogeneous, and it consists of type b individuals. In period $t = -2$, however, a very small fraction of the adult population gives birth to mutants of type a, whose quality parameter, β^a, is higher than that in the existing adult population. In period $t = -1$, the mutants are adults who make fertility decisions. Their income is identical to that of type b individuals, but their fertility rate is nevertheless lower, due to their higher preference for child quality. In period $t = 0$, the mutants are "regular" individuals of type a whose potential income is higher than that of type b individuals. Finally, in all periods $t \geq 0$, all individuals of type a have parents who are of type a as well. Hence, mutation has a real affect on output only in period 0.

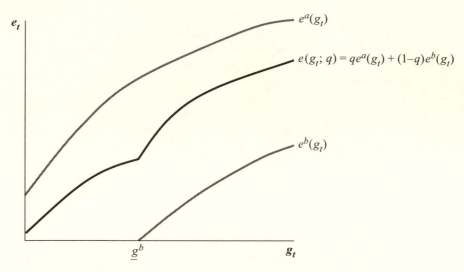

FIGURE 7.2. Investment in quality as a function of the rate of technological progress. *Summary:* The figure depicts the effect of the rate of technological progress, g_t, on offspring quality chosen by parents with high valuation of quality, e_t^a, and low valuation of quality, e_t^b, and on the average quality of the population, e_t, weighted according to the fraction q_t of individuals with high valuation of quality.

Figure 7.2, investment in child quality in each dynasty of type $i = a, b$ is

$$e_t^a = e^a(g_t) > 0 \quad \text{for all } t$$

$$e_t^b = e^b(g_t) > 0 \quad \text{for } g_t > \underline{g}(\beta^b) \equiv \underline{g}^b > 0; \tag{7.13}$$

$$e^a(g_t) > e^b(g_t) \quad \text{for all } t.$$

The argument behind (7.13), which follows from (7.10) and the definition of β, is straightforward. For individuals of type a, $\beta^a > \beta$, where β denotes the threshold level of the quality parameter (above which individuals of generation t invest in the education of their offspring even if $g_{t+1} = 0$). Hence, within a dynasty with high valuation of quality (type a), investment in child quality, e_t^a, is strictly positive for all t. For individuals with low valuation of quality (type b), however, $\beta^b < \beta$ and investment in child quality takes place if and only if the rate of technological change and hence the return on quality is sufficiently large. Hence, as follows from (7.6), the level of human capital within dynasties with high valuation of quality is higher (i.e., $h_t^a > h_t^b$ for all t).

Let q_t be the fraction of individuals with high valuation of quality (type a) in generation t:

$$q_t \equiv L_t^a / L_t. \tag{7.14}$$

The average level of education, e_t, as depicted in Figure 7.2, is therefore a weighted average of the level of education of the two types of individuals:

$$e_t = q_t e^a(g_t) + (1 - q_t) e^b(g_t) \equiv e(g_t, q_t). \tag{7.15}$$

As depicted in Figure 7.2, following (7.10), (7.13), and Assumption (7.A2), the function $e(g_t, q_t)$ is increasing in both arguments and is piecewise strictly concave with respect to g_t.[25]

The aggregate supply of efficiency units of labor in period t, H_t, is

$$H_t = L_t^a f_t^a h_t^a + L_t^b f_t^b h_t^b = L_t[q_t f_t^a h_t^a + (1 - q_t) f_t^b h_t^b], \tag{7.16}$$

where f_t^i is the fraction of time devoted to labor force participation by an individual of type $i = a, b$. As follows from (7.8), noting that $z_t^i = x_t^\alpha h^i(g_t)$,

$$f_t^i \equiv f^i(g_t, x_t) = \begin{cases} 1 - \gamma, & \text{if } z_t^i \geq \tilde{z}; \\ \tilde{c}/z_t^i, & \text{if } z_t^i \leq \tilde{z}, \end{cases} \tag{7.17}$$

where, as follows from (7.4) and Assumption (7.A3), $f_x^i(g_t, x_t) < 0$ and $f_g^i(g_t, x_t) > 0$ for $z_t^i \leq \tilde{z}$.

7.3.6 Time Path of the Macroeconomic Variables

Technological Progress
Suppose that technological progress, g_{t+1}, which takes place between periods t and $t + 1$, depends on the average quality (education) among the working generation in period t, e_t:

$$g_{t+1} \equiv \frac{A_{t+1} - A_t}{A_t} = \psi(e_t), \tag{7.18}$$

where the rate of technological progress, g_{t+1}, is an increasing, strictly concave function of the average level of education of the working generation in period t, e_t, and $\psi(0) = 0$.[26]

The level of technology in period $t + 1$, A_{t+1}, is, therefore,

$$A_{t+1} = [1 + g_{t+1}]A_t = [1 + \psi(e_t)]A_t, \tag{7.19}$$

where the technological level in period 0 is historically given as A_0.

---

[25] It should be noted that although the kink in the function $e(g_t, q_t)$ is an artifact of the existence of two types of individuals, the inflection in the curve would emerge under a wide range of continuous distributions.

[26] The abstraction from the complementary role of the scale of the economy (i.e., the size of the population) in the determination of technological progress is designed to sharpen the focus on the role of the evolutionary process in the transition to modern growth.

Hence, as follows from (7.15), (7.18), (7.10), and (7.13), g_{t+1} is uniquely determined by g_t and q_t:

$$g_{t+1} = \psi(e(q_t, g_t)) \equiv g(g_t, q_t), \tag{7.20}$$

where $g_q(g_t, q_t) > 0$, $g_g(g_t, q_t) > 0$, and $g_{gg}(g_t, q_t) < 0$.

Population and Fertility Rates across Types
The evolution of the working population over time is given by

$$L_{t+1} = n_t L_t, \tag{7.21}$$

where $L_t = L_t^b + L_t^a$, is the population size of generation t; L_0^a, L_0^b, and therefore L_0 are given, and n_t is the average fertility rate in the population. That is,

$$n_t \equiv q_t n_t^a + (1 - q_t) n_t^b, \tag{7.22}$$

where, as defined in (7.14), $q_t \equiv L_t^a/L_t$ is the fraction of adult individuals of type a in generation t (born to type a individuals), and n_t^i is the number of children of each individual of type $i = a, b$. Given that $g_{t+1} = g(g_t, q_t)$, it follows from (7.12) that

$$n_t^i = n^i(g_t, x_t, q_t), \quad i = a, b. \tag{7.23}$$

The evolution of the fraction q_t of individuals with high valuation of quality (type a) is governed by the evolution of the population of the two types over time. Since for $i = a, b$, $L_{t+1}^i = n_t^i L_t^i$, where L_t^i is the population size of type i in generation t, it follows from (7.14), (7.20), and (7.23) that

$$q_{t+1} = \frac{n_t^a}{n_t} q_t \equiv q(g_t, x_t, q_t). \tag{7.24}$$

The analysis of the relationship between the economic environment and the evolutionary advantage of different types of individuals indicates that in the early Malthusian Epoch, when humans merely struggle for survival, individuals of type a (i.e., individuals with a preference for offspring quality) have an evolutionary advantage over those of type b. That is, the fraction of individuals of type a, q_t, rises in the population, despite their bias against quantity. However, once the economic environment improves sufficiently, the evolutionary pressure weakens, the significance of quality for survival (fertility) declines, and type b individuals—the quantity type—gain the evolutionary advantage.

As follows from (7.12) $n_t^a > n_t^b = 0$ for $x_t = [\tilde{c}/h^b(g_t)]^{1/\alpha}$, and $n_t^b > n_t^a$ for $x_t \geq [\tilde{z}/h^b(g_t)]^{1/\alpha}$. Hence, since $\forall x_t \in ([\tilde{c}/h^b(g_t)]^{1/\alpha}, [\tilde{z}/h^b(g_t)]^{1/\alpha})$ (i.e., for the range under which $\partial n^b(g_t, x_t; q)/\partial x_t > 0$), $\partial n^b(g_t, x_t; q)/\partial x_t >$

$\partial n^a(g_t, x_t; q)/\partial x_t$. Noting that, as follows from (7.13), $e_t^a > e_t^b$, $\forall t > 0$, it follows from the Intermediate Value Theorem that under Assumption (7.A1), for any given $g_t \geq 0$, as depicted in Figure 7.3, there exists a unique $\check{x}_t \in ([\tilde{c}/h^b(g_t)]^{1/\alpha}, [\tilde{z}/h^b(g_t)]^{1/\alpha}) \equiv \check{x}(g_t; q)$ such that $\forall x_t > [\tilde{c}/h^b(g_t)]^{1/\alpha}$ (i.e., $\forall z_t^b > \tilde{c}$),

$$n_t^a \begin{cases} > n_t^b & \text{for } x_t < \check{x}_t; \\ = n_t^b & \text{for } x_t = \check{x}_t; \\ < n_t^b & \text{for } x_t > \check{x}_t. \end{cases} \tag{7.25}$$

Figure 7.3 depicts the fertility rates, n_t^b and n_t^a, of individuals of the two types as functions of effective resources per efficiency unit of labor, x_t, given the rate of technological progress g_t. In the early stages of development, effective resources per efficiency unit of labor are low (less than $\check{x}(g_t; q)$) and the fraction

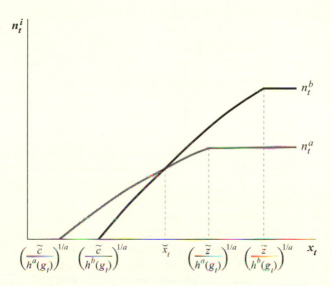

FIGURE 7.3. Fertility rates across types.
Summary: The figure depicts the reversal of evolutionary advantage in the process of development, as effective resources per worker, x_t, increase over time. In the predemographic transition era, fertility rates of individuals with high valuation of quality, n_t^a, are higher than those of individuals with low valuation of quality, n_t^b, and the quality trait increases its representation in the population. In the post-demographic transition era, this evolutionary advantage is reversed.

of individuals with high valuation of quality (type a) increases. However, as the level of effective resources per efficiency unit of labor increases sufficiently (i.e., $x_t > \check{x}(g_t; q)$) and the Malthusian pressure relaxes, the rate of population growth among individuals of type b (the quantity type) overtakes the rate among type a (the quality type).[27] It should be noted that, as follows from the properties of (7.10) and (7.12), the increase in the rate of technological progress (which brings about the increase in effective resources) initially generates an increase in fertility rates of both types of individuals, but ultimately, due to the substitution of quality for quantity, a demographic transition takes place and fertility rates decline.[28]

If the economy is populated only with individuals of the quantity type, b, fertility rates of individuals of type b are at replacement level. As follows from (7.12),

$$n_t^b \begin{cases} = 0, & \forall x_t \leq [\tilde{c}/h^b(g_t)]^{1/\alpha}; \\ > 1, & \forall x_t \geq [\tilde{z}/h^b(g_t)]^{1/\alpha}; \end{cases} \quad \text{for} \quad g(g_t, q_t) \leq \underline{g}^b. \qquad (7.26)$$

Hence, since n_t^b is continuous and monotonically increasing in x_t, it follows from the Intermediate Value Theorem that, for g_t and q_t such that $g_{t+1} = g(g_t, q_t) \leq \underline{g}^b$, there exists a unique level of effective resources per efficiency unit of labor, $\grave{x}(g_t, q_t) \in ([\tilde{c}/h^b(g_t)]^{1/\alpha}, [\tilde{z}/h^b(g_t)]^{1/\alpha})$, such that the fertility rate of type b individuals is at a replacement level; that is,

$$n^b(g_t, \grave{x}(g_t, q_t), q_t) = 1 \quad \text{for} \quad g(g_t, q_t) \leq \underline{g}^b. \qquad (7.27)$$

Suppose that the entire population in the economy is of type b (i.e., $q = 0$) and the economy is in a steady-state equilibrium where the rate of technological progress is 0 (and accordingly $e = 0$). Furthermore, since n_t^b increases in x_t, and x_t decreases when $n_t^b > 1$ and increases when $n_t^b < 1$, it follows from (7.27) that in this steady-state equilibrium fertility rate is precisely at the replacement level (i.e., $n_t^b = 1$) and effective resources per efficiency unit of labor equal $\grave{x}$.

The Neolithic Revolution facilitated the division of labor and fostered trade relationships among individuals and communities, enhancing the complexity of human interaction and raising the return on human capital. The distribution of valuation of quality lagged behind the evolutionarily optimal level, and dynasties characterized by higher valuation of quality therefore had an evolutionary advantage. They generated higher income, and in the Malthusian Epoch

---

[27] Fertility rates of type b individuals exceed those of type a, when type b individuals are still constrained by subsistence consumption. However, for type a, the constraint may not be binding. Figure 7.3 is drawn for the case in which the constraint is binding for both types.

[28] An increase in g_t shifts the curves $n^a(g_t, x_t; q)$ and $n^b(g_t, x_t; q)$ in Figure 7.3 rightward and downward.

(when income is positively associated with aggregate resources allocated to child rearing), a larger number of offspring; they therefore gained an evolutionary advantage.

Hence, it is assumed that when g and q are infinitesimally small, the return on quality is sufficiently high to ensure that the income of type a individuals (the quality type) is sufficient to permit their fertility rates to be above replacement; namely,

$$\dot{x}(0,\, 0) < \check{x}(0;0), \tag{7.A4}$$

where $\dot{x}(0,\, 0) = (\tilde{c}/[1 - \tau])^{1/\alpha}$ is the level of effective resources under which fertility rates of individuals of type b are at a replacement level, and $\check{x}(0;0)$ is the level of effective resources under which fertility rates of individuals of both types are equal.

Since the size of the population which has high valuation of quality (type a) is assumed to be very small, it has a negligible effect on the size of x_0 and therefore in period 0, $x_0 = \check{x}(0;0) < \check{x}_0$. Hence, as follows from (7.25) and (7.27), the fertility rate of individuals of the quality type in period 0, n_0^a, is above replacement and it exceeds the fertility rate of individuals of the quantity type in this period, n_0^b; that is,

$$n_0^a > n_0^b = 1. \tag{7.28}$$

Hence, in the early stages of development, Malthusian pressure provides an evolutionary advantage for the quality type. The income of individuals of the quantity type is near subsistence, and fertility rates are therefore near the replacement level. In contrast, the wealthier, quality type can afford higher fertility rates (of higher quality offspring). As technological progress brings about an increase in income, Malthusian pressure relaxes, and the domination of wealth in fertility decisions diminishes. The inherent advantage of the quantity type in reproduction gradually dominates, and fertility rates of the quantity type eventually overtake those of the quality type.

Human Capital and Effective Resources

The growth rate of efficiency units of labor, μ_{t+1}, as follows from (7.16), is

$$\mu_{t+1} \equiv \frac{H_{t+1}}{H_t} - 1 = \frac{q_t n_t^a f_{t+1}^a h_{t+1}^a + (1 - q_t) n_t^b f_{t+1}^b h_{t+1}^b}{q_t f_t^a h_t^a + (1 - q_t) f_t^b h_t^b} - 1. \tag{7.29}$$

Substituting (7.12) and (7.20) into (7.29) and noting (7.17), it follows from the properties of (7.10) and (7.12) that under Assumptions (7.A1) and (7.A3), $\forall x_t > [\tilde{c}/h^b(g_t)]^{1/\alpha}$ or equivalently, $\forall z_t^b > \tilde{c}$ (i.e., for the range in which individuals of type b, and hence of type a, do not become extinct),

$$\mu_{t+1} = \mu(g_t,\, x_t,\, q_t), \tag{7.30}$$

where $\forall z_t^b \geq \tilde{z}$, $\mu_g(g_t, x_t, q_t) < 0$ and

$$\mu_x(g_t, x_t, q_t) \begin{cases} > 0, & \text{if } x_t < [\tilde{z}/h^b(g_t)]^{1/\alpha}; \\ = 0, & \text{otherwise,} \end{cases} \qquad (7.31)$$

$$\mu_q(g_t, x_t, q_t)\big|_{g_{t+1}=g_t} \gtreqless 0 \quad \text{if and only if} \quad n_t^a \gtreqless n_t^b.$$

The evolution of effective resources per efficiency unit of labor, $x_t \equiv A_t X / H_t$, as follows from (7.20) and (7.29), is

$$x_{t+1} = \frac{1 + g_{t+1}}{1 + \mu_{t+1}} x_t \equiv x(g_t, x_t, q_t). \qquad (7.32)$$

Resources depend, therefore, on the rate of technological progress and the growth rate of efficiency units of labor.

7.4 The Dynamical System

The development of the economy is characterized by the trajectory of output, population, technology, education, and human capital. The dynamic path of the economy is fully determined by a sequence $\{x_t, g_t, q_t\}_{t=0}^{\infty}$, which describes the time path of effective resources per efficiency unit of labor, x_t, the rate of technological progress, g_t, and the fraction q_t of individuals of the quality type in the population. It is governed by a three-dimensional first-order autonomous dynamical system given by (7.20), (7.24), and (7.32):

$$\begin{cases} x_{t+1} = x(g_t, x_t, q_t); \\ g_{t+1} = g(g_t, q_t); \\ q_{t+1} = q(g_t, x_t, q_t). \end{cases} \qquad (7.33)$$

The analysis of the dynamical system can be greatly simplified, since, as established in the following subsection, the evolution of g_t and therefore of $e_t = e(g_t; q)$ is determined independently of x_t, provided that q_t is held constant.

7.4.1 Conditional Dynamics of Technology and Education

The conditional dynamical subsystem, $g_{t+1} = g(g_t; q)$, which describes the time path of the rate of technological change for a given q, is a one-dimensional system. The geometric analysis is more revealing, however, if the equation of motion, $g_{t+1} = \psi(e(g_t; q_t)) \equiv g(g_t; q_t)$, is decomposed into the joint evolution of technology, $g_{t+1} = \psi(e_t)$, and education, $e_t = e(g_t; q_t)$.

The evolution of the rate of technological progress and education, conditional on a given fraction, q, of individuals with high valuation of quality, is characterized by the sequence, $\{g_t, e_t; q\}_{t=0}^{\infty}$, which satisfies in every period t the conditional two-dimensional system

$$\begin{cases} e_t = e(g_t; q); \\ g_{t+1} = \psi(e_t). \end{cases} \tag{7.34}$$

In light of the properties of the functions $e_t = e(g_t; q)$ and $g_{t+1} = \psi(e_t)$, given by (7.15) and (7.18), it follows that in any time period, this conditional dynamical subsystem may be characterized by one of two qualitatively different configurations, which are depicted in Figures 7.4(a), 7.5(a), and 7.6(a) and derived formally in Section 7.9.1. The economy shifts endogenously from one configuration to another as the fraction of individuals with high valuation of quality, q, increases and the curve $e_t = e(g_t; q)$ shifts upward to account for the positive effect of an increase in q on the average investment in quality, e_t.

As depicted in Figures 7.4(a), 7.5(a), and 7.6(a), the set of steady-state equilibria of the conditional dynamical system (7.34) changes qualitatively as the value of q passes a threshold level $\hat{q}$ (formally derived in Section 7.9.1). That is, for all $q < \hat{q}$ the system is characterized by two locally stable steady-state equilibria, $(\bar{g}^L(q), \bar{e}^L(q))$ and $(\bar{g}^H(q), \bar{e}^H(q))$, and an unstable equilibrium, $(\bar{g}^U(q), \bar{e}^U(q))$, whereas for all $q > \hat{q}$ it is characterized by a unique globally stable steady-state equilibrium, $(\bar{g}^H(q), \bar{e}^H(q))$:

$$\begin{cases} \{(\bar{g}^L(q), \bar{e}^L(q)), (\bar{g}^U(q), \bar{e}^U(q)), (\bar{g}^H(q), \bar{e}^H(q))\} & \text{for } q < \hat{q}; \\ (\bar{g}^H(q), \bar{e}^H(q)) & \text{for } q \geq \hat{q}, \end{cases} \tag{7.35}$$

where $\bar{g}^L(q) < \underline{g}^b < \bar{g}^H(q)$ and $\partial(\bar{g}^j(q), \bar{e}^j(q))/\partial q > 0$ for $j = L, H$.

As depicted in Figure 7.4(a) (for $q = 0$) and Figure 7.5(a) (for $0 < q < \hat{q}$), if the fraction of individuals with high preference for quality is low (i.e., if $q < \hat{q}$), the economy is characterized by multiple locally stable steady-state equilibria: a low steady-state equilibrium $(\bar{g}^L(q), \bar{e}^L(q))$, where $\bar{g}^L(q) < \underline{g}^b$ (and therefore only individuals with high valuation of quality invest in human capital) and a high steady-state equilibrium $(\bar{g}^H(q), \bar{e}^H(q))$, where $\bar{g}^H(q) > \underline{g}^b$ (and therefore both types of individuals invest in human capital). As the fraction q of individuals with high valuation of quality increases, the rate of technological progress and the average level of education in each of the two stable steady-state equilibria increase as well.[29]

---

[29] In the knife-edged case in which $q = \hat{q}$, the system is characterized by multiple steady-state equilibria. However, only the uppermost one, $[\bar{g}^H(q), \bar{e}^H(q)] > [\underline{g}^b, 0]$, is locally stable.

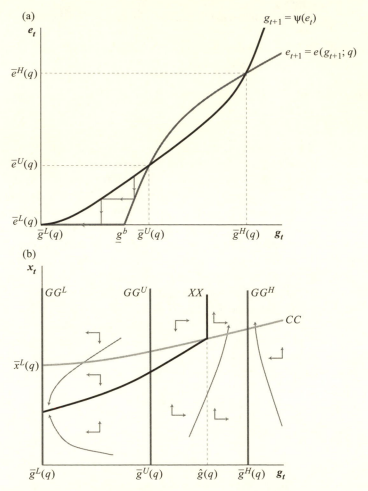

FIGURE 7.4. Evolution of technology, g_t, education, e_t, and effective resources, x_t: no individuals are of the quality type (i.e., $q = 0$).

Summary: Panel (a) describes the evolution of education, e_t, and technological progress, g_t, when the fraction q of individuals with high valuation of quality is zero. The curve $g_{t+1} = \psi(e_t)$ shows the effect of the average quality of the population on technological progress. The curve $e_{t+1} = e(g_{t+1}; q)$ shows the effect of expected technological change on the average investment in offspring quality. In the early stages of development, the economy is in the vicinity of the locally stable temporary Malthusian steady-state equilibrium (the intersection of the two curves at the origin). There is no investment in education, and the rate of technological progress is zero. Panel (b) describes the evolution of technological progress, g_t, and effective resources per efficiency units of labor, x_t, when the fraction q of individuals with high valuation of quality is zero. The CC locus is the curve below which the subsistence constraint is binding for at least part of the population. The GG loci are the curves for which technological progress is constant. The XX locus is the curve for which effective resources per efficiency unit of labor are constant. In the early stages of development, the economy is in the vicinity of a locally stable Malthusian temporary steady-state equilibrium (the intersection of GG and XX at $g_t = 0$). There is no investment in education, technological progress is zero, fertility rate is at the replacement level, and output per capita is constant.

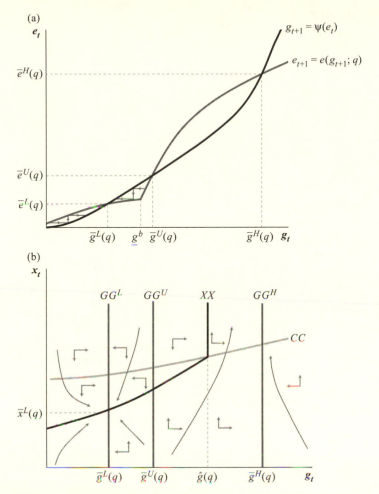

FIGURE 7.5. Evolution of technology, g_t, education, e_t, and effective resources, x_t: a small fraction of individuals are of the quality type (i.e., $q \in (0, \hat{q})$).

Summary: Panel (a) describes the evolution of education, e_t, and technological progress, g_t, for a fraction of individuals of the quality type that is below a threshold level that would trigger take-off from the Malthusian Epoch (i.e., $q \in (0, \hat{q})$). Given the initial conditions, in the absence of large shocks, the economy remains in the vicinity of a low steady-state equilibrium $(\bar{g}^L, \bar{e}^L)$, where both the level of education and technological progress are low but positive. The evolutionary advantage of individuals of the quality type raises their fraction in the population, q, and consequently the curve $e_t = e(g_t; q)$ shifts upward. Panel (b) describes the evolution of technological progress, g_t, and effective resources per efficiency unit of labor, x_t, for a fraction of individuals of the quality type below a threshold level that would trigger a take-off from the Malthusian Epoch (i.e., $q \in (0, \hat{q})$). In the absence of large shocks, the economy remains in the vicinity of the low steady-state equilibrium $(\bar{g}^L, \bar{x}^L)$, where technological progress and education are low, and the level of effective resources permits fertility rates above replacement. The evolutionary advantage of individuals of the quality type raises their fraction in the population, q, and consequently GG^L and GG^U shift toward one another.

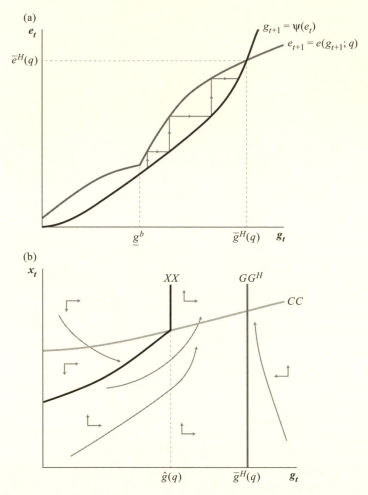

FIGURE 7.6. Evolution of technology, g_t, education, e_t, and effective resources, x_t. A large fraction of individuals are of the quality type ($q > \hat{q}$).

Summary: Panel (a) describes the evolution of education, e_t, and the rate of technological change, g_t, once the fraction of individuals with high valuation of quality in the population has grown sufficiently, due to the evolutionary process, and is above the threshold level that triggers the take-off from the Malthusian Epoch (i.e., $q > \hat{q}$). The dynamical system is characterized by a unique globally stable steady-state equilibrium ($\bar{g}^H$, $\bar{e}^H$). The economy converges to this steady state characterized by a high level of education, rapid technological progress, and sustained economic growth. Panel (b) describes the evolution of technological progress, g_t, and effective resources per labor, x_t, once, due to the evolutionary process, the fraction of the quality type exceeds the threshold that triggers a take-off from the Malthusian Epoch (i.e., $q > \hat{q}$). The economy converges to a steady-state equilibrium characterized by a high level of education, rapid technological progress, and a positive growth rate of effective resources and output per capita.

As depicted in Figure 7.6(a), for a sufficiently high fraction of individuals with high preference for quality (i.e., as long as $q \geq \hat{q}$), the economy is characterized by a unique globally stable steady-state equilibrium $(\bar{g}^H(q), \bar{e}^H(q))$, where both types of individuals invest in human capital.

7.4.2 Conditional Dynamics of Technology and Effective Resources

The evolution of the rate of technological progress, g_t, and effective resources per efficiency unit of labor, x_t, for a given fraction q of individuals of the quality type is characterized by the sequence $\{g_t, x_t; q\}_{t=0}^{\infty}$, which satisfies in every period t the conditional two-dimensional system

$$\begin{cases} g_{t+1} = g(g_t; q); \\ x_{t+1} = x(g_t, x_t; q). \end{cases} \tag{7.36}$$

The phase diagrams of this conditional dynamical system, depicted in Figures 7.4(b), 7.5(b), and 7.6(b), contain three loci: the CC locus, the GG locus, and the XX locus. The properties of these loci and the dynamics of (g_t, x_t) in relation to these loci are derived in Section 7.9.

The CC Locus: The Subsistence Consumption Frontier.
This locus is the set of all pairs (g_t, x_t) such that the income of low-income individuals (the quantity type, type b) is at a level above which the subsistence consumption constraint is no longer binding (i.e., $z_t^b = \tilde{z}$). The locus separates the regions in which the subsistence constraint is binding for at least individuals of type b from those regions in which it is not binding for both types. As depicted in Figures 7.4(b), 7.5(b), and 7.6(b), the CC locus is an upward sloping curve in the plane (g_t, x_t) with a positive vertical intercept.

The GG Locus
This locus is the set of all pairs (g_t, x_t) such that, for a given level of q, the rate of technological progress, g_t, is in a steady state (i.e., $g_{t+1} = g_t$). As follows from (7.20), along the GG locus $g_{t+1} = g(g_t; q) = g_t$. The GG locus is therefore not affected by the effective resources per efficiency unit of labor, x_t, and, as depicted in Figures 7.4(b), 7.5(b), and 7.6(b), the GG locus consists of vertical line(s) at the steady-state level(s) of g, listed in (7.35) and depicted in Figures 7.4(a), 7.5(a), and 7.6(a). There are two qualitatively different configurations. For $q < \hat{q}$, as depicted in Figures 7.4(b) and 7.5(b), the GG locus consists of three vertical lines at the conditional steady-state levels of g : $\{\bar{g}^L(q), \bar{g}^U(q), \bar{g}^H(q)\}$. For $q > \hat{q}$, as depicted in Figure 7.6(b)

(and corresponding to Figure 7.6(a)), the GG locus consists of a unique vertical line at the conditional steady-state level of g, $\bar{g}^H(q)$.[30]

The XX Locus

This locus is the set of all pairs (g_t, x_t) such that the level of effective resources per efficiency unit of labor, x_t, for a given level of q, is in a steady state (i.e., $x_{t+1} = x_t$). As follows from (7.32), along the XX locus, $x_{t+1} = [(1 + g_{t+1})/(1 + \mu_{t+1})]x_t \equiv x(g_t, x_t; q) = x_t$. Hence, along the XX locus, the growth rate of efficiency units of labor, μ_t, and the rate of technological progress, g_t, are equal. As depicted in Figures 7.4(b), 7.5(b), and 7.6(b), the XX locus has a positive vertical intercept at $g = 0$, it increases monotonically with g_t, and it becomes vertical once the XX locus intersects the CC locus (at $g_t = \hat{g}(q)$). Furthermore, as q increases, the value of $\hat{g}(q)$ declines.

7.4.3 Conditional Steady-State Equilibria

This subsection describes the properties of the conditional steady-state equilibria of the conditional dynamical system (7.36) that governs the evolution of $\{g_t, x_t; q\}_{t=0}^{\infty}$, based on the phase diagrams depicted in Figures 7.4(b), 7.5(b), and 7.6(b).

The set of steady-state equilibria of this dynamical system consists of constant growth rates of both the technological level and the effective resources per efficiency unit of labor, and therefore a constant growth rate of output per capita. Let χ_t denote the growth rate of effective resources per worker. As follows from (7.32),

$$\chi_t \equiv \frac{x_{t+1} - x_t}{x_t} = \frac{g_{t+1} - \mu_{t+1}}{1 + \mu_{t+1}} \equiv \chi(g_t, x_t; q). \tag{7.37}$$

As depicted in Figures 7.4(b), 7.5(b), and 7.6(b), the set of steady-state equilibria of the conditional dynamical system (7.36) changes qualitatively as the fraction of individuals with high valuation of quality surpasses the threshold level $\hat{q}$. That is, for all $q < \hat{q}$, the system is characterized by two locally stable steady-state equilibria, $(\bar{g}^L(q), \bar{\chi}^L(q))$ and $(\bar{g}^H(q), \bar{\chi}^H(q))$, and an unstable equilibrium $(\bar{g}^U(q), \bar{\chi}^U(q))$, whereas for all $q > \hat{q}$ it is characterized by a unique globally stable steady-state equilibrium $(\bar{g}^H(q), \bar{\chi}^H(q))$, where the growth rate of output per capita is equal to that of effective resources per efficiency unit of labor:[31]

[30] For the knife-edged case of $q = \hat{q}$, $\bar{g}^L(\hat{q}) = \bar{g}^U(\hat{q}) = \hat{g}^b$, and the GG locus consists of two vertical lines at the steady-state levels of g: $\{\hat{g}^b, \bar{g}^H(\hat{q})\}$.

[31] Note that for $q = \hat{q}$, the system is characterized by multiple steady-state equilibria. However, only the uppermost one is locally stable.

$$\left\{[\bar{g}^L(q), \bar{\chi}^L(q)], [\bar{g}^U(q), \bar{\chi}^U(q)], [\bar{g}^H(q), \bar{\chi}^H(q)]\right\} \quad \text{for } q < \hat{q};$$

$$[\bar{g}^H(q), \bar{\chi}^H(q)] \qquad\qquad\qquad\qquad\qquad \text{for } q \geq \hat{q},$$

(7.38)

where $\bar{g}^L(q) < \underline{g}^b < \bar{g}^H(q)$, $\bar{\chi}^H(q) > \bar{\chi}^L(q) = 0$, $\partial \bar{\chi}^L(q)/\partial q = 0$, $\partial \bar{\chi}^H(q)/\partial q > 0$, and for $j = L, H$, $\partial \bar{g}^j(q)/\partial q > 0$.

Hence, in the early stages of development, when the fraction q of individuals with high valuation of quality in the population is sufficiently small, the conditional dynamical system (depicted in Figures 7.4(b) and 7.5(b) in the space (g_t, x_t)) is characterized by two locally stable steady-state equilibria. However, since the initial levels of g and q are sufficiently small, the economy converges to the Malthusian steady-state equilibrium $(\bar{g}^L(q), \bar{x}^L(q))$, where the rate of technological progress is positive, but output per capita is constant.

In later stages of development, as q_t increases sufficiently, the Malthusian conditional steady-state equilibrium vanishes. The dynamical system (depicted in Figure 7.6(b)), is characterized by a unique steady-state equilibrium, where the growth rates of the level of technology and effective resources per efficiency unit of labor are constant at $[\bar{g}^H(q), \bar{\chi}^H(q)] > 0$. The steady-state growth rate of output per capita is equal to the growth rate of effective resources per efficiency unit of labor.

7.4.4 Human Evolution and the Transition from Stagnation to Growth

This section analyzes the relationship between the evolution of humans and economic growth since the emergence of the human species. The analysis demonstrates that the inherent evolutionary pressure that has been associated with the Malthusian Epoch brought about the transition from Malthusian stagnation to sustained economic growth. The Malthusian pressure generated a process of natural selection in which the representation of individuals with high valuation of child quality increased, raising the average level of human capital and inducing higher rates of technological progress that eventually brought about the Modern Growth Regime.

Suppose that in the early era of the human species, the population of the world consisted of two types of individuals: individuals of the quantity type, who place a lower weight on the quality of their offspring, and an infinitesimally small fraction of individuals of the quality type, who place a higher weight on the quality of their offspring. Since the fraction q of individuals of the quality type is infinitesimally small, they have no impact on the rate of technological progress. Given the initial conditions, the economy is therefore in a steady-state equilibrium, where the rate of technological progress, g_t, is nearly zero, parents of type b have no incentive to invest in the quality of their children; and the average quality in the population is therefore nearly zero. Hence, as depicted in Figure 7.4(a) in the plane (g_t, e_t) for $q = 0$, this conditional dynamical system is in a locally stable steady-state equilibrium, where $\bar{g}^L(0) = 0$ and $\bar{e}^L(0) = 0$. As depicted in Figure 7.4(b) in the plane (g_t, x_t), the economy is in a locally stable Malthusian steady-state equilibrium, where effective resources are constant at a level $\bar{x}^L(0) > 0$, the level of human capital is constant, and hence, output per capita is constant as well. In this steady-state equilibrium, the population is constant, and fertility rate is therefore at the replacement level (i.e., $n_t^b = 1$). Furthermore, (small) shocks to population or resources would be undone in a classic Malthusian fashion.

As long as the fraction of individuals of the quality type is sufficiently small, (i.e., $q_t < \hat{q}$), as depicted in Figure 7.5(a) in the space (g_t, e_t), the economy is in the vicinity of a conditional locally stable steady-state equilibrium $(\bar{g}^L(q), \bar{e}^L(q))$, where $\bar{g}^L(q) < \underline{g}^b$. As established in (7.13), as long as the rate of technological progress is below $\underline{g}^b$ (the threshold level above which individuals of type b start investing in the quality of their children), the quality chosen by type b individuals is $e_t^b = 0$, and the quality chosen by type a individuals is $e_t^a > 0$. Since the fraction of individuals of type a is small, the average level of education, e_t, is positive but small (i.e., $g_{t+1} = \psi(e_t) < \underline{g}^b$). Furthermore, as depicted in Figure 7.5(b) in the space (g_t, x_t), this conditional locally stable steady-state equilibrium corresponds to a locally stable conditional Malthusian steady-state equilibrium, $(\bar{g}^L(q), \bar{x}^L(q))$, where $\bar{g}^L(q) < \underline{g}^b$. The existence of a small fraction of individuals of the quality type generates a slow rate of technological progress. Investment in quality is negligible, and resources above subsistence are devoted to child rearing. The Malthusian mechanism therefore generates a proportional increase in output and population, and the economy is in the vicinity of a temporary locally stable Malthusian steady-state equilibrium.

In this early Malthusian era, individuals of type a (i.e., individuals with a preference for quality of offspring) have an evolutionary advantage over individuals of type b. That is, the fraction of individuals of type a rises in the population, despite their bias against the quantity of their offspring. Hence, in the early stages of development, Malthusian pressure provides an evolutionary advantage to the quality type. The income of individuals of the quantity type is near subsistence, and fertility rates are therefore near replacement level. In contrast, the wealthier, quality type can afford higher fertility rates (of higher quality offspring). As depicted in Figure 7.3 (and analyzed in Section 7.9.2), in the Malthusian Epoch, $n_t^a > n_t^b$ for all $q_t < \hat{q}$, and hence the fraction q_t of individuals of the quality type in the population increases monotonically over this Malthusian regime. As q_t increases, the locus $e(g_{t+1}, q_t)$ in Figure 7.5(a) shifts upward and the corresponding conditional steady-state equilibrium reflects a higher rate of technological progress along with higher average quality.

Eventually as q_t crosses the threshold level $\hat{q}$, the conditional dynamical system changes qualitatively. The $e(g_{t+1}, q_t)$ locus in Figure 7.5(a) shifts sufficiently upward so as to eliminate the lower intersection with the locus

$g_{t+1} = \psi(e_t)$, and the loci GG^L and GG^U depicted in Figure 7.5(b) vanish, whereas the GG^H locus shifts rightward and the XX locus above the Subsistence Consumption Frontier shifts leftward. As depicted in Figure 7.6, the Malthusian conditional steady-state equilibrium vanishes, and the economy is no longer trapped in the vicinity of this equilibrium. The economy converges gradually to a unique globally stable conditional steady-state equilibrium $(\bar{g}^H(q), \bar{e}^H(q), \bar{\chi}^H(q)) > (g^b, 0, 0)$, where both types of individuals invest in human capital, the rate of technological progress is high, and the growth rate of effective resources per efficiency unit of labor is positive. Once the rate of technological progress exceeds $\underline{g}^b$ (the threshold level above which individuals of type b start investing in the quality of their children), the growth rate of the average level of education increases, and consequently there is an acceleration in the rate of technological progress that may be associated with the Industrial Revolution. The positive feedback between the rate of technological progress and the level of education reinforces the growth process. The economy eventually crosses the Subsistence Consumption Frontier, setting the stage for a demographic transition in which the rate of population growth declines and the average level of education increases. The economy converges to the unique stable conditional steady-state equilibrium above the Subsistence Consumption Frontier with a positive growth rate of output per worker.[32]

Technological progress has two effects on the evolution of the population. First, by inducing parents to give their children more education, it *ceteris paribus* lowers the rate of population growth. But second, by raising potential income, technological progress increases the fraction of time that parents devote to raising children. Initially, while the economy is in the Malthusian region (depicted in Figure 7.5(b)), the effect of technology on the parental budget constraint dominates, and the growth rate of the population increases. As the economy eventually crosses the Subsistence Consumption Frontier, further improvements in technology no longer have the effect of changing the amount of time devoted to child rearing. Faster technological change therefore raises the quality of children while reducing their number.

During the transition from the Malthusian Epoch to sustained economic growth, once the economic environment improves sufficiently, evolutionary pressure weakens, the significance of quality for survival declines, and type b individuals—the quantity type—gain the evolutionary advantage. Namely, as technological progress brings about an increase in income, the Malthusian pressure relaxes, and the domination of wealth in fertility decisions diminishes. The inherent advantage of the quantity type in reproduction gradually dominates,

---

[32] It should be noted that once the fraction of individuals of the quality type exceeds $\hat{q}$ and therefore $g_t > \underline{g}^b$, the demographic transition occurs regardless of the evolutionary process.

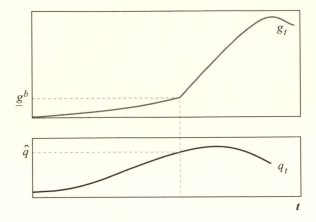

FIGURE 7.7. The dynamics of the fraction of individuals of the quality type and the rate of technological progress.
Summary: The figure shows that the fraction of individuals of the quality type in the population, q, increases gradually in the Malthusian Epoch, and once it reaches the critical level, $\hat{q}$, it triggers an intensive interaction between technological progress and investment in quality that brings about the Industrial Revolution. The onset of the demographic transition reverses the evolutionary advantage, q declines gradually, and the rate of technological progress declines but remains positive.

and fertility rates of the quantity type ultimately overtake those of the quality type (i.e., as the level of effective resources exceeds $\check{x}$). Hence, the fraction q_t of individuals who have high valuation of quality starts declining as the economy approaches the Subsistence Consumption Frontier. The model predicts, therefore, that the long-run equilibrium is characterized by a complete domination of the quantity type (i.e., $q = 0$). Nevertheless, the growth rate of output per worker remains positive, although at a lower level than the one that existed at the peak of the transition. As the level of q declines below the threshold level $\hat{q}$, depicted in Figure 7.7, the conditional dynamical system that describes the economy is once again characterized by multiple locally stable steady-state equilibria, as depicted in Figures 7.4 and 7.5. However, unlike the situation in the early stages of development, the position of the economy prior to the decline in q_t ensures that the economy converges to the high steady-state equilibrium.[33]

---

[33] If mutations reduce the lower bound of the valuation of quality, an additional assumption will be needed to ensure the existence of a sustained-growth steady-state equilibrium. In particular,

The incorporation of some additional plausible factors into the analysis, such as environmental effects on preferences (i.e., learning and imitation of the behavior of the quality type) would permit heterogeneity of types in the long run. Furthermore, the incorporation of a positive effect of the scale of the population (given quality) on the rate of technological progress might prevent the decline in the growth rate of output per capita, depicted in Figure 7.7, in the advanced stages of the evolution of the economy as it approaches the (unconditional) long-run equilibrium.

Finally, fertility differentials across income groups evolve nonmonotonically in the process of development. As depicted in Figure 7.3, in any period during the Malthusian Regime (i.e., as long as $g_t \leq \underline{g}^b$ and therefore $x_t < \check{x}$), fertility rates among richer individuals are predicted to be higher than those among poorer individuals, whereas in any period after the take-off (i.e., once $x_t \geq x^{CC}(g_t)$ and therefore $x_t > \check{x}$), fertility rates among richer individuals are predicted to be lower than those among poorer individuals. Hence, in the course of the transition from the Malthusian Epoch to the Modern Growth Regime, the cross-sectional relationship between income and fertility is reversed. In the Malthusian Epoch there is a positive cross-sectional correlation between income and fertility rates, whereas in the Modern Growth Regime this correlation is negative.

7.5   Failed Take-off Attempts

The analysis suggests that the interaction between the composition of the population and the rate of technological progress is the critical factor that determines the timing of the transition from stagnation to growth. In particular, the theory indicates that waves of rapid technological progress before the Industrial Revolution did not generate a sustainable economic growth due to the shortage of individuals of the quality type in the population, whereas sustained economic growth after the Industrial Revolution may be attributed to the presence of a sufficiently high fraction of individuals of the quality type in the population.

As depicted in Figures 7.4(b) and 7.5(b), if the fraction of individuals of the quality type is low, the economy is characterized by two locally stable equilibria: a Malthusian steady-state equilibrium, where output per capita is constant near a subsistence level of consumption, and a steady-state equilibrium where the growth rate of output per capita is positive and constant.

---

these mutations would generate an evolutionary disadvantage if, for a sufficiently high rate of technological progress, the erosion effect dominates the productivity effect for individuals who do not invest in human capital, and consequently available resources for child rearing would not permit fertility rates above replacement.

Initial conditions place the economy in the vicinity of the Malthusian steady-state equilibrium. However, a sufficiently large technological shock would place the economy on a trajectory that leads to a sustained-growth regime. The composition of the population determines the effectiveness of a technological shock. The smaller the fraction of individuals of the quality type in the population, the larger is the size of the shock necessary to generate a sustained take-off from Malthusian stagnation. As the fraction of the quality type in the population increases (i.e., q_t rises), the distance between the loci GG^L and GG^U (depicted in Figure 7.5(b)) narrows, and the necessary jump in the rate of technological progress to facilitate a sustained take-off decreases. Ultimately, as depicted in Figure 7.6(b), once q crosses the threshold level $\hat{q}$, the dynamical system changes qualitatively. It is characterized by a unique globally stable steady-state equilibrium with sustained economic growth, and the transition from Malthusian stagnation occurs without the need for a technological shock.

The analysis suggests therefore that those nonsustainable growth episodes before the Industrial Revolution may be attributed to the presence of a relatively small fraction of individuals of the quality type in the population that would have invested sufficiently in education in response to the change in the technological environment and therefore would have allowed this rapid change in technology to be sustained.[34] Furthermore, one may meaningfully argue that, given the finiteness of a technological leap, an adverse composition of the population could have virtually prevented a sustained take-off from a Malthusian steady state. Unlike the unsuccessful take-off attempts before the Industrial Revolution, the theory suggests that the successful take-off during the Industrial Revolution (which has been attributed largely to the acceleration in the pace of technological progress) is partly due to the gradual evolution of the composition of the population, which generated a sufficiently large fraction of quality type individuals on the eve of the Industrial Revolution. This compositional change has allowed the pace of technological progress to be sustained by generating an impressive increase in the average level of education.

7.6 Main Hypotheses and Their Empirical Assessment

This unified evolutionary growth theory generates several hypotheses about human evolution and the process of development, emphasizing the role of natural

---

[34] The effect of nonsustainable technological advance on output growth would vanish gradually. It would generate an increase in the average human capital of the population, but at a level that would sustain only slower technological progress. This lower rate, however, would not sustain the return on human capital. The average human capital in the population would decline, leading to a decline in the rate of technological change that would ultimately end in a state of stagnation.

selection in (i) the gradual process of human capital formation and thus technological progress prior to the Industrial Revolution and (ii) the acceleration of the interaction between human capital and technological progress in the second phase of the Industrial Revolution, the associated demographic transition, and the emergence of an era of sustained economic growth.

H1 *During the initial phases of the Malthusian Epoch, the growth rate of output per capita is nearly zero and the growth rate of population and literacy rates is minuscule, reflecting the sluggish pace of technological progress, the low representation of individuals with high valuation of child quality, and the slow pace of the evolutionary process.*

This hypothesis is consistent with the characteristics of the Malthusian Epoch, as described in Section 2.1.

H2 *In the pre-demographic transition era, traits for higher valuation of offspring quality generated an evolutionary advantage. Namely, individuals with higher valuation of the quality of children had a larger number of surviving offspring, and their representation in the population increased over time. In contrast, in the post-demographic transition era, when income per capita has no longer been the binding constraint on fertility decisions, individuals with higher valuation of offspring quantity have an evolutionary advantage, bearing a larger number of surviving offspring. Thus, in the pre-demographic transition era, the number of surviving offspring was affected positively by parental education and parental income, whereas in the post-demographic transition era this pattern is reversed and more educated, higher income individuals have a smaller number of surviving offspring.*

Clark and Hamilton (2006) examine empirically this hypothesis on the basis of data from wills written in England in 1620–1636. The wills were written near the time of death, in urban and rural areas, and across a large variety of occupations and wealth. They contain information about the number of surviving offspring, literacy of the testator (indicated by whether the will was signed), occupation of testator, and the amounts of money, houses, and land that were bequeathed. The study finds a positive and statistically significant association between literacy (and wealth) and the number of surviving offspring.[35] They confirm the hypothesis that literate people (born, according to the theory, to parents with quality bias) had an evolutionary advantage in this (pre-demographic

---

[35] In addition, Boyer (1989) argues that in early nineteenth century England, agricultural laborers' income had a positive effect on fertility: birth rates increased by 4.4% in response to a 10% increase in annual income. Further evidence is surveyed by Lee (1987).

transition) period.[36] The negative relationship between education and fertility within a country in the post-demographic transition era has been documented extensively, as discussed in Section 4.3.

H3 *The rise in the representation of individuals with higher valuation of quality gradually increased the average level of investment in human capital, permitting slow growth of output per capita.*

The prediction about the rise in human capital prior to the Industrial Revolution is consistent with historical evidence. Various measures of literacy rates demonstrate a significant rise during the two centuries that preceded the Industrial Revolution in England.[37] As depicted in Figure 7.8, male literacy rates increased gradually during 1600–1760. Literacy rates for men doubled over this period, rising from about 30% in 1600 to more than 60% in 1760. Similarly, as reported by Cipolla (1969), literacy rates of women more than tripled from less than 10% in 1640 to more than 30% in 1760.[38] Moreover, recent evidence suggests that human capital formation prior to industrialization played an important role in technological progress and in the industrial take-off (Boucekkine et al., 2007; Baten and van Zanden, 2008).

Moreover, human capital accumulation in England began in an era when the market rewards for skill acquisition were at historically low levels, consistent with the argument that the rise in human capital reflected a rise in the preference for quality offspring.

H4 *The acceleration in the rate of technological progress, which was reinforced by investment in human capital by individuals with high valuation of offspring quality, increased the demand for human capital in the late Post-Malthusian Regime, generating a universal investment in human capital, a demographic transition, and a rapid pace of economic growth.*

The hypothesis is consistent with the evidence (provided in Section 2.3) on the significant rise in industrial demand for human capital in the second phase of

---

[36] Interestingly, in New France, where land was abundant, and thus fertility decisions were not constrained by the availability of resources, the number of surviving offspring was higher among less educated individuals. These findings are consistent with the theory as well. If resource constraint is not binding for fertility decisions (e.g., in the post-demographic transition era, or due to a positive shock to income in the Malthusian Epoch), individuals with higher valuation of quantity gain an evolutionary advantage.

[37] Moreover, this hypothesis appears consistent with the increase in the number and size of universities in Europe since the establishment of the first university in Bologna in the eleventh century, significantly outpacing the population growth rate.

[38] This pattern is robust and is observed in various dioceses over this period. For instance, Cressy (1980) reports a gradual rise in average literacy rate of yeomen, husbandmen, and tradesmen in Norwich from 30% in 1580 to nearly 61% in 1690 (Table 6.3, p. 113) and a gradual rise in literacy in the diocese of Durham between 1565 and 1624 (Table 7.1, p. 143).

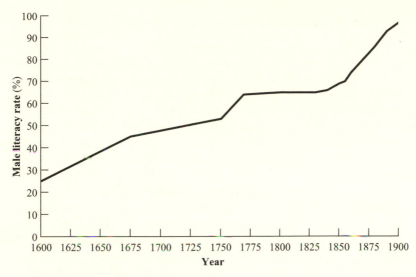

FIGURE 7.8. The rise in male literacy rates prior to and during the Industrial Revolution: England, 1600–1900.
Data sources: Cipolla (1969); Stone (1969); Schofield (1973).

the Industrial Revolution, the marked increase in educational attainment, the emergence of universal education toward the end of the nineteenth century in association with a decline in fertility rates, and a transition to an era of sustained economic growth.

7.7 Complementary Mechanisms

The theory suggests that during the Malthusian Epoch, hereditary human traits associated with higher earning capacity generated an evolutionary advantage and had dominated the population over time. Hereditary traits that stimulated technological progress or raised the incentive to invest in offspring's human capital (e.g., ability, longevity, and a preference for quality) may have triggered a positive feedback loop between investment in human capital and technological progress that brought about a take-off from an epoch of Malthusian stagnation, a demographic transition, and a shift to an era of sustained economic growth. Hence, the struggle for existence that had characterized most of human history stimulated a process of natural selection that generated an evolutionary advantage to individuals whose characteristics were complementary to the growth process.

7.7.1 Evolution of Entrepreneurial Spirit and Economic Growth

The potential impact of evolutionary processes on the prevalence of entrepreneurial spirit has been the subject of a complementary hypothesis about the role of natural selection in the emergence of sustained economic growth. Galor and Michalopoulos (2006) advanced the hypothesis that the evolution of entrepreneurial spirit played a significant role in the process of economic development and the time path of inequality within and across societies.

The theory suggests that the prevalence of entrepreneurial traits evolved nonmonotonically in the course of human history. In the early stages of development, risk-tolerant, growth-promoting entrepreneurial traits generated an evolutionary advantage, and their increased representation accelerated the pace of technological advancement, contributing significantly to the process of development and the transition from stagnation to growth. Natural selection had magnified growth-promoting activities in relatively wealthier economies as well as in the upper segments of societies, enlarging the income gap within as well as across societies. As economies matured, however, this evolutionary pattern was reversed, and individuals characterized by entrepreneurial traits had an evolutionary disadvantage, diminishing the growth potential of advanced economies and contributing to the convergence of intermediate-level economies and advanced ones.

Unlike the commonly emphasized forces for economic convergence (i.e., higher returns to investments in human capital, physical capital, and technological adoption for laggard countries), the research proposes that a higher prevalence of growth-promoting entrepreneurial traits in middle-income economies contributed to economic convergence. Moreover, the analysis demonstrates that in the least advanced economies, selection of growth-promoting traits has been delayed, contributing to the persistence of poverty. Thus, historical variations in geographical, environmental, and social factors affected the pace of this evolutionary process and thus the prevalence of growth-promoting entrepreneurial traits across economies. These variations thus contribute to the sustained contemporary differences in productivity and income per capita across countries.

The predictions of the proposed theory provide further understanding of the path of income inequality in a society over time. Consistent with the observed pattern of inequality during development, the theory suggests that in the early stages of development, inequality widens due to a more rapid selection of entrepreneurial individuals among the elites. However, as the economy matures, inequality subsides, because of increased representation of entrepreneurial individuals among the middle and lower classes. In particular, this prediction is consistent with the class origin of entrepreneurs during the Industrial Revolution. The failure of the landed aristocracy to lead the innovative process of industrialization can be attributed to the low representation of growth-promoting entrepreneurial traits within the landed gentry, and their prevalence among the middle and even lower classes.[39]

Consider an economy that, due to the forces of natural selection, evolves endogenously from a Malthusian Epoch to an era of sustained economic growth. The growth process is fueled by technological progress, which is positively affected by the level of income per capita as well as by the prevalence of risk-tolerant entrepreneurial individuals in the economy.[40] Variations in entrepreneurial spirit among individuals are modeled as differences in the degree of risk aversion with respect to consumption. Differences in the degree of risk aversion with respect to consumption among individuals affect their reproductive success differentially and are transmitted across generations, either genetically or culturally.

The reversal in the evolutionary advantage of the risk-tolerant entrepreneurial types stems from the effect of the level of income on the relative cost of consumption and child rearing. At the early stages of development, countries in a stationary equilibrium undergo a change in (latent) distribution of entrepreneurial spirit. As the economy progresses and wage income increases, the opportunity cost of child rearing increases relative to consumption. Consequently, at sufficiently low levels of income, the cost of children (whose production is time intensive) is lower than that of consumption, and the less risk-averse individuals (whose choices are more responsive to relative prices) optimally allocate more resources to child rearing, and the representation of their type increases in the population over time. As the economy develops and wage income increases, the cost of raising children is eventually higher than the cost of consumption. The less risk-averse individuals then optimally allocate more resources to consumption and less to children. Hence, the more

---

[39] The implications of the theory for the class origin of entrepreneurs during the Industrial Revolution are complementary to Doepke and Zilibotti (2008). Their theory suggests that middle-class families in occupations requiring effort, skill, and experience develop patience and a work ethic among their children, whereas upper-class families relying on rental income cultivate a refined taste for leisure. These class-specific attitudes become key determinants of success, once industrialization transforms the economic landscape, eventually permitting the middle class to surpass the pre-industrial landed elite.

[40] Technological adoption and creation is associated with uncertainty, and a population with more risk-tolerant individuals would engage more frequently in innovative, risky projects, thus technologically outperforming a population of similar size comprised of more risk-averse individuals. The positive association between the fraction of entrepreneurial individuals in the population and the rate of technological growth is well documented in the literature. It is at the foundation of the Schumpeterian viewpoint (e.g., Schumpeter, 1934; Aghion and Howitt, 1992), according to which the role of entrepreneurs is instrumental in the process of innovation. In particular, the role of risk-taking behavior in facilitating innovation and technological adoption in the industrial as well as the agricultural sectors is well documented (Moscardi and de Janvry, 1977; van Praag and Cramer, 2001).

risk-averse individuals allocate relatively more resources to fertility and gain the evolutionary advantage. Thus, entrepreneurial spirit declines over time in advanced stages of development.

A low degree of entrepreneurial spirit has an adverse effect on fertility and reproductive success, raising the frequency of the entrepreneurial, risk-tolerant, growth-promoting individuals in the economy and stimulating the growth process. However, as economies mature, a higher degree of risk aversion (i.e., lower level of entrepreneurial spirit) has a beneficial effect on reproductive success, diminishing the growth potential of the economy. The non-monotonic effect of entrepreneurial spirit on fertility across different levels of income per capita is the driving force behind the changing distribution of the entrepreneurial, risk-tolerant individuals in the population along the path of economic development. It contributes to the nonmonotonic effect of natural selection on inequality across nations, stimulating divergence in the early stages of development and convergence in more mature phases.

The predictions of the theory regarding the reversal in the evolutionary advantage of entrepreneurial risk-tolerant individuals in more advanced stages of development could be examined, based on the effect of the degree of risk aversion on fertility choices in contemporary developed and less developed economies. Existing evidence is consistent with the proposed hypothesis, suggesting that entrepreneurial propensity, proxied by risk tolerance, is positively correlated with the number of children in less developed economies and negatively in developed economies (Feinerman and Finkelshtain, 1996; Miyata, 2003; Dohmen et al., 2006).

Furthermore, evidence from twin studies strongly suggests that a substantial component of the observed variation in degrees of novelty seeking may be attributed to genetic variation (Kohler et al. 1999; Rodgers et al. 2001a).[41] Furthermore, the dopamine receptor D4 (D4DR) gene has been studied extensively in the biological literature as a potential candidate for moderating novelty-seeking behavior. Although the evidence is still inconclusive, a positive association between a certain polymorphism in the D4DR (the 7R allele) and novelty-seeking behavior is most widely documented. The available genetic, biochemical, and physiological data suggest that the 7R allele has been subjected to positive selection. This finding implies that once more entrepreneurial

---

[41] Cloninger (1987) proposed four genetically homogeneous and independent dimensions of personality: novelty seeking, harm avoidance, reward dependence, and persistence that are hypothesized to be based on distinct neurochemical and genetic substrates. In particular, novelty seeking is closely associated with the notion of entrepreneurial spirit in the economics literature (Köse, 2003). Human personality traits that can be reliably measured by rating scales show a considerable heritable component. One such rating scale is the Tridimensional Personality Questionnaire (TPQ), which was designed by Cloninger (1987) to measure harm avoidance, novelty seeking, and reward dependence. Several studies have shown that a large component of the observed variation in the behavioral traits as measured by the TPQ can be attributed to genetic differences.

individuals were introduced in the human population, they started procreating at higher rates throughout most of human history, corroborating the focal prediction of the theory. As to the genetic evolution of the dopamine receptor D4 locus, Ding et al. (2002), studying a worldwide population sample, proposed that the 7R allele originated as a rare mutational event about 40,000 years ago that nevertheless increased to high frequency in human populations by positive selection. To the extent that the 7R allele is associated with novelty-seeking behavior, the findings of Ding et al. (2002) confirm the basic prediction of the model. Individuals characterized by high elasticity of substitution at low levels of economic development have an evolutionary advantage, and the introduction of such traits in an environment characterized by very low income levels (i.e., the emergence of the 7R allele bearers about 40,000 years ago) should have led to an appreciable increase in their representation in the population.

7.7.2 Evolution of Life Expectancy and Economic Growth

The potential impact of evolutionary processes on the rise in life expectancy during development has been the subject of a complementary hypothesis about the role of natural selection in the emergence of sustained economic growth. The theory suggests that social, economic, and environmental changes associated with the transition from hunter-gatherer tribes to agricultural communities and urban societies affected the nature of environmental hazards confronted by the human population and triggered an evolutionary process that had a significant impact on the time path of human longevity.

The rise in population density, the domestication of animals, and the increase in work effort during the Neolithic Revolution increased the exposure and vulnerability of humans to environmental hazards, such as infectious diseases and parasites. It increased the extrinsic mortality risk (i.e., risk associated with environmental factors) and led to the observed temporary decline in life expectancy during the Neolithic period, as depicted in Figure 7.9.[42] Nevertheless, as argued by Galor and Moav (2005, 2008), the rise in the extrinsic mortality risk generated an evolutionary advantage to individuals who were genetically predisposed

---

[42] Most comparisons between hunter-gatherers and farmers (e.g., Cohen, 1991) suggest that, in the same locale, farmers suffered higher rates of infection due to the increase in human settlements, poorer nutrition from reduced meat intake, and less effective mineral absorption because of the cereal-based diet. Consequently, Neolithic farmers were shorter and had a lower life expectancy relative to Mesolithic hunter-gatherers. Although it is difficult to draw a reliable conclusion about relative life expectancy in these periods, because skeletal samples are often distorted and incomplete, available evidence suggests that prehistorical hunter-gatherers often fared relatively well compared to later populations, particularly with reference to the survival of children. The Illinois Valley provides life tables for hunter-gatherers which confirm the assessment that their life expectancies matched or exceeded those of later groups. Additional evidence, mostly from the Old World, is provided in Galor and Moav (2005, Table 1).

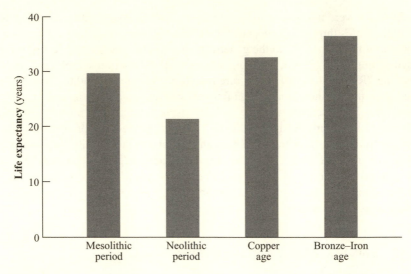

FIGURE 7.9. Nonmonotonic evolution of life expectancy during the Neolithic Revolution.
Data Source: Galor and Moav (2005).

to longer life expectancy, leading to the observed increase in life expectancy in the post-Neolithic period.

The theory suggests, therefore, that the increase in extrinsic mortality risk in the course of the Neolithic Revolution triggered an evolutionary process that gradually altered the composition of the population. Individuals who were characterized by a higher genetic predisposition to somatic investment, repairs, and maintenance (e.g., enhanced immune system, DNA repairs, tumor suppression, and antioxidants) and thus to longer life expectancy gained the evolutionary advantage during this transition, and their representation in the population increased over time.[43] Despite the increase in extrinsic mortality risk that brought about a temporary decline in life expectancy, longevity eventually increased beyond the peak that existed in hunter-gatherer society, due to changes in the composition of the population in favor of individuals with genetic predispositions to higher life expectancy. Moreover, the biological upper bound of longevity (i.e., longevity in a risk-free environment) gradually increased, generating the traits that contributed significantly to the impact of recent improvements in medical technology on the dramatic prolongation of life expectancy.

The evolutionary process that was triggered by the transition to agriculture was reinforced by the gradual rise in extrinsic mortality risk since the Neolithic

---

[43] For the effect of somatic maintenance systems on longevity, see Kirkwood (1979).

Revolution, prior to improvements in health infrastructure. The gradual increase in population density in the Malthusian Epoch generated an additional increase in extrinsic mortality risk, further elevating the evolutionarily optimal level of resources that were devoted to somatic investment, repairs, and maintenance, which further contributed to the prolongation of life expectancy.[44]

The process of urbanization and the associated rise in population density further contributed to the increase in the extrinsic mortality risk.[45] During the initial process of European urbanization in which the percentage of urban population increased sixfold from about 3% in 1520 to nearly 18% in 1750 (De Vries, 1984; Bairoch, 1988), the rapid increase in population density generated a rise in mortality rates and a decline in life expectancy.[46] For instance, as depicted in Figure 2.6, in England life expectancy (at birth) fell from about 40 at the end of the sixteenth century to about 33 in the beginning of the seventeenth century, while mortality rates increased by nearly 50% (Wrigley and Schofield, 1981). This rise in extrinsic mortality risk further increased the representation of individuals who were genetically predisposed to higher life expectancy (Livi-Bacci, 2001), contributing to the observed rise in the eighteenth century and the first half of the nineteenth century, prior to significant advancements in medical technologies.

The theory predicts that the interaction between the rise in extrinsic mortality risk and the evolutionary process has manifested itself in the observed nonmonotonic time path of life expectancy in the process of development. In the short run—while the composition of the population was nearly stationary—the rise in mortality risk reduced life expectancy. However, socioeconomic changes and the associated increase in population density triggered an evolutionary process that increased the representation of individuals characterized by a higher life expectancy and a higher biological upper bound on longevity. In particular, as the composition of the population shifted sufficiently in favor of individuals with genetic predispositions to longer life expectancy, the population's life expectancy increased to a higher level than the one that existed prior

[44] The eventual trend of increasing life expectancy was accompanied by regional fluctuations, reflecting local environmental and climatic conditions. For instance, life expectancy fluctuated in the Malthusian Epoch, ranging from 24 in Egypt in 33–258 CE to 42 in England at the end sixteenth century.

[45] Major epidemics, such as the Black Death in Europe in the middle of the fourteenth century, further contributed to the increase in extrinsic mortality risk, bringing about an initial decline in life expectancy and potentially enhancing the evolutionary process associated with the trend of increased life expectancy.

[46] For instance, in the early nineteenth century the infant mortality rate in London was in excess of 400 per 1,000 (Laxton and Williams, 1989), whereas infant mortality in the population as a whole was 104 per 1,000 in the first half of the eighteenth century and 49 per 1,000 in 1825–1837 (Wrigley and Schofield, 1981).

to the increase in mortality risk. Moreover, the rise in extrinsic mortality risk increased the gap between the biological upper bound of longevity (i.e., life expectancy in a risk-free environment) and actual life expectancy, and it generated the necessary traits for the momentous effect of rapid improvements in health infrastructure and medical technology on the prolongation of life expectancy.

Galor and Moav (2005) explore the impact of economic development on the evolution of the distribution of somatic investment and maintenance over the life cycle (i.e., life-history profiles) in humans. The theory demonstrates that if the effect of a rise in extrinsic mortality risk on the survival probability can be mitigated by an increase in somatic investment, then it would necessarily generate an evolutionary advantage to individuals with higher genetic predisposition to somatic investment and may therefore increase life expectancy.

Evolutionary biologists have advanced two complementary theories for the evolution of senescence (i.e., the persistent decline in the somatic function of an organism with age) and thus of life expectancy, based on the premise that selection weakens with age. The mutation accumulation theory of aging (Medawar, 1952) suggests that late-acting deleterious mutations have a smaller negative effect on the survival of the genes, and therefore aging is an inevitable outcome of the declining force of natural selection in older age. The antagonistic pleiotropy theory (Williams, 2001) suggests that late-activating deleterious genes may be favored by natural selection and may actively accumulate in a population if they have beneficial reproductive effects in the early stages of life. In particular, the disposable soma theory (Kirkwood and Holliday, 1979) examines the optimal allocation of metabolic resources between reproduction and maintenance.[47]

Galor and Moav (2005) explore the evolution of the life cycle distribution of somatic investment and its effect on life expectancy in light of the fundamental trade-off between parental somatic investment in each offspring and the number of offspring that can be supported.[48] Resources that are channeled into higher somatic investment in each offspring generate higher life expectancy but limit

---

[47] Most of the literature on evolutionary biology has focused on the effect of a rise in extrinsic mortality rate that cannot be mitigated by an increase in somatic investment, arguing therefore that in this type of environment, an increase in extrinsic mortality rate generates a decline in somatic investment and thereby a decline in life expectancy. Recently, however, in light of a wide range of compelling evidence, it has been recognized that the adverse effect of a rise in extrinsic mortality risk can be counteracted by an increase in somatic investment (Kirkwood and Holliday, 1979). In particular, Reznick et al. (2004) demonstrate that guppies exposed to a higher extrinsic mortality risk had lower intrinsic mortality rates.

[48] The allocation of resources between offspring caring and bearing is subject to evolutionary changes (Lack, 1954).

the number of offspring that can be raised.[49] Thus, there is an evolutionary trade-off, regarding reproduction success, between the life expectancy of each offspring and the number of offspring that can be supported.

The probability that an individual will survive to reproductive age is affected positively by the genetically predetermined somatic investment and negatively by extrinsic mortality risk associated with socio-environmental characteristics, such as population density. The rise in mortality risk triggers a process of natural selection that alters the distribution of types in the population. Nature selects the life-history profile and thereby the life expectancy that maximizes reproductive success in any given environment, and the distribution of these hereditary life-history traits evolves over time due to changes in the environment. As long as the adverse effect of population density on survival probability is lower for individuals who are genetically predisposed for higher somatic investment, the evolutionarily optimal level of somatic investment is an increasing function of extrinsic mortality risk. Thus, the evolutionary process in the human population may lead to a reduction in mortality rates and an increase in life expectancy, despite the increase in extrinsic mortality risk.

The theory suggests that individuals who are characterized by low somatic investment and thus low life expectancy have an evolutionary advantage in an environment characterized by reduced population density and small extrinsic mortality risk. In contrast, those characterized by high somatic investment and thus high life expectancy have an evolutionary advantage in an environment characterized by greater population density and thus a larger extrinsic mortality risk.

Thus, as population density increased in the process of development, increasing the extrinsic mortality risk, the evolutionary advantage shifted from individuals with low somatic investment to those with high somatic investment. Furthermore, the increase in population density and its interaction with

---

[49] Evidence shows that the evolved capacity of somatic cells to carry out effective maintenance and repairs (e.g., DNA repairs, accurate gene regulation, tumor suppression, and antioxidants) governs the time taken for damage to accumulate, thus regulating longevity. Evidence at the molecular and cellular levels suggests that longevity is correlated with effort devoted to repair and cellular maintenance. A positive correlation is found among captive mammals between longevity and DNA repair capacity, genomic integrity, and mitochondrial reactive oxygen species production. Furthermore, cell resistance to external stress is greater among long-lived species. Moreover, long-run adaptations that reduce extrinsic mortality (e.g., larger brains) are generally linked to increased longevity. These long-run adaptations, however, are not the focus of Galor and Moav (2005). Experiments on and observation of nonhuman species indicate that this trade-off exists (Williams and Day, 2003). Furthermore, using a historical dataset from the British aristocracy, Westendorp and Kirkwood (1998) argue that human life histories involve a trade-off between longevity and reproduction.

the forces of natural selection induced a nonmonotonic time path of life expectancy. As population density increased and extrinsic mortality risk rose, life expectancy declined as long as the distribution of types in the population had not considerably evolved.[50] Ultimately, however, as individuals with a genetic predisposition toward a higher life expectancy have dominated the population, life expectancy has risen. Moreover, the biological upper bound of longevity has increased, generating the biological infrastructure for the recent prolongation of life expectancy that was brought about by the decline in extrinsic mortality risk due to improvements in health infrastructure and medical technology.[51]

As examined in Section 6.4.2, empirical findings indicate that, indeed, a significant portion of the variations in life expectancy across countries can be traced to the variation in the timing of the Neolithic Revolution. In particular, as depicted in Figure 6.14, every 1,000 years of earlier Neolithic transition of the current population's ancestors in each country is estimated to contribute about 2 years to contemporary life expectancy, accounting for geographical characteristics, income, education, and health expenditure per capita.

7.8 Concluding Remarks

Unified Growth Theory explores the dynamic interaction between human evolution and the process of economic development and advances the hypothesis that the forces of natural selection played a significant role in the evolution of the world economy from stagnation to growth. The Malthusian pressures have acted as the key determinant of population size, and conceivably, via natural selection, have shaped the composition of the population as well. Lineages of individuals whose traits were complementary to the economic environment generated higher levels of income and thus enjoyed a larger number of surviving offspring. This evolutionary process gradually increased the representation of favorable traits in the population, which contributed to furthering the process of development and the take-off from stagnation to growth.

---

[50] In the long run, the decline in extrinsic mortality risk due to improvements in medical technology and health infrastructure may reverse the outlined evolutionary process.

[51] Abstracting from the process of economic development, Robson and Kaplan (2003) examine the evolutionarily optimal human brain size and life expectancy in the context of hunter-gatherer societies that were prevalent during the 2 million years that preceded the Neolithic Revolution. They argue that a decrease in extrinsic mortality risk that was faced by the human population led to an increase in somatic investment, leading to larger brain size and higher life expectancy. In contrast to the basic premise of Robson and Kaplan (2003) that extrinsic mortality risk decreased in the course of human existence, evidence about the rise of population density and lack of significant improvements in technology prior to the Mesolithic period suggests in fact that extrinsic mortality risk increased in this era.

The Neolithic Revolution facilitated the division of labor and fostered trade relationships among individuals and communities, enhancing the complexity of human interaction and raising the return on human capital. Thus, individuals born to parents with traits that complemented the development of human capital were able to generate higher incomes and, in the Malthusian Epoch when child rearing was positively correlated with aggregate resources, a large number of offspring. Consequently, traits that contributed to higher child quality gained an evolutionary advantage, and their representation in the population increased over time. This selection process and its effect on investment in human capital stimulated growth in technology and initiated a reinforcing interaction between investment in human capital and technological progress that ultimately brought about the decline in population growth and the transition to an era of sustained economic growth.[52]

7.9 Appendix

7.9.1 Conditional Dynamics of Technology and Education

This section derives the properties of the phase diagrams of the conditional dynamical system (7.34) that describes the dynamics of technology and education, $\{g_t, e_t; q\}_{t=0}^{\infty}$, depicted in Figures 7.4(a), 7.5(a), and 7.6(a), for specific levels of q.

To allow for the existence of a long-run steady state with a positive growth rate, it is necessary to assume that

$$\exists g > 0 \quad \text{such that} \quad e(g; 0) > \psi^{-1}(g). \tag{7.A5}$$

That is, as depicted in Figure 7.4(a), for $q = 0$, there exists a positive rate of technological progress such that, in the plane (g_t, e_t), the curve $e(g, 0)$ lies above the curve $\psi(e_t)$.

Lemma 7.1 *Under Assumptions (7.A1), (7.A2), and (7.A5), as depicted in Figure 7.4(a), for $q = 0$, the conditional dynamical system (7.34) is characterized by two locally stable steady-state equilibria:*

$$(\bar{g}^L(q), \bar{e}^L(q)) = (0, 0);$$
$$(\bar{g}^H(q), \bar{e}^H(q)) > (\underline{g}^b, 0).$$

---

[52] Thus, in contrast to the nonevolutionary theory presented in Chapter 5, the gradual change in the composition (rather than the size) of the population is a sufficient trigger for the take-off from stagnation to growth, and a scale effect therefore is not essential for the take-off.

Proof. This lemma follows from the properties of $e_t = e(g_t; q)$ and $g_{t+1} = \psi(e_t)$, given by (7.15) and (7.18), Assumption (7.A5), (7.10), and (7.13).

Lemma 7.2 *Under Assumptions (7.A1), (7.A2), and (7.A5), there exists a critical level $\hat{q} \in (0, 1)$ such that*

$$e(\underline{g}^b, \hat{q}) = \psi^{-1}(\underline{g}^b).$$

Proof. It follows from the properties of $e_t = e(g_t; q)$ and Lemma 7.1 that $e(\underline{g}^b; 1) > \psi^{-1}(\underline{g}^b)$ and $e(\underline{g}^b; 0) < \psi^{-1}(\underline{g}^b)$. Therefore, the lemma follows from the continuity of $e(g_t; q)$ in q.

7.9.2 Conditional Dynamics of Technology and Effective Resources

This section derives the properties of the phase diagrams of the conditional dynamical system (7.36) that describes the dynamics of technology and effective resources, $\{g_t, x_t; q\}_{t=0}^{\infty}$, depicted in Figures 7.4(b), 7.5(b), and 7.6(b), for specific levels of q. It derives the properties of the CC locus, the GG locus, the XX locus, and the dynamics of (g_t, x_t) in relation to these loci.

The CC Locus
Let the CC locus be the set of all pairs (g_t, x_t) for which $z_t^b = \tilde{z}$: $CC \equiv \{(g_t, x_t) : z_t^b = \tilde{z}\}$, where $z_t^b = x_t^{\alpha} h^b(g_{t+1})$ and $\tilde{z} = \tilde{c}/(1 - \gamma)$.

Lemma 7.3 *Under Assumptions (7.A1) and (7.A3), there exists a single-valued, strictly increasing function*

$$x_t = (\tilde{c}/[(1 - \gamma)h^b(g_t)])^{1/\alpha} \equiv x^{CC}(g_t),$$

such that for all $g_t \geq 0$,

$$(g_t, x^{CC}(g_t)) \in CC,$$

where

$$x^{CC}(0) = (\tilde{c}/[1 - \gamma])^{1/\alpha};$$
$$\partial x^{CC}(g_t)/\partial g_t > 0.$$

Proof. This lemma follows from Assumptions (7.A1) and (7.A3), noting that $h(0, 0) = 1$ and $e^b(0) = 0$.

Hence, as depicted in Figures 7.4(b), 7.5(b), and 7.6(b), the CC locus is an upward sloping curve in the plane (g_t, x_t) with a positive vertical intercept.

The GG Locus

Let the GG locus be the set of all pairs (g_t, x_t) such that, for a given level of q, the rate of technological progress, g_t, is in a steady state: $GG \equiv \{(g_t, x_t; q) : g_{t+1} = g_t\}$.

As follows from (7.20), along the GG locus, $g_{t+1} = g(g_t; q) = g_t$. The GG locus is therefore not affected by the effective resources per efficiency unit of labor, x_t. Furthermore, as depicted in Figures 7.4(b), 7.5(b), and 7.6(b), the GG locus consists of vertical line(s) at the steady-state level(s) of g, derived in Lemma 7.1, stated in (7.35), and depicted in Figures 7.4(a), 7.5(a), and 7.6(a).

The dynamics of g_t in relation to the GG locus follow from the properties of (7.20):

$$g_{t+1} - g_t \begin{cases} > 0, & \text{if } g_t < \bar{g}^L(q) \quad \text{or} \quad g_t \in (\bar{g}^U(q), \bar{g}^H(q)); \\ = 0, & \text{if } g_t \in \{\bar{g}^L(q), \bar{g}^U(q), \bar{g}^H(q)\}; \qquad \text{for } q < \hat{q}, \\ < 0, & \text{if } g_t \in (\bar{g}^L(q), \bar{g}^U(q)) \quad \text{or} \quad g_t > \bar{g}^H(q), \end{cases}$$

(7.39)

$$g_{t+1} - g_t \begin{cases} > 0, & \text{if } g_t < \bar{g}^H(q); \\ = 0, & \text{if } g_t = \bar{g}^H(q); \qquad \text{for } q > \hat{q}. \\ < 0, & \text{if } g_t > \bar{g}^H(q), \end{cases}$$

(7.40)

The XX Locus

Let the XX locus be the set of all pairs (g_t, x_t) such that, for a given level of q, the level of effective resources per efficiency unit of labor, x_t, is in a steady state: $XX \equiv \{(g_t, x_t; q) : x_{t+1} = x_t\}$.

As follows from (7.32), along the XX locus, $x_{t+1} = [(1 + g_{t+1})/(1 + \mu_{t+1})]x_t \equiv x(g_t, x_t; q) = x_t$. Thus, as follows from (7.20) and (7.31), along the XX locus, $\mu(g_t, x_t; q) = g(g_t; q)$.

To simplify the exposition and ensure the existence of the XX locus, it is further assumed that[53]

$$\mu_g(g_t, x_t; q) \le 0;$$

$$\lim_{g_t \to \infty} \mu(g_t, x^{CC}(g_t); q) \le 0;$$

(7.A6)

$$\mu(0, x^{CC}(0); q) > g(0; q).$$

---

[53] A sufficient condition for the negativity of $\mu_g(g_t, x_t; q)$ is a sufficiently small value of $|\partial h^i(g_t)/\partial g_t|$, $i = a, b$. The second condition is consistent with $\mu_g(g_t, x_t; q) \le 0$, given the feasible range of μ (i.e., $\mu \ge -1$). The third condition is satisfied if $g(0, q)$ is sufficiently small, since for $g_t = g_{t+1} = 0$, $\mu > 0$ is weakly above the Malthusian Frontier.

The following lemma and corollary derive the properties of the XX locus.

Lemma 7.4 *Under Assumptions (7.A3)–(7.A6), given q, there exists a critical level of the rate of technological progress, $\hat{g}(q) > 0$, such that the XX locus in the plane (g_t, x_t) is:*

1. *vertical at $g_t = \hat{g}(q)$, where $\hat{g}'(q) < 0$ for all x_t above the CC locus, that is,*

$$(\hat{g}(q), x_t) \in XX \quad \forall x_t \geq x^{CC}(\hat{g}(q));$$

2. *represented by a strictly increasing single-valued function, $x_t = x^{XX}(g_t; q) > 0$, in the interval $[0, \hat{g}(q))$, that is,*

$$(g_t, x^{XX}(g_t; q)) \in XX \quad \forall g_t \in [0, \hat{g}(q));$$

3. *below the CC locus in the interval $[0, \hat{g}(q))$, that is,*

$$x^{XX}(g_t; q) < x^{CC}(g_t; q) \quad \forall g_t \in [0, \hat{g}(q));$$

4. *empty for $g_t > \hat{g}(q)$, that is,*

$$(g_t, x_t) \notin XX \quad \forall g_t > \hat{g}(q).$$

Proof.

1. If the XX locus is nonempty weakly above the CC frontier, it is necessarily vertical in this range, since, as follows from (7.31), $\mu_x(g_t, x_t, q) = 0$ above CC. Hence it is sufficient to establish that there exists a unique value $g_t = \hat{g}(q)$ such that $(\hat{g}(q), x^{CC}(\hat{g}(q))) \in XX$. As follows from Assumption (7.A6), $\mu(0, x^{CC}(0); q) > g(0; q)$ and $\lim_{g_t \to \infty} \mu(g_t, x^{CC}(0); q) < \lim_{g_t \to \infty} g(g_t; q)$. Hence, since $\mu(g_t, x_t; q)$ is monotonically decreasing in g_t and $g(g_t; q)$ is monotonically increasing in g_t, there exists a unique value $g_t = \hat{g}(q)$ such that $(\hat{g}(q), x^{CC}(\hat{g}(q))) \in XX$. Since along the XX locus, $\mu(g_t, x^{CC}(g_t); q) = g(g_t; q)$, it follows from the properties of these functions, as derived in (7.20) and (7.31), that $\hat{g}'(q) < 0$.

2. Given the existence of a unique value $g_t = \hat{g}(q)$ such that $(\hat{g}(q), x^{CC}(\hat{g}(q))) \in XX$, the existence of $x_t = x^{XX}(g_t; q)$ follows from continuity and the Implicit Function Theorem, noting that along the XX locus, $\mu(g_t, x_t; q) = g(g_t; q)$ and the positivity of $\mu_x(g_t, x_t; q)$ in the interval $[0, \hat{g}(q))$, as established in (7.31). In particular,

$$\frac{\partial x^{XX}(g_t; q)}{\partial g_t} = \frac{g_g(g_t; q) - \mu_g(g_t, x_t, q)}{\mu_x(g_t, x_t, q)} > 0 \quad \forall g_t \in [0, \hat{g}(q)). \quad (7.41)$$

(Note that, as established in (7.31), $\mu_x(g_t, x_t; q) = 0$ for $g_t = \hat{g}(q)$, and the verticality of the XX locus follows.) Furthermore, since $\mu(0, 0; q) =$

$-1 < g(0; q)$, it follows that the vertical intercept of the XX locus is strictly positive. In particular, $x^{XX}(0, 0) = (\tilde{c}/[1 - \tau])^{1/\alpha}$.

3. Given the uniqueness of the value $g_t = \hat{g}(q)$ such that $(\hat{g}(q), x^{CC}(\hat{g}(q))) \in XX$, it follows that the XX locus and the CC frontier do not intersect in the interval $[0, \hat{g}(q))$. In addition, the XX locus is vertical above the CC frontier. Hence, the XX locus is below the CC frontier in the range $[0, \hat{g}(q))$. In particular, $x^{XX}(0, 0) = (\tilde{c}/[1 - \tau])^{1/\alpha} < x^{CC}(0, 0) = (\tilde{c}/[1 - \gamma])^{1/\alpha}$, since $\gamma > \tau$.

4. Given the uniqueness of the value of $g_t = \hat{g}(q)$ such that $(\hat{g}(q), x^{CC}(\hat{g}(q))) \in XX$, it follows that if the XX locus exists in the interval $(\hat{g}(q), \infty)$, then it must lie below the CC frontier. However, since $\mu_x(g_t, x_t; q) > 0$ and since along the XX locus, $\mu(g_t, x_t; q) = g(g_t; q)$, it follows that along the CC frontier, in the interval $(\hat{g}(q), \infty)$, $\mu(g_t, x_t; q) > g(g_t; q)$, in contradiction to the fact that in the interval $(\hat{g}(q), \infty)$, $\mu(g_t, x_t; q) < g(g_t; q)$, as follows from Assumption (7.A6) and established in part 1 of this proof.

Hence, as depicted in Figures 7.4(b), 7.5(b), and 7.6(b), the XX locus has a positive vertical intercept at $g = 0$; it increases monotonically with g_t, as long as $g_t \in [0, \hat{g}(q))$; and it becomes vertical at $g_t = \hat{g}(q)$. Furthermore, as q increases, the value of $\hat{g}(q)$ declines.

Corollary 7.1 *Given* q, *there exists a unique pair* $g_t = \hat{g}(q)$ *and* $x_t = x^{XX}(\hat{g}(q), q)$ *such that* $\{g_t, x_t; q\} \in XX \cap CC$.

The dynamics of x_t with respect to the XX locus are

$$
x_{t+1} - x_t \begin{cases} > 0, & \text{if } x_t < x^{XX}(g_t) \quad \text{or} \quad g_t > \hat{g}(q); \\ = 0, & \text{if } x_t = x^{XX}(g_t); \\ < 0, & \text{if } x_t > x^{XX}(g_t) \quad \text{and} \quad g_t < \hat{g}(q). \end{cases} \tag{7.42}
$$

To ensure the existence of a long-run (unconditional) steady-state equilibrium with sustained economic growth, it is further assumed that[54]

$$
\hat{g}(0) < \bar{g}^H(0). \tag{7.A7}
$$

---

[54] As follows from the dynamics of x_t, Assumption (7.A7) holds if and only if for all x_t, $x_{t+1} - x_t = x(\bar{g}^H(0), x_t; 0) - x_t > 0$; that is, noting (7.32), if an only if for all x_t $\mu(\bar{g}^H(0), x_t; 0) \leq \bar{g}^H(0)$. As follows from (7.29), $\mu(\bar{g}^H(0), x_t; 0) = n_t^b - 1$. Hence, it follows from (7.12) that Assumption (7.A7) holds if and only if $\gamma \leq [\bar{g}^H(0) + 1][\tau + e^b(\bar{g}^H(0))]$. Assumption (7.A7) holds, therefore, for sufficiently (i) high preference for quality by individuals of type b, β^b (since e^b and hence $\bar{g}^H(0)$ increase with β^b); (ii) high cost of child raising, τ; and (iii) low weight, γ, for children relative to consumption in the utility function.

Hence, since $\bar{g}^H(q)$ increases with q (as follows from (7.35)) and $\hat{g}(q)$ decreases with q (as follows from Lemma 7.4), $\hat{g}(q) < \bar{g}^H(q) \, \forall q$.

Hence, as depicted in Figures 7.4(b), 7.5(b), and 7.6(b), and as established in the lemma below, Assumption (7.A7) ensures that if the economy crosses the CC locus and enters into the sustained-growth regime, it will not cross back into the Malthusian regions.

Furthermore, to ensure that the economy takes off from the Malthusian regime, as is apparent from Figures 7.4(a), 7.5(a), and 7.6(a), it is necessary that the value of q increases sufficiently so as to pass the critical level, $\hat{q}$. Hence, it is necessary to ensure that the fraction of individuals of type a in the population increases as long as $q \in [0, \hat{q}]$ and $g_t \in [0, \underline{g}^b]$. Since $n_t^a > n_t^b$ as long as $x_t < \check{x}_t$, it is therefore sufficient to assume that

$$x^{XX}(g_t; q) < \check{x}(g_t; q) \quad \text{for} \quad g_t \in [0, \underline{g}^b] \text{ and } q \in [0, \hat{q}]. \tag{7.A.8}$$

Lemma 7.5 *Under Assumptions (7.A2)–(7.A6) and (7.A8), $\forall q \in [0, \hat{q}]$, $\hat{g}(q) > \underline{g}^b$.*

Proof. As follows from the properties of (7.12), $n_t^b > n_t^a$ weakly above the CC locus, and therefore $\check{x}(g_t; q) < x^{CC}(g_t)$ for all g_t and q. Hence, it follows from Assumption (7.A8) that $x^{XX}(g_t; q) < x^{CC}(g_t; q)$ for $g_t \in [0, \underline{g}^b]$ and $q \in [0, \hat{q}]$. As established in Lemma 7.4, $x^{XX}(g_t; q) < x^{CC}(g_t; q) \, \forall g_t \in [0, \hat{g}(q))$. It follows therefore that $\hat{g}(q) > \underline{g}^b$.

Thus, as long as the economy is in the range of low rates of technological progress, (i.e., as long as $g_t < \underline{g}^b$), individuals of type b do not invest in the quality of their offspring, and the economy cannot take off from the Malthusian regime.

It should be noted that since the dynamical system is discrete, the trajectories implied by the phase diagrams do not necessarily approximate the actual dynamic path, unless the state variables evolve monotonically over time. The evolution of g_t is monotonic, whereas the evolution and convergence of x_t may be oscillatory. Nonmonotonicity may arise only if $g < \hat{g}$. Nonmonotonicity in the evolution of x_t does not affect the qualitative description of the system. Furthermore, if $\partial x(g_t, x_t; q)/\partial x_t > -1$ for $q \leq \hat{q}$, the conditional dynamical system is locally nonoscillatory. The local stability of the steady-state equilibrium $(0, \bar{x}(g_t))$ can be derived formally. The eigenvalues of the Jacobian matrix of the conditional dynamical system evaluated at the conditional steady-state equilibrium are both smaller than 1 (in absolute value) under Assumptions (7.A1)–(7.A3).

CHAPTER 8

Concluding Remarks

The transition from stagnation to growth and the associated divergence in income per capita across the globe have been the subject of intensive research in the growth literature in the past two decades. The inconsistency of the predominant theories of economic growth with some of the most fundamental characteristics of the growth process and their limited ability to shed light on the origins of the vast global disparity in living standards have led to the development of a unified theory of economic growth that captures the growth process in its entirety.

The advancement of Unified Growth Theory has been fueled by the conviction that the understanding of global variation in economic development would be fragile and incomplete unless the prevailing theory of economic growth would reflect the principal driving forces behind the entire process of development and would capture the central role that historical factors have played in bringing about the current disparities in living standards. Moreover, it has been fostered by the realization that a comprehensive understanding of the hurdles faced by less developed economies in reaching a state of sustained economic growth will remain obscure unless the factors that facilitated the transition of the currently developed economies can be identified and modified to account for the differences in the growth structure in an increasingly interdependent world.

The theory suggests that the transition from an epoch of stagnation to an era of sustained economic growth has been an inevitable by-product of the process of development. It argues that the stagnation in income per capita during the Malthusian Epoch masked a dynamism that may have ultimately brought about the transition from stagnation to growth. Although the growth of income per capita was miniscule during this era, technological progress intensified and world population significantly increased in size—a dynamism that was instrumental for the emergence of economies from the Malthusian trap. Nevertheless, the counterbalancing effect of population growth on the growth of income per capita and the diminishing effect of the scale of the population on knowledge accumulation prevented a sustained break from Malthusian forces prior to the emergence of human capital formation.

The acceleration in the pace of technological progress ultimately raised the importance of education in coping with the rapidly changing technological environment, increasing industrial demand for education. The rise in the profitability of investment in human capital, and the increasing resources that were channeled into investment in education, limited the ability of households to sustain their fertility rates. The onset of the demographic transition has liberated the growth process from the counterbalancing effect of rapid population growth. It enabled economies to divert a larger share of the fruits of factor accumulation and technological progress toward the enhancement of human capital formation and the growth of income per capita, paving the way for the emergence of sustained economic growth.

Unified Growth Theory sheds light on the remarkable divergence in income per capita across the globe during the past two centuries. It advances the understanding of three fundamental aspects of comparative economic development. First, it identifies the factors that have governed the pace of the transition from stagnation to growth and have thus contributed to the observed worldwide disparity in economic development. Second, it uncovers the forces that have sparked the emergence of convergence clubs and unveils the characteristics that determine the association of different economies with each club. Third, it highlights the persistent effects that variations in historical and prehistorical factors have had on the composition of human capital and economic development across countries.

Unified Growth Theory has planted the seeds for a renaissance in the fields of economic growth and economic history. It has generated novel testable predictions that will enable researchers to revisit their interpretations of existing evidence, while guiding them in their important mission of data collection. Recent research on the validity of the Malthusian hypothesis, the sources of the demographic transition, and the role of human capital in the advancement of industrialization is an early indication of the potential impact of Unified Growth Theory on the field of economic history.

Further, Unified Growth Theory suggests that the exploration of the role of cultural, institutional, and geographical factors in the differential pace of the transition from stagnation to growth and the emergence of a great disparity in economic development across the globe could generate significant insights about the growth process and comparative economic development. In particular, the hypothesis that the pace of the transition from stagnation to growth has been influenced by cultural and institutional factors—which may have evolved in response to the economic incentives that the process of development has generated—could benefit from further exploration. Have the institutional and cultural factors that have been associated empirically with the disparity in economic development been the oil that lubricated the wheels of development once economies emerged from the Malthusian trap, or were they the initial trigger that set those wheels in motion?

Finally, the most promising and challenging future research in the field of economic growth in the next decades will be: (i) the examination of the role of historical and prehistorical factors in the prevailing disparity across the globe, and (ii) the analysis of the interaction between human evolution and the process of economic development. The exploration of these vast and largely uncharted territories may revolutionize the understanding of the process of development and the persistent effect that deep-rooted factors have had on the composition of human capital and economic outcomes across the globe, fostering the design of policies that could promote economic growth and poverty alleviation.

References

Abramovitz, M., and David, P. A. (2000). American macroeconomic growth in the era of knowledge-based progress: The long-run perspective, *in* S. L. Engerman and R. E. Gallman (eds), *The Cambridge Economic History of the United States, Vol. 2*, Cambridge University Press, New York.

Abu-Lughod, J. L. (1989). *Before European Hegemony: The World System A.D. 1250–1350*, Oxford University Press, New York.

Acemoglu, D., and Robinson, J. A. (2000). Why Did the West Extend the Franchise? Democracy, Inequality, and Growth in Historical Perspective, *Quarterly Journal of Economics* **115**(4): 1167–1199.

Acemoglu, D., Johnson, S., and Robinson, J. A. (2001). The Colonial Origins of Comparative Development: An Empirical Investigation, *American Economic Review* **91**(5): 1369–1401.

————. (2002). Reversal of Fortune: Geography and Institutions in the Making of the Modern World Income Distribution, *Quarterly Journal of Economics* **117**(4): 1231–1294.

————. (2005a). Institutions as the fundamental cause of long-run growth, *in* P. Aghion and S. N. Durlauf (eds), *Handbook of Economic Growth*, Vol. IA, Elsevier North-Holland, Amsterdam.

————. (2005b). The Rise of Europe: Atlantic Trade, Institutional Change, and Economic Growth, *American Economic Review* **95**(3): 546–579.

Acemoglu, D., Aghion, P., and Zilibotti, F. (2006). Distance to Frontier, Selection, and Economic Growth, *Journal of the European Economic Association* **4**(1): 37–74.

Acemoglu, D., Johnson, S., Robinson, J. A., and Yared, P. (2008). Income and Democracy, *American Economic Review* **98**(3): 808–842.

Aghion, P., and Howitt, P. (1992). A Model of Growth through Creative Destruction, *Econometrica* **60**(2): 323–351.

Aghion, P., Bloom, N., Blundell, R., Griffith, R., and Howitt, P. (2005). Competition and Innovation: An Inverted-U Relationship, *Quarterly Journal of Economics* **120**(2): 701–728.

Aghion, P., Howitt, P., and Mayer-Foulkes, D. (2005). The Effect of Financial Development on Convergence: Theory and Evidence, *Quarterly Journal of Economics* **120**(1): 173–222.

Alesina, A., and Angeletos, G.-M. (2005). Fairness and Redistribution, *American Economic Review* **95**(4): 960–980.

Alesina, A., and La Ferrara, E. (2005). Ethnic Diversity and Economic Performance, *Journal of Economic Literature* **43**(3): 762–800.

Alesina, A., Devleeschauwer, A., Easterly, W., Kurlat, S., and Wacziarg, R. (2003). Fractionalization, *Journal of Economic Growth* **8**(2): 155–194.

Alger, I., and Weibull, J. W. (2010). Kinship, Incentives and Evolution, *American Economic Review* **100**(3): 1725–1758.

Allen, R. C. (2006). Economic Structure and Agricultural Productivity in Europe, 1300–1800, *European Review of Economic History* **4**(1): 1–25.

Andersen, T. B., Dalgaard, C.-J., and Selaya, P. (2010). Eye Disease and Development: The Impact of Cataract. Discussion paper, University of Copenhagen, Copenhagen.

Anderson, R. D. (1975). *Education in France 1848–1870*, Clarendon Press, Oxford.

Andorka, R. (1978). *Determinants of Fertility in Advanced Societies*, Taylor & Francis, Washington, DC.

Angrist, J. D., Lavy, V., and Schlosser, A. (2008). New Evidence on the Causal Link between the Quantity and Quality of Children. Working paper, Massachusetts Institute of Technology, Cambridge, MA.

Artzrouni, M., and Komlos, J. (1990). Mathematical Investigations of the Escape from the Malthusian Trap, *Mathematical Population Studies* **2**(4): 269–287.

Ashraf, Q., and Galor, O. (2007). Cultural Assimilation, Cultural Diffusion, and the Origin of the Wealth of Nations. Working paper, Brown University, Providence, RI.

———. (2009). The Out-of-Africa Hypothesis, Human Genetic Diversity, and Comparative Economic Development. Working paper, Brown University, Providence, RI.

———. (2011). Dynamics and Stagnation in the Malthusain Epoch, *American Economic Review* **101**. Forthcoming.

Ashton, T. S. (1948). *The Industrial Revolution: 1760–1830*, Oxford University Press, Oxford, UK.

Azariadis, C., and Drazen, A. (1990). Threshold Externalities in Economic Development, *Quarterly Journal of Economics* **105**(2): 501–526.

Bairoch, P. (1982). International Industrialization Levels from 1750 to 1980, *Journal of European Economic History* **11**(2): 269–333.

———. (1988). *Cities and Economic Development: From the Dawn of History to the Present*, University of Chicago Press, Chicago.

Baldwin, R. E., Martin, P., and Ottaviano, G.I.P. (2001). Global Income Divergence, Trade, and Industrialization: The Geography of Growth Take-Offs, *Journal of Economic Growth* **6**(1): 5–37.

Banerjee, A. V., and Duflo, E. (2005). Growth theory through the lens of development economics, *in* P. Aghion and S. N. Durlauf (eds), *Handbook of Economic Growth*, Vol. IA, Elsevier North-Holland, Amsterdam.

Banerjee, A. V., and Iyer, L. (2005). History, Institutions, and Economic Performance: The Legacy of Colonial Land Tenure Systems in India, *American Economic Review* **95**(4): 1190–1213.

Banerjee, A. V., and Newman, A. (1993). Occupational Choice and the Process of Development, *Journal of Political Economy* **101**(2): 274–298.

Bar, M., and Leukhina, O. (2010). Demographic Transition and Industrial Revolution: A Macroeconomic Investigation, *Review of Economic Dynamics* **13**(2): 424–451.

Barro, R. J., and Becker, G. S. (1989). Fertility Choice in a Model of Economic Growth, *Econometrica* **57**(2): 481–501.

Barro, R. J., and Lee, J.-W. (2001). International Data on Educational Attainment: Updates and Implications, *Oxford Economic Papers* **53**(3): 541–563.

Barro, R. J., and McCleary, R. M. (2003). Religion and Economic Growth across Countries, *American Sociological Review* **68**(5): 760–781.

Baten, J., and van Zanden, J. L. (2008). Book Production and the Onset of Modern Economic Growth, *Journal of Economic Growth* **13**(3): 217–235.

Baten, J., Foldvari, P., van Leeuwen, B., and van Zanden, J. L. (2010). World Income Inequality 1820–2000. Working paper, University of Tübingen, Germany.

Becker, G. S. (1960). An economic analysis of fertility, *in* G. S. Becker (ed.), *Demographic and Economic Change in Developed Countries*, Princeton University Press, Princeton, NJ.

———. (1981). *A Treatise on the Family*, Harvard University Press, Cambridge, MA.

Becker, G. S., and Lewis, H. G. (1973). On the Interaction between the Quantity and Quality of Children, *Journal of Political Economy* **81**(2, Part II): S279–S288.

Becker, G. S., Murphy, K. M., and Tamura, R. (1990). Human Capital, Fertility, and Economic Growth, *Journal of Political Economy* **98**(5): S12–S37.

Becker, S. O., and Woessmann, L. (2009). Was Weber Wrong? A Human Capital Theory of Protestant Economic History, *Quarterly Journal of Economics* **124**(2): 531–596.

Becker, S. O., Cinnirella, F., and Woessmann, L. (2010). The Trade-Off between Fertility and Education: Evidence from before the Demographic Transition, *Journal of Economic Growth* **15**(3): 177–204.

Benabou, R. (1996). Equity and Efficiency in Human Capital Investment: The Local Connection, *Review of Economic Studies* **63**(2): 237–264.

———. (2005). Inequality, Technology and the Social Contract, *in* P. Aghion and S. N. Durlauf (eds), *Handbook of Economic Growth*, Vol. IA, Elsevier North-Holland, Amsterdam.

Benabou, R., and Tirole, J. (2006). Belief in a Just World and Redistributive Politics, *Quarterly Journal of Economics* **121**(2): 699–746.

Benhabib, J., and Spiegel, M. M. (2005). Human Capital and Technology Diffusion, *in* P. Aghion and S. N. Durlauf (eds), *Handbook of Economic Growth*, Vol. IA, Elsevier North-Holland, Amsterdam.

Berdugo, B., Sadik, J., and Sussman, N. (2009). Delays in Technology Adoption, Appropriate Human Capital, Natural Resources and Growth. Working paper, Department of Economics, Hebrew University, Israel.

Bertocchi, G. (2006). The Law of Primogeniture and the Transition from Landed Aristocracy to Industrial Democracy, *Journal of Economic Growth* **11**(1): 43–70.

Bertocchi, G., and Canova, F. (2002). Did Colonization Matter for Growth? An Empirical Exploration into the Historical Causes of Africa's Underdevelopment, *European Economic Review* **46**(10): 1851–1871.

Bisin, A., and Verdier, T. (2000). Beyond the Melting Pot: Cultural Transmission, Marriage, and the Evolution of Ethnic and Religious Traits, *Quarterly Journal of Economics* **115**(3): 955–988.

Black, S. E., Devereux, P. J., and Salvanes, K. G. (2005). The More the Merrier? The Effect of Family Size and Birth Order on Children's Education, *Quarterly Journal of Economics* **120**(2): 669–700.

Bleakley, H., and Lange, F. (2009). Chronic Disease Burden and the Interaction of Education, Fertility, and Growth, *Review of Economics and Statistics* **91**(1): 52–65.

Bloom, D. E., Canning, D., and Sevilla, J. (2003). Geography and Poverty Traps, *Journal of Economic Growth* **8**(4): 355–378.

Boldrin, M., and Jones, L. E. (2002). Mortality, Fertility, and Saving in a Malthusian Economy, *Review of Economic Dynamics* **5**(4): 775–814.

Bonilla, F. (1965). Brazil, *in* J. S. Coleman (ed.), *Education and Political Development*, Princeton University Press, Princeton, NJ.

Boserup, E. (1965). *The Conditions of Agricultural Growth: The Economics of Agrarian Change under Population Pressure*, Aldine Publishing, Chicago.

Botticini, M., and Eckstein, Z. (2005). Jewish Occupational Selection: Education, Restrictions, or Minorities?, *Journal of Economic History* **65**(4): 922–948.

Boucekkine, R., de la Croix, D., and Licandro, O. (2003). Early Mortality Declines at the Dawn of Modern Growth, *Scandinavian Journal of Economics* **105**(3): 401–418.

Boucekkine, R., de la Croix, D., and Peeters, D. (2007). Early Literacy Achievements, Population Density, and the Transition to Modern Growth, *Journal of the European Economic Association* **5**(1): 183–226.

Bourguignon, F., and Morrisson, C. (2002). Inequality among World Citizens: 1820–1992, *American Economic Review* **92**(4): 727–744.

Bourguignon, F., and Verdier, T. (2000). Oligarchy, Democracy, Inequality and Growth, *Journal of Development Economics* **62**(2): 285–314.

Bowles, S. (1998). Endogenous Preferences: The Cultural Consequences of Markets and Other Economic Institutions, *Journal of Economic Literature* **36**(1): 75–111.

Bowles, S., and Gintis, H. (1975). Capitalism and Education in the United States, *Socialist Revolution* **5**(25): 101–138.

Boyd, R., and Richerson, P. J. (1985). *Culture and the Evolutionary Process*, University of Chicago Press, Chicago.

Boyer, G. R. (1989). Malthus Was Right After All: Poor Relief and Birth Rates in South-Eastern England, *Journal of Political Economy* **1**(97): 93–114.

Brezis, E. S., and Temin, P. (2008). Elites and Economic Outcomes, *in* S. N. Durlauf and L. E. Blume (eds), *New Palgrave Dictionary of Economics*, Macmillan, Basingstoke, UK.

Brezis, E. S., Krugman, P. R., and Tsiddon, D. (1993). Leapfrogging in International Competition: A Theory of Cycles in National Technological Leadership, *American Economic Review* **83**(5): 1211–1219.

Broadberry, S. (2007). Recent Developments in the Theory of Very Long Run Growth: A Historical Appraisal. Warwick Economics Research Paper 818, University of Warwick, UK.

Brown, J. C., and Guinnane, T. W. (2007). Regions and Time in the European Fertility Transition: Problems in the Princeton Project's Statistical Methodology, *Economic History Review* **60**(3): 574–595.

Caldwell, J. C. (1976). Toward a Restatement of Demographic Transition Theory, *Population and Development Review* **2**(3–4): 321–366.

Cameron, R. (1993). *A Concise Economic History of the World: From Paleolithic Times to the Present*, Oxford University Press, New York.

Cann, H. M., de Toma, C., Cazes, L., Legrand, M.-F., Morel, V., Piouffre, L., et al. (2002). A Human Genome Diversity Cell Line Panel, *Science* **296**(5566): 261–262.

Caselli, F. (2005). Accounting for Cross-Country Income Differences, *in* P. Aghion and S. N. Durlauf (eds), *Handbook of Economic Growth*, Vol. IA, Elsevier North-Holland, Amsterdam.

Caselli, F., and Coleman, W. J. (2001). The US Structural Transformation and Regional Convergence: A Reinterpretation, *Journal of Political Economy* **109**(3): 584–616.

———. (2006). The World Technology Frontier, *American Economic Review* **96**(3): 499–522.

Caselli, F., and Feyrer, J. (2007). The Marginal Product of Capital, *Quarterly Journal of Economics* **122**(2): 535–568.

Cavalli-Sforza, L. L. (2005). The Human Genome Diversity Project: Past, Present and Future, *Nature Reviews Genetics* **6**(4): 333–340.

Cavalli-Sforza, L. L., and Feldman, M. W. (1981). *Cultural Transmission and Evolution: A Quantitative Approach*, Princeton University Press, Princeton, NJ.

Cervellati, M., and Sunde, U. (2005). Human Capital Formation, Life Expectancy, and the Process of Development, *American Economic Review* **95**(5): 1653–1672.

———. (2008). The Economic and Demographic Transition, Mortality, and Comparative Development. Working paper, Institute for the Study of Labor.

Chakraborty, S., Papageorgiou, C., and Sebastián, F. P. (2008). Diseases and Development: A Theory of Infection Dynamics and Economic Behavior. Working paper, International Monetary Fund, Washington, DC.

Chandler, T. (1987). *Four Thousand Years of Urban Growth: An Historical Census*, Edwin Mellen Press, Lewiston, NY.

Chaudhuri, K. N. (1990). *Asia before Europe: Economy and Civilization of the Indian Ocean from the Rise of Islam to 1750*, Cambridge University Press, Cambridge, UK.

Chen, C. (1961). *Land Reform in Taiwan*, China Publishing Company, Taipei.

Chesnais, J. (1992). *The Demographic Transition: Stages, Patterns, and Economic Implications*, Clarendon Press, Oxford.

Cipolla, C. M. (1969). *Literacy and Development in the West*, Penguin Books, Harmondsworth, UK.

Clark, G. (2005). The Condition of the Working Class in England, 1209–2004, *Journal of Political Economy* **113**(6): 1307–1340.

Clark, G., and Hamilton, G. (2006). Survival of the Richest: The Malthusian Mechanism in Pre-Industrial England, *Journal of Economic History* **66**(3): 707–736.

Cloninger, R. C. (1987). A Systematic Method for Clinical Description and Classification of Personality Variants. A Proposal, *Archives of General Psychiatry* **44**(6): 573–588.

Coale, A. J., and Treadway, R. (1986). A summary of the changing distribution of overall fertility, marital fertility, and the proportion married in the provinces of Europe, *in* A. J. Coale and S. Watkins (eds), *The Decline of Fertility in Europe*, Princeton University Press, Princeton, NJ.

Coatsworth, J. H. (1993). Notes on the comparative economic history of Latin America and the United States, *in* W. Bernecker and H. W. Tobler (eds), *Development and Underdevelopment in America*, Walter de Gruyter, New York.

Cody, M. L. (1966). A General Theory of Clutch Size, *Evolution* **20**(2): 174–184.

Cohen, M. (1991). *Health and the Rise of Civilization*, Yale University Press, New Haven, CT.

Comin, D., Easterly, W., and Gong, E. (2010). Was the Wealth of Nations Determined in 1000 B.C.?, *American Economic Journal: Macroeconomics* **2**(3): 65–97.

Crafts, N. (1985). *British Economic Growth during the Industrial Revolution*, Oxford University Press, Oxford, UK.

Crafts, N., and Harley, K. C. (1992). Output Growth and the British Industrial Revolution: A Restatement of the Crafts-Harley View, *Economic History Review* **45**(4): 703–730.

Crafts, N., and Mills, T. C. (2009). From Malthus to Solow: How Did the Malthusian Economy Really Evolve?, *Journal of Macroeconomics* **31**(1): 68–93.

Crafts, N., and Thomas, M. (1986). Comparative Advantage in UK Manufacturing Trade, 1910–1935, *Economic Journal* **96**(383): 629–645.

Craig, F.W.S. (1989). *British Electoral Facts, 1832–1987*, Gower Press, Brookfield, VT.

Cressy, D. (1980). *Literacy and the Social Order: Reading and Writing in Tudor and Stuart England*, Cambridge University Press, Cambridge, UK.

Cubberley, E. P. (1920). *The History of Education*, Riverside Press, Cambridge, MA.

Dahan, M., and Tsiddon, D. (1998). Demographic Transition, Income Distribution, and Economic Growth, *Journal of Economic Growth* **3**(1): 29–52.

Dalgaard, C.-J., and Strulik, H. (2010). The Physiological Foundations of the Wealth of Nations. Discussion paper, Leibniz Universität, Hannover, Germany.

Darwin, C. (1859). *On the Origin of Species by Means of Natural Selection*, John Murray, London.

Dawkins, R. (1989). *The Selfish Gene*, Oxford University Press, Oxford, UK.

De Vries, J. (1984). *European Urbanization 1500–1800*, Taylor & Francis, Washington, DC.

Deininger, K., and Squire, L. (1998). New Ways of Looking at Old Issues: Inequality and Growth, *Journal of Development Economics* **57**(2): 259–288.

de la Croix, D., and Licandro, O. (2009). The Child Is Father of the Man: Implications for the Demographic Transition. Working paper, CORE, Louvain-la-Neuve, Belgium.

Dell, M. (2010). The Persistent Effects of Peru's Mining Mita, *Econometrica* **78**(6): 1863–1903.

Dennis, G. (1961). Education, *in* M. T. Florinsky (ed), *Encyclopedia of Russia and the Soviet Union*, McGraw-Hill, New York.

Desmet, K., and Parente, S. L. (2009). The Evolution of Markets and the Revolution of Industry: A Quantitative Model of England's Development, 1300–2000. CEPR Discussion Paper DP7290, Center for Economic Policy Research, London.

Diamond, J. (1997). *Guns, Germs and Steel: The Fates of Human Societies*, W. W. Norton & Co., New York.

———. (2002). Evolution, Consequences and Future of Plant and Animal Domestication, *Nature* **418**(6898): 700–707.

Ding, Y. C., Chi, H. C., Grady, D. L., Morishima, A., Kidd, J. R., Kidd, K. K., Flodman, P., Spence, M. A., Schuck, S., Swanson, J. M., Zhang, Y., and Moyzis, R. K. (2002). Evidence of Positive Selection Acting at the Human Dopamine Receptor D4 Gene Locus, *Proceedings of the National Academy of Sciences of the United States of America* **99**(1): 309–314.

Dinopoulos, E., and Thompson, P. (1998). Schumpeterian Growth without Scale Effects, *Journal of Economic Growth* **3**(4): 313–335.

Diwan, I., and Rodrik, D. (1991). Patents, Appropriate Technology, and North-South Trade, *Journal of International Economics* **30**(1–2): 27–47.

Doepke, M. (2004). Accounting for Fertility Decline during the Transition to Growth, *Journal of Economic Growth* **9**(3): 347–383.

———. (2005). Child Mortality and Fertility Decline: Does the Barro-Becker Model Fit the Facts?, *Journal of Population Economics* **18**(2): 337–366.

Doepke, M., and Tertilt, M. (2009). Women's Liberation: What's in It for Men?, *Quarterly Journal of Economics* **124**(4): 1541–1591.

Doepke, M., and Zilibotti, F. (2005). The Macroeconomics of Child Labor Regulation, *American Economic Review* **95**(5): 1492–1524.

———. (2008). Occupational Choice and the Spirit of Capitalism, *Quarterly Journal of Economics* **123**(2): 747–793.

Dohmen, T., Falk, A., Huffman, D., Schupp, J., Sunde, U., and Wagner, G. (2006). Individual Risk Attitudes: New Evidence from a Large, Representative, Experimentally-Validated Survey. CEPR Discussion Paper 5517, Center for Economic Policy Research, London.

Dowrick, S., and Nguyen, D.-T. (1989). OECD Comparative Economic Growth 1950–85: Catch-up and Convergence, *American Economic Review* **79**(5): 1010–1030.

Durante, R. (2009). Risk, Cooperation and the Economic Origins of Social Trust: An Empirical Investigation. Mimeo, Department of Economics, Brown University, Providence, RI.

Durham, W. H. (1982). Interactions of Genetic and Cultural Evolution: Models and Examples, *Human Ecology* **10**(3): 289–323.

Durlauf, S. N. (1996). A Theory of Persistent Income Inequality, *Journal of Economic Growth* **1**(1): 75–93.

Durlauf, S. N., and Johnson, P. A. (1995). Multiple Regimes and Cross-Country Growth Behaviour, *Journal of Applied Econometrics* **10**(4): 365–384.

Durlauf, S. N., and Quah, D. (1999). The new empirics of economic growth, *in* J. B. Taylor and M. Woodford (eds), *Handbook of Macroeconomics*, Elsevier North-Holland, Amsterdam.

Durlauf, S. N., Johnson, P. A., and Temple, J. R. (2005). Growth Econometrics, *in* P. Aghion and S. N. Durlauf (eds), *Handbook of Economic Growth*, Vol. IA, Elsevier North-Holland, Amsterdam.

Dyson, T., and Murphy, M. (1985). The Onset of Fertility Transition, *Population and Development Review* **11**(3): 399–440.

Easterlin, R. (1981). Why Isn't the Whole World Developed?, *Journal of Economic History* **41**(1): 1–19.

Easterly, W., and Levine, R. (1997). Africa's Growth Tragedy: Policies and Ethnic Divisions, *Quarterly Journal of Economics* **112**(4): 1203–1250.

———. (2003). Tropics, Germs and Crops: How Endowments Influence Economic Development, *Journal of Monetary Economics* **50**(1): 3–39.

Eckert, C. (1990). *Korea Old and New: A History*, Ilchokak, Seoul.

Eckstein, Z., and Zilcha, I. (1994). The Effects of Compulsory Schooling on Growth, Income Distribution and Welfare, *Journal of Public Economics* **54**(3): 339–359.

Eckstein, Z., Mira, P., and Wolpin, K. (1999). A Quantitative Analysis of Swedish Fertility Dynamics: 1751–1990, *Review of Economic Dynamics* **2**(1): 137–165.

Ehrlich, I., and Lui, F. T. (1991). Intergenerational Trade, Longevity, and Economic Growth, *Journal of Political Economy* **99**(5): 1029–1059.

Eicher, T. S., and García-Peñalosa, C. (2001). Inequality and Growth: The Dual Role of Human Capital in Development, *Journal of Development Economics* **66**(1): 173–197.

Endler, J. (1986). *Natural Selection in the Wild*, Princeton University Press, Princeton, NJ.

Engerman, S. L., and Sokoloff, K. L. (2000). History Lessons: Institutions, Factor Endowments, and Paths of Development in the New World, *Journal of Economic Perspectives* **14**(3): 217–232.

———. (2002). Factor Endowments, Inequality, and Paths of Development among New World Economies, *Economia* **3**(1): 41–109.

Estevadeordal, A., Frantz, B., and Taylor, A. (2003). The Rise and Fall of World Trade, 1870–1939, *Quarterly Journal of Economics* **118**(2): 359–407.

Feinerman, E., and Finkelshtain, I. (1996). Introducing Socioeconomic Characteristics into Production Analysis under Risk, *Agricultural Economics* **13**(3): 149–161.

Feinstein, C. (1972). *National Income, Expenditure and Output of the United Kingdom, 1855–1965*, Cambridge University Press, Cambridge, UK.

Fernández, R., and Fogli, A. (2009). Culture: An Empirical Investigation of Beliefs, Work, and Fertility, *American Economic Journal: Macroeconomics* **1**(1): 146–177.

Fernández, R., and Rogerson, R. (1996). Income Distribution, Communities, and the Quality of Public Education, *Quarterly Journal of Economics* **111**(1): 135–164.

Fernández, R., Fogli, A., and Olivetti, C. (2004). Mothers and Sons: Preference Formation and Female Labor Force Dynamics, *Quarterly Journal of Economics* **119**(4): 1249–1299.

Fernández-Villaverde, J. (2001). Was Malthus Right? Economic Growth and Population Dynamics. Working paper, Department of Economics, University of Pennsylvania, Philadelphia.

Feyrer, J. D. (2008). Convergence by Parts, *The B.E. Journal of Macroeconomics* **8**(19).

Fiaschi, D., and Lavezzi, A. M. (2003). Distribution Dynamics and Nonlinear Growth, *Journal of Economic Growth* **8**(4): 379–401.

Field, A. (1976). Educational Reform and Manufacturing Development in Mid-Nineteenth Century Massachusetts, *Journal of Economic History* **36**(1): 263–266.

Findlay, R., and Kierzkowski, H. (1983). International Trade and Human Capital: A Simple General Equilibrium Model, *Journal of Political Economy* **91**(6): 957–978.

Findlay, R., and O'Rourke, K. H. (2001). Commodity market integration, 1500–2000, *in* A.M.T.M.D. Bordo and J. G. Williamson (eds), *Globalization in Historical Perspective*, University of Chicago Press, Chicago.

Flora, P., Kraus, F., and Pfenning, W. (1983). State Economy and Society in Western Europe 1815–1975, Vol. 1, Palgrave Macmillan, London.

Fogel, R. W. (1994). Economic Growth, Population Theory, and Physiology: The Bearing of Long-Term Processes on the Making of Economic Policy, *American Economic Review* **84**(3): 369–395.

Foster, A. D., and Rosenzweig, M. R. (1996). Technical Change and Human-Capital Returns and Investments: Evidence from the Green Revolution, *American Economic Review* **86**(4): 931–953.

Frank, A. G. (1998). *Re-Orient: Global Economy in the Asian Age*, University of California Press, Berkeley.

Frankel, J. A., and Romer, D. (1999). Does Trade Cause Growth?, *American Economic Review* **89**(3): 379–399.

Friedman, B. M. (2005). *The Moral Consequences of Economic Growth*, Alfred A. Knopf, New York.

Galiani, S., Heymann, D., Dabús, C., and Tohmé, F. (2008). On the Emergence of Public Education in Land-Rich Economies, *Journal of Development Economics* **86**(2): 434–446.

Gallup, J. L., Sachs, J. D., and Mellinger, A. D. (1999). Geography and Economic Development, *International Regional Science Review* **22**(2): 179–232.

Galor, O. (1992). A Two-Sector Overlapping-Generations Model: A Global Characterization of the Dynamical System, *Econometrica* **60**(6): 1351–1386.

————. (1996). Convergence? Inferences from Theoretical Models, *Economic Journal* **106**(437): 1056–1069.

————. (2005). From Stagnation to Growth: Unified Growth Theory, *in* P. Aghion and S. N. Durlauf (eds), *Handbook of Economic Growth*, Vol. IA, Elsevier North-Holland, Amsterdam.

————. (2007). *Discrete Dynamical Systems*, Springer, Berlin.

————. (2010). The 2008 Lawrence R. Klein Lecture—Comparative Economic Development: Insights from Unified Growth Theory, *International Economic Review* **51**(1): 1–44.

Galor, O., and Michalopoulos, S. (2006). The Evolution of Entrepreneurial Spirit and the Process of Development. Working paper, Department of Economics, Brown University, Providence, RI.

Galor, O., and Moav, O. (2000). Ability-Biased Technological Transition, Wage Inequality, and Economic Growth, *Quarterly Journal of Economics* **115**(2): 469–497.

————. (2002). Natural Selection and the Origin of Economic Growth, *Quarterly Journal of Economics* **117**(4): 1133–1191.

————. (2004). From Physical to Human Capital Accumulation: Inequality and the Process of Development, *Review of Economic Studies* **71**(4): 1001–1026.

————. (2005). Natural Selection and the Evolution of Life Expectancy. Working paper, Department of Economics, Brown University, Providence, RI.

————. (2006). Das Human-Kapital: A Theory of the Demise of the Class Structure, *Review of Economic Studies* **73**(1): 85–117.

————. (2008). The Neolithic Origins of Contemporary Variations in Life Expectancy. Working paper, Department of Economics, Brown University, Providence, RI.

Galor, O., and Mountford, A. (2006). Trade and the Great Divergence: The Family Connection, *American Economic Review* **96**(2): 299–303.

————. (2008). Trading Population for Productivity: Theory and Evidence, *Review of Economic Studies* **75**(4): 1143–1179.

Galor, O., and Ryder, H. E. (1989). Existence, Uniqueness, and Stability of Equilibrium in an Overlapping-Generations Model with Productive Capital, *Journal of Economic Theory* **49**(2): 360–375.

Galor, O., and Tsiddon, D. (1997). Technological Progress, Mobility, and Economic Growth, *American Economic Review* **87**(3): 363–382.

Galor, O., and Weil, D. N. (1996). The Gender Gap, Fertility, and Growth, *American Economic Review* **86**(3): 374–387.

————. (1999). From Malthusian Stagnation to Modern Growth, *American Economic Review* **89**(2): 150–154.

————. (2000). Population, Technology, and Growth: From Malthusian Stagnation to the Demographic Transition and Beyond, *American Economic Review* **90**(4): 806–828.

Galor, O., and Zeira, J. (1993). Income Distribution and Macroeconomics, *Review of Economic Studies* **60**(1): 35–52.

Galor, O., Moav, O., and Vollrath, D. (2009). Inequality in Landownership, the Emergence of Human-Capital Promoting Institutions, and the Great Divergence, *Review of Economic Studies* **76**(1): 143–179.

Gerber, J. (1991). Public School Expenditures in the Plantation States, 1910, *Explorations in Economic History* **28**(3): 309–322.

Gershman, B. (2010). The Two Sides of Envy. Working paper, Department of Economics, Brown University, Providence, RI.

Glaeser, E. L., and Shleifer, A. (2002). Legal Origins, *Quarterly Journal of Economics* **117**(4): 1193–1229.

Glaeser, E. L., La Porta, R., Lopez-de-Silanes, F., and Shleifer, A. (2004). Do Institutions Cause Growth?, *Journal of Economic Growth* **9**(3): 271–303.

Goldin, C. (1990). *Understanding the Gender Gap: An Economic History of American Women*, Oxford University Press, New York.

———. (1998). America's Graduation from High School: The Evolution and Spread of Secondary Schooling in the Twentieth Century, *Journal of Economic History* **58**(2): 345–374.

Goldin, C., and Katz, L. F. (1998). The Origins of Technology-Skill Complementarity, *Quarterly Journal of Economics* **113**(3): 693–732.

———. (2001). The Legacy of US Educational Leadership: Notes on Distribution and Economic Growth in the 20th Century, *American Economic Review* **91**(2): 18–23.

———. (2002). The Power of the Pill: Oral Contraceptives and Women's Career and Marriage Decisions, *Journal of Political Economy* **110**(4): 730–770.

Gollin, D., Parente, S., and Rogerson, R. (2002). The Role of Agriculture in Development, *American Economic Review* **92**(2): 160–164.

Goodfriend, M., and McDermott, J. (1995). Early Development, *American Economic Review* **85**(1): 116–133.

Goody, J. (1996). *The East in the West*, Cambridge University Press, Cambridge, UK.

Gradstein, M. (2007). Inequality, Democracy and the Protection of Property Rights, *Economic Journal* **117**(516): 252–269.

Gradstein, M., and Justman, M. (2002). Education, Social Cohesion, and Economic Growth, *American Economic Review* **92**(4): 1192–1204.

Grant, B. R., and Grant, P. R. (1989). *Evolutionary Dynamics of a Natural Population: The Large Cactus Finch of the Galápagos*, University of Chicago Press, Chicago.

Green, A. (1990). *Education and State Formation*, Macmillan Palgrave, Hampshire, UK.

Greenwood, J., Hercowitz, Z., and Krusell, P. (1997). Long-Run Implications of Investment-Specific Technological Change, *American Economic Review* **87**(3): 342–362.

Greenwood, J., Seshadri, A., and Vandenbroucke, G. (2005a). The Baby Boom and Baby Bust, *American Economic Review* **95**(1): 183–207.

Greenwood, J., Seshadri, A., and Yorukoglu, M. (2005b). Engines of Liberation, *Review of Economic Studies* **72**(1): 109–133.

Greif, A. (1993). Contract Enforceability and Economic Institutions in Early Trade: The Maghribi Traders' Coalition, *American Economic Review* **83**(3): 525–548.

———. (2006). *Institutions and the Path to a Modern Economy: Lessons from Medieval Trade*, Cambridge University Press, Cambridge, UK.

Grossman, G. M., and Helpman, E. (1991). *Innovation and Growth in the Global Economy*, MIT Press, Cambridge, MA.

Gubbins, J. H. (1973). *The Making of Modern Japan*, Scholarly Resources, Wilmington, DE.

Guinnane, T. W., Okun, B. S., and Trussell, J. (1994). What Do We Know about the Timing of Fertility Transitions in Europe?, *Demography* **31**(1): 1–20.

Guiso, L., Sapienza, P., and Zingales, L. (2006). Does Culture Affect Economic Outcomes?, *Journal of Economic Perspectives* **20**(2): 23–48.

Guzman, M. (2010). Human Physiology and Comparative Development, Working paper, Brown University.

Gylfason, T. (2001). Natural Resources, Education, and Economic Development, *European Economic Review* **45**(4–6): 847–859.

Hall, R. E., and Jones, C. I. (1999). Why Do Some Countries Produce So Much More Output per Worker Than Others?, *Quarterly Journal of Economics* **114**(1): 83–116.

Hansen, G. D., and Prescott, E. C. (2002). Malthus to Solow, *American Economic Review* **92**(4): 1205–1217.

Hanushek, E. A. (1992). The Trade-Off between Child Quantity and Quality, *Journal of Political Economy* **100**(1): 84–117.

Hanushek, E. A., and Woessmann, L. (2008). The Role of Cognitive Skills in Economic Development, *Journal of Economic Literature* **46**(3): 607–668.

Hassler, J., and Mora, J.V.R. (2000). Intelligence, Social Mobility, and Growth, *American Economic Review* **90**(4): 888–908.

Hausmann, R., Hwang, J., and Rodrik, D. (2007). What You Export Matters, *Journal of Economic Growth* **12**(1): 1–25.

Hayami, Y. (1975). *A Century of Agricultural Growth in Japan*, University of Minnesota Press, Minneapolis.

Hazan, M. (2009). Longevity and Lifetime Labor Supply: Evidence and Implications, *Econometrica* **77**(6): 1829–1863.

Hazan, M., and Berdugo, B. (2002). Child Labour, Fertility, and Economic Growth, *Economic Journal* **112**(482): 810–828.

Hazan, M., and Zoabi, H. (2006). Does Longevity Cause Growth? A Theoretical Critique, *Journal of Economic Growth* **11**(4): 363–376.

Heckman, J. J., and Walker, J. R. (1990). The Relationship between Wages and Income and the Timing and Spacing of Births: Evidence from Swedish Longitudinal Data, *Econometrica* **58**(6): 1411–1441.

Helpman, E. (2004). *The Mystery of Economic Growth*, Belknap Press of Harvard University Press, Cambridge, MA.

Helpman, E., and Trajtenberg, M. (1998). Diffusion of general purpose technologies, *in* E. Helpman (ed.), *General Purpose Technologies and Economic Growth*, MIT Press, Cambridge, MA.

Hendricks, L. (2010). Cross-Country Variation in Educational Attainment: Structural Change or within Industry Skill Upgrading?, *Journal of Economic Growth* **15**(3): 205–233.

Hernandez, D. J. (2000). Trends in the Well Being of America's Children and Youth. U.S. Department of Health and Human Services, Washington, DC.

Herzer, D., Strulik, H., and Vollmer, S. (2010). The Long-Run Determinants of Fertility: One Century of Demographic Change 1900–1999. Working paper, University of Hannover, Hannover, Germany.

Hindle, S. (2004). *On the Parish: The Micro-Politics of Poor Relief in Rural England c. 1550–1750*, Clarendon Press, Oxford, UK.

Hobson, J. M. (2004). *The Eastern Origins of Western Civilization*, Cambridge University Press, Cambridge, UK.

Horrell, S., and Humphries, J. (1995). The Exploitation of Little Children: Child Labor and the Family Economy in the Industrial Revolution, *Explorations in Economic History* **32**(4): 485–516.

Howitt, P. (1999). Steady Endogenous Growth with Population and R. & D. Inputs Growing, *Journal of Political Economy* **107**(4): 715–730.

Hsieh, C.-T., and Klenow, P. J. (2009). Misallocation and Manufacturing TFP in China and India, *Quarterly Journal of Economics* **124**(4): 1403–1448.

Hurt, J. (1971). *Education in Evolution*, Paladin, London.

Iyigun, M. (2008). Luther and Suleyman, *Quarterly Journal of Economics* **123**(4): 1465–1494.

Johnson, W. (1969). *Russia's Educational Heritage*, Octagon Books, New York.

Jones, C. I. (1995). R&D-Based Models of Economic Growth, *Journal of Political Economy* **103**(4): 759–784.

———. (1997). Convergence Revisited, *Journal of Economic Growth* **2**(2): 131–153.

———. (2001). Was an Industrial Revolution Inevitable? Economic Growth Over the Very Long Run, *Advances in Macroeconomics* **1**(2): 1–43.

Jones, E. L. (1981). *The European Miracle: Environments, Economies and Geopolitics in the History of Europe and Asia*, Cambridge University Press, Cambridge, UK.

Jones, L. E., and Tertilt, M. (2006). An Economic History of Fertility in the US: 1826–1960. NBER Working Paper 12796, National Bureau of Economic Research, Cambridge, MA.

Kalaitzidakis, P., Mamuneas, T. P., Savvides, A., and Stengos, T. (2001). Measures of Human Capital and Nonlinearities in Economic Growth, *Journal of Economic Growth* **6**(3): 229–254.

Kalemli-Ozcan, S. (2002). Does the Mortality Decline Promote Economic Growth?, *Journal of Economic Growth* **7**(4): 411–439.

Keller, W. (2004). International Technology Diffusion, *Journal of Economic Literature* **42**(3): 752–782.

Kelly, M., and O'Grada, C. (2010). Living Standards and Mortality in England since the Middle Ages: The Poor Law versus the Positive Check. Discussion paper, University College, Dublin.

Kettlewell, B. (1973). *The Evolution of Melanism*, Clarendon Press, Oxford, UK.

Kirkwood, T. (1979). Evolution of Aging, *Nature* **270**: 301–304.

Kirkwood, T., and Holliday, R. (1979). The Evolution of Ageing and Longevity, *Proceedings of the Royal Society of London, Series B, Biological Sciences* **205**(1161): 531–546.

Klemp, M.P.B., and Weisdorf, J. L. (2010). The Child Quantity-Quality Trade-off: Evidence from the Population History of England. Mimeo, Department of Economics, University of Copenhagen, Copenhagen.

Klenow, P. J., and Rodriguez-Clare, A. (1997). The Neoclassical Revival in Growth Economics: Has It Gone Too Far?, *NBER Macroeconomics Annual* **12**: 73–103.

Knack, S., and Keefer, P. (1995). Institutions and Economic Performance: Cross-Country Tests Using Alternative Institutional Measures, *Economics & Politics* **7**(3): 207–227.

———. (1997). Does Social Capital Have an Economic Payoff? A Cross-Country Investigation, *Quarterly Journal of Economics* **112**(4): 1251–1288.

Kohler, H.-P., Rodgers, J. L., and Christensen, K. (1999). Is Fertility Behavior in Our Genes? Findings from a Danish Twin Study, *Population and Development Review* **25**(2): 253–288.

Köse, S. (2003). A Psychobiological Model of Temperament and Character: TCI, *Yeni Symposium*, **41**(2): 86–97.

Kremer, M. (1993). Population Growth and Technological Change: One Million B.C. to 1990, *Quarterly Journal of Economics* **108**(3): 681–716.

Kremer, M., and Chen, D. (2002). Income Distribution Dynamics with Endogenous Fertility, *Journal of Economic Growth* **7**(3): 227–258.

Krugman, P., and Venables, A. J. (1995). Globalization and the Inequality of Nations, *Quarterly Journal of Economics* **110**(4): 857–880.

Krusell, P., and Rios-Rull, J.-V. (1996). Vested Interests in a Positive Theory of Stagnation and Growth, *Review of Economic Studies* **63**(2): 301–329.

Kuhn, T. S. (1957). *The Copernican Revolution*, Harvard University Press, Cambridge, MA.

Kurian, G. (1994). *Datapedia of the United States, 1790–2000: America Year by Year*, Bernan Press, Lanham, MD.

Kuznets, S. (1967). Quantitative Aspects of the Economic Growth of Nations: X. Level and Structure of Foreign Trade: Long-Term Trends, *Economic Development and Cultural Change* **15**(2): 1–140.

Lack, D. (1954). *The Natural Regulation of Animal Numbers*, Clarendon Press, Oxford, UK.

Lagerlöf, N.-P. (2003a). From Malthus to Modern Growth: Can Epidemics Explain the Three Regimes?, *International Economic Review* **44**(2): 755–777.

———. (2003b). Gender Equality and Long-Run Growth, *Journal of Economic Growth* **8**(4): 403–426.

———. (2006). The Galor-Weil Model Revisited: A Quantitative Exercise, *Review of Economic Dynamics* **9**(1): 116–142.

———. (2009). Malthus in Sweden. Working paper, York University, York, Canada.

Landes, D. S. (1969). *The Unbound Prometheus: Technical Change and Industrial Development in Western Europe from 1750 to the Present*, Cambridge University Press, Cambridge, UK.

———. (1998). *The Wealth and Poverty of Nations: Why Some Are So Rich and Some So Poor*, W. W. Norton & Co., New York.

Laxton, P., and Williams, N. (1989). Urbanization and infant mortality in England: A long term perspective and review, *in* M. Nelson and J. Rogers (eds), *Urbanization and the Epidemiological Transition*, Uppsala University, Uppsala, Sweden.

Lee, R. D. (1987). Population Dynamics of Humans and Other Animals, *Demography* **24**(4): 443–465.

———. (1997). Population dynamics: Equilibrium, disequilibrium, and consequences of fluctuations, *in* O. Stark and M. Rosenzweig (eds), *The Handbook of Population and Family Economics*, Elsevier, Amsterdam.

Lehr, C. S. (2009). Evidence on the Demographic Transition, *Review of Economics and Statistics* **91**(4): 871–887.

Levine, R. (2005). Finance and Growth: Theory and Evidence, *in* P. Aghion and S. N. Durlauf (eds), *Handbook of Economic Growth*, Vol. IA, Elsevier North-Holland, Amsterdam.

Li, H., Zhang, J., and Zhu, Y. (2008). The Quantity-Quality Trade-off of Children in a Developing Country: Identification Using Chinese Twins, *Demography* **45**(1): 223–243.

Lin, C. J. (1983). The Republic of China (Taiwan), *in* R. M. Thomas and T. N. Postlethwaite (eds), *Schooling in East Asia*, Pergamon Press, Oxford, UK.

Livi-Bacci, M. (2001). *A Concise History of World Population*, 3rd edition, Blackwell Publishers, Oxford, UK.

Livingstone, F. B. (1958). Anthropological Implications of Sickle Cell Gene Distribution in West Africa, *American Anthropologist* **60**: 533–562.

Lloyd-Ellis, H., and Bernhardt, D. (2000). Enterprise, Inequality and Economic Development, *Review of Economic Studies* **67**(1): 147–168.

Lorentzen, P., McMillan, J., and Wacziarg, R. (2008). Death and Development, *Journal of Economic Growth* **13**(2): 81–124.

Lucas, R. E., Jr. (1988). On the Mechanics of Economic Development, *Journal of Monetary Economics* **22**(1): 3–42.

———. (2002). The Industrial Revolution: Past and Future, *in* R. E. Lucas, Jr. (ed.), *Lectures on Economic Growth*, Harvard University Press, Cambridge, MA.

———. (2009). Ideas and Growth, *Economica* **76**(301): 1–19.

MacArthur, R. H., and Wilson, E. O. (2001). *The Theory of Island Biogeography*, Princeton University Press, Princeton, NJ.

Macaulay, V., Hill, C., Achilli, A., Rengo, C., Clarke, D., Meehan, W., et al. (2005). Single, Rapid Coastal Settlement of Asia Revealed by Analysis of Complete Mitochondrial Genomes, *Science* **308**(5724): 1034–1036.

Maddison, A. (2001). *The World Economy: A Millennial Perspective*, Organisation for Economic Co-operation and Development, Paris.

———. (2003). *The World Economy: Historical Statistics*, Organisation for Economic Co-operation and Development, Paris.

———. (2008). The West and the Rest in the World Economy: 1000–2030, *World Economics* **9**(4): 75–99.

Malthus, T. R. (1798). *An Essay on the Principle of Population*, J. Johnson, in St. Paul's Church-Yard, London, UK.

Mankiw, N. G., Romer, D., and Weil, D. N. (1992). A Contribution to the Empirics of Economic Growth, *Quarterly Journal of Economics* **107**(2): 407–437.

Manuelli, R. E., and Seshadri, A. (2009). Explaining International Fertility Differences, *Quarterly Journal of Economics* **124**(2): 771–807.

Matsuyama, K. (1992). Agricultural Productivity, Comparative Advantage, and Economic Growth, *Journal of Economic Theory* **58**(2): 317–334.

Matthews, R., Feinstein, C., and Odling-Smee, J. (1982). *British Economic Growth, 1856–1973*, Stanford University Press, Stanford, CA.

McClelland, C. (1980). *State, Society, and University in Germany, 1700–1914*, Cambridge University Press, Cambridge, UK.

McDermott, J. (2002). Development Dynamics: Economic Integration and the Demographic Transition, *Journal of Economic Growth* **7**(4): 371–409.

McEvedy, C., and Jones, R. (1978). *Atlas of World Population History*, Penguin Books, New York.

Medawar, P. B. (1952). *An Unsolved Problem of Biology*, HK Lewis & Co., London.

Mekel-Bobrov, N., Gilbert, L., Evans, P., Vallender, E., Anderson, J., Hudson, R., Tishkoff, S., and Lahn, B. (2005). Ongoing Adaptive Evolution of ASPM, a Brain Size Determinant in *Homo sapiens*, *Science* **309**(5741): 1720–1722.

Michalopoulos, S. (2008). The Origins of Ethnolinguistic Diversity: Theory and Evidence. Working paper, Tufts University, Medford, MA.

Michalopoulos, S., and Papaioannou, E. (2010). Divide and Rule or the Rule of the Divided? Evidence from Africa. Working paper, Tufts University, Medford, MA.

Milanovic, B. (2009). Global Inequality and the Global Inequality Extraction Ratio: The Story of the Past Two Centuries. World Bank Policy Research Working Paper 5044, World Bank, Washington, DC.

Milionis, P., and Klasing, M. (2010). Innovation-Based Growth and Long-Run Economic Development. Working paper, University of Gröningen, Gröningen, The Netherlands.

Mitch, D. F. (1992). *The Rise of Popular Literacy in Victorian England: The Influence of Private Choice and Public Policy*, University of Pennsylvania Press, Philadelphia.

————. (1993). The role of human capital in the first Industrial Revolution, *in* J. Mokyr (ed.), *The British Industrial Revolution: An Economic Perspective*, Westview Press, Boulder, CO.

Mitchell, B. R. (1975). *European Historical Statistics, 1750–1970*, Columbia University Press, New York.

Miyata, S. (2003). Household's Risk Attitudes in Indonesian Villages, *Applied Economics* **35**(5): 573–583.

Moav, O. (2005). Cheap Children and the Persistence of Poverty, *Economic Journal* **115**(500): 88–110.

Modelski, G. (2003). *World Cities: –3000 to 2000*, FAROS 2000, Washington, DC.

Mokyr, J. (1985). *The Economics of the Industrial Revolution*, Rowman and Littlefield, New Jersey.

————. (1990). *The Lever of Riches: Technological Creativity and Economic Progress*, Oxford University Press, New York.

————. (2001). The Rise and Fall of the Factory System: Technology, Firms, and Households since the Industrial Revolution, *Carnegie-Rochester Conference Series on Public Policy* **55**(1): 1–45.

————. (2002). *The Gifts of Athena: Historical Origins of the Knowledge Economy*, Princeton University Press, Princeton, NJ.

Mookherjee, D., and Ray, D. (2003). Persistent Inequality, *Review of Economic Studies* **70**(2): 369–393.

Moscardi, E., and de Janvry, A. (1977). Attitudes toward Risk among Peasants: An Econometric Approach, *American Journal of Agricultural Economics* **59**(4): 710–716.

Mourmouras, A., and Rangazas, P. (2009). Reconciling Kuznets and Habbakuk in a Unified Growth Theory, *Journal of Economic Growth* **14**(2): 149–181.

Murphy, T. E. (2009). Old Habits Die Hard (Sometimes): What Can Département Heterogeneity Tell Us About the French Fertility Decline?. Working paper, Bocconi University, Italy.

Murtin, F. (2009). *On the Demographic Transition*. Organisation for Economic Co-operation and Development, Paris.

Neher, P. A. (1971). Peasants, Procreation, and Pensions, *American Economic Review* **61**(3): 380–389.

Nelson, R. R., and Phelps, E. S. (1966). Investment in Humans, Technological Diffusion, and Economic Growth, *American Economic Review* **51**(2): 69–75.

Ngai, R. L. (2004). Barriers and the Transition to Modern Growth, *Journal of Monetary Economics* **51**(7): 1353–1383.

North, D. C. (1981). *Structure and Change in Economic History*, W. W. Norton & Co., New York.

Nugent, J., and Robinson, J. (2002). Are Endowments Fate?. CEPR Discussion Paper 3206, Center for Economic Policy Research, London.

Nunn, N. (2008). The Long-Term Effects of Africa's Slave Trades, *Quarterly Journal of Economics* **123**(1): 139–176.

Nunn, N., and Qian, N. (2011). The Potato's Contribution to Population and Urbanization: Evidence from an Historical Experiment, *Quarterly Journal of Economics*, forthcoming.

Ofek, H. (2001). *Second Nature: Economic Origins of Human Evolution*, Cambridge University Press, Cambridge, UK.

Olson, M. (1982). *The Rise and Decline of Nations: Economic Growth, Stagflation, and Social Rigidities*, Yale University Press, New Haven, CT.

Olsson, O., and Hibbs, Jr., D. A. (2005). Biogeography and Long-Run Economic Development, *European Economic Review* **49**(4): 909–938.

Oppenheimer, S. (2003). *The Real Eve: Modern Man's Journey out of Africa*, Carroll & Graf, New York.

O'Rourke, K. H., and Williamson, J. G. (1999). *Globalization and History*, MIT Press, Cambridge, MA.

———. (2005). From Malthus to Ohlin: Trade, Industrialisation and Distribution since 1500, *Journal of Economic Growth* **10**(1): 5–34.

O'Rourke, K. H., Rahman, A. S., and Taylor, A. M. (2008). Luddites and the Demographic Transition. NBER Working Paper 14484, National Bureau of Economic Research, Cambridge, MA.

Owen, A. L., Videras, J., and Davis, L. (2009). Do All Countries Follow the Same Growth Process?, *Journal of Economic Growth* **14**(4): 265–286.

Parente, S. L., and Prescott, E. C. (2000). *Barriers to Riches*, MIT Press, Cambridge, MA.

Passin, H. (1965). Japan, *in* J. S. Coleman (ed.), *Education and Political Development*, Princeton University Press, Princeton, NJ.

Pelling, M., and Smith, R. M. (1991). *Life, Death and the Elderly: Historical Perspectives*, Routledge, London.

Peregrine, P. N. (2003). Atlas of Cultural Evolution, *World Cultures: Journal of Comparative and Cross-Cultural Research* **14**(1): 1–75.

Peretto, P. F. (1998). Technological Change and Population Growth, *Journal of Economic Growth* **3**(4): 283–311.

Persson, T., and Tabellini, G. (2002). *Political Economics: Explaining Economic Policy*, MIT Press, Cambridge, MA.

———. (2006). Democracy and Development: The Devil in the Details, *American Economic Review* **96**(2): 319–324.

Piketty, T., and Saez, E. (2006). The Evolution of Top Incomes: A Historical and International Perspective, *American Economic Review* **96**(2): 200–205.

Pomeranz, K. (2000). *The Great Divergence: Europe, China and the Making of the Modern World Economy*, Princeton University Press, Princeton, NJ.

Pritchett, L. (1997). Divergence, Big Time, *Journal of Economic Perspectives* **11**(3): 3–17.

Prugnolle, F., Manica, A., and Balloux, F. (2005). Geography Predicts Neutral Genetic Diversity of Human Populations, *Current Biology* **15**(5): R159–R160.

Putterman, L. (2008). Agriculture, Diffusion, and Development: Ripple Effects of the Neolithic Revolution, *Economica* **75**(300): 729–748.

Quah, D. T. (1997). Empirics for Growth and Distribution: Stratification, Polarization, and Convergence Clubs, *Journal of Economic Growth* **2**(1): 27–59.

Ramachandran, S., Deshpande, O., Roseman, C. C., Rosenberg, N. A., Feldman, M. W., and Cavalli-Sforza, L. L. (2005). Support from the Relationship of Genetic and Geographic Distance in Human Populations for a Serial Founder Effect Originating in Africa, *Proceedings of the National Academy of Sciences of the United States of America* **102**(44): 15942–15947.

Ramankutty, N., Foley, J. A., Norman, J., and McSweeney, K. (2002). The Global Distribution of Cultivable Lands: Current Patterns and Sensitivity to Possible Climate Change, *Global Ecology and Biogeography* **11**(5): 377–392.

Razin, A., and Ben-Zion, U. (1975). An Intergenerational Model of Population Growth, *American Economic Review* **65**(5): 923–933.

Reher, D. S. (2004). The Demographic Transition Revisited as a Global Process, *Population Space and Place* **10**(1): 19–42.

Reznick, D. N., Bryant, M. J., Roff, D., Ghalambor, C. K., and Ghalambor, D. E. (2004). Effect of Extrinsic Mortality on the Evolution of Senescence in Guppies, *Nature* **431**(7012): 1095–1099.

Ringer, F. (1979). *Education and Society in Modern Europe*, Indiana University Press, Bloomington.

Robson, A. J. (2001). The Biological Basis of Economic Behavior, *Journal of Economic Literature* **39**(1): 11–33.

Robson, A. J., and Kaplan, H. S. (2003). The Evolution of Human Life Expectancy and Intelligence in Hunter-Gatherer Economies, *American Economic Review* **93**(1): 150–169.

Rodgers, J. L., Hughes, K., Kohler, H.-P., Christensen, K., Doughty, D., Rowe, D. C., and Miller, W. B. (2001a). Genetic Influence Helps Explain Variation in Human Fertility: Evidence from Recent Behavioral and Molecular Genetic Studies, *Current Directions in Psychological Science* **10**(5): 184–188.

Rodgers, J. L., Kohler, H.-P., Kyvik, K. O., and Christensen, K. (2001b). Behavior Genetic Modeling of Human Fertility: Findings from a Contemporary Danish Twin Study, *Demography* **38**(1): 29–42.

Rodrik, D., Subramanian, A., and Trebbi, F. (2004). Institutions Rule: The Primacy of Institutions over Geography and Integration in Economic Development, *Journal of Economic Growth* **9**(2): 131–165.

Romer, P. (1990). Endogenous Technological Change, *Journal of Political Economy* **98**(5): S71–S102.

Rosenzweig, M. R., and Wolpin, K. I. (1980). Testing the Quantity-Quality Fertility Model: The Use of Twins as a Natural Experiment, *Econometrica* **48**(1): 227–240.

Rosenzweig, M. R., and Zhang, J. (2009). Do Population Control Policies Induce More Human Capital Investment? Twins, Birth Weight and China's "One-Child" Policy, *Review of Economic Studies* **76**(3): 1149–1174.

Sah-Myung, H. (1983). The Republic of Korea (South Korea), *in* R. M. Thomas and T. N. Postlethwaite (eds), *Schooling in East Asia*, Pergamon Press, Oxford, UK.

Saint-Paul, G. (2007). On Market Forces and Human Evolution, *Journal of Theoretical Biology* **247**(3): 397–412.

Sala-i-Martin, X. (2006). The World Distribution of Income: Falling Poverty and . . . Convergence, Period, *Quarterly Journal of Economics* **121**(2): 351–397.

Sanderson, M. (1995). *Education, Economic Change, and Society in England, 1780–1870*, Cambridge University Press, Cambridge, UK.

Schofield, R. (1973). Dimensions of Illiteracy, 1750–1850, *Explorations in Economic History* **10**(4): 437–454.

Schultz, T. P. (1985). Changing World Prices, Women's Wages, and the Fertility Transition: Sweden, 1860–1910, *Journal of Political Economy* **93**(6): 1126–1154.

———. (1997). Demand for Children in Low Income Countries, *in* M. R. Rosenzweig and O. Stark (eds), *Handbook of Population and Family Economics*, Elsevier Science, Amsterdam.

Schultz, T. W. (1975). The Value of the Ability to Deal with Disequilibria, *Journal of Economic Literature* **13**(3): 827–846.

Schumpeter, J. A. (1934). *The Theory of Economic Development: An Inquiry into Profits, Capital, Credit, Interest, and the Business Cycle*, Harvard University Press, Cambridge, MA.

Segerstrom, P. S. (1998). Endogenous Growth without Scale Effects, *American Economic Review* **88**(5): 1290–1310.

Sheshinski, E. (2009). Uncertain Longevity and Investment in Education. Working paper, Hebrew University, Israel.

Shiue, C. H., and Keller, W. W. (2007). Markets in China and Europe on the Eve of the Industrial Revolution, *American Economic Review* **97**(4): 1189–1216.

Simon, B. (1987). Systematization and segmentation in education: The case of England, *in* D. Muller, F. Ringer, and B. Simon (eds), *The Rise of the Modern Educational System*, Cambridge University Press, Cambridge, UK.

Smith, A. (1776). *An Inquiry into the Nature and Causes of the Wealth of Nations*, E. Cannan (ed), 1904, Methuen & Co., London.

Snowdon, B. (2008). Towards a Unified Theory of Economic Growth: Oded Galor on the Transition from Malthusian Stagnation to Modern Economic Growth, *World Economics* **9**(2): 97–151.

Soares, R. R. (2005). Mortality Reductions, Educational Attainment, and Fertility Choice, *American Economic Review* **95**(3): 580–601.

Solow, R. (1956). A Contribution to the Theory of Economic Growth, *Quarterly Journal of Economics* **70**(1): 65–94.

Spolaore, E., and Wacziarg, R. (2009). The Diffusion of Development, *Quarterly Journal of Economics* **124**(2): 469–529.

Steckel, R. H. (2004). The Best of Times, the Worst of Times: Health and Nutrition in Pre-Columbian America. NBER Working Paper 10299, National Bureau of Economic Research, Cambridge, MA.

Stokey, N. L. (1991). The Volume and Composition of Trade between Rich and Poor Countries, *Review of Economic Studies* **58**(1): 63–80.

———. (2001). A Quantitative Model of the British Industrial Revolution, 1780–1850, *Carnegie-Rochester Conference Series on Public Policy* **55**(1): 55–109.

Stone, L. (1969). Literacy and Education in England 1640–1900, *Past & Present* **42**(1): 69–139.

Strulik, H., and Weisdorf, J. L. (2008). Population, Food, and Knowledge: A Simple Unified Growth Theory, *Journal of Economic Growth* **13**(3): 195–216.

Sussman, N., and Yafeh, Y. (2000). Institutions, Economic Growth, and Country Risk: Evidence from Japanese Government Debt in the Meiji Period, *Journal of Economic History* **60**(2): 442–467.

Tabellini, G. (2010). Culture and Institutions: Economic Development in the Regions of Europe, *Journal of the European Economic Association* **8**(4): 677–716.

Tamura, R. (2006). Human Capital and Economic Development, *Journal of Development Economics* **79**(1): 26–72.

University of California, Berkeley, and Max Planck Institute. (2003). Human Mortality Database. University of California, Berkeley, and Max Planck Institute for Demographic Research, Germany.

U.S. Bureau of the Census (1975). *Historical Statistics of the United States: Colonial Times to 1970*, part 1, Series D 830-844, p. 172.

van Praag, C., and Cramer, J. (2001). The Roots of Entrepreneurship and Labour Demand: Individual Ability and Low Risk Aversion, *Economica* **68**(269): 45–62.

Vaughan, M. (1982). *The State, Education, and Social Class in Mexico, 1880–1928*, Northern Illinois University Press, DeKalb, IL.

Voight, B. F., Kudaravalli, S., Wen, X., and Pritchard, J. K. (2006). A Map of Recent Positive Selection in the Human Genome, *PLoS Biology* **4**(3): 446–458.

Voigtländer, N., and Voth, H.-J. (2006). Why England? Demographic Factors, Structural Change and Physical Capital Accumulation during the Industrial Revolution, *Journal of Economic Growth* **11**(4): 319–361.

———. (2009). Malthusian Dynamism and the Rise of Europe: Make War, Not Love, *American Economic Review* **99**(2): 248–254.

Voth, H.-J. (2003). Living Standards during the Industrial Revolution: An Economist's Guide, *American Economic Review* **93**(2): 221–226.

———. (2004). Living standards and the urban environment, *in* P. Johnson and R. Floud (eds), *The Cambridge Economic History of England*, Cambridge University Press, Cambridge, UK.

Wang, S., Jr., Lewis, C. M., Jakobsson, M., Ramachandran, S., Ray, N., Bedoya, G., et al. (2007). Genetic Variation and Population Structure in Native Americans, *PLoS Genetics* **3**(11): 2049–2067.

Weber, M. (1905). *The Protestant Ethic and the Spirit of Capitalism*, Talcott Parsons and Anthony Giddens (translators), 1930, Allen & Unwin, London.

Weibull, J. W. (1997). *Evolutionary Game Theory*, MIT Press, Cambridge, MA.

Weisdorf, J. L. (2005). From Foraging to Farming: Explaining the Neolithic Revolution, *Journal of Economic Surveys* **19**(4): 561–586.

Westendorp, R. G., and Kirkwood, T. B. (1998). Human Longevity at the Cost of Reproductive Success, *Nature* **396**(6713): 743–746.

White, R. E., Thornhill, S., and Hampson, E. (2006). Entrepreneurs and Evolutionary Biology: The Relationship between Testosterone and New Venture Creation, *Organizational Behavior and Human Decision Processes* **100**(1): 21–34.

Wiesenfeld, S. L. (1967). Sickle-Cell Trait in Human Biological and Cultural Evolution: Development of Agriculture Causing Increased Malaria Is Bound to Gene-Pool Changes Causing Malaria Reduction, *Science* **157**(3793): 1134–1140.

Williams, G. C. (2001). Pleiotropy, Natural Selection, and the Evolution of Senescence, *Evolution* **11**(4): 398–411.

Williams, P. D., and Day, T. (2003). Antagonistic Pleiotropy, Mortality Source Interactions, and the Evolutionary Theory of Senescence, *Evolution* **57**(7): 1478–1488.

Wolthuis, J. (1999). *Lower Technical Education in the Netherlands, 1798–1993: The Rise and Fall of a Subsystem*, Garant, Apeldoorn, The Netherlands.

Wong, R. B. (1997). *China Transformed: Historical Change and the Limits of European Experience*, Cornell University Press, Ithaca, NY.

World Bank. (2001). World Development Indicators. World Bank, Washington, DC.

Wright, D. G. (1970). *Democracy and Reform, 1815–1885*, Longman, London.

Wrigley, E. A., and Schofield, R. (1981). *The Population History of England, 1541–1871: A Reconstruction*, Cambridge University Press, Cambridge, UK.

Yates, P. L. (1959). *Forty Years of Foreign Trade: A Statistical Handbook with Special Reference to Primary Products and Underdeveloped Countries*, Allen & Unwin, London.

Yoong-Deok, J., and Kim, Y. (2000). Land Reform, Income Redistribution, and Agricultural Production in Korea, *Economic Development and Cultural Change* **48**(2): 253–268.

Young, A. (1991). Learning by Doing and the Dynamic Effects of International Trade, *Quarterly Journal of Economics* **106**(2): 369–405.

———. (1998). Growth without Scale Effects, *Journal of Political Economy* **106**(1): 41–63.

———. (2005). The Gift of the Dying: The Tragedy of AIDS and the Welfare of Future African Generations, *Quarterly Journal of Economics* **120**(2): 423–466.

Zeira, J. (1998). Workers, Machines, and Economic Growth, *Quarterly Journal of Economics* **113**(4): 1091–1117.

Name Index

Subject Index